7-30-93

NOTORIOUS:
FROM THE FILES OF
AMERICA'S MOST DANGEROUS
CAREER CRIMINALS

CHRISTOPHER BERNARD WILDER: Born in Australia, he came to America and started a killing spree from Florida to California to New Hampshire, leaving behind a trail of murdered young women and grieving families

WILLIAM FRANCIS SUTTON: His friends called the diminutive bank robber "the Actor" because of his ability to alter his appearance. A man of cunning and style, Willie Sutton was finally nailed on February 18, 1952 in New York City.

WAI-CHIU (TONY) NG: The first Asian to make the Most Wanted List, he tied, robbed, and shot fourteen customers in a private gambling club in Seattle.

ALTON COLEMAN: He graduated from sex crime to murder. With a woman accomplice, he set off a midwestern murder spree and the longer he was free, the higher the body count climbed.

DONALD ROGERS SMELLEY: After vowing that he would "never be taken alive" the repeat offender surrendered to G-men on November 7, 1966, saying, "I'm glad it's over. You guys are too hot for me."

QUANTITY SALES

Most Dell books are available at special quantity discounts when purchased in bulk by corporations, organizations, or groups. Special imprints, messages, and excerpts can be produced to meet your needs. For more information, write to: Dell Publishing, 1540 Broadway, New York, NY 10036. Attention: Special Markets.

INDIVIDUAL SALES

Are there any Dell books you want but cannot find in your local stores? If so, you can order them directly from us. You can get any Dell book currently in print. For a complete up-to-date listing of our books and information on how to order, write to: Dell Readers Service, Box DR, 1540 Broadway, New York, NY 10036.

■ THE FBI MOST WANTED

AN ENCYCLOPEDIA

Michael and Judy Ann Newton

A DELL BOOK

Published by
Dell Publishing
a division of
Bantam Doubleday Dell Publishing Group, Inc.
1540 Broadway
New York, New York 10036

ISBN: 0-440-21437-8

Reprinted by arrangement with Garland Publishing, Inc.

Printed in the United States of America

Published simultaneously in Canada

August 1993

10 9 8 7 6 5 4 3 2 1

OPM

To the twenty-nine
Special Agents
of the FBI
who gave their lives
in active service,
1925–1986.
God keep.

CONTENTS

ACKNOWLEDGMENTS

Special thanks are owed to Melanie McElhinney, "Top Ten" Materials Coordinator for the Federal Bureau of Investigation, and to Mike Marler, of the St. Louis *Post-Dispatch*, for providing eleventh-hour information, without which this book would literally have gone unfinished. Others deserving of mention are listed below, geographically.

ALABAMA: The Mobile *Register*

ARIZONA: Laurie Devine, with the Phoenix Public Library; the *Arizona Republic*; Marge Purcell, with Tribune Newspapers; and Laura Harkins, of the Tucson *Arizona Daily Star*

ARKANSAS The Pine Bluff-Jefferson County Public Library

CALIFORNIA: The Fresno *Bee*; Larry Odom, of the Oakland Public Library; the Redding *Record-Searchlight*; the *Sacramento Bee*; T. Miller, with the *Sacramento Union*; Anita Kaschube, of the San Bernardino *Sun*; S. Lowell, with the San

Jose *Mercury News*; the Santa Clara County Free Library; and Laurel Doud, with SOUTHNET

CANADA: The Montreal *Gazette;* the National Library and Public Archives; and Pat Wilson, of the Toronto *Star*

COLORADO: Betty Carnes, with the Pueblo *Chieftain*

CONNECTICUT: The New Haven Public Library; and the Norwalk Public Library

DISTRICT OF COLUMBIA: The Federal Bureau of Investigation; and the *Washington Post*

FLORIDA: The Daytona Beach *News-Journal*; Katherine Sours and Debrah Priest, with the Broward County Division of Libraries; the *Miami Herald*; Jim Jones, with the *News & Observer*, of New Smyrna Beach; the Orlando Public Library; Emily Johnson, of the West Florida Regional Library in Pensacola; and Greg Hamilton, with the St. Petersburg *Times*

GEORGIA: The Atlanta Public Library

IDAHO: Lorraine Kunze, with the *Idaho State Journal*; and the Idaho State University Library, in Pocatello

ILLINOIS: The *Daily Herald*, in Arlington Heights; Betty Carr, with the *Daily Calumet*; the Columbia *Star*; Marjorie Fanning, with the Peoria *Journal Star*; Edith Piercy, with the Rockford *Register Star*; Linda Garvert, with Springfield's Lincoln Library; and the Alton *Telegraph*

INDIANA: The Indiana University Library, in Bloomington; the Monroe County Public Library; Nadine Moore, with the *Indianapolis News* and *Indianapolis Star*; the Michigan City *News-Dispatch*; and Betty Menges, with the New Albany-Floyd County Public Library

IOWA: Mary Herr, of the Davenport Public Library; and Cheri Ritchhart, of the Des Moines *Register and Tribune*

KANSAS: Anne Gould, of the Dodge City *Daily Globe*; Patsy Ruddick, of the Garden City Community College Library; and Mark Enoch, of the Hutchinson *News-Herald*

KENTUCKY: The Lexington *Herald-Leader*; Robin Rader, of the Lexington Public Library; the Louisville *Courier-Journal*; and the *Mt. Washington Star*

LOUISIANA: Betty Dees, of the East Baton Rouge Parish Library; and Beverly Barkley, of the Shreve Memorial Library

MAINE: Marcia MacVane, of the Portland *Press Herald*

MASSACHUSETTS: William Boles, of the *Boston Globe*; the Boston Public Library; the Holyoke *Transcript-Telegram*; Irene Montague, of the *Daily Hampshire Gazette*; and the Springfield City Library

MICHIGAN: The Detroit *Free Press*; the *Detroit News*; the Detroit Public Library; Robert Groat, of the Hamtramck *North Detroit Citizen*; the Jackson *Citizen Patriot*; Marge Mc-Bee, of the Monroe *Evening News*; and Ron Cotton, of the *St. Ignace News*

MINNESOTA: The St. Paul Public Library; Judith Matzung, of the St. Paul *Pioneer Press Dispatch*; Sheila Godava, of the Minneapolis *Star Tribune*; the Sandstone Community Library; and Kim Jevne, of the Warren *Sheaf*

MISSISSIPPI: Marilyn Pustay, of the Biloxi *Sun-Daily Herald*; and Harold Andrews, of the New Albany *Gazette*

MONTANA: The *Montana Standard*, in Butte; Marge Foot, of the Great Falls *Tribune*; and Don Spritzer, of the Missoula Public Library

NEBRASKA: Stephen Allars, of the Omaha *World-Herald*

NEVADA: The Clark County Library System, in Las Vegas

NEW JERSEY: Pat Straub, with the Camden *Courier Post*; and the Jersey City Public Library (Jersey City, New Jersey)

NEW MEXICO: Patricia Seligman, of the Albuquerque *Tribune*

NEW YORK: The Buffalo *News*; the Nyack Public Library; the Rochester *Times-Union*; and the Spring Valley Public Library

NORTH CAROLINA: Susan McClure, of the Chapel Hill Public Library; Cheryl Wolf, with the Charlotte *Observer* and *News*; Barbara Semonche, with the Durham *Herald-Sun*; the *Sentinel*, in Winston-Salem; and Marilyn Rollins, with the Winston-Salem *Journal*

OHIO: Cathy Tierney, with the Akron *Beacon Journal*; the Stark District Library, in Canton; the Clinton *Repository*; the Cincinnati *Enquirer*; Genevieve Aziz and Sara Edwards, with the Cleveland *Plain Dealer*; Diane Gagel, with the Toledo-Lucas Country Public Library; Steve Long, with the Uhrichsville *Times Reporter*; Jane Strachan, with the Willoughby *News-Herald*; and Martha Clonis, with the Youngstown *Vindicator*

OKLAHOMA: Juanita Russell, with the Chelsea *Reporter*

OREGON: Barbara Kahl, with the Multnomah County Library; Sandra Macomber, with the Portland *Oregonian*; and the Springfield *News*

PENNSYLVANIA: Linda DiSante, with the *Beaver County Times*; Carol Jensen, with the Pittsburgh *Post-Gazette*; the *Daily Free Press*, in Quakertown; and Katie Searle, of the York *Dispatch*

RHODE ISLAND: The John F. Kennedy Library at Brown University

SOUTH CAROLINA: Sally Farris, with the Aiken County Public Library; the Charleston *News & Courier*; and Anne Kuickel, with the Columbia *State-Record*

SOUTH DAKOTA: The *Daily Capital Journal*

TENNESSEE: Annette Morrison, with the Nashville *Tennessean*; and James Earl Ray

TEXAS: Alice Gilroy, with the *Floyd County Hisperian*; Rachel Orozco, with the Fort Worth Public Library; Kristine Carr and Melissa Mantel, with the Houston *Chronicle*; Audie Thompson, with the Lubbock *Avalanche-Journal*; the Plainview *Daily Herald*; and the San Antonio *Express-News*

VIRGINIA: The South Hill *Enterprise*; Maureen Powers Watts, with the *Virginian Pilot* and the *Ledger-Star*, in Norfolk

WEST VIRGINIA: Leah Godby, of the Logan *Banner*; and Diane Thomas, of the Moundsville City-County Public Library

WISCONSIN: The *Capital Times;* and the Milwaukee *Journal*

WYOMING: Marci Turner, of the Casper *Star-Tribune*; the Park County Library System; and the Thermopolis *Independent Record*

INTRODUCTION

America has always been a nation of superlatives. We thrive on recognition of the best and brightest, eager to know everything about the fastest car or tallest building, anxious to discover for ourselves which movie star or athlete is the highest paid. We publish lists and books of lists, recording every detail of the largest, smallest, best, or worst in every field of human enterprise or natural phenomena. From the ridiculous to the sublime, we dote on categories, ranks, and ratings.

What, therefore, could be more natural—and more American—than an official list of outlaws who are deemed the worst and most notorious in our society?

Throughout the 1930s, "public enemies" were named and numbered by the press, contenders moving up the ladder as their predecessors were consigned to prison or the grave. With notoriety came nicknames—Scarface, Mad Dog, Pretty Boy—designed to make the headlines sing, surrounding thieves and killers with an air of romance and adventure, elevating some to the undeserved status of folk heroes before they were finally cut down. And yet, for all the fanfare, there existed no official list of public enemies until the decade after World War II.

As 1949 was drawing to a close, a feature writer for the International News Service—predecessor of United Press International—asked the FBI to name the "toughest guys" whom Bureau agents were pursuing at the moment. The resultant story proved so popular and generated so much positive publicity that FBI Director J. Edgar Hoover officially inaugurated the Bureau's "Ten Most Wanted Fugitives" program a few weeks later, on March 14, 1950.

Criteria for the selection of a "Top Ten" fugitive is specialized, befitting designation as among the worst of several hundred thousand criminals at large on any given day. For openers, the individual must have a lengthy history of conflict with the law or, if a new offender, must be counted as a special danger to society because of pending charges. Sheer ferocity is not enough, however. It must also be determined that publicity afforded by the program, coast to coast, will be of positive assistance in the apprehension of a fugitive. Accordingly, the candidate should not already be notorious from prior publicity—like Patty Hearst and her abductors in the 1970s—as this defeats the purpose of the "Top Ten" list.

The single purpose of the "Ten Most Wanted" list, like other "top ten" programs, is the generation of publicity. Unlike the other lists, however, ego and commercialism play no part in execution of the Bureau's program. In the case of wanted fugitives, publicity becomes a searing spotlight, stripping them of precious anonymity, applying heat that leads directly to their capture and confinement.

How effective is the program? In the past four decades, 420 fugitives have been named to the FBI's list. Of those, 391 have been apprehended by authorities; process was dismissed against another fifteen (discussed below), and four were ultimately dropped because they no longer fit "Top Ten" criteria in some manner. Of the fugitives arrested, some 115—29 percent—were caught as a direct result of citizen cooperation: many others were corraled by local officers who memorized the information on their federal WANTED bulletins.

In short, the program works.

The average "Top Ten" fugitive is thirty-six years old and

male, though seven female fugitives have also graced the list. He measures five feet nine and weighs 167 pounds. The average time between a fugitive's addition to the list and apprehension is 157 days, and he will travel some 969 miles between commission of his crime and the point of arrest. (The shortest time on record was a mere two hours: the longest, eighteen years, four months, nine days.) Six men have made the roster twice, while brothers have been added to the list as "family acts" on four occasions.

As we noted earlier, not every "Top Ten" fugitive is apprehended. Federal warrants were dismissed in fifteen cases, generally at the request of local prosecutors, after time eliminated evidence or witnesses required for a successful prosecution. Several "Top Ten" outlaws have been found—or are presumed to be—deceased. Four others were deleted from the list as passing time reduced the likelihood of new publicity resulting in arrests.

Since June of 1961, the "Top Ten" list has occasionally been expanded to include eleven fugitives, when special circumstances—such as public danger from a homicidal maniac at large—were thought to justify exceptional additions. In September 1970, the list was bumped to fourteen names, including radicals connected with the bombing of a university. One month later, in October 1970, the roster hit its all-time high of sixteen fugitives, including two more radicals indicted after "liberating" money from a bank at gunpoint.

Agents of the FBI may enter cases on a wide variety of legal grounds. Some "Top Ten" fugitives are sought for federal statute violations—racketeering, civil rights infringement, interstate transportation of stolen property or vehicles—but most are sought initially for local felonies. The Bureau, as a rule, does not have jurisdiction in a case of murder, rape, assault, or robbery (aside from banks), but federal laws enacted over forty years have granted agents greater latitude in the pursuit of fugitives.

In 1934, an act of Congress made it a federal offense to flee across state lines in avoidance of prosecution for murder, assault with a deadly weapon, mayhem, burglary, rape, kidnapping, extortion accompanied by threats of violence, robbery, or attempts to commit any of the above. (Arson was added to the list in 1956.) In 1946, amendments made interstate flight from confinement following a conviction for these crimes a federal offense. New amendments passed in 1960, 1961, and 1962 made it illegal to escape across state lines from prosecution, custody, or confinement for *any* felony or capital crime, or to avoid giving testimony in felony proceedings. With these statutes in hand, unlawful flight to avoid prosecution (UFAP) and unlawful flight to avoid confinement (UFAC) have become the most common grounds for FBI pursuit of "Most Wanted" fugitives.

Critics of the bureau's "Top Ten" program emphasize three main concerns. For some, the program is a mere "publicity event," and so a waste of time and money. Others criticize the list for the attention paid to "small-time" criminals, while leaders of the Mafia and major traffickers in drugs remain at large. A final criticism deals with brief expansion of the program in the 1970s, with emphasis on left-wing radicals, asserting that the list was therby made "political."

The first complaint—publicity—appears to be no grounds for a complaint at all. As noted earlier, publicity has always been the "Top Ten" program's purpose, not for any exaltation of the FBI, but to produce arrests. In this the effort must be rated a success. Unlike some other Bureau uses of the media —including frequent manipulation of the press by former director J. Edgar Hoover—the "Top Ten" program serves a basic law enforcement function by enlisting public aid in the pursuit of desperate criminals.

As noted earlier, selection of a fugitive for posting to the "Ten Most Wanted" list is predicated on established guidelines—notably the outlaw's record, his potential as a public menace, and the estimated contribution of publicity toward his apprehension. Ranking mobsters seldom "take it on the lam," preferring to remain at home in luxury while high-priced lawyers fight their battles in the courts. When they do take flight, publicity is commonplace, making a posting to the "Top Ten" list redundant. Nor is it entirely fair to single out "disorganized" offenders as "small-time" and hence unworthy of attention. Loners some may be, but they are no less lethal for their isolationism. Three such human tumbleweeds—Ted Bundy, Alton Coleman, and Christopher Wilder—were responsible for slaying at least 37 persons and raping, brutalizing, and abducting at least 20 others in a single decade. Publicity in such a case may ring the curtain down before a homicidal monster claims more lives.

The third complaint, the brief expansion of the program to include six violent radicals in 1970 "politicized" the list, is understandable in light of FBI Director Hoover's well-known hatred for the left. A case may theoretically be made that "special" postings to the list diminish impact on the public mind, but "Top Ten" fugitives have alway represented a cross-section of criminal America, reflecting modern trends in crime along with FBI priorities. From 1950 through the early 1960s, bank robbers, burglars and car thieves dominated the roster. During the late 1960s and early 1970s, as violence sputtered in the ranks of left-wing militants, the list reflected changing times, with emphasis on sabotage, destruction of government property and kidnapping. In the latter 1970s and the 1980s, Bureau emphasis on organized crime, terrorism, and serial murder has populated the list with mobsters, homicidal deviants, and violent activists of all political persuasions, from the revolutionary left to the reactionary, neo-fascist right. The "Top Ten" list, per se, has never been "political," except where outlaws have attempted to "legitimize" their crimes as "wars of liberation" or "defense of God and country."

Imitation, we are told, is the sincerest form of flattery. With that in mind, it is significant to note that many other law enforcement agencies have borrowed freely from the Bureau in the past four decades, publishing their own "Most Wanted" lists of desperate fugitives. The Royal Canadian Mounted Police inaugurated the "Canadian Top Ten" in January 1952, and other agencies have followed suit. Kentucky's state police created a "Top Five" list in June 1965, followed closely by Ohio. United States marshals stalk their own "Top Fifteen," and the concept has filtered down to a number of big-city police departments, as well. A weekly television program on "America's Most Wanted" has been credited with more than one arrest per week since its debut in February 1988 (including three of the FBI's own "Top Ten" felons).

What follows is a case-by-case description of fugitives who

made the FBI's "Most Wanted" list from its inception through
the summer months of 1988. Their stories, taken in conjunction, are a profile and a history of criminal America. Because
most of the felons on the FBI's "Most Wanted" lists are eventually tried for state and local crimes, the FBI's records often
end with their apprehension. Anyone who has additional information about the subjects described in this book is invited
to share it with the authors c/o Garland Publishing, 136 Madison Avenue, New York, NY 10016.

1 ■ THOMAS JAMES HOLDEN

The first man listed on the FBI's new "Ten Most Wanted" roster, Thomas Holden was a veteran of crime whose record dated from the bygone era of such desperadoes as John Dillinger, "Baby Face" Nelson, and "Pretty Boy" Floyd. In the early 1920s, teamed with partner Francis Keating, Holden earned a reputation as a daring bank and payroll robber who was not averse to raiding mail trains on the side. Other notorious members of the Holden-Keating gang included Harvey Bailey, Frank "Jelly" Nash, and brutal Verne Miller (later identified as one of the triggermen in Kansas City's Union Station massacre).

For all their ruthlessness, the leaders of the Holden-Keating gang had certain scruples. When two members of the gang, Frank Weber and Charles Harmon, wantonly murdered a hostage after a bank robbery at Menomonie, Wisconsin, Holden and Keating passed a death sentence on their trigger-happy confederates. Weber and Harmon were shot execution-style, their bodies dumped in a roadside ditch for police to discover next morning.

Holden and Keating ran out of luck in 1928, following the holdup of a train in Evergreen Park, a Chicago suburb. Dubbed the "Evergreen bandits," both were sentenced to lengthy terms in Leavenworth prison. They escaped in 1931, with the assistance of a bootlegger, George Barnes, who worked in the prison's office. Barnes forged passes for Holden and Keating, allowing the bandits to simply walk out, unopposed.

They fled to Kansas City, teaming up with members of the violent Barker-Karpis gang on several bank robberies in the next twelve months. On July 8, 1932, Holden, Keating, and Harvey Bailey were surrounded by federal agents while playing golf at the Old Mission course, a resort popular with underworld figures. The arresting agents missed Frank Nash, another fugitive, whose inability to hit the ball had left him far behind his foursome. (One of those who arrested Holden and his partners, Special Agent Raymond Caffrey, would go down before Verne Miller's guns in Union Station, twelve months later. So, ironically, would "Jelly" Nash, who was at the time in the custody of Agent Caffrey and a number of his colleagues.)

Paroled in November 1947, Holden returned home to Chicago after spending most of eighteen years in prison. On June 5, 1949, a drunken family get-together led to angry words between Tom Holden and his wife. Holden drew a gun and killed her with a single shot, then turned the weapon on her brothers when they rushed to her defense. Aware that he could offer no defense to triple murder charges, Holden fell back on his instincts and immediately fled.

When leaders of the FBI devised the "Ten Most Wanted" list in March of 1950, as a means of tracking down especially elusive fugitives, Tom Holden was a natural to head the roster. Spokesmen for the Bureau publicly announced that Holden was "a menace to every man, woman, and child in America."

While agents scoured the countryside for Holden, their quarry was living quietly in Beaverton, Oregon, working as a plasterer under the alias of "John McCullough." On June 23, 1951, an alert citizen recognized Holden's mugshot in a local paper's roundup of the "Top Ten" fugitives, and G-men were dispatched to seize him at his latest job site. Convicted of murder in Chicago, Holden died two years later in the Illinois state prison.

2 ■ MORLEY VERNON KING

Nothing was precisely what it seemed within the world of Morley King. For openers, the name was wrong. He had been christened Stanis Ludwig at his birth, in Wheeling, West Virginia, and had run away from home to join the United States Navy during World War I, at age fifteen. He spoke four languages and had been known by many names. The wife he murdered during 1947 cherished secrets of her own.

The long pursuit of Morley King began on July 9, 1947, when the cook at a hotel in San Luis Obispo, California, noted foul aromas emanating from a trunk beneath the hotel's porch. Police were summoned, and they found a woman's decomposing body in the trunk, a scarf wound tight around her neck. She was identified, from fingerprints, as Helen King, wife of the hotel dining room's manager. When Morley King did not report for work that afternoon, or any day thereafter, the authorities prepared a warrant charging him with homicide.

A background check on "Morley King" revealed his navy record, and a great deal more. As Stanis Ludwig, he had been arrested during 1923 for passing bogus checks. He had resided in the Middle East from 1927 through the summer months of 1934. In 1943, he had been questioned in the death of a New Orleans gambler, which was later ruled a suicide. His marriage to the victim had been solemnized in Casablanca, in September 1931, and they had come to the United States in August 1934.

Although she had no future, "Helen King" possessed a past as colorful as anything her husband's record had to offer. Born in Turkey, she became the Countess Christina de Zoheb in 1915, via marriage to a nobleman from Portugal. A short year later she was widowed, when her husband died in combat. Serving out the war years as an ambulance attendant and interpreter, the countess suffered battle wounds a short time later. Back in Turkey, in the early 1920s, she was nearly killed by bayonet wounds suffered in a local insurrection. On recovery, she toured northern Africa as the traveling representative of a dressmaking firm, and so met Morley King in Casablanca, where he owned a small hotel.

Arriving in America, the Kings spent fifteen months in New York City, moving on from there to pass a decade in Louisiana. Morley drifted in and out of jobs with several restaurants and shipped out as a merchant seaman on occasion, when he tired of life on shore. Between September and November 1946, the couple wandered aimlessly through Texas, Mexico, and Southern California, finally settling in Pacoima. There were stormy arguments and talk of separation. Morley found a job and lodgings for himself in San Luis Obispo, but he made the journey "home" to Helen faithfully, at weekly intervals. The last time she was seen alive—June 30, 1947—they had been together.

Homicide detectives theorized that Helen had been strangled in Pacoima, with her body shipped from there by Morley King for ultimate disposal in the desert. Listed as a federal fugitive from justice, King was added to the FBI's "Most Wanted" list as number two, on March 15, 1950.

It took another nineteen months to bring him in, and federal officers would not reveal their source of information on King's whereabouts. A team of agents found him shucking oysters, at a restaurant in Philadelphia, the evening of October 31, 1951. King had been working at the restaurant, as "William Wilson," for a period of several weeks. He offered no resistance, and was soon returned to California, where he drew a term of life imprisonment.

3 ■ WILLIAM RAYMOND NESBIT

Sought by federal agents on a charge of unlawful flight to avoid confinement, William Nesbit was a jewel thief with a taste for homicide. In league with two accomplices, he staged a daring robbery in Sioux City, Iowa, which netted the gang $37,000 worth of gems, but then he ran afoul of paranoia and the roof fell in.

Suspecting two associates, a man and a woman, as potential squealers, Nesbit and his cronies opted for assassination as a cheap insurance policy. Transported to a rural area, the man was shot and killed, the woman gravely wounded. Nesbit thought her dead, but he could not be satisfied with less than absolute obliteration of the bodies. Dragging both victims into a shack jammed with 3,500 pounds of dynamite and 7,000 pounds of black powder, Nesbit lit the fuse and beat a swift retreat. Incredibly, the wounded woman managed to escape before the blast, which rattled windows in a five-mile radius. She lived to testify against the gunmen, sending them away for terms of life which were reduced, by order of the court, to twenty years.

Nesbit escaped from the South Dakota state penitentiary on September 4, 1946. Evidence of interstate flight made him a federal fugitive, and he was still at large when the FBI created its "Most Wanted" program in the spring of 1950. Posted to the list as number three, on March 16, Nesbit became the program's first arrestee, two days later.

Living off the land since his escape from prison, Nesbit was holed up in a cave beside the Mississippi River, outside St. Paul, Minnesota, when a pair of teenaged boys observed him early Saturday. The boys, James Lewis and James Radeck, recognized his face from mug shots printed in a local paper and immediately summoned the police. While Nesbit made his journey back to prison, facing extra time for the escape, the youths were flown to Washington, where they received the personal congratulations of FBI Director J. Edgar Hoover.

4 ■ HENRY RANDOLPH MITCHELL

A daring gambler who loved to bet the ponies, Henry Mitchell passed a fair amount of time at race tracks, where the regulars remembered him as "Little Mitch." Unfortunately, Mitchell rarely backed a winner, and his quest for capital propelled him into crime. In early January 1948, he was released from prison on completion of a ten-year term in Florida, where he had been convicted of burglary and grand larceny. He should have gone straight, but the nags were running at Hialeah, and Little Mitch had never been much good at staying out of trouble.

On January 21, with an accomplice at his side, Mitchell celebrated his return to freedom with a visit to the Perkins State Bank in Williston, Florida. Brandishing pistols, the bandits walked out with $10,353, becoming instant fugitives under the federal bank robbery statutes.

Mitchell's accomplice was captured soon after the crime, but Henry was still at large when the "Top Ten" list was created two years later. Posted as number four, he became the first of the worst to confound federal agents. The fugitive warrant against Mitchell was dismissed on July 18, 1958, after eight years and four months of fruitless searching. "Little Mitch" would have been sixty-three years old at the time, and an FBI spokesman in Mitchell's hometown, Louisville, Kentucky, conceded that dismissal of the warrant "might mean he was dead."

5 ■ OMAR AUGUST PINSON

The Bureau's fifth addition to its "Top Ten" list was sought on federal charges of escape from prison in the state of Oregon, where he had been confined on murder charges. Omar Pinson's trouble started on the afternoon of April 27, 1947, when a traffic officer in Hood River, Oregon, pulled him over in a truck containing several weapons. Rather than surrender, Pinson shot the officer to death and drew a term of life imprisonment. He was a restless prisoner, undisciplined and prone to "rabbit." Twice he tried escape before he finally got it right.

On May 30, 1949, Pinson and a crony, William Benson, were confined inside a special block of cells as punishment for prior escape attempts. With smuggled saws, they cut through tempered bars, then used a wrench to force the latches on a cell block door. Outside, they crossed the yard and scaled the prison's wall with bullets whistling around their ears, escaping in a stolen car. Cornered, briefly, on the afternoon of August 25, in Gooding County, Idaho, Pinson shot his way out of a police trap and escaped a second time. His name was added to the "Ten Most Wanted" list on March 18, 1950.

Federal agents had a fair idea of where Pinson was before he ever made the Bureau's "honor roll." On February 3, the fugitive applied by mail for transfer of the title to a car in South Dakota; Pinson listed an address in Aberdeen, but mail dispatched to the address came back, unclaimed. He wrote the South Dakota motor vehicle authorities a second time, in mid-July, and once again their answer was returned, unopened. Routine contact with the FBI revealed that Pinson was a fugitive from justice. Special Agent Milton Kuhl requested that a hold be placed on any transfer of a vehicle in Pinson's name.

His third attempt to register the car was one too many. When he surfaced in Pierre, on August 28, to do the job himself, authorities were waiting. Taken into custody by Clayton

Vickmark, special agent with the state attorney general's office, Pinson made a final effort to escape. He begged a drink of water, threw the glass in Vickmark's face and made a break for freedom, but pursuers caught him before he reached the street. A search of Pinson's car revealed four guns, a cache of dynamite, a gas mask, and a set of burglar's tools.

In custody, the fugitive identified himself as "Dan Andell," of Kansas City, but a fingerprint comparison revealed his true identity. With life plus extra time awaiting him in Oregon, he faced new charges in a string of burglaries around Pierre and Arlington, committed on the weekend prior to his arrest.

6 ■ LEE EMORY DOWNS

In the predawn hours of June 4, 1948, two gunmen forced their way inside the offices of the Pacific Telephone and Telegraph Company in San Jose, California. Tying up two janitors, the outlaws blew an office safe and fled with some $2,000 worth of cash and checks. The fingerprints they left behind identified Lee Downs and his accomplice, Walter Lennon.

Downs possessed a record spanning many years, with prison time invested in the states of Idaho, Oregon, Utah, and Washington. In 1945, his wife had helped him flee captivity in Utah, but his freedom had been brief. Lee's spouse did time for aiding his escape. The robbery in San Jose, with evidence of flight across state lines to Butte, Montana, made the gunmen federal fugitives, and Downs was added to the FBI's "Most Wanted" list on March 20, 1950.

Federal agents knew that Lennon had acquired a lavish, thirty-two-foot trailer—in the name of one "George Clarkson"—from a dealership in Butte. A photographic lineup indicated "Clarkson" was, in fact, a ringer for Lee Downs. The trailer had been traced as far as Florida, and there, in the winter of 1949, the trail went cold.

Creation of the "Ten Most Wanted" list, with Downs as number six, rejuvenated the pursuit. On April 5, Walt Lennon was surprised by state and federal officers outside Mojave, California. Topping speeds of seventy MPH, Lennon led FBI agents and California Highway Patrol officers on a wild desert chase, finally losing control of his car. Emerging from the vehicle with gun in hand, he tried to shoot it out and was killed by return fire from his pursuers.

Two days later, local officers and agents of the FBI traced Lennon's partner to Daytona Beach, in Florida. "George Clarkson" and his wife had been residing at a local trailer park since mid-December 1949. Along with the outstanding California charges, Downs was now suspected of a recent heist at Marineland Studios.

Converging on the trailer park, arresting officers stood by and waited for their quarry to reveal himself. When Downs emerged and climbed into his car, four agents moved to block him, weapons leveled at his face. He made no move to reach the loaded pistol in his pocket, and was taken into custody without resistance. Searchers turned up two more pistols in the trailer, with six rifles, nine sticks of dynamite, twelve electric detonating fuses, and two leather briefcases filled with ammunition.

Downs resisted extradition briefly, but in vain. Returned to San Jose, he was convicted and imprisoned for the robbery, but doing time had never taught Downs anything. Paroled in 1968, he tried to burglarize the Colombian consulate in San Francisco. A security guard surprised him, took his crowbar, and administered a beating which left Downs relieved to see police arriving on the scene. He was returned to prison for a violation of parole.

7 ■ ORBA ELMER JACKSON

A Missouri farm boy weary of the hard life, Orba Jackson ran afoul of the police in 1924, at age eighteen. Convicted on a charge of auto theft, he served four years in prison, but within months of his release, he was arrested on a federal charge of crossing state lines in a stolen car. Another three years, spent in Leavenworth, inspired a fling at going straight, but Jackson apparently could not tolerate the thought of working for a living. With an armed accomplice, Orba robbed a store in

Poplar Bluff, Missouri, taking time to pistol-whip the elderly proprietor before they fled the scene. Because the store contained a post office, federal charges were preferred; upon conviction, Jackson was dispatched to serve another quarter-century in Leavenworth. In time, he earned a trusty's status, and the extra freedom helped him to escape in mid-September 1947.

Posted to the FBI's "Most Wanted" list as number seven, on March 21, 1950, Jackson had been living on the run for thirty months. With the publicity surrounding his addition to the list, he lasted two more days. A resident of Portland, Oregon, identified the fugitive from published photographs and telephoned authorities. Converging on a nearby poultry farm, where Jackson was employed, police and special agents of the FBI were waiting when their quarry came back from a movie at 11:45 p.m., March 23. Surrendering without resistance, Jackson told his captors that he had been hiding in the Portland area since early 1948. Employees at the farm regarded Jackson as a "perfect gentleman," but character endorsements scarcely helped his case. He was returned to Leavenworth, with extra time appended to his standing sentence for the prison break.

8 ■ GLEN ROY WRIGHT

Born and raised in Malvern, Arkansas, Glen Wright was an old-fashioned gangster from the 1930s. Wounded twice in shootouts with police, he also bore the scars of knife fights on his face. A chain smoker who coughed incessantly, he felt undressed without a gun or two concealed about his person.

With numerous felony convictions behind him, including terms for burglary and armed robbery, Wright's luck ran out in 1934. Arrested for armed robbery in Oklahoma, he was convicted as an habitual criminal and sentenced to life imprisonment. Wright had fourteen years behind him when, on September 14, 1948, he obtained a smuggled gun and shot his way out of the state penitentiary. Federal warrants were issued, charging Wright with unlawful flight to avoid confinement,

and his name was added to the "Ten Most Wanted" list on
March 22, 1950.

Nine months later, in Salina, Kansas, Wright was recognized by citizens who telephoned the FBI. A team of agents
found their man and took him into custody, without resistance, on December 13.

9 ■ HENRY HARLAND SHELTON

An Indiana native, Henry Shelton was arrested during 1933
for his participation in a Michigan bank robbery which left
one cashier dead. Sentenced to a minimum of sixty years, he
made his first escape attempt in 1935, without success. His
luck was better in the first week of September 1949, when he
obtained a pistol, shot it out with guards, and fled the prison
grounds accompanied by Samuel Lieb, an inmate serving life
for murder.

On September 17, the convicts seized a motorist in northern Michigan. Abducted at knifepoint, their hostage escaped
after driving his captors across Wisconsin and Illinois, into
Indiana. There the trail went cold, but agents of the FBI were
joining in the hunt. In flight, the fugitives had racked up federal kidnap charges, in addition to their violation of the Dyer
Act, forbidding transportation of a stolen car across state
lines.

The outlaws surfaced in Kentucky, on the evening of October 2, when they tried to rob a Mayfield resident outside his
home. Inside the house, the victim's wife observed the crime
in progress, phoning for police, and officers arrived to find the
fugitives still rifling their victim's pockets. Gunfire was exchanged; Sam Lieb was captured when he tried to jump a
fence and cracked his skull instead. In the confusion, Shelton
managed to escape once more.

He surfaced in Paducah nine days later, holding up a liquor
store and fleeing with $1,100. When the FBI created its "Most
Wanted" program, Shelton's name was posted to the list as
number nine. Exactly three months later, he was captured.

A native of Indianapolis, Shelton had never strayed far

from home in his travels. Scouring the city, federal officers were told Shelton liked to patronize a certain tavern, turning up with clockwork regularity to slake his thirst. On June 23, 1950, special agents staked out Shelton's favorite bar and settled down to wait.

When Shelton finally appeared, with two companions, G-men moved to intercept, but months of living on the run had honed the convict's paranoia to a razor's edge. He tried to draw the .45 concealed beneath his coat, but agents opened fire before he had a chance to use the weapon, dropping Shelton in his tracks. Upon recovery, the fugitive faced trial in federal court and was sentenced to a forty-five year term in Leavenworth. In the event that he survived to make parole, the term of sixty years to life, with extra time for his escape, would still be waiting for him, back in Michigan.

10 ■ MORRIS GURALNICK

The final slot on the original "Most Wanted" list was occupied by an explosive psychopath whose furious, impulsive violence made him dangerous to everyone with whom he came in contact. During March of 1948, Guralnick stabbed a Kingston, New York, woman who had spurned his crude advances. Cornered by police in New York City one month later, Morris bit off a patrolman's finger as arresting officers attempted to subdue him. Jailed in Kingston and awaiting trial in mid-July, he tore out plumbing in his cell and used the pipe to brutally assault his jailers, fleeing in the company of other inmates.

With charges of escape and multiple assault on file in New York State, Guralnick was declared a federal fugitive. No trace of him was found within the twenty months before inauguration of the FBI's "Most Wanted" program, and his violent record earned Guralnick instant nomination to the roster. Added to the list March 24, 1950, he received immediate publicity which signalled the beginning of the end.

Guralnick's flight had taken him to Madison, Wisconsin, where he worked a few days at a luggage shop before securing a job at Campus Clothes. His luck ran out when patron Edward Yudin, a law student at the University of Wisconsin, recognized his photograph and called police. They in turn made contact with the FBI, and local officers accompanied federal agents when they cornered Moe Guralnick at his place of business, on the fifteenth of December.

Never one to give up peacefully, Guralnick fought a vicious battle with arresting officers at Campus Clothes, but he was finally subdued and held for extradition to New York. His reputation had preceded him in court, and there would be no hint of leniency when he was called before the bar for sentencing.

11 ■ WILLIAM FRANCIS SUTTON

Willie Sutton always had a sense of style. To friends and enemies alike, he was "The Actor," capable of altering appearance, personality, to suit his needs in any given situation. Armed with keen intelligence where many of his criminal contemporaries struggled through on nerve alone, he operated in the upper strata of an industry where life expectancies and careers are sometimes measured out in hours. Willie played the game for nearly forty years, and there are those who would suggest he won more often than he lost.

Born in Brooklyn's "Irishtown," young Willie Sutton ran with street gangs as a youth, but he already had his sights on bigger things. While friends were stealing food from pushcarts, playing smash-and-grab with local merchants, Sutton dreamed of going on to law school and defending those whose company he cherished. He could never raise the cash for college, and in 1917, romance propelled him into trouble with the law. He burglarized a store belonging to his girlfriend's father, stealing $16,000 which he hoped would finance their elopement. On arrest, he was indicted for abduction, burglary, and grand larceny, but the imposing charges bargained down to mere unlawful entry. Willie spent a year in the reformatory, and his sentence was suspended.

Sutton disappeared from the official records for a time, returning with a vengeance on July 10, 1921. With an acquaintance, Sutton was indicted on a double charge of murder after two known enemies were shot outside his favorite pool hall. Running for his life, he joined a team of robbers and safe-crackers, picking up an education on the lam before he was arrested and returned for trial. To everyone's surprise, he was acquitted by a jury of his peers.

In April 1926, he was sentenced to serve five to ten years for burglarizing banks in New York City. Turned out on parole in August 1929, he spent the early years of the Depression robbing banks and jewelry stores, unloading stolen merchandise through cronies in the Bronx affiliated with the Dutch Schultz syndicate. On June 5, 1931, he was returned to Sing Sing on conviction for a bank job. He escaped from prison in December 1932, surviving on the run for fourteen months before his luck went sour in Philadelphia. A prison term of twenty-five to fifty years was waiting for him there, accumulated from a string of holdups where he frequently impersonated a policeman. Willie's reputation as "The Actor" was established.

Chafing at confinement, Sutton made four unsuccessful bids for freedom over thirteen years. He was successful in his fifth attempt, in February 1947, when a snowstorm covered his escape. By this point in his life, there was no question of the Actor "going straight." He only knew one trade, and he was still the best in town.

On March 9, 1950, three armed bandits struck the offices of Manufacturer's Trust Company, in Sunnyside, Queens, escaping with $63,933. Bank employees picked out Sutton's mug shot as a likeness of the leader, and his name was added to the "Ten Most Wanted" list on March 20, replacing that of William Nesbit.

The end came suddenly, on February 18, 1952, when subway rider Arnold Schuster recognized the Actor from his wanted flyers. Summoning police, he watched as Sutton casually surrendered and was taken into custody. The fugitive's accomplices in Queens had been identified as Thomas Kling (# 15) and John De Venuta, both of whom were captured two days later by police in New York City.

On April 1, the Actor and his sidekick, Kling, were both convicted of the robbery in Queens, and each was sentenced to a term of twenty-nine years in prison. Sutton received two additional terms of fifteen years to life on weapons charges unrelated to the heist, those terms to run consecutively with his sentence in the robbery. Venuta saved himself by testifying for the state; his sentence was suspended.

Willie Sutton's long career in crime was over, but there was a grisly postscript to the case. Informant Arnold Schuster had become an overnight celebrity by fingering the Actor, but his fame would be short-lived. Observing Schuster in a television interview, a local chieftain of the Mafia, psychotic Albert Anastasia, flew into a homicidal rage. "I hate squealers!" he shouted. "Hit that guy!" The contract was fulfilled on March 8, 1952, when Schuster was assassinated near his Brooklyn home. According to the testimony of defecting mobster Joe Valachi, Schuster's execution was arranged and carried out by Frederick J. Tenuto (# 14), yet another member of the Bureau's "Top Ten" list.

12 ■ STEPHEN WILLIAM DAVENPORT

The Bureau's twelfth "Most Wanted" fugitive had thirty years of crime behind him by the time his name was posted to the list in April 1950. At an early age, in 1920, he was dubbed incorrigible and committed to a boy's reformatory in the town of Eldorado, Iowa. Enlistment in the army failed to curb his wild streak; in November 1927, he was sentenced to a term of two years for desertion and assault. Reentry to civilian life, in 1929, brought no end to his problems. Bungling a robbery in Hammond, Indiana, Davenport was cornered by police and shot one officer to death before he was disarmed. Imprisoned for a term of life, he was paroled in 1946.

Seized in Quincy, Illinois, on federal charges stemming from a violation of the Dyer Act (forbidding transportation of a stolen car across state lines), he was consigned to Leavenworth. Successful for perhaps the first time, Davenport escaped from prison in July 1949 by using what authorities described, in classic understatement, as "a lot of razor blades" to cut the bars securing a window of his cell.

The fugitive's audacity, together with his record as a thief and murderer, won Davenport a nomination to the "Ten Most Wanted" roster. He was added to the list on April 4, 1950, and survived another month outside captivity.

Davenport's apprehension, when it came, epitomized his long and bumbling career outside the law. Arrested in Las Vegas as a simple vagrant, on May 5th, he gave his name as "William Stephen Daniels." Standard scrutiny of fingerprints revealed his true identity, and Davenport was automatically returned to Leavenworth, where extra charges of escape appended further years to his already-lengthy sentence.

13 ■ HENRY CLAY TOLLETT

Henry Tollett's criminal record dated from 1923, including convictions for larceny, auto theft, and bank robbery. On his first arrest, for theft of livestock, he was sentenced to a two-year prison term. In 1925, he drew five years for robbery. In 1932, the charge was robbery with firearms and the sentence thirty years. Released on April 16, 1946, after serving fourteen years for the armed robbery of a Konawa, Oklahoma, bank, Tollett seemed incapable of avoiding trouble with the law.

In early 1947, he was arrested in Bakersfield, California, on another robbery charge, and won release on bail. On May 5 of that year, Tollett and a male accomplice robbed a bank in Oakland, Oregon, of $31,000 in cash and $1,225 in blank U.S. savings bonds. On July 10, he was arrested in Tulare, California, on charges of child stealing and contributing to the delinquency of a minor; two weeks later, again in Bakersfield, he was charged with carrying a concealed weapon.

The sporadic arrests failed to slow Tollett down. On August 29, 1947, he joined a male accomplice in raiding a Sweet Home, Oregon, bank for $58,000—then the largest haul from a bank robbery in Oregon history. On September 10, he was held on a concealed weapons charge in Tulare. Then he was arrested by federal officers, in Bakersfield, on September 17. Sentenced to twenty-five years on federal bank robbery charges, Tollett faced another term of five years to life in California upon his release.

On November 22, 1949, Tollett escaped from the federal prison on McNeil Island, Washington, by hiding in an outbound shipment of prison-made furniture. He was seen bailing out of the truck in Tacoma, and the hunt was on. As an escaped federal prisoner with a quarter-century of violent felonies behind him, Tollett made the "Ten Most Wanted" list on April 11, 1950.

In the end, his penchant for returning to his favorite haunts in California spelled the end for Tollett. FBI investigation turned up evidence that he was traveling the Golden State in spring of 1951, and officers of the California Highway Patrol picked him up near Redding, on June 3. Tollett was returned to federal prison for completion of his sentence, with a list of brand new charges filed against him.

14 ■ FREDERICK J. TENUTO

The trigger man in Arnold Schuster's murder was a thirty-seven-year-old murderer and fugitive from justice, known with certain irony among his gangland cronies as "the Angel," or "St. John." His execution of the man who fingered Willie Sutton may have been an act of friendship, but the better evidence suggests Tenuto acted under orders from the "Lord High Executioner" of Brooklyn mafiosi, Albert Anastasia. Either way, it was a move which proved as lethal for the gunman as it did his human target.

Fred Tenuto served his first time in reform school at eleven years of age, committed as a chronic runaway from home. At age sixteen, he gained a reputation for arrests as a "suspicious person." At eighteen, he was convicted of robbery and burglary, sentenced to three years probation. Picked up again, he was packed off for a ten-year stretch in the state's industrial school at Huntington, Pennsylvania. In and out of prison through the 1930s, Tenuto was convicted of murdering a Philadelphia man in 1940. Sentenced to a term of ten to twenty years, he managed to escape in 1942, but was swiftly recaptured. Another prison break, in 1945, won Tenuto a short month of freedom before he was recaptured in New York. Transferred to Holmesburg Prison, on the outskirts of Philadelphia, he staged another break in 1947, fleeing in the company of four other convicts. One of his companions in the break was Willie Sutton.

After his escape, Tenuto surfaced in the gangland haunts of Brooklyn, wearing two guns in his belt and bragging that the only way police would ever take him was by shooting him in bed. He sought protection from the Mafia, and won an audience with Anastasia, who was always on the lookout for reliable assassins. Posted to the FBI's "Most Wanted" list on May 24, 1950, the Angel was still at large two years later, when Anastasia flew into a rage one night and ordered Schuster's execution as an example to "stool pigeons" everywhere.

Tenuto took the contract, but it blew up in his face. According to the testimony of informant Joe Valachi, Anastasia realized the risks involved in killing a "civilian"—someone not affiliated with the mob—and took swift measures to protect himself. Once he had murdered Schuster, Fred Tenuto was himself assassinated, and his body disappeared. (One theory has it that Tenuto got a "double-decker" funeral, his corpse concealed inside a coffin built for two.)

Tenuto's name was formally removed from the "Most Wanted" list on March 9, 1964, in light of Joe Valachi's evidence. The federal warrant naming him a fugitive from justice was dismissed.

15 ■ THOMAS KLING

Another member of the "Ten Most Wanted" list associated with the Willie Sutton case was Thomas Kling, a gunman in the robbery which netted $63,933 from a bank in Sunnyside, New York, on March 9, 1950. It was not Kling's first experience in crime, nor would it be his last.

Arrested for the first time at the tender age of ten, in 1916, Kling had managed to collect a bulky record, leaning heavily towards counts of robbery and assault. The latter charges stemmed primarily from Kling's employment as a strongarm goon for crooked labor unions on the New York waterfront, where he was known as "Mad Dog," an enforcer with a reputation for brutality. Kling served a term of fifteen years in a New Jersey prison, finally emerging on September 18, 1947. Two years later, he was suspected as the bandit in a New York tavern robbery, but he remained at large, eluding the police. His work with Sutton followed swiftly, and his name was added to the FBI's "Most Wanted" list in mid-July of 1950.

Kling's good fortune, while it lasted, seemed caught up with Sutton's. When the Actor was arrested by New York police, responding to a tip from witness Arnold Schuster, Kling had only two more days of freedom left. Arrested February 20, 1952, with three associates, he was confined and held for trial with Sutton, on assorted charges stemming from the robbery at Sunnyside. A third accomplice, John De Venuta, turned state's evidence to save himself, and testified against his cronies at their trial. Kling and Sutton each drew sentences of twenty-nine years for the heist, effectively putting both men out of action forever.

16 ■ MEYER DEMBIN

A native of New York City's Lower East Side, Meyer Dembin grew up on the streets, running with gangs of local toughs. By the early 1930s, he had racked up six arrests for larceny, assault and robbery, along with one—in 1934—on suspicion of murder. All the charges were dismissed for lack of evidence, but Dembin's luck ran out in early 1935. On February 8, with three accomplices, he robbed a bank in Sparkill, New York, of $19,799. Two of the bandits were traced through the license plates on their abandoned getaway car and arrested days later, each receiving terms of 25 years in prison. A third participant was arrested in 1946, and sentenced to fifteen years, but Dembin was still at large when his name was added to the "Top Ten" list on September 5, 1950.

Fourteen months later, on November 26, 1951, the fugitive surrendered voluntarily to federal agents in New York.

Dembin told his captors that he had "gone straight" a decade earlier, around the time he married, but refused to say where he had been since 1935. He carried no wallet or identification at the time of his surrender, and the labels had been carefully removed from all his clothing.

Picked up once for investigation in El Paso while living on the run, Dembin had been released before officers realized his true identity. Otherwise, he told the FBI, he had been earning $75 to $100 a week selling hooked rugs. (Agents doubted his story, linking his name with unsolved bank robberies in Detroit, Los Angeles, El Paso, and elsewhere.) Pleading guilty on federal charges the same day he surrendered, Dembin faced a maximum term of forty-seven years in prison for the Sparkill robbery.

17 ■ COURTNEY TOWNSEND TAYLOR

A classic "paper hanger," Courtney Taylor had a flair for passing bogus checks. Despite his bulk—in excess of 200 pounds— the forger never stooped to violence. Questioned on his methods, Taylor once produced a fountain pen and gloated, "This is all the gun I need."

And it was true. In his pursuit of other people's money, Taylor used more than a hundred pseudonyms, inscribing countless rubber checks from coast to coast. The FBI had evidence sufficient to connect him with 225 bad checks, written in an estimated 100 cities. Taylor's lethal fountain pen had earned him more than $100,000 by the time his name was posted to the "Ten Most Wanted" list on January 8, 1951. Charged with forgery and interstate transportation of stolen property, Taylor had a month and seven days of freedom left.

Ironically, his capture stemmed from Taylor's urge to take a short vacation. He traveled south to Alabama, stopping in Mobile, where he discovered he could not resist the urge to write more checks. In recent weeks, he had been using stolen checks from the Reynolds Tobacco Company, enjoying good results as he impersonated an employee of the firm. Unknown to Taylor, though, the FBI had recently identified his favorite checks, and warnings had been sent to merchants nationwide.

In Mobile, Taylor's fondness for expensive jewelry got the better of him. On February 16, 1951, his check was readily accepted at one store, but his second target had a more suspicious credit manager. A note was made of Taylor's license number, and employees telephoned the FBI while their superior flagged down a traffic officer. Before patrolmen had a chance to study Taylor's "Rodney Hickson" driver's license, federal agents had converged upon the scene with warrants, sample fingerprints, and mug shots of their man.

High living has its price, and Courtney Taylor's indiscretions carried rigid penalties. Each worthless check entitled him to ten years of prison time, plus a $10,000 fine—and he had penned 225. The prospect of 2,250 years in jail and $2,250,000 in fines was intimidating, to say the least, but Taylor got off "easy" at his trial, in June. A judge inclined toward mercy settled for a prison term of fifteen years.

18 ■ JOSEPH FRANKLIN BRENT , JR.

The desperate career of Joseph Brent epitomizes the type of fugitive for whom the FBI's "Most Wanted" program was initiated. Charged in three states with assault and robbery, Brent fled the San Diego area when he was charged with an attempted murder there. In Colorado, he received a twenty-five-year sentence for the robbery of a post office at Grand Junction, but escaped once more, before the prison gates could close behind him. Captured, briefly, in Louisiana, he escaped from Gretna's jail and shot it out with officers who gave pursuit. Brent's friends repeated boasts that he would not be taken in alive.

Brent's name was added to the "Ten Most Wanted" list on January 9, 1951. His life of violence stood in striking contrast to the methods of another fugitive, Courtney Taylor, who had made the list the day before.

A rootless nomad, Brent evaded federal agents for a period of nineteen months. In August 1952, his photograph was run in *Pageant* magazine, producing a reaction from Alaska. An informant there, whose anonymity was closely guarded by the FBI, remembered Brent and thought he might be bound for Mexico. Investigation in the neighborhood of Monterey brought G-men back to Texas City, Texas, where they caught Brent on August 29.

A team of special agents had surrounded Brent's apartment building, ready for a siege, believing him to be inside. The fugitive surprised them, moments later, by arriving in a yellow Ford coupe. Surrounded in an instant as he tried to park, Brent scrambled from the car and tried to draw a pistol from his belt. A bullet in the thigh reduced his urge to fight, and he was hustled off for treatment in the jail ward of a local hospital. With Colorado's sentence waiting, followed by accumulated time in California and assorted other states, his run was over.

19 ■ HARRY H. BURTON

As such things go, the holdup—in October 1947—had been perfectly routine until its final moments. Men with guns had crashed a party in Los Angeles, commanding those present to lie on the floor while their pockets and handbags were rifled for cash, jewelry stripped from their fingers and wrists. All was well until one of the guests, Robert Crane, tried to rise from the floor and was shot through the head. He was dead when the ambulance came, and the robbery charge became murder. The case was no longer mundane.

Among the several bandits, one had captured the attention of surviving witnesses. He had been wearing heavy pancake makeup, a peculiarity which jogged the memories of homicide detectives. Suspect Harry Burton, with a history of forgery and robbery arrests that dated back to 1921, had worn such makeup in the past, and once a warrant had been issued, cryptic references were made to "other evidence" recovered at the scene. A three-year local search revealed no trace of Burton in Los Angeles, and he was added to the Bureau's

"Top Ten" list on February 18, 1951. It took another year for agents of the FBI to bring him in.

Unlike some fugitives, who trust in constant movement for protection, Burton found himself a hiding place and burrowed in. He spent four years in Cody, Wyoming, changing jobs periodically, before a "True Detective" broadcast on the radio betrayed him. A description of distinctive facial scars, the relics of a welding accident, alerted listeners and brought a tip to federal agents. Burton was arrested at a local auto dealership, where he had been employed for several weeks before the fateful broadcast.

Ironically, considering the time and effort spent to run him down, the fugitive would not remain in jail for long. When Burton went to trial that May, assorted witnesses could not identify him as the gunman who had murdered Robert Crane in 1947. Burton's lawyer called two witnesses who swore that he was at the bedside of a dying man when Crane was killed, and in the absence of substantial evidence, he was acquitted by a jury.

20 ■ JOSEPH PAUL CATO

It may be fairly said that Joseph Cato was a hoodlum all his life. In Prohibition, he enlisted with the California bootleg mob run by Eddie Quinones, earning his keep as a hired gun and rum runner. Cato was not above hijacking shipments consigned to his rivals, a practice which sparked many long-running feuds in the twenties and thirties. Aside from his dealings in liquor, he sometimes branched out on his own, serving hard time for robbery and impersonating a federal officer. For all of that, it was a crime of passion which eventually landed Cato on the "Ten Most Wanted" list.

Paroled in California from a robbery conviction, Cato took a shot at going straight in San Francisco. He was married, making decent money in a little sandwich shop, when he became enamored of a patron, Phyllis McCullough. The lady returned his affections, her own marriage notwithstanding. There was talk of divorce from encumbering spouses, and

Phyllis, as good as her word, parted ways with her husband. Joe Cato was slower, and soon Phyllis tired of the wait. She came up with a new paramour, Herbert Wallander, brushing her former lover aside.

Cato's strong point had never been tolerance. Faced with rejection, he fired back with threats. Phyllis spoke to the district attorney, but bridled at signing a formal complaint. Herb Wallander was present on March 22, 1946, when Cato broke into the woman's house, a pistol in his hand, and chased her upstairs to the bedroom. There, he shot her in the head, then beat a hasty exit with her Doberman attack dog in pursuit. The dog returned a short time later, and by then, police were on the scene.

They learned that Cato had cleaned out his bank account before the shooting. He was gone without a trace, and five years would pass before he surfaced. In the meantime, homicide detectives had a hunch that Cato was relying on his syndicate connections as a cover. During 1949, as gangland violence sputtered in Los Angeles, he traveled south. The Mafia was squaring off against a hoodlum army led by Mickey Cohen, and assorted witnesses in Hollywood named Cato as the gunman who had ambushed Neddie Herbert, Cohen's right-hand man.

His long-established history of violence earned Joe Cato a position on the "Ten Most Wanted" list, and he was added to the roster on June 7, 1951. Precisely two weeks later, he was apprehended in Cleveland, where he had secured a machinist's job under the alias of "Joseph Lombardo." Ray Abbaticchio, special agent in charge, led a raiding party composed of three special agents and Cleveland Chief of Detectives James McArthur. Cato offered slight resistance, and was easily subdued. Returned to San Francisco and a murder trial, he tried to write the fatal shooting off as "accidental." Members of the jury disagreed, and he was jailed for life.

21 ■ ANTHONY BRANCATO

Anthony Brancato was a hard case, living on the fringes of the underworld and serving bigger mobsters than himself when there was work available, content to rape and rob and push narcotics when the times were lean. A Kansas City native, he had gravitated to Los Angeles, and there compiled a record of arrests for gambling, dealing drugs and bootleg liquor, plus suspicion in a string of gangland murders. When a sniper murdered Bugsy Siegel, during June 1947, homicide detectives hustled Tony in for questioning. They called him back in 1948, when Hooky Rothman, one of Mickey Cohen's goons, was murdered in Los Angeles, and in July 1949 he was interrogated after an attack on Cohen. To the north, in Fresno, California, he was suspect in the drug-related death of Abe Davidian.

Brancato's bosom pal, another Kansas City boy gone bad, was Anthony Trombino. They had been hauled in together, on occasion, and between them they could boast of forty-six arrests, including rape and robbery, assault, and other major crimes. They were considered renegades within a world of outlaws, and they had devoted years to making enemies.

On May 28, 1951, four bandits robbed the sports book at the Fabulous Flamingo, in Las Vegas, making off with $3,500 in cash. The heist was ill-conceived at best, considering the hidden ownership of the casino, doubly so considering the fact that Anthony Brancato did not bother with a mask. Considering his long and violent record, he was posted to the "Ten Most Wanted" list June 27. Two days later, with a lawyer at his side, he voluntarily surrendered to the FBI in San Francisco, posting a $10,000 bond. Before he had a chance to leave the building, Anthony was rearrested on Nevada's warrant, naming him a fugitive from justice. This time, he was out of cash and could not post the necessary bail.

Brancato's case became a minor *cause célèbre* for students of the Constitution, who accused the state and federal governments of violating Tony's civil rights. Released without bond on a writ of habeas corpus, Brancato fled south to Los Angeles, there teaming up with his sidekick, Trombino. They both needed cash for their various lawyers, and neither could stomach the thought of an honest day's work. Their last days are described by author Ovid Demaris in *The Last Mafioso*, a biography of syndicate killer Jimmy "The Weasel" Fratianno.

According to Fratianno, "the Two Tonys," swindled a gambler, Sam Lazes, out of $3,000 he owed to a syndicate bookie. Posing as collection agents for the mob, Brancato and Trombino pocketed the cash, and later tried to pressure Lazes for another payment. Added to Brancato's sheer audacity in robbing the Flamingo, it was more than local mobsters were inclined to tolerate.

On orders from the syndicate, Fratianno approached Brancato and Trombino, offering to help them execute a robbery in Hollywood. On August 6, the Weasel kept his date, with gunman Charles Battaglia in tow. Brancato and Trombino occupied the front seat of a car parked on Hollywood Boulevard, Fratianno and Battaglia seated behind them, when the shooting started. Both Brancato and Trombino were killed instantly by multiple shots to the head, their murder "unsolved" until Fratianno entered the federal witness protection program twenty years later.

22 ■ FREDERICK EMERSON PETERS

A swindler and bad check artist in the mold of Courtney Taylor, Frederick Peters used 130 different names before he reached the age of sixty-five. His record spanned four decades, in the course of which he had impersonated federal officers and clergymen, physicians and professors, even presidents of the United States. One foolish victim had mistaken him for Franklin Roosevelt, an error helped along by Peters and his polished line of patter. Even members of his family were not immune. On one occasion, Peters used an alias to wire his parents with the information that their son was dead; two hundred dollars was required "to send the body home." Grief-stricken, Frederick's parents sent the money off at once, and Peters used it to inaugurate another swindle on the spot.

At sixty-five, Fred Peters was a felon with a record, sought for violation of parole in Tampa, Florida. A fraud indictment had been filed against him in St. Petersburg, with other charges pending in Chicago, Philadelphia, and Birmingham. The federal government was seeking him on charges of impersonation and for moving stolen goods across state lines. His name was added to the Bureau's "Ten Most Wanted" list on July 2, 1951. The king of bunco artists had six months of freedom left.

Ironically, it was a swindle in the making which betrayed Fred Peters at the end. On January 15, 1952, a special agent of the FBI saw Peters in the lobby of a Washington hotel, and detained him for questioning. The fugitive identified himself as one "Paul Carpenter," just in from New York City to discuss production of a music festival in Uruguay with spokesmen for the State Department. Unimpressed, the agent offered to accompany him, but on arrival at their destination, Peters suddenly "remembered" his appointment had not been with State at all, but rather with a member of the Pan American Union. When his new companion showed no signs of losing interest in the tour, Fred folded and confessed his true identity. He was returned to Florida for sentencing on violation of parole and trial on other pending charges.

23 ■ ERNEST TAIT

The burglary should never have resulted in a shootout. It was scheduled for a simple in-and-out, a two-man job devoid of complications. Knocking off the Elks Club in New Castle, Indiana, should have been easy but police surprised the burglars who tried to pull it off on April Fool's Day, 1951. The bandits came out shooting, and police replied in kind. One of the suspects clubbed an officer unconscious and escaped; his partner, Richard Schmidt, was captured at the scene, his legs permanently paralyzed by a bullet which had clipped his spine.

Schmidt managed to survive, and there were those among investigating officers who ventured a suggestion that his partner was responsible for Richard's wound. They may have been correct, for Schmidt was talking freely by the time he left intensive care. He named his comrade in the burglary as Ernest Tait, an Indiana native known to officers around the state.

Tait's record of arrests spanned twenty years, beginning as a juvenile in Indianapolis. In 1935, he had been wounded there, in an attempt to burglarize a local bank. Upon recovery, he was sentenced to a stretch in prison, but escaped. Arrested by police in Illinois for trying to illegally procure explosives, he was jailed again; upon release, he was returned to finish off his time in Indiana, with another hitch tacked on for his escape. Detectives knew him as a frequenter of race tracks, recognizable by his distinctive lisp. His name and face were added to the Bureau's "Top Ten" list July 11, 1951.

The day of Tait's addition to the roster, he was featured in a story published by a paper in Miami, Florida. Employees at a restaurant in Coral Gables saw his photograph and recognized the likeness of a frequent customer. He drove a brand-new Oldsmobile, the FBI was told, and agents started hitting local dealers, calling on garages, passing out Tait's mug shot to mechanics, salesmen, anyone at all who might have contact with the fugitive.

No more than half an hour after G-men called at Finchley Motors, on July 12, 1951, Tait brought his new car in for servicing. Mechanic Jesse Marrs identified the fugitive and put his car up on the grease rack, to prevent escape while an urgent call was put through to the FBI. R. W. Wall, Special Agent in Charge, arrived moments later, with Agent Webb Burke in tow. Tait's matching pair of .45s was out of reach, inside the elevated car, and he submitted meekly to arrest. Returned to Indiana, Tait pled guilty to a charge of burglary in mid-October receiving a term of two to five years in the state penitentiary.

24 ■ OLLIE GENE EMBRY

Ollie Embry was a self-styled ladies' man and two-gun bandit who relied on benzedrine to quicken his reactions on a holdup. Born in Arkansas, he was arrested for the first time, as a highway robber, at the tender age of fifteen years. By early 1951, he had served time in California, Texas, Colorado, with a stint in the United States reformatory at El Reno, Oklahoma.

On the sixth of February 1951, four gunmen entered the Monroe National Bank, in Columbia, Illinois, ten minutes after it reopened from lunch. They lined employees up and swept $8,943 from the cages, scattering two-inch roofing nails in the street to halt pursuers as they fled the scene. Their getaway had been meticulously planned—three different cars were used—but luck was running hard against the outlaws. Teenage wheelman Frank Daubauch was soon arrested on a tip from neighbors, and he started naming names. His cronies, Jack McAllister and Patrick Kane—reputed organizer of the raid—were picked up hours later, some $8,000 of the loot recovered by arresting officers. In unison, they gave up Ollie Embry as the one who got away.

The robbery itself had been a federal crime, ordained by statutes dating from the 1930s; other charges lodged against the fugitive included interstate transportation of stolen property and violation of the Dyer Act, the driving of a stolen car across state lines. Embry's name was posted to the "Ten Most Wanted" list on July 25. He had ten days of freedom left.

On August 5, a local plainclothes officer, James Messick, spotted Embry pumping gas in Kansas City. Messick tipped the FBI, and Lee Boardman, special agent in charge, led a raiding party to the service station where Embry was employed. The agents posed as customers, surrounding Ollie as he bent to check beneath their hood. Comparison of fingerprints, conducted at the scene, confirmed their recognition of the fugitive, and he was carted back to Illinois for trial.

25 ■ GIACHINO A. BACCOLIA

A mobster based in Paterson, New Jersey, Baccolia earned his keep by smuggling narcotics and hiring out from time to time as "muscle" for his underworld associates. According to police informants, he was not afraid to pull a trigger if the price was right, and federal officers suspected him of murder in at least one case. The victim, jeweler Albert Swarz, was killed in May 1951, a week before he was supposed to testify against Chicago hoodlums charged with stealing $25,000 worth of film. Baccolia was sought on federal charges of obstructing justice, plus a local charge of murder in Detroit; his name was added to the "Ten Most Wanted" list on August 20, 1951.

FBI surveillance of his favorite haunts resulted in the fugitive's arrest, in New York City, on December 10, 1951. A year later, he was acquitted of murder charges by a Detroit jury, but the victory did not put Baccolia back on the street. In the interim, a federal court had convicted him of smuggling narcotics into the United States, an offense which earned him seven years in prison.

26 ■ RAYMOND EDWARD YOUNG

The son of an affluent contractor in Lincoln, Nebraska, Raymond Young described himself as a "wild kid" who "learned too much in the reformatory" and was doomed to lead a life of crime as the result. He failed to mention that his first incarceration, during 1932, was a result of his deliberate attempt to rob a bank. The poor, misguided "kid" was twenty years old at the time.

Upon release, Young traveled to Los Angeles, where he began to trade in stolen jewelry. Convicted of receiving stolen property, he drew a sentence of two and a half years. Parole freed him a year later, but he was soon back inside, serving one to five for burglary. Paroled again in three years he hung around Los Angeles until police surprised him during another burglary and he was sentenced to a term of five years to life in Folsom prison. On August 31, 1948, Young and forty-seven other convicts were dispatched to fight a forest fire near San Luis Obispo. He escaped on foot, returning to Los Angeles, where cars were waiting to be stolen, houses to be burglarized. In mid-September, arguing with an acquaintance, "wild kid" Raymond Young produced a .38 and fired six shots at point-blank range, but poor aim spared him from a murder charge. His target fled, unscathed.

Young had been living on the run for two months, when a pair of beat patrolmen stopped him on the street in late October 1948. Their questions struck too close to home, and he responded violently, punching one officer, ripping his gun from its holster and shooting the other. Young fled north to San Francisco, east from there to Wyoming, and on to Colorado, settling in Denver in December. He was married there in February 1949, as "Donald Sherman," and it seems that marriage altered Young's approach to life. He worked a wide variety of jobs throughout the next three years, but never drifted back to crime. When he was added to the "Ten Most Wanted" list, on November 12, 1951, Young was working nights at a bakery, running errands for a mortuary in the daylight hours.

Federal agents found him at the bakery four nights later, acting on a tip from local sources who had recognized his photograph. They found him loading bread trucks, and Young offered no resistance, readily admitting his identity. When news of his arrest was broadcast, neighbors circulated a petition asking Colorado's governor to block the extradition of a man they all regarded as "a darn swell fellow." It was a touching effort, ultimately wasted. Raymond Young, a "wild kid" who reformed himself too late, was taken back to California for trial.

27 ■ JOHN THOMAS HILL

The brief career of fugitive John Hill was more a rampage than a crime wave. His behavior, vicious as it was, seemed more a product of his inner rage and cultivated taste for alcohol than any real intent to make a living on the wrong side of the law. In May of 1950, Hill was leader of a six-man gang that robbed a store in Willoughby, Maryland; before they fled, the elderly proprietor was murdered with an ax. Five members of the gang were caught almost immediately, in a local dragnet. Only Hill escaped, and with him went the cash box, their pathetic loot inside.

Hill drove to Portsmouth, in Virginia, turning up at the

home of his estranged wife. She invited him in, they shared numerous drinks, and old arguments were rekindled by liquor. Enraged, Hill seized an ice pick and inflicted five deep wounds about the woman's head and breast. She would survive to testify, and so Virginia charged him only with felonious assault. In Maryland, the pending charge was murder in the first degree.

Hill's name was added to the "Ten Most Wanted" list on December 10, 1951. Eight months elapsed before a citizen in Hamtramck, Michigan, identified his wanted flyer, notifying agents of the FBI. Investigation turned up Hill's address, and Special Agent in Charge James Robey led the raiding party which caught Hill in bed, fast asleep as they crashed through his door. He offered no resistance, and was extradited back to Maryland for trial.

28 ■ GEORGE ARTHUR HEROUX

A veteran stickup artist who specialized in bank robberies, Heroux joined accomplice Gerhard Puff (#30) to rob a bank in Kansas City, Missouri, on October 10, 1951. Six weeks later, on November 23, they cracked another bank in Prairie Village, Kansas, walking out with $62,650. By the time FBI agents began tracking him on federal charges, Heroux was also suspected in the murder of Massachusetts State Trooper Alje Savela, slain at Barre on August 31, 1951. The fugitive's name was added to the "Top Ten" list on December 19, 1951, with his partner following a month later.

Evidence recovered from an abandoned car led G-men to scour the state of New Hampshire on July 19, 1952, but the trail was already cold. Six days later, in the Miami suburb of El Portal, Florida, Police Chief Barron Shields and Patrolman Robert Dubray responded to reports of a disturbance at a local residence. Arriving on the scene, they were confronted by Heroux, with gun in hand. He forced the officers to take him on a drive, which soon became a high-speed, bullet-punctuated chase as other squad cars joined the lineup. Chief Shields finally brought the pursuit to a close by swerving his car into a tree, stunning Heroux long enough for the fugitive to be disarmed.

In custody, Heroux refused to offer any information, but an inadvertent comment led the FBI to New York City, where his partner, Puff, was captured on July 26.

29 ■ SYDNEY GORDON MARTIN

Sydney Martin's troubles started in the army. Stationed in the Panama Canal Zone, during 1941, he tried to hang himself when it appeared he might be posted overseas for combat duty. Martin twice deserted during World War II, finally winning a dishonorable discharge after serving twelve months at hard labor.

The reentry to civilian life was rocky for a man who had been booted from the service of his country in disgrace. The discharge had a way of closing doors in Sydney's face, and things were not improved when it became apparent that he hated honest work. On June 1, 1950, Martin lured farmer Edward Pinski from his chores with stories of a nonexistent car stalled on the road near Pinski's farm, outside of Belchertown, Massachusetts. As the farmer climbed down from his tractor, Martin drew a pistol, firing three shots into Pinski's neck and chest. Unsatisfied, he used a heavy stone to crush his victim's skull, stole some $440 from the farmer's house, and fled in Pinski's truck.

Arrested by police in Holyoke on June 18, his birthday, Martin soon confessed his crime. Jailed at Northampton, pending the October grand jury session, Martin scaled a barbed wire fence and made his getaway, with other inmates, on September 4. His two accomplices were soon recaptured, earning eighteen months in prison for the break, but Martin was at large on January 7, 1952, when he was added to the FBI's "Most Wanted" list.

The end came one day short of three weeks later, when a resident of Corpus Christi, Texas, recognized the fugitive from mug shots published in a magazine. The FBI was notified, and agents apprehended him in Corpus Christi on November 27.

Martin was returned to Massachusetts, where, in the absence of capital punishment, he was sentenced to life imprisonment.

30 ■ GERHARD ARTHUR PUFF

Sought, with George Heroux (#28), for robbery of banks in Kansas and Missouri, Puff was traced to New York City after Heroux's arrest in Florida, on July 25, 1952. FBI agents discovered that the fugitives had registered at the Congress Hotel on July 20, with their wives, using the names "J. Burns" (for Puff) and "John Hanson" (for Heroux). Heroux afterwards drove to Florida, where he was captured, while Puff and the women remained in New York.

On the morning of July 26, five federal agents hid themselves in a small waiting room off the lobby of the Congress Hotel, maintaining radio contact with a sixth agent outside. They observed "Mrs. Burns" and "Mrs. Hanson" leaving the hotel with heavy luggage, later found to be packed full of guns and ammunition. Gerhard Puff returned to the hotel a short time later, riding upstairs in the elevator, and the agents took their places to arrest him when he reappeared. Four men were stationed in the lobby, while a fifth—Special Agent Joseph Brock—crouched down behind a frosted glass door, separating the lobby from a hallway in the rear.

Puff managed to surprise the agents by descending on the stairs, ambushing Agent Brock and shooting him five times, with fatal results. Believing himself in the clear, Puff bolted through the lobby and was halted by a bullet in his leg. A charge of murder in the first degree was added to the federal counts against him, while the women captured in his company were charged with aiding and abetting federal fugitives.

31 ■ THOMAS EDWARD YOUNG

For Thomas Young, the joys of married life were simply an extension of his chosen criminal career. When Young went out on "jobs," he took his mate along as an accomplice and as driver for their getaways. For her part, Margaret Young had no complaints about the curious arrangement, even when it landed her in jail.

By 1951, the couple faced indictments for an auto theft in Denver. They had used the stolen car to cross state lines, becoming federal fugitives through violation of the Dyer Act. Arrested by police in Fargo, North Dakota, after burglarizing two post offices, they managed to escape together. On December 30, they burglarized a small Santana, Kansas, bank and left their fingerprints behind as evidence. Young's name was posted to the "Ten Most Wanted" list on February 21, 1952; his wife, considered a subordinate accomplice, was not added to the roster.

In mid-September, federal agents got a tip which placed the Youngs in Idaho's Boise National Forest. Local officers and G-men fanned out through the area, approaching campsites cautiously, with weapons drawn. The fugitives were spotted at a site near Lowman, Idaho, September 23, and plans were made to attack the camp by night. A guard was posted, but the Youngs surprised their would-be captors, breaking camp that afternoon and packing all their goods inside the one-ton trailer they had hooked up to their car. Inside the trailer was an arsenal with which the outlaws practiced frequently, in preparation for a showdown with the law.

Compelled to change their plans or lose their quarry, sixteen agents formed a hasty roadblock on the narrow, unpaved track which offered access to the campsite. They were waiting as the Youngs approached, and neither fugitive resisted in the face of so much concentrated weaponry. Inside the trailer, safely out of reach, the agents seized two rifles, two shotguns, and two cases of ammunition. In the car, a shortwave radio had been installed to monitor police calls, but it did the Youngs no good as they were cornered and disarmed.

32 ■ KENNETH LEE MAURER

Lawrence Maurer came home in a decent mood that Monday, looking forward to a peaceful evening with his family. In three more days, Thanksgiving would provide him with a paid day off from work, and he was looking forward to a break from the routine of hustling as a salesman at a Detroit auto dealership. He loved the quiet times at home.

And yet, it seemed a bit too quiet as he closed the door behind him on the evening of November 26, 1951. No answer came when he called out that he was home. He crossed the living room, checked out the kitchen—no one there; no supper on the stove—and started down the hallway, stopping short as he saw a trail of rusty bloodstains on the carpet, leading toward the master bedroom. Maurer tried the door and found it locked. He knocked, but got no answer, moving swiftly toward his daughter's room.

A shape was huddled underneath the blankets in his daughter's bed. When Maurer stripped the covers back, he found a doll reposing on the bloody sheets. The missing girl, young Janet Maurer, was discovered huddled in her closet, stabbed four times, her skull split open by a vicious blow which had exposed the brain.

Unable to continue with his search, the stricken father telephoned police. Patrolmen forced the master bedroom's door and found his wife stretched out beside the bed, dispatched with thirty-four distinct and separate stab wounds, as well as crushing blows delivered with a hatchet.

Another member of the Maurer family, eighteen-year-old Kenneth, turned up missing in the search, and homicide detectives first believed he might have been abducted. Their opinion changed when they discovered evidence that someone had conducted a deliberate search for family snapshots, stealing every photo that depicted Kenneth Maurer. Instantly, the missing boy was shifted from the status of potential victim to a leading suspect in the case. (Police discovered that the purge of family photographs had missed a single snapshot; it would be retrieved to illustrate the wanted posters charging Maurer with two counts of murder in the first degree.)

Initially, Ken Maurer seemed to be a most unlikely suspect

in the vicious crime. A shy assistant Boy Scout leader, Maurer loved stray animals and spent his free time gardening. However, homicide investigators soon heard tales of raging arguments between the murdered woman and her son. Observers in the neighborhood recalled that Ken was prone to violent outbursts, rages which were swift and unpredictable. A coroner's report suggested that the killing wounds had been inflicted with a Boy Scout knife and hatchet.

The pursuit of Kenneth Maurer led police and federal agents on a far-flung chase, as "positive" reports were filed by witnesses in California, Mexico, New Jersey. In Detroit, the female victim of a stabbing two days after Maurer's disappearance named the missing boy as her assailant, but police by then possessed conclusive evidence that he had fled the state. Their fugitive had left a paper trail of payroll checks and bus tickets from Michigan to Dayton, Ohio, on from there to Nashville, Tennessee. Ken Maurer's photo was selected as the likeness of a customer who shopped for cars in Tampa, Florida, November 27, showing special interest in a car that turned up stolen one day later.

There, the trail went cold, and there had been no further news of Maurer when his name was added to the "Ten Most Wanted" list on February 27, 1952. By that time, Maurer had already settled in Miami, known to neighbors and the woman who became his live-in mistress as "John Arthur Blotz." The couple moved into a trailer park together. She began to introduce herself as "Mrs. Blotz," while Maurer found employment at a local cabinet shop.

The job turned out to be a steady one, and "Blotz" might well have reached retirement there, had it not been for national publicity surrounding the "Most Wanted" program. Several customers identified his published photograph in early January 1953, and more than one saw fit to telephone the FBI. Agents Robert Wall and Webb Burke found Maurer at work on January 8, and he submitted meekly to arrest. Afraid to fly, the killer was permitted to return by train for trial on murder charges in Detroit.

Interrogation yielded a confession to his mother's murder, but the suspect still professed amnesia in his sister's case. A panel of psychiatrists reported him insane in February 1953, and Maurer was committed to Ionia State Hospital until such time as he might be considered fit for trial. On May 12, 1964, it was announced that Maurer had escaped from the asylum, but the bulletin was cancelled one day later, with discovery of his body floating in a reservoir inside the compound. Whether Maurer killed himself or drowned by accident remains a mystery.

33 ■ ISAIE ALDY BEAUSOLEIL

On Wednesday afternoon, August 17, 1949, a teenage boy returning home from school stepped off his bicycle beside a culvert in Monroe County, Michigan. He meant to check the water level in the ditch, and he was unprepared for the discovery of a woman's lifeless body, floating face-down in the stagnant stream. A coroner's report declared the woman had been stunned by blows about the head, then dumped in the canal, where she had drowned without regaining consciousness. It took a week for a review of fingerprints to yield the victim's name. Rose Tabram, forty-seven, was a visitor from Canada, last seen alive in company with a fellow Canadian, one Isaie Beausoleil.

The latter name was only too familiar to authorities. A drifter from Ontario, the suspect alternated time between assorted prisons and the open road. His record started with a bootlegging arrest in 1927; two years later, he was picked up for attempted robbery in New York City. Charged with robbing a $2,500 payroll at Providence, Rhode Island, Beausoleil had managed to escape from prison during 1939. Since then, he had been drifting back and forth across the border, finally reentering the United States illegally, in 1946.

The FBI tagged Beausoleil a federal fugitive, but finding him was something else. In 1950, G-men narrowly missed him in Massachusetts. Hiding at a house in Worcester, Isaie slipped out through a back door, leaving warm food on the table, as a raiding party massed out front. In summer 1951, Wisconsin was the scene of an intensive search, when an employee at a rural filling station fingered Beausoleil as one of three men who had stopped for gas. According to the story, Beausoleil had occupied the back seat, with the body of "a young boy with a bullet hole in his forehead." State and federal officers were scrambling to trace the gang when their informant finally admitted it was all a hoax, concocted to relieve the boredom of his lonely job. On March 3, 1952, the Bureau added Beausoleil to its "Most Wanted" list.

By then, the fugitive had settled in Chicago, marrying a widow whom he courted after meeting at a dance. He used the name of "Raymond Blair," but marriage brought the running man no peace of mind. Disturbed by the appearance of his photograph in local papers, Beausoleil took off for a vacation in New Orleans, but his likeness also graced the walls of federal buildings there. In desperation, he conceived a plan which would—he thought—allow him to live safely in Chicago. In the actual event, his scheme produced the most humiliating capture of a "Top Ten" fugitive in Bureau history.

On June 25, 1953, Chicago officers were summoned to the beach, along North Avenue. A "pervert" had been sighted in the women's dressing area, and female officers moved in to make the collar. Speaking in a strange, falsetto voice, the suspect grudgingly identified "herself" as "Rita Bennett," giving up her handbag for inspection. A frisk resulted in arrest when the suspicious officers discovered that their subject had "a more than average need" for padding in "her" bra. Chicago had its share of deviants in 1953, but only one was posted on the "Ten Most Wanted" list, and a review of fingerprints led Beausoleil to finally admit his true identity. The feminine disguise, worn every time he left his house, was Beausoleil's attempt to circumvent arrest. Condemned to life imprisonment in Michigan, the drifter would be forced to get along in prison denims, purchased off the rack.

34 ■ LEONARD JOSEPH ZALUTSKY

A burglar, car thief, and convicted cop-killer, Leonard Zalutsky became number thirty-four on the FBI's "Most Wanted" list as a result of his escape from Florida's maximum-security prison at Raiford, in September 1951. Jailed for the murder of a Miami police officer at the time of his escape, Zalutsky had a reputation as a "rabbit," with a string of daring jailbreaks in at least three states.

A Pennsylvania native, Leonard Zalutsky had been in trouble with the law since age sixteen, when he was busted on a charge of burglary. Sentenced to a decade in Pennsylvania's Huntington reformatory, Zalutsky served less than three years before he was paroled in March 1933.

Five months later, Leonard was in trouble again, charged with an Allentown payroll robbery which netted $5,000. Zalutsky was returned to prison—and again, he was released after serving only a fraction of his allotted time. He had already earned the nickname "Bad Eye," from his fellow inmates, and Zalutsky was convinced no prison in America could hold him for a substantial period of time.

By 1937, Florida had "Bad Eye" Leonard in its Raiford lock-up, facing a variety of now-familiar charges. He escaped on August 1, with the assistance of a former cellmate from the Pennsylvania reformatory, firing several shots at guards before they fled. The fugitives were captured by authorities in Georgia, hours later, and returned to Florida for trial on charges of escape.

In April 1938, Zalutsky fled a prison road camp with another inmate, firing two shots at a guard as he escaped. They were recaptured three weeks later, in Denver, Colorado, following the abduction of a local businessman. The victim's car was stolen by Zalutsky and his sidekick, after which they robbed the man of pocket change and tied him to a tree beside the highway.

En route back to Florida, Zalutsky escaped from a jail in Lawrenceburg, Tennessee. This time, he felt the homing instinct, fleeing north to Pennsylvania. Police in Philadelphia arrested "Bad Eye" on July 20, 1938, charging him with burglary and auto theft, but they had no more luck in holding Leonard than their counterparts in Florida. A few days prior to trial, Zalutsky made another break and armed himself. Aware of "Bad Eye's" reputation as a cop-killer, officers were quick to return fire, and Zalutsky was wounded in the fierce exchange.

Convicted of assorted felonies in August 1938, Zalutsky was given a prison term of ten to twenty years. He was paroled to Florida authorities in 1944, to finish out his sentence in the Sunshine State. On May 14, 1945, he fled another road camp, eluding police for nearly two years before he was recaptured in Newton Falls, Ohio, in March 1947.

"Bad Eye's" final break from Raiford, on September 1, 1951, was his most dramatic yet. In concert with another con, Zalutsky firebombed a guard tower, escaping in the confusion, holding the prison dentist and his wife at knifepoint. The pair eluded their pursuers in a hectic chase, and Leonard made the "Top Ten" roster when a vacancy occurred in August 1952.

Aware of Leonard's tendency to run for home, authorities were watching out for him in Pennsylvania. On September 8, 1952, two citizens of Beaver Falls identified Zalutsky's mug shots as a likeness of one "Dominic Bulaski," locally employed. Detective Theodore Smith arrested Zalutsky at his place of business, and following a foiled attempt at suicide in jail, he was returned to Florida. This time, there would be no escape for "Bad Eye."

35 ■ WILLIAM MERLE MARTIN

William Martin was twenty years old when he was first arrested for public drunkenness, in 1929. Within a year, St. Louis officers arrested him for burglary, and he was sentenced to a five-year prison term, enlivened by a one-day breakout during 1931. In 1936, he earned three years for stealing chickens near Miami, Oklahoma. Three years later, in Missouri, Martin drew an eight-year sentence for receiving stolen property and carrying a weapon. He "cracked up" in 1940, and was transferred to the state-run hospital at Fulton. Two weeks later, he escaped.

By January 1941, the fugitive had earned a widespread reputation as the "pillow case burglar," after his method of hauling loot away from jobs in Kansas, Illinois, and his native Missouri. An explosive argument with Charlie Reed, his closest friend, resulted in Reed's death, but Martin had not been connected with the killing when he was arrested for violation of the Dyer Act, involving transportation of a stolen car across state lines. He finished seven years of a suggested ten-year term in Leavenworth, before he was remanded to Missouri for completion of his sentence there. Paroled on May 9, 1952, he managed to avoid collision with the law for barely seven weeks.

A farmer near Olathe, Kansas, called the local sheriff on June 23, reporting that his pickup truck had just been stolen. Deputies were answering the call when they observed the truck approaching, slithering along the muddy, one-lane track. They tried to flag the pickup down, and lawman Willard Carver stopped a bullet when the driver opened fire. The wound was fatal, but his partner had no time to linger as one suspect left the truck, attempting to escape on foot. The driver, meanwhile, revved the pickup's engine, briefly spinning out before the tires found traction and he sped away. Ex-convict Charles Isgrigg was captured in a nearby cornfield. Under questioning, he named the trigger man in Carver's death as William Martin, late of the Missouri prison system.

Martin's name was added to the "Ten Most Wanted" list on August 11. On the twenty-fourth, a burglar matching his description pistol-whipped a woman and her son in Birmingham. Police secured descriptions of a car seen near the plundered home, and one day later they picked up Roberta Carter, Martin's mistress, as she drove through town, a rifle and a pistol on the seat behind her. Federal charges were invoked, because the car had been reported stolen one week earlier, in Valparaiso, Indiana.

On August 27, traffic officers pursued another stolen car, outside St. Louis, closing as the driver lost control and fled on foot, evading capture in the nearby woods. Descriptions and a hasty check of fingerprints confirmed that they were tracking William Martin, drawn inexorably to his old, familiar hunting grounds.

On August 28, the fugitive was sighted by a posse, but escaped in darkness as the hunters peppered him with gunfire. Two days later, Martin sat behind the wheel of yet another stolen car—this one belonging to a deputy from Cedar Hill—when cruisers forced him to the curb and officers with leveled guns surrounded him on every side. Emaciated, bruised and filthy from his flight, the fugitive submitted meekly to arrest.

36 ■ JAMES EDDIE DIGGS

James Diggs had earned the reputation of an honest man who did a good day's work before he left North Carolina, settling in Norfolk during 1933. He married there, in 1937, and appeared to be a quiet, happy family man. In World War II, he held the local post of air raid warden, chosen by his neighbors as a gesture of respect. Then came the armistice, and things began to change.

By April 1946, it was reported that James Diggs had started drinking heavily. There were suspicions that he cheated on his wife, repeatedly, with several different women. He was picked up by police four times in 1948, for public drunkenness and reckless driving, carrying a concealed weapon, assault and battery. Each time, he paid a fine and managed to escape the harsher punishment of jail time. The home once singled out for comment as a prime example of domestic bliss became a battleground of violent arguments and stony silence. Diggs was separated, briefly, from his wife in 1948, but it appeared that they could no more live apart than get along together.

On the morning of May 26, 1949, a burst of gunfire rocked the neighborhood where Diggs had made his home. Police were summoned, and they found a scene of carnage in the house. Ruth Diggs had been shot twice; her two sons, ages six and four, had been cut down by three shots each. All three were dead. James Diggs was nowhere to be found.

The fugitive was charged with triple murder five days later, and a warrant issued in his name. That afternoon, May 31, a traffic officer in Hamlet, North Carolina, stopped a car with Norfolk plates and three black passengers, requesting that the occupants identify themselves. Two of the men were reaching for their wallets when the third produced a pistol, squeezing off a shot that struck the officer, Rex Howell, in the mouth.

Howell would survive to name James Diggs as his assailant, while the other men, surrendering that night in Norfolk, spun a tale of being snatched at gunpoint, forced to drive their captor south. Immediately after Howell was shot, Diggs left the car near Hamlet, striking off on foot in the direction of some nearby woods. His captives had returned to Norfolk, acting out of fear that local whites might organize a lynching mob before they learned the facts.

No trace of Diggs had been discovered at the time his name was posted to the "Ten Most Wanted" list, on August 27, 1952. Nine years and four months later, when he was dropped from the list, he had still not surfaced. His fate remains a mystery, but by the early 1960s, other desperate felons were demanding equal time.

37 ■ NICK GEORGE MONTOS

Born in Tampa, Florida, in 1916, Montos was first arrested at age fourteen, receiving brief probation on an accusation of possessing stolen property. In 1934, he drew a term of eighteen months for auto theft, and two years later he escaped from the Miami jail where he had been confined for owning burglar's tools. Recaptured quickly, he was sentenced to a year in Raiford prison. On release, he moved to Alabama, quickly racking up convictions there for burglary and grand larceny. Sentenced to the road gang, Montos made a break for freedom, winding up in Kilby Prison, near Montgomery. At Kilby, Montos picked up further training with machinery and tools, while stamping license plates. Unwilling to complete the course, he fled from custody on October 20, 1942, and was recaptured as a federal fugitive in June 1943.

Returned to Kilby, Montos staged another break in February 1944. Four other inmates joined him as he propped a ladder up against the prison wall and scrambled clear. Police arrested him in Illinois, where he was a suspect in a string of burglaries, and shipped him back to Alabama, where, incredibly, he won parole in 1949. Arrested for a burglary in Anniston, he bargained down to a charge of possessing burglar's tools, and escaped with a $500 fine. Shifting to Georgia, Montos was indicted for a burglary in Coweta County, jumping bond before the case was called for trial. In March 1951, a burglary in Hattiesburg, Mississippi resulted in conviction. The case was on appeal when Montos earned himself a nomination to the "Ten Most Wanted" list.

On August 11, 1951, Montos and two cronies entered the home which Render Carter, age seventy-four, shared with his sixty-five-year-old sister near Alma, Georgia. Both were bound, the old man cruelly pistol-whipped, before the thieves ransacked their house, absconding with a thousand dollars. As they fled, the woman managed to untie herself and telephoned police, resulting in a hot pursuit. Near Waycross, Montos and a veteran hard case by the name of Robert Mathus, bailed out of the speeding car. Their wheelman subsequently lost control, and he was captured when he rolled the vehicle.

By summer, 1952, the FBI knew Montos and a mistress, traveling as "Mr. and Mrs. James Lewis," had been sighted in Chicago. A raiding party missed the fugitive in June, when Nick abandoned his apartment suddenly, without informing neighbors he was leaving. Added to the "Top Ten" list September 8, he was the subject of reports which placed him anywhere from Texas to the isle of Puerto Rico. None of the reports were accurate. In fact, by early 1953 the fugitive had run back to Chicago.

Nick's old accomplice from the Georgia robbery, Bob Mathus (#47), had been added to the "Top Ten" list on March 16; he was arrested three days later, in Louisiana. Four weeks later, William Ellison was busted in Chicago, for participation in a $15,000 bank job. Burglar tools recovered from his car were covered with the fingerprints of Nick George Montos, and the hunt moved back to northern Illinois.

An auto dealer in Chicago told the FBI that he had sold a car to Montos and a woman, three days prior to Ellison's arrest. The fugitive had listed an address in Caseyville, five miles from East St. Louis. Federal agents showed Nick's mug shots to the current occupants, and they in turn identified a former tenant, "Jimmy Hastings," who had occupied the house from mid-September 1952 through early April 1953.

On May 6, 1953, the missing vehicle was purchased by a used car dealer in Reno, Nevada. Airline ticket records, pur-

chased under pseudonyms, tracked Montos and his lady
friend to Denver, then to Oklahoma City. In the meantime,
agents in Chicago had connected Montos with a local ring of
burglars who struck off far and wide to execute their heists.
Four members of the gang had been arrested in Kentucky,
with an arsenal of weapons in their car, while they were robbing a bank at Fulton. In February 1954, Montos was identified as one of three men who invaded the home of a wealthy
Kenosha, Wisconsin, art collector, waltzing out again with
paintings valued at $200,000. One of Nick's accomplices had
been Chicago mobster Americo De Pietto. When the stolen
art work was recovered by authorities in Melrose Park, on
February 28, the loot bore fingerprints from De Pietto and his
crony, Montos.

In the spring of 1954, a friend of Montos, deportee Arthur
Colucci, turned up in Chicago after illegally reentering the
United States. The FBI allowed Colucci to remain at liberty,
establishing surveillance of his home in the belief that Montos
would eventually pay a visit to his chum. The bet paid off on
August 23, and Nick made no resistance as he found himself
surrounded by a ring of weapons. Sentenced to a term of
seven years for the Wisconsin art theft, Montos first owed
fourteen years to state and federal authorities in Mississippi,
for the burglary at Hattiesburg. In case he ever won parole, a
Georgia prosecutor put in dibs to try him for the brutal robbery of Render Carter, which had drawn a term of life for
Nick's accomplices.

38 ■ THEODORE ROBERT BYRD , Jr.

Byrd was first arrested in 1944, at age eighteen, and then
racked up criminal convictions in seven states. He earned a
reputation as an expert "penman"—bad check artist—in the
mold of Courtney Taylor and Frederick Peters. Agents of the
FBI connected him with passing worthless checks which to-
taled more than $40,000 in the fourteen months before he
made the "Ten Most Wanted" list, on September 9, 1952.

Five months later, Byrd was passing through El Reno,

Oklahoma, and he missed his midnight train to Phoenix. Dropping by a local coffee shop, he was identified by Robert Harvey, a clerk in the local FBI office who had been working the late shift. Harvey, who was taking correspondence courses in the hope of graduating to a special agent's status, had prepared and circulated WANTED flyers on the fugitive when Byrd was added to the "Top Ten" list. On recognizing Byrd, the would-be agent sprinted three blocks to the El Reno police station, returning with officers who took the penman into custody.

39 ■ HARDEN COLLINS KEMPER

Harden Kemper was the leader of a huge Southwestern auto theft ring, broken up by state and federal officers in 1951. Convicted of a Dyer Act violation on October 8, in Santa Fe, New Mexico, he drew a five-year prison term but was released on temporary stay of execution, to defend himself against a pending civil suit. He failed to keep a date with federal marshals on December 17, and was declared a federal fugitive from justice. Nine months later, to the day, his name was added to the FBI's "Ten Most Wanted" list.

An expert mechanic whose flair for Western clothing earned him a reputation as "the cowboy car thief," Kemper had a record dating back to 1926, including convictions for forgery and white slavery. His biggest break had been the car-theft ring, which operated from a large estate near Taos, ripping off an estimated sixty cars in two years' time. A cagey veteran of crime, his weaknesses were an attachment to his family and a fascination with the great Southwestern desert. In the end, these were enough to bring him down.

Around the time that Kemper disappeared from Santa Fe, a "Harvey Charley Kennedy" turned up in Glendale, Arizona, a Phoenix suburb. "Kennedy" rented a house, where he lived with his two grown-up sons, and found work at a local garage for a hundred dollars a week. It was a quiet life, but Kemper's confidence betrayed him. Customers and neighbors recognized his published photographs, the FBI was called, and they arrested him at home on New Year's Day of 1953.

40 ■ JOHN JOSEPH BRENNAN
41 ■ CHARLES PATRICK SHUE

On August 1, 1952, four gunmen robbed a bank in Lyons, Illinois, of $40,000. Two were quickly captured, and identified their comrades still at large, John Brennan and Charles Shue. A scan of Bureau records showed that both men had encountered prior difficulties with the law. At thirty-three, John Brennan had spent fourteen years in jail, beginning with his first arrest at age fifteen. His partner's sheet was less impressive, but it included several felony arrests, the first of which—for robbery—was logged at seventeen.

John Brennan's name was added to the "Top Ten" list October 6, but three more months would pass before the Bureau found a vacancy for Shue. The New Year's Day arrest of Harden Kemper cleared a place, and Shue was added to the list on January 15, 1953. By then, the fugitives from justice were already running out of time.

John Brennan liked to boast that federal agents would not take him in alive. On January 23, they made a liar out of Brennan in Chicago, seeing through his lame "disguise" of horn-rimmed spectacles as Brennan and his wife sat drinking in a tavern. Caught without a weapon, Brennan offered no resistance as the two of them were led away in handcuffs.

Charlie Shue was also in Chicago, but he had another three weeks left to run. On February 13, 1953, a team of federal agents collared him at home, relying on the fruits of their investigation into Brennan's local movements and acquaintances. At trial, the partners were convicted and dispatched for yet another term in jail.

42 ■ LAWSON DAVID SHIRT BUTLER

Lawson Butler cultivated a respectable facade. Well-dressed, soft-spoken, he was fond of joining local churches when he settled in a given town for any length of time. He worked odd jobs, and seemed content to labor long for minor compensation.

So much for appearances. Behind the "front," he also specialized in daring daylight robberies, in which he often worked alone, without a driver or accomplice. By 1947, he had served two terms behind San Quentin's walls, and California officers were hunting him for violation of parole when he was seized in Oregon, in June, convicted of a new armed robbery—his fourth, officially—and sentenced to a ten-year term. The state of California placed a "hold" on Butler, anxious to receive him when he finished off his time in Oregon.

The prospect was discouraging, and Butler opted not to wait around. His first two bids for freedom had been unsuccessful. Sawing through the prison bars had merely tired him out, and later, when he threw a pinch of pepper in a jailer's face, en route to court, he had been pummeled to the ground. On February 8, 1952, he got a helping hand from Mother Nature as a fog bank rolled across the prison yard at Salem, covering his movements as he propped a wooden plank against the outer wall and scrambled clear. He had a long three-hour lead before a roving guard discovered Butler's makeshift ladder and a head-count showed him missing.

Butler headed back to Southern California, where, as "Albert Caine," he managed to avoid detection for the next eleven months. His name was added to the Bureau's "Ten Most Wanted" list on January 22, 1953, and the resultant fanfare of publicity sealed Butler's fate. On April 21, a team of federal agents, acting on a tip, arrested Butler in Los Angeles. There would be ample time ahead of him in Salem, Oregon—and later, in San Quentin—for the fugitive to analyze his failure and begin to plan his next escape.

43 ■ JOSEPH JAMES BRLETIC

A hard-luck drifter, Joe Brletic liked the ponies, pool halls, and the gambling joints where dice and customers alike were often loaded. Semi-literate and semi-skilled, he worked odd jobs as pin boy in a bowling alley, sometimes as a shill for gamblers who let him win a hand or two, and thereby lured suckers to the table. Nicknamed "Zump" by friends, he liked the name enough to have it tattooed on his arm. A violent temper sometimes got Brletic into trouble; once, he broke into a pool hall after closing time and vandalized the building, out of spite.

But it was greed, not anger, which eventually got Joe in trouble. With a comrade, he began a two-month crime spree in the tiny town of Robertson, Missouri, ripping off a service station for the cash on hand. More holdups followed—six of them in Allegheny County, Pennsylvania—with a string of auto thefts designed to give the bandits wheels. Arrested in St. Louis, during August 1948, Brletic was confined in lieu of bond, awaiting trial on counts of robbery and car theft. On September 6, he used a pair of barber's shears to gouge himself an exit from the county jail. Brletic hopped a westbound freight and was reported from Las Vegas prior to dropping out of sight.

His goal, as Joe would later tell arresting officers, had simply been to put the past behind him. He was "going straight," and chose the desert town of Lancaster, California, as the setting for his new, improved life. As "Jimmy Rizzo," he was married to a local secretary, fathering two children in as many years. When Joe was not at work, he liked to bowl, and he became the star of Lancaster's champion team. For the first time in years, Joe felt lucky. Everything seemed to be going his way.

Brletic's good fortune ended on February 9, 1953, when he was added to the FBI's "Most Wanted" list, with charges of unlawful flight. Before the day was out, a citizen of Lancaster had recognized his published photograph and telephoned police. Brletic was arrested at his home on February 10, without resistance. Waiving extradition to Missouri, he was tried, convicted, and imprisoned for his crimes.

44 ■ DAVID DALLAS TAYLOR

In 1948, while serving time for grand larceny, David Taylor staged a violent jailbreak in Jasper, Alabama, killing one of his guards. Quickly recaptured, he was sentenced to an additional twenty years for the murder, but Alabama's prisons could not hold him. Late in 1950, with another convict, he escaped from Atmore's prison camp in a dump truck, remaining at large until July 1951.

Fourteen months later, in September 1952, Taylor was en route to Kilby Prison, near Montgomery, when he leaped from the moving train in Birmingham's switchyard. Picking the lock on his handcuffs with a hair pin, he boarded a north-bound freight train and thus made his way to Chicago. He was still at large on March 3, 1953, when his name was posted to the FBI's "Most Wanted" list.

Investigation had convinced the FBI that Taylor must be hiding in Chicago. On the afternoon of May 26, 1953, two special agents recognized him behind the wheel of a passing car, and they immediately took off in pursuit. The chase went on for several blocks, until Taylor tried to pass a bus on the wrong side and was blocked by oncoming traffic. Taken into custody without further resistance, Taylor was returned to Alabama and a waiting cell in maximum-security.

45 ■ PERLIE MILLER

Perlie Miller took five years to make the "Ten Most Wanted" list, but it was not for lack of trying. Serving time for armed robbery in North Carolina, he bludgeoned a guard at the Yancey County prison camp, in 1948, and led six other convicts in a daring break for freedom. Only Miller still remained at large on March 4, 1953, when he was posted to the Bureau's list. The federal charge: unlawful flight to avoid confinement.

Five years of unearned freedom may have softened Miller's instincts, or he may have simply used up his allotted time. In either case, he was arrested one day after being posted to the list, in Somersworth, New Hampshire, by a team of local officers and federal agents. Miller had been hiding out in Somersworth since 1950, working at a local diner, as the counterman. His neighbors, and the live-in mistress he had picked up four months earlier, had no cause to suspect that "Leroy Calvin Miller" was a fugitive from justice, but a sharp-eyed customer had recognized his published photograph and tipped authorities. Surrendering without resistance at his home, he was returned to Carolina for completion of his sentence at the prison farm.

46 ■ FRED WILLIAM BOWERMAN

A veteran holdup man whose record spanned two decades, Fred Bowerman was pushing sixty years old when he became number forty-six on the FBI's "Most Wanted" list. Within two months of his ascension to the limelight, Bowerman's luck— and his life—ran out in a flurry of violence which served to characterize his long career in crime.

Fred Bowerman was one more in the old tradition of the hard-core stickup artists, men like Tommy Holden, Harvey Bailey, Alvin Karpis, who could never turn their backs upon an easy woman—or an easy bank. Arrested for armed robbery by Illinois authorities, in 1932, Bowerman served five years for his first major offense, winning parole in 1937.

A year later, he was back inside, but not before committing numerous robberies in the Chicago area. Adhering to the bandit's maxim that "you don't live where you pull your jobs," Bowerman resided in Michigan, commuting to Chicago in stolen cars for a series of heists—thirty-six in all—which he committed between June and October of 1938. Conviction in the epic string of holdups brought more time in Joliet, but Fred was on the street by 1946, looking for action.

Bowerman was able to avoid detection for a while, but in September 1952, he was identified as one of those who took a South Bend, Indiana, bank for $53,000 in a violent daylight raid. A bank employee had been shot and wounded when he raised his hands too slowly for the bandit's taste, and

Bowerman was added to the Bureau's "Ten Most Wanted" list when a vacancy became available, on March 3, 1953.

The heist that finished Bowerman was a chaotic, bloody fracas in the worst Wild West tradition. Bowerman and three accomplices descended on the Southwest Bank, in north St. Louis, on the afternoon of April 24. The robbery went well, at first, the raiders plucking some $140,000 from the tellers' cages, stuffing it inside a nylon satchel. But a bank employee had been quick enough to trigger a silent alarm, and as Bowerman's gang prepared to evacuate, a strike force of nearly 100 police officers converged on the bank, preparing for a siege. In seconds, as employees scrambled for the safety of the vault, a full-scale firefight was in progress, bandits firing through the windows, gagging on the fumes of tear gas which was pumped into the bank. A sergeant stopped two bullets, in the head and neck, before the tide of battle turned.

Attempting to escape, Fred Bowerman was toppled by a bullet in the chest, which pierced a lung and lodged against his spine. Accomplice William Scholl, armed with a shotgun and pushing a woman ahead of him, made it as far as the sidewalk. Surrounded, he shoved his hostage to the pavement, breaking both her wrists, before a bullet knocked him sprawling. He was digging in his pocket for a backup weapon when police rushed forward to disarm him, dragging him away in handcuffs.

Trapped inside the bank, Bowerman's remaining accomplices panicked. One, Frank Vito, put a pistol to his head and killed himself. The lone survivor, one-time college football star Glenn Chesnick, managed to escape on foot—without a dime—but he was captured three days later by alert detectives.

At the hospital, Fred Bowerman identified himself as "John W. Frederick," a ruse which fell apart once G-men had a chance to scrutinize his fingerprints. He died on May 1, 1953, of injuries sustained in his last battle with police.

47 ■ ROBERT BENTON MATHUS

Robert Mathus had a record of arrests which dated back to 1943, when he was fined, at age sixteen, for carrying a concealed weapon. From that point on, the charges filed against him would include armed robbery, attempted robbery, and violation of parole. He liked to carry guns, and if intimidation failed to cow his victims, he was not opposed to using violence.

An accomplice of Nick George Montos (# 94) in the brutal robbery of an elderly couple at Alma, Georgia, on August 11, 1951, Mathus was nominated to the "Top Ten" list with Montos, but his posting had to wait upon a vacancy. With the arrest of Perlie Miller, Mathus made the list on March 16, 1953 and was apprehended three days later.

Immediately after their escape from officers at Waycross, Georgia, which had left their driver to be captured in the wreckage of his car, the fugitives had separated, Montos heading northward, toward Chicago, where his syndicate connections offered sanctuary and the opportunity for other scores. Bob Mathus felt more comfortable in the South. He settled in near Lafayette, Louisiana, thinking he was safe.

Addition to the "Top Ten" roster changed all that. In Lafayette, a citizen observed his published photograph and recognized him as a current resident of Duson, fifteen miles away. Police and federal agents visited his home on March 19, uncovering a pistol and a set of burglar's tools inside. Despite their find, the fugitive insisted he was "Robert Conway," of Chicago, giving up the pose when fingerprint comparisons removed all doubt of his identity. Returned to Georgia, Mathus was convicted of his crimes and sentenced to a term of life imprisonment.

48 ■ FLOYD ALLEN HILL

Evicted from the family home when he was ten years old, the target of a cruel stepfather's rage, Floyd Hill grew up the hard way, living hand-to-mouth. At age eighteen, in 1930, he was jailed for auto theft. It was his first encounter with police, but Hill was only getting started. He would make three trips to Alcatraz in years to come, collecting state and local sentences for auto theft, armed robbery, and burglary. In 1947, Houston officers pursued him in a running shootout, killing Hill's companion, ex-con Martin Rosser, in a wild exchange of gunfire. One year later, he was swept up in a dragnet near Elizabethtown, North Carolina, climaxing a five-hour chase that began when a traffic officer tried to stop Hill's car for a moving violation.

Hill was on the street again by autumn 1952, and ready for the holdup of a lifetime. On October 3, he joined accomplice Gene Paul Norris at a plush hotel in Ft. Worth, Texas, where they met a pair of Cuban revolutionaries seeking weapons for their war against Fulgencio Batista. Hill and Norris had been posing as a pair of weapons dealers, but the only guns they carried to the meeting on October 3 were those they leveled at the Cubans, walking off with a quarter of a million dollars from the revolutionary war chest.

One month later, to the day, police were tipped that money from the robbery was buried in a wooded area near Azle, Texas, roughly ten miles from Ft. Worth. Converging on the site, detectives soon unearthed a Thermos jug with $128,000 jammed inside; they also dug up $4,250 worth of bonds, which had been stolen from a home in Kilgore, Texas, sometime earlier. Surveillance paid off hours later, when Floyd Hill arrived to claim his loot. He was arrested and transported to the Tarrant County jail.

Confinement was an unattractive prospect for the veteran thief. Aside from any time he might receive upon conviction for the robbery, Hill knew that he had angered agents of the CIA—then backing Cuban revolutionaries in an ill-conceived attempt to institute "agrarian reform"—and there were rumors of a contract on his head, commissioned by guerilla leader Fidel Castro.

On February 17, Hill led nine other inmates in a breakout from the Tarrant County jail. A deputy assigned to place the men inside their cells for nightly lockup was attacked and battered with a pipe, relieved of keys which opened outer doors and granted access to the street. The other nine were swiftly captured and returned to jail. Hill's name was added to the "Ten Most Wanted" list March 20, 1953.

Hill's love for Texas scenery undid him in the end. A tip, on April 18, sent police and federal agents to a Dallas home where residents had sheltered Hill since his escape from Tarrant County. Hill was armed with a revolver, but he had no chance to use it as he found himself surrounded. His companions were arrested on the charge of harboring a fugitive, and Hill served ten years on conviction for the Ft. Worth robbery. Upon completion of his sentence, he was shuttled to a federal lockup, there to serve 400 days for violation of parole.

Inside the walls, Hill turned to art, and finished 1,000 paintings while he waited for release. "I've never served time," he informed reporters. "I make time serve me." Apparently reformed, he moved to California after paying off his several debts in state and federal jails, and died of cancer in 1971.

49 ■ JOSEPH LEVY

Born in 1897, Joseph Levy earned a reputation as a truant by the age of nine. His first arrest—for "false pretenses" at the age of seventeen—displayed an early interest in the con games which would soon become a way of life. Dispatched to the New Jersey state reformatory as a first offender, Levy was paroled in November 1915. Less than two years later, he was arrested for impersonating a federal officer. Over the next decade, he would be picked up, most commonly for running swindles, by police in Buffalo, Chicago, Louisville, Miami Beach, New York, New Orleans, Hot Springs, Kansas City, Atlanta, and Los Angeles. He served two federal prison terms, at Leavenworth, and later in Atlanta. Illinois confined him twice, in prisons at Menard and Joliet. At Riker's Island, in New York, he was assigned to duties in the prison's purchasing department, there accumulating knowledge which would help him pass bad checks in later years.

At liberty once more, in April 1948, Joe Levy surfaced at a bank in Baltimore, and introduced himself as an employee of the New York City prison system. The check he cashed was drawn upon a bank in Philadelphia; the fact that his account with that establishment was nonexistent made his act a federal crime. In May and June of 1948, he left a trail of worthless checks from California to New York, his luck expiring on October 6, when he was finally arrested at a bank in Syracuse. Returned to Riker's Island on a charge of violating his parole, he was delivered to the federal prison system to begin another term on Christmas Eve. Conditional release was granted in mid-January 1951, and Levy settled down to hold his first legitimate employment, at a sanitarium in Rye, New York.

The daily grind of nine-to-five was hard on Levy, and he failed to punch the clock on February 19. Soon, his rubber checks were bouncing coast-to-coast, in Boston, in Chicago, and in San Francisco. Trying out a new technique, Joe started wooing lonely women, tapping their accounts in California banks, ranging as far east as Detroit to swindle one victim in early 1952. In April of that year, he dumped one lady at the altar, in Las Vegas, surfacing in Brooklyn, where he swiftly robbed another of her savings. As a cover for his lavish lifestyle, Levy started shipping gifts to national celebrities—including golf clubs, silver punch bowls, and assorted other tokens of esteem dispatched to President Eisenhower and Vice President Nixon. Neither man had ever heard of Levy, but the gifts kept rolling in, while Levy's chosen victims stood in awe of his "connections" at the White House.

By the early days of 1953, the FBI had ninety-four known pseudonyms on file for Levy, and the list was growing by the day. Joe earned a nomination to the "Ten Most Wanted" list March 17; Floyd Hill's arrest in April left the necessary vacancy, and agents planned a press release on Levy's graduation for the first of May.

Joe never made it.

On the afternoon of April 30, the day before his name was slated for addition to the list, a federal agent working on an unrelated case at Churchill Downs, near Louisville, Kentucky, spotted Levy in the crowd and collared him before he had a chance to slip away. Released from prison on probation after several years, he was arrested by the FBI again in 1958, in 1962, and yet again in 1963. The last arrest, for violation of probation, bought him five years in a federal penitentiary. Paroled in May of 1966, he was arrested two months later in St. Petersburg, for shoplifting, and paid a thirty-nine dollar fine. Another violation of parole, departing Florida without permission for a trip to Reno, put him back inside. When he was freed once more, in 1967, age and crippling disease combined to guarantee that Levy, finally, was going straight.

50 ■ ARNOLD HINSON

In retrospect, it is impossible to say if Arnold Hinson's problems stemmed from mental illness, or if Hinson tried to use the system for his own advantage, building up a reputation as a "psycho" in an effort to escape incarceration for his crimes. In either case, his sixteen years of criminal activity were marked by violence, climaxed with a lethal act of savagery.

In January 1935, Hinson was committed to the U.S. Veterans Hospital for the Insane, near Augusta, Georgia, where he spent three months under observation by staff psychiatrists. Their reports were inconclusive, but they found no evidence that Hinson posed a danger to society. He proved them wrong in April 1936, with an arrest for auto theft which put him in the United States reformatory outside Chillicothe, Ohio. An unruly inmate, he was transferred to the federal penitentiary at Lewisburg, from which he won conditional release in February 1937.

Arnold did not last long on the street. The ink was barely dry on his parole before he stood convicted of grand larceny in Florida, a rap that earned him two consecutive one-year sentences in Raiford prison. April 1940 brought him two more years for auto theft; he fled from custody and was recaptured in July of 1941. Hinson got off easy that time, sentenced to a four-year term of supervised probation, but he soon turned up in Quitman, Texas, with another stolen car. The vehicle had been obtained in Alabama, and a violation of the Dyer Act drew Hinson three years at the federal prison in Atlanta. In addition to the federal time, his violation of probation added two more years to his existing sentences.

Psychiatrists examined Hinson in Atlanta, finding him "psychotic." He was transferred to the federal prisoners' medical center at Springfield, Missouri in September 1945, and won conditional release in mid-July of 1947. Violation of his contract with the feds resulted in another six-month term, but Arnold was discharged for good on June 1, 1948.

During the next four years, it seemed that Hinson might be able to exist outside of prison. He married, tried his hand at honest work, and avoided conflict with the law—for a while.

On June 16, 1952, the Hinsons spent their evening drinking with a ranch hand, Edward Howard, at a Millegan, Montana, tavern. They were seen to leave together, and when Howard was found dead the next day, his battered body in a nearby field with four bullets in his head and chest, the Hinsons were immediately suspect. Federal agents joined the chase when Hinson's luggage was discovered underneath a bridge near Burlington, in Colorado. Arnold's name was added to the "Top Ten" list on May 4, 1953.

Investigators traced the couple south, to Memphis, Tennessee, where they were sighted by a pair of federal agents on November 7. Hinson and his wife were seated in a car, perusing local papers, when the G-men closed on either side, with weapons drawn. Unarmed, the fugitives surrendered, waiving extradition to Montana. Charges naming Judy Hinson in the case were dropped when Arnold filed a guilty plea, in March; on June 11, 1954, he tried to change his mind, accusing Judy of the murder, but the court rejected his attempt to gain a jury trial. In January 1964, he broke out of the prison mental ward, but was recaptured after three days on the road.

51 ■ GORDON LEE COOPER

Arrested for the first time as a ten-year-old, for burglary, Gordon Cooper was sent to a Missouri reformatory. He failed to reform, and his record later spanned the area from California to Louisiana, listing auto theft, burglary, forgery, and grand larceny among his crimes. By early 1952, he had spent time in federal penitentiaries at Terre Haute, Indiana, and El

Reno, Oklahoma, with state time served in Arkansas and his native Missouri.

On May 27, 1952, Cooper sat in jail at Poplar Bluff, Missouri, awaiting his trial for robbery of the post office in Painton, his hometown. That night, with the assistance of another inmate, Cooper slugged his jailer, Leonard Landreth, with a homemade blackjack, robbed his fallen victim of $160, and escaped by climbing down an elevator shaft. His awkward comrade fell and broke a leg, unable to continue with his flight, but Cooper stole a pickup truck outside and made his getaway. The truck was found at Maryville, in Tennessee, a few days later, putting him in violation of the Dyer Act. Cooper also faced charges of unlawful flight. His name was added to the Bureau's "Top Ten" list on May 11, 1953. By that time, federal hunters had already focused their attention on St. Louis.

One month later, to the day, a team of G-men spotted Cooper as he drove a car reported stolen from Detroit, where he had previously held a job on an assembly line. They forced him to the curb, relieved him of a sawed-off shotgun, after which the fugitive surrendered peacefully. In custody, he startled officers with a confession listing several crimes around St. Louis in the past two years.

According to his statement, Cooper and another man had burglarized a local home in mid-October 1951, obtaining pistols and $550 cash. (The man whom Cooper named as his accomplice was already serving federal time for income tax evasion.) In November 1951, he found employment with a Catholic charity and subsequently stole the payroll, $936 in all. On February 20, 1952, he robbed a tavern with another bandit, already convicted at the time of Cooper's statement.

Back in Butler County, Gordon Cooper drew a term of life for robbery and the assault upon his keeper. Marathon appeals saw Cooper in and out of court until the state supreme court ratified his sentence in the early part of 1961, but in the meantime, he had other problems. In November 1958, he stabbed another inmate—convicted killer Warren McConville—in an altercation on the yard. The wound proved fatal, and a murder charge insured that Cooper would be living out his days behind the walls of the Missouri penitentiary.

52 ■ FLEET ROBERT CURRENT

When Current robbed a San Francisco restaurant of $1,500, during January 1953, he was behaving true to form. His record dated back to 1942, with a conviction for a burglary, in Oakland, which had earned him nine months in the county jail. Upon release, he would be linked with holdups on the West Coast, and around the area of Minneapolis-St. Paul.

In August 1948, Fleet Current won a grudging compliment from Minneapolis police for what they called "the smoothest stickup in a generation." Smooth it may have been, but Current's robbery of a local loan company earned him five years in prison. Paroled in May 1951, he traveled west again, and picked up with the only trade he knew. The San Francisco robbery cinched Current's nomination to the "Ten Most Wanted" list, and he was added to the roster on May 18, 1953.

Fleet Current was the kind of thief who stood out in a crowd. A victim of severe tuberculosis, he was so emaciated that his prison comrades dubbed him "The Apple," after his prominent larynx. Witnesses remembered Current easily, and linked him with a string of holdups in 1952 and 1953. In late November 1952, he robbed a Minneapolis tavern of $2,500. The San Francisco holdup placed him back in California, during January, but The Apple traveled widely. On the first of March, he joined accomplices in robbing a St. Paul dairy to the tune of $22,000. Unsatisfied, he popped up two weeks later for a puny score in Minneapolis, robbing a hotel of $275. Addition to the "Top Ten" list did not slow Current down: On June 25, he joined two other Oakland, California, gunmen, ripping off the American Trust Company for $5,148.

Weary from his illness, harried by the need to be in constant motion, Current sought a sanctuary in the great Midwest. He settled on Nebraska, packing up his teenage bride and moving east, to Omaha, where he believed that he would not be recognized. It was a fatal error. Agents of the FBI received a tip which put them on The Apple's track, and on July 12 he was taken, with his wife, by G-men acting in coordination with the local sheriff. Caught without a weapon, Current offered no resistance as the agents took him into custody. He was returned to California, there to spend his final days in prison.

53 ■ DONALD CHARLES FITTERER

A native of Burlington, Iowa, Fitterer possessed a record of arrests beginning at the age of nine. Across the next two decades, he was picked up frequently for larceny, armed robbery, and forgery. Convictions followed some of the arrests, and on release, he added violation of parole to his assorted other crimes. Ironically, for all his larcenous intent, it was an act of drunken rage which brought Don Fitterer to grief and placed him on the "Ten Most Wanted" list.

Charles Harrison, a grocer from Alexis, Illinois, was killing time in Denmark, Iowa, when he met Fitterer and sidekick Patrick Russell in a tavern, August 11, 1952. They drank together, seeming friendly for a while, but drunken tempers flared as time wore on, and Harrison was found next morning, murdered, in a ditch outside of town. Pat Russell was arrested quickly, sentenced to a term of life, but Fitterer was still at large on June 8, 1953, when he was posted to the "Top Ten" list on charges of unlawful flight.

The end came one day short of two weeks later, when the FBI received an anonymous tip that Fitterer would be crossing the San Francisco-Oakland Bay Bridge between 3:30 and 4:00 that afternoon. The caller said their man would be alone, driving a gray 1952 sedan. A team of federal agents, acting in conjunction with the California Highway Patrol, were waiting when the fugitive approached the toll booths. Fitterer, unarmed, did not resist when suddenly confronted with a ring of pistols, riot guns and submachine guns. On September 18, 1953, he was convicted on a charge of murder in the first degree; his jury recommended life.

54 ■ JOHN RALEIGH COOKE

A Fitchburgh, Massachusetts, native, Cooke was first arrested at the age of fourteen years, for vandalism. Later, he drew a term of fifteen years in New York state, for robbery, and on release was rearrested twice for violating terms of his parole. By 1952, he had returned to Massachusetts, but he was not going straight. He simply wanted different targets, in an area where he felt more at home.

September 4. Four gunmen barged into the home of a cafe proprietor in Lowell, Massachusetts, stealing fifty dollars from the occupants. Unsatisfied, two bandits drove the owner to his restaurant, where he obtained $300 from the till without alerting customers or his employees. Back at home, the loot was split, one outlaw left to guard the hostages while his companions left to raid a tavern at the Highland Hotel, shortly before closing time. They ran afoul of Francis McMahon, city councilman, who stopped in for a pack of cigarettes, observed the robbery, and ran for help. One robber's gun misfired three times, and thus McMahon's life was spared. The thieves escaped with some $250 cash—a total average of thirty bucks an hour for the time they had invested in their string of holdups.

Two participants, Robert Kelly and Paul Duteau, had been identified by witnesses before the week was out. Duteau's arrest and swift confession named the other two, but Cooke was still at large in June 1953. His name was added to the FBI's "Most Wanted" list June 22.

On October 20, in Roseville, Michigan, a sheriff's deputy named Raymond Tessier was startled when a friend approached him with the news that a suspicious stranger, matching Cooke's description, had been working as a welder at a nearby shopping center. Tessier checked it out, confirmed the tentative ID, and notified the FBI. When agents came for him at work, Cooke offered no resistance, smiling as they led him to the car. "It's a relief," he said. "I knew it was coming, but I didn't know when."

55 ■ JACK GORDON WHITE

A veteran criminal, White compiled a lengthy record of escapes from Southern jails before his final breakout, from a Florida state prison camp, in August 1952. Picking up his criminal career where it had earlier been interrupted by arrest and trial, he launched a string of armed robberies, looting business establishments throughout the Carolinas. White was sought on federal charges of unlawful flight to avoid prosecution for armed robbery, and his name was added to the Bureau's "Ten Most Wanted" list on July 6, 1953.

White's downfall, as with many criminals before him, came when he attempted to survive outside familiar territory. After years of working the southeastern states, he fled to Washington, with Bureau agents close behind him. Their investigation traced him to Seattle, and they bagged him there on August 27, less than eight weeks after his name was added to the roster.

56 ■ ALEX RICHARD BRYANT

Alex Bryant's history of conflict with the law was traceable to 1924, when he was jailed for rape. Paroled in 1928, he joined a gang of stickup artists, knocking off a dozen stores and service stations in the state of Michigan before he was arrested during 1929. Convicted in the string of robberies, he drew a term of life imprisonment as an habitual offender. By the end of 1951, he had spent only seven months of his adult life outside prison walls.

But Bryant meant to change all that. On January 14, 1952, his presence was required at the administration building of the Michigan state penitentiary, at Jackson. In the station wagon, riding with the driver and a guard for company, he pulled a homemade knife and took his captors hostage, forcing them to drive him off the prison grounds. Outside, he dumped his prisoners and drove on to Ohio, violating federal statutes which forbid the transportation of a stolen car across state lines. A search was mounted, but the fugitive was still at large when he was added to the FBI's "Most Wanted" list on July 14, 1953.

Bryant's run had taken him cross-country, westward, to Los Angeles. He settled there, as "Edward Lawson," and was married in October 1952. The wife who bore his child in August 1953 knew nothing of his past, the fact that he was being sought by federal officers from coast to coast. Co-workers at the local cartage company respected "Lawson" and admired his friendly attitude. He was the very model of a new man, going straight.

The roof fell in on January 26, 1954. Acting on a tip from undisclosed sources, agents of the FBI arrested Bryant in downtown Los Angeles, picking him off the street without resistance. Despite protests from his wife and friends, he was returned to Michigan to finish out his sentence.

57 ■ GEORGE WILLIAM KRENDICH

George Krendich was a pilot with the U.S. Army Air Force during World War II. He kept his hand in as a pilot after V-J Day, occasionally renting planes for pleasure flights or business. There was nothing in his background to suggest a violent nature, but in April 1951, a secret, pent-up rage exploded into lethal action, shattering two lives at once and making him a fugitive from justice.

On April 27, Akron resident Juanita Bailey, an expectant mother, was reported missing from her home. In fact, she had been last seen on the twenty-second, when she left the house with Krendich, and a neighbor watched them drive away together. When the woman's mutilated, decomposing corpse was found on May 10, weighted with metal and wire, in a creek near Augusta, Kentucky, Krendich became an immediate suspect. His role in the crime was confirmed by a fingerprint match from the FBI's files, and Kentucky issued a murder warrant on December 7. Three days later, federal officers charged Krendich with unlawful flight to avoid prosecution. His name was added to the Bureau's "Top Ten" list on July 27, 1953.

The killer's motivation has remained obscure, but federal agents had no trouble picking up his trail. He was identified in Scobey and Four Buttes, Montana, on September 13, two days later, Krendich cashed a paycheck in Grenora, North Dakota. He had earned the money working on a nearby farm.

The trail stopped cold on October 11, when some hunters found a jeep abandoned thirty-five miles east of Watford, North Dakota. They were startled to observe a hose, attached to the exhaust pipe, which had been inserted through the window on the driver's side. Behind the wheel, a corpse lay slumped and decomposing in the autumn sun.

The jeep was registered to Krendich, and a fingerprint comparison identified the corpse as his. He had been dead at least three weeks when he was found, and death was ruled a suicide. Whatever private demons had compelled him to the act of murder, they apparently had come back to haunt him, with a vengeance.

58 ■ LLOYD REED RUSSELL

Born in Ohio in 1921, Lloyd Russell was the product of a family notorious for breeding criminals. By 1950, he had registered arrests for robbery, assault, and burglary, continuing the grand tradition of his family, and he was serving thirty-seven years in the Ohio penitentiary. One of his brothers was inside the walls, to keep Lloyd company, and they worked overtime to plot a prison break. Their plans bore fruit in May, and they escaped to Michigan, where officers began to track them in the single greatest manhunt in state history. A string of running shootouts left Lloyd's brother wounded on May 20. Before he was apprehended, Lloyd Russell shot a cop, and was sentenced to ten years in the Michigan state prison, at Marquette.

A taste of freedom, brief and violent though it may have been, encouraged Lloyd to try another break. Recruiting six confederates, he set about collecting homemade knives and making final preparations for their flight. On May 22, 1953, the inmates overpowered several guards and locked them up in cells, escaping through a window after they had sawed the bars away. Outside the prison walls, they scattered. All had been recaptured by June 10, except for Russell, who remained at large when he was added to the FBI's "Most Wanted" list, September 8.

A change of scene was clearly indicated. Russell ran for Washington, and there—as "Raymond Kidd"—joined forces with a local tough guy, Norman Wyatt, in a string of burglaries in summer 1954. They robbed a tavern in Spokane, along with markets in the towns of Valley and Dishman. Office safes resisted their explosive charges in Pullman and Priest River, Idaho, but the outlaws fared better in Deer Park, Washington, cracking the box at a grocery on August 2.

The night of August 3, they parked outside a Spokane supermarket, working up their nerve, a jar of gelatin explosive in the car. Around 9:30, cruising deputies saw two men sitting in their car, outside a market closed for hours, and became suspicious. As the squad car drew abreast, Lloyd panicked, leaping from the car and taking off on foot, with a patrolman on his heels. Behind him, as the shooting started, Wyatt huddled on the floorboards of their car.

Accustomed to resisting the police with force, Lloyd Russell drew a gun and opened fire on his pursuer. It had worked before, in other confrontations, but the fugitive was out of luck. A single bullet from the deputy's revolver struck Lloyd in the head and killed him instantly. It took six officers to drag Norman Wyatt from the car, but once in custody he offered full confessions to the crimes he had committed with the man he knew as "Raymond Kidd."

59 ■ EDWIN SANFORD GARRISON

Edwin Garrison selected crime as a career the way some people choose the law, or medicine. Beginning with his first arrest in 1925, he was confined on various occasions for robbery, burglary, kidnapping, grand larceny, parole violation, and prison escapes. Linked with organized crime in the days of the syndicate's infancy, Garrison's reputation as a "human adding machine"—capable of doing complicated math without a pad or pencil—readily endeared him to Dutch Schultz, the boss of numbers racketeers in New York and New Jersey. Working with the likes of wizard "Abbadabba" Berman, Garrison helped Schultz rig odds at local race tracks, thus deciding what the winning number for the day must be. If many players bet a given number, thus creating the potential for a heavy loss, last-minute betting at the track would change the odds and wipe out the potential winners in a single stroke.

In late October 1935, returning from the track at River Downs, in Cincinnati, with the Dutchman's daily loot, Ed missed his train and had to wait around the station for another. If the move was strictly accidental, luck was smiling on him, for he missed the massacre that wiped out Schultz and several of his closest friends in Newark's Palace Chop House. Dutch lay babbling for hours on his deathbed, but he never named Ed Garrison, and so the human adding machine was free to seek other employment.

He found it with the Cleveland syndicate, in early 1936. The mob was moving in on independent gamblers in Kentucky, and their first offensive targeted Pete Schmidt's Beverly Hills Club, in Newport. Schmidt refused to sell, and in the early morning hours of February 3 his club burned to the ground. A child, the daughter of a maintenance employee, died of burns, and the enraged community demanded action. Garrison was chosen as the scapegoat, but his wealthy friends insured that any time he served would be both brief and pleasant. Soon paroled, he found a soft job waiting in the outfit's plushest club.

Respectability, albeit once removed, was hard for Garrison to take. He wanted action, and he found it in the state of Alabama, where a string of robberies and burglaries resulted in his being sent to jail for life. On August 27, 1952, he joined eleven other inmates in escaping from the penitentiary in Atmore. Breaking out of temporary barracks, Garrison—with two attempted prison breaks behind him—led the others through a tunnel which brought gas and water to the prison compound. Ed was added to the Bureau's "Ten Most Wanted" list October 27, 1953.

Between his breakout and addition to the "Top Ten" roster, Garrison had found his sanctuary in Kentucky, hiding out in Covington, where Cleveland mobsters ruled the roost and paid the local sheriff's bills to guarantee official blindness. He made no attempt to hide in Covington—it was not necessary, after all—but new publicity surrounding his addition to the list forced Garrison to reevaluate his situation. Fleeing to Detroit, he holed up with a friend November 1, believing he was safe.

Police received a call from one of Garrison's new neighbors on November 3. He had been recognized, and agents of the FBI were notified. Four G-men and a pair of local officers went to the house that night, found Garrison alone, and made the collar. Edwin called himself "James Brown" at first, but finally owned up to his identity before comparison of fingerprints was necessary. Since his escape, the fugitive allegedly had paid his way with race track winnings, and by working as an income tax consultant. "I knew I'd be caught eventually," he told his captors. "Every night I'd say to myself, 'Well, at least I've had one more day of freedom.'"

60 ■ FRANKLIN JAMES WILSON

A native of Chicago, Franklin Wilson had a criminal record spanning 23 years, including two terms in the Illinois state prison at Joliet. Paroled the second time in July 1951, he lasted for less than a month without running afoul of the law.

On August 4, with three accomplices, Wilson invaded the apartment occupied by Walter and Violet Wolfner, owners of the Chicago Cardinals football team. Mrs. Wolfner escaped in the confusion of the holdup, scrambling through a bathroom window to alert police, but her husband and several other hostages were herded into the basement, where the outlaws expected to find a safe brimming with cash. Forced to settle for a paltry $800 and a diamond watch, the hoodlums were preparing to leave when a hundred policemen surrounded the building.

One of the gang, a 44-year-old ex-convict named John Piech, chose to shoot it out with police and was killed on the spot, mowed down by a withering barrage of gunfire. Their comrade's fate persuaded Wilson and the others to surrender, later posting $30,000 bail which Wilson promptly forfeited by leaving town. (The other two survivors stayed to take their medicine in court, receiving prison terms of twenty years each.) Still at large two years later, Wilson's name was added to the "Top Ten" list November 2, 1953.

The outlaw's hometown ties eventually spelled disaster, as he found that he could not resist just one more visit to Chicago. Federal agents traced him to the Lenox Hotel on January 18, 1954, and took him into custody without resistance. Held initially for forfeiture of bond, Wilson also faced reinstatement of the original robbery charges, which had lapsed in his absence.

61 ■ CHARLES E. JOHNSON

Charles Johnson's record dated back to 1921, with an arrest for burglary while he was still a juvenile. In 1934, his first adult arrest—for robbery, in New York—earned Johnson a term of four to eight years in Sing Sing. After shooting a policeman in a foiled escape attempt, he would be transferred north to Dannemora, the "Siberia" of the New York state penal system. Except for six short months of freedom, Johnson was confined from 1935 to 1952. A year later, New York authorities were seeking him for three-time violation of parole.

On August 28, 1952, Johnson and four other gunmen held up a bankrobber, relieving the outlaw of loot he had gained from a $50,000 bank heist at Lakesville, North Carolina, four months earlier. Their victim was in no position to complain, but when arrested for the robbery, he would be quick to point a finger. Federal statutes made Charles Johnson and the others guilty of receiving stolen property, as if the members of his gang had robbed the bank themselves. His name was added to the "Ten Most Wanted" list on November 12, 1953.

Approximately six weeks later, on November 28, a resident of Central Islip, New York, recognized Johnson's photograph in a magazine article covering the "Top Ten" fugitives. The FBI was notified that afternoon. A dozen G-men, backed by local officers, converged upon a ranch-style home at midnight, bursting in to find their man, unarmed, in his pajamas and a robe. The fugitive did not resist as he was taken into custody.

62 ■ THOMAS JACKSON MASSINGALE

Sentenced to the reformatory at Hutchinson, Kansas, on October 8, 1952, with his conviction for a robbery in Wichita, Massingale wasted no time in planning his escape. On May 14, 1953, with two other inmates, he clubbed one guard unconscious and captured two others at knifepoint, using them as human shields to cross the prison compound under fire. Escaping with a hostage, in a stolen car, the inmates dumped their wheels and prisoner in Wichita, stealing a fresh car for the road. Sighted next day by police in Guadalupe County, New Mexico, the fugitives escaped once more with bullets whistling around their ears. Short hours later, Massingale's companions were surprised and apprehended in Tucumcari, taken back to Kansas where they each received another sixty years for kidnapping. Only Massingale remained at large, and he was added to the FBI's "Most Wanted" list November 8.

Eighteen days elapsed before a resident of Las Vegas, New Mexico, recognized Massingale's mug shot in an issue of the *Saturday Evening Post*. Police and agents of the FBI were summoned to a local motel, where the fugitive was captured without resistance. Smiling, he informed his captors, "It was a good run while it lasted."

Possibly, but it would be expensive. On return to Kansas, Massingale would face conviction and renewed imprisonment on two counts of assault with a deadly weapon (twenty years on each count), escape (ten years), auto theft (ten to thirty years), and kidnapping (sixty years). The fugitive's "good run" was over.

63 ■ PETER EDWARD KENZIK

Born in Pittsburgh on June 29, 1907, Peter Kenzik settled in Chicago as an adult, variously working as a fireman, merchant seaman, tailor, and as a valet in various hotels around the Windy City. Finding work was never Kenzik's problem, and his trouble with the law revolved around his family life. Despite the mark of familial respect he carried on his right forearm—the tattoo of a headstone with the words "In Memory of Mother"—Kenzik had no luck at all in his relationships with loved ones still alive.

Convicted of attempted murder in a knife assault upon his wife, Kenzik was sentenced to a term of one to twenty years on the state prison farm at London, Ohio. He escaped from custody on March 2, 1948, and was still at large five years later, when his estranged spouse was stabbed to death, in Chicago, on March 13, 1953. Local authorities charged Kenzik with the murder, and federal charges of unlawful flight to avoid prosecution were added on June 12. His name was added to the Bureau's "Ten Most Wanted" list on December 7, 1953.

As family relationships had led to Kenzik's conflict with the law, so a fondness for liquor led to his capture. FBI flyers identified the fugitive as a heavy drinker, and Kenzik's taste for the sauce betrayed him on January 26, 1955, when San Diego police arrested him on a charge of public intoxication. Routine fingerprint comparisons revealed that Kenzik was no ordinary drunk, and he was swiftly returned to Chicago for trial on murder charges.

64 ■ THOMAS EVERETT DICKERSON

Allergic to discipline in any form, Thomas Dickerson had been expelled by a Virginia military school in 1939. Thereafter, as a juvenile delinquent and an adult felon, he compiled a record of arrests which testified to his devotion to the "high life." As it turned out, though, his efforts to become a big-time thief were sadly limited by lack of talent. Jailed for ten to twenty-five years on an Ohio robbery conviction, Dickerson was finally paroled in January 1953. He lasted barely seven months before he tried another robbery, and failed again.

On July 14, 1953, Dickerson held up a loan company in Bethesda, Maryland, fleeing in a car driven by a female accomplice. Arrested the next day in Arlington, Virginia, he first attempted suicide, then launched a hunger strike designed to dramatize his "cause." Requesting medical attention for the pains of self-imposed starvation, he was transferred to the Spring Grove State Hospital, at Cantonsville, September 28. With a companion, also lately transferred, he escaped next day, severely beating a guard in the process. A federal warrant for unlawful flight was issued on October 2, and his name was posted to the "Ten Most Wanted" list October 10.

Reliance on his family for shelter finally betrayed Tom Dickerson. In mid-December, federal agents warned a second cousin in Verdunsville, West Virginia, that they thought the fugitive might try to get in touch. When Dickerson arrived December 21, in company with an uncle, state police and G-men sprang their trap. Dickerson and his uncle—later charged with harboring a fugitive—were taken into custody without a fight.

65 ■ CHESTER LEE DAVENPORT

Born too late to be a cowboy, Chester Davenport became a cattle rustler, instead. His brother, Norman, helped, and prior to their arrest the Davenports were linked with thefts of stock in Oklahoma, Arkansas, and Texas. Formally charged with rustling at Idabel, Oklahoma, in 1950, the brothers jumped bail, remaining at large into 1951, when they were surprised by a state trooper at Locust Grove. Together, they overpowered the officer, disarming him, but they were soon arrested by a larger force and sentenced to twenty-five years for assaulting an officer.

In July 1953, Chester Davenport was one of several inmates driven to another prison for a baseball game. The playing field was outside prison walls, and during the excitement of the game, he simply "walked away." He had not been recaptured five months later, when his name was added to the "Ten Most Wanted" list on January 6.

Escape had given Davenport a brand-new lease on life. He fled to Sacramento, California, joined by his wife and child. The state employment office found him a position at a dairy farm near Dixon, in Solano County, where his long experience with livestock earned him a reputation as "an excellent dairy-man."

Publicity surrounding Davenport's addition to the list produced immediate results. A local veterinarian, Dr. R. J. Cobble, recognized the published mug shots as a likeness of "Floyd Walker," a ranch hand at the Dixon dairy. Federal officers and local lawmen visited the farm on January 7, surrounding Davenport in the barn. He was milking a cow at the time, and offered no resistance to arresting officers.

66 ■ ALEX WHITMORE

Indicted during January 1950 on a charge of hit-and-run, Alex Whitmore did not fit the profile of an average "Top Ten" criminal. He had no lengthy record of arrests, and the collision which had injured a pedestrian, in Norfolk, Virginia, seemed relatively minor in comparison with the atrocious rap sheets of others on the FBI list. Still, the incident suggested certain disregard for human life, and Whitmore had not tried his hand at robbery thus far.

On August 14, 1950, Whitmore picked up Norfolk resident Ralph Williams in his car. Instead of dropping Williams at his destination, Whitmore pulled a hatchet and demanded money. Williams drew a knife, resisting, slashing Whitmore's face and arms before he was subdued by hatchet blows. Robbing his mark of a watch, two rings, three cigarette lighters, and eighteen dollars in cash, Whitmore dumped him on the sidewalk, leaving him for dead.

Ralph Williams was not dead, however, and he readily identified Whitmore for police. Arrested the same evening, Whitmore was taken to a local hospital for treatment of his wounds, and there gave officers the slip, escaping in the darkness. Formally indicted for assault and robbery September 7, he was still at large on January 11, 1954, when his name was added to the FBI's "Most Wanted" list.

The end came one day short of four months later, in the Belltown district of Seattle, Washington. A neighbor recognized the fugitive from mug shots televised some weeks before, while agents tracked him from Florida to Texas, Mexico, Los Angeles, Tacoma. Constantly in motion as his wanted flyers turned up everywhere, Whitmore still told the arresting officers, "I wasn't exactly hiding. I knew it was just a matter of time, but I kept putting it off as long as I could."

67 ■ EVERETT LOWELL KRUEGER

A native of Laramie, Wyoming, Krueger launched his criminal career in 1936, at age fourteen, when he was committed to the Wyoming Industrial School at Worland, officially deemed an incorrigible youth. Paroled in July 1937, he was returned to the institution in January 1939, following a Nebraska arrest for carrying concealed weapons. Paroled again in February 1940, Krueger joined the army seven months later, but quickly went AWOL, chalking up a federal arrest for interstate transportation of a stolen car. Conviction on that charge, in May 1941, earned him four years probation, but Krueger learned nothing from the experience. On February 22, 1942, he was charged with burglarizing three business establishments in Casper, Wyoming, and his probation was revoked. Packed off to the federal lockup at Englewood, Colorado, to serve a four-year term, Krueger was paroled on November 19, 1943.

Incredibly, the army took him back, and Krueger's second enlistment ended with an honorable discharge on May 4, 1946. By December 7 of that year, he was back behind bars in Wyoming, sentenced to thirteen months on conviction of burglary. Released on August 10, 1947, Krueger soon botched another break-in and was returned to prison in January 1948, facing a term of three to five years. He escaped and was recaptured during May, somehow earning commutation of his sentence that August, after spending thirty days in a Veterans Administration hospital.

Briefly detained by officers at Guymon, Oklahoma, in March 1950, Krueger made it home to Wyoming in time to be convicted of grand larceny before the end of the month. His two-to-three-year sentence expired on January 30, 1952, and Krueger was at large for less than ten months before his ar-

rest, in Jackson, Wyoming, on charges of burglary and aiding
a prisoner to escape from the local jail. Everett pleaded "not
guilty by reason of insanity" on those counts, but psychiatrists
found no trace of mental illness, and he was returned to the
local jail, awaiting trial, on April 1, 1953.

Following the evening meal on May 8, Krueger and two
other inmates overpowered their jailer, locking him in a cell
after seizing his pistol and car keys. A patrolman in Driggs,
Iowa, sighted the fugitives an hour later, but was forced to
abandon pursuit when his car struck a deer on the highway.
Abandoning their vehicle near Tetonia, Idaho, the escapees
stole a pickup truck which was later recovered near Last
Chance, Idaho. Federal charges of driving a stolen car across
state lines were filed on May 13, 1953, and Krueger's
cellmates were soon arrested by local authorities. The mastermind behind the jailbreak was at large when his name
made the FBI's "Top Ten" roster on January 25, 1954.

Three weeks later, federal agents caught Krueger in Las
Cruces, New Mexico, while he was making preparations to
leave town. G-men refused to explain how Krueger was
traced, but the answer most probably lies in massive publicity
and the initials "E.K." tattooed on the fugitive's left arm.

68 ■ APEE HAMP CHAPMAN

Born in Greenwood County, South Carolina, in January 1919,
Apee Chapman avoided conflict with the law until August
1939, when he was committed to the State Industrial School at
Huntingdon, Pennsylvania, on conviction of burglary. Although sentenced to serve ten years, he was paroled on December 20, 1940, working through World War II and the post-
war years as a longshoreman and laborer. An inveterate crap
shooter and poolroom hustler, Chapman played the odds
close enough to face violence on several occasions, picking up
noteworthy scars on his nose, chin, right shoulder and left
buttock.

On November 23, 1949, Chapman and a male accomplice,
masked and armed, forced their way into the payroll office of

a Philadelphia construction firm, making off with $11,000 in cash. Chapman's sidekick was convicted, naming his companion in the heist, but Apee was still at large on February 8, 1953, when a marital spat erupted into lethal violence.

Chapman and his wife were attending a party in Cleveland, Ohio, that evening, when they began to quarrel during supper. Chapman stormed out of the apartment but soon returned with gun in hand, killing his wife with two shots before moving on to murder their hostess and wound two bystanders. Acquaintances reported that Chapman had fled to Pennsylvania after the shootings, and federal charges of unlawful flight to avoid prosecution were filed against him by the Justice Department.

On November 21, 1953, Chapman was identified as the gunman who robbed a Norfolk, Virginia, grocery store of $1,586, narrowly evading a cordon of police to make his getaway. Local warrants were issued on November 25, and Chapman made the "Ten Most Wanted" list on February 3, 1954.

Exactly one week later, Bureau agents traced Chapman to Silver Springs, Maryland, where the self-styled cop-hater was captured without resistance, given no opportunity to use his chrome-plated .45 automatic. Chapman was returned to Cleveland for his trial and subsequent conviction on multiple murder charges.

69 ■ NELSON ROBERT DUNCAN

The alleged leader of an interstate auto theft ring, Nelson Duncan was also an expert burglar and safe cracker, based in Atlanta, Georgia. On November 24, 1949, he burglarized the ticket office of Grant Field, an Atlanta sports stadium, making off with $2,000 in gate receipts from a Scottish Rite football game. Fingerprints recovered from the scene identified the suspect, and a warrant was issued, with federal charges alleging unlawful flight to avoid prosecution, interstate transportation of a stolen car, and violations of the federal firearms act. Five years elapsed before Duncan's name was added to the

"Ten Most Wanted" list, on February 8, 1954. At that time, he had less than two weeks left to run.

In retrospect, it seems that Duncan's own refusal to depart Atlanta for another field of operations sealed his fate. On April 21, a pair of beat patrolmen noticed strange activity inside a supermarket which had closed for the night. Noting a hole in the skylight, Officer A. E. McKinnon scrambled up to the roof for a better view, leaving his partner to call for backup. Peering through the skylight, McKinnon caught two men in the act of trying to crack the store's safe. Covering his prisoners, McKinnon marched them through the door, where reinforcements were arriving, anxious to receive them. The catch included Duncan and a partner, Thomas Sircy, late of Tennessee. Convicted on a list of state and federal violations, Duncan was effectively removed from circulation.

70 ■ CHARLES FALZONE

Possessing a criminal record spanning twenty-two years, Charles Falzone logged his first arrest in 1932. A charge of larceny lodged him in the Massachusetts State Reformatory at West Concord until 1935, but parole brought no change of habits. Convictions for burglary and armed robbery soon packed him off to the state prison at Charleston, from which he was paroled in 1944. Moving to New York, Falzone found employment with the Richardson Boat Company, at North Tonawanda, but the straight life suffered in comparison to easy money and a life of crime.

On May 3, 1947, Falzone kidnapped two co-workers, stealing the company's $6,085 payroll and taking his hostages on the road. He released them near Buffalo, staying in town long enough to court a local widow, who became his wife in June. They moved to Pennsylvania that September, settling at New Bedford, where—as "James LaValle"—Falzone found employment as a carpenter.

This time, it seemed that going straight had finally captured his imagination. More than six years passed before his name was added to the "Ten Most Wanted" list, on February 24,

1954, and while he seemed obsessed with firearms, keeping more than twenty in his modest home, there is no evidence to link Falzone with a crime while he resided in New Bedford.

In June of 1958, Falzone's wife was visiting the local post office, when her granddaughter—the child of her daughter by a previous marriage—pointed out a poster on the wall. It bore a photograph of "Daddy," with notations of his true identity and criminal career. Falzone's home became a battleground, with daily quarrels erupting as his wife attempted to distinguish truth from lies. Six weeks of constant bickering eventually drove Falzone to distraction; furious, he promised he would kill his wife, together with her adult daughter, if the questions did not cease.

On August 17, Falzone's wife alerted members of the Pennsylvania State Police, in New Castle, and the FBI was quickly notified. That afternoon, a raiding party took Falzone at his home, surrounded by a cache of thirteen pistols, seven rifles, and a shotgun. Even with the arsenal at hand, he offered no resistance, and was brought back to New York State for trial.

71 ■ BASIN KINGSLEY BECK

Born on March 1, 1933, Beck was officially declared a juvenile delinquent at eleven years of age. From 1944 to 1949, he was confined in state-run Oklahoma "homes" and training schools for boys in trouble with the law. The "training" did not take, and Basin Beck emerged from "school" determined to pursue a criminal career.

Suspected of a Kansas City burglary, committed on September 5, 1953, Beck fled to Arkansas, and a federal fugitive warrant was issued three days later. Picked up by the Arkansas authorities, he was returned to Kansas, lodged in the Oswego jail awaiting trial. Recruiting three more inmates to assist him, Basin overpowered guards and made his getaway before a jury had an opportunity to hear his case.

In flight, the fugitive proved lethal. He was connected with a homicide in Philadelphia, September 21, and in the first week of November, Basin burglarized a cafe in Milwaukee.

He was added to the "Top Ten" list on March 1, 1954, on his twenty-first birthday. Two days later, federal agents got a present of their own.

The FBI knew Beck had visited San Pablo, California, briefly during June of 1953, and they suspected that he might return in search of sanctuary. On March 3, they got a tip that he was back, employed—as "Charles Wright"—at a local auto wrecking yard. Five cars were stationed at the intersection nearest to the yard, and Beck was boxed in as he drove to work. Surrounded by a ring of guns, he offered no resistance to arrest.

72 ■ JAMES WILLIAM LOFTON

A native of Owassa, Alabama, with a record spanning twenty years, James Lofton also had a reputation as a "rabbit," noted for his several escapes from prison. More than once, he fled the Kilby lockup at Montgomery, hiding out in nearby swamps and creeping into town by night, committing burglaries to keep himself in food and spending money. Always captured in the end, he never gave up trying for that one clean break.

A robbery conviction, with assorted other charges, sent him to the prison farm near Atmore, Alabama in the early 1950s, facing an accumulated thirty-five-year sentence. Never one to stick around and do his time, on August 27, 1952, James led ten other inmates in a daring bid for freedom. They demolished prison doors with a hydraulic jack, gained access to a tunnel exiting the camp, and scattered through the countryside. Of the eleven "rabbits," ten were soon captured. Only Lofton was at large by early 1954, and he was added to the FBI's "Most Wanted" list on March 16.

Next day, the Bureau got a tip that Lofton had been seen in Morgan City, Louisiana. Supported by local police, federal officers traced their man to a shell-crushing plant, where he had been employed—under the alias of "Fred Moore"—for several months. Unarmed, he offered no resistance to arrest and was returned to Alabama, no doubt confident that there would always be another chance to slip away.

73 ■ CLARENCE DYE

Dye launched his criminal career with burglary in the Depression era, but he never really had the knack of pulling a successful job. In 1931, a West Virginia heist earned him a year in jail. By 1933, a second burglary conviction resulted in a ten-year term. Dye managed to escape from prison during February 1938, but he was captured three days later, serving out the full ten years before he hit the streets in 1943. Discouraged by his luck so far, he tried his hand at daylight robbery—and had no luck at all.

On July 29, 1946, Dye and an accomplice, Orris Gaines, held up two restaurants in Akron, Ohio. The first job went smoothly, but the second fell apart when owner Gus Ballas drew a pistol from under the counter, opening fire on the bandits. Gaines was dead before he hit the floor, and Dye left Ballas wounded as he fled with cash in hand. Identified from mug shots, he was charged with robbery, attempted murder, and a list of lesser crimes. Still at large in early 1954, on March 8 he was added to the "Ten Most Wanted" list.

Dye chose to stay in Milwaukee while the federal government began to narrow down its search. From April through October 1954, he worked as a chef at a local country club, unrecognized by co-workers and clientele. There would be other jobs in months to come, but Clarence stubbornly refused to leave his chosen town for any length of time.

On August 3, 1955, city detectives received a tip that Dye was visiting Milwaukee's Friendship Club. They staged a raid without informing agents of the FBI beforehand, bagging Dye as he attempted to evade detection, slipping out a back door while they entered through the front. Unarmed, he offered no resistance and was extradited to Ohio for his trial.

74 ■ STERLING GROOM

Convicted for the murder of a Raccoon Ford, Virginia, woman, Sterling Groom was sentenced to a term of life imprisonment in April 1934. State authorities paroled Groom in

July of 1951, but if the parole board thought he was rehabilitated, they could scarcely have been farther from the truth.

By mid-December, Groom was serving thirty days in jail for larceny, in Orange County, Virginia. On December 15, he attacked a jailer and escaped, resurfacing in Winston two days later, where he choked the owner of a general store to death. With evidence in hand suggesting Groom had fled the state, the FBI began its search for him on charges of unlawful flight. His name was added to the "Ten Most Wanted" list on April 2, 1954.

On April 21, a resident of Baltimore saw Sterling's wanted flyer in the local post office, recognizing him as one "John Waugh," who had been living in the city, working at a local foundry, for the past two years. Arrested on the job, Groom clung tenaciously to his assumed identity, but fingerprint comparisons removed all doubt. Returned for trial on murder charges in Virginia, this time Sterling Groom had no hope of receiving leniency.

75 ■ RAYMOND LOUIS OWEN MENARD

A veteran thief, by February 1953 Menard had been convicted on a list of charges that included robbery, burglary, and assault with intent to rob. Unlike so many of his criminal compatriots, Menard appeared to learn from his mistakes, although the nature of his lessons never leaned toward "going straight." Instead, he graduated from simple burglary to safecracking, heading up his own gang in St. Louis, pulling off an estimated thirty jobs in one year's time, before a team of federal agents cracked the ring, arresting fourteen of Menard's associates in February 1954. At that, Menard was quicker than his adversaries, and he managed to escape, in company with his wife. Both fugitives were named in federal warrants for unlawful flight, and Raymond's name was added to the "Ten Most Wanted" list on May 3, 1954.

New Orleans was the kind of town where a determined fugitive could lose himself in style. Ray found employment for his wife—as an "exotic" dancer in a club on Bourbon Street—

while he stayed close to home and kept an eye peeled for the feds. On May 4, one day after his addition to the list, his photograph was published in a local paper, neighbors recognized his face, and the authorities were notified. A squad of federal agents and police surrounded the Menards in their apartment on May 5, and captured them without resistance. Neither fugitive was armed.

76 ■ JOHN ALFRED HOPKINS

Arrested for the first time at age seventeen, in hometown Spokane, Washington, Hopkins received a sentence of two years, suspended, on conviction for attempted burglary. Six years later, in Los Angeles, he faced a five-count charge of forgery, but managed to escape from the police en route to court. Arrested one month later, in November 1938, in Fort Worth, Texas, Hopkins was returned to California, where he drew a term of eighteen months in L.A.'s county jail. Released in August 1940, he was free for less than thirty days before arrest for auto theft and violation of parole brought home a term of one to fourteen years in prison. This time, John would serve his time inside San Quentin, winning a conditional release in mid-September 1942.

From California, Hopkins made his way to Maricopa County, Arizona, where he tried his hand at mining in the Vulture Mountains, outside Wickenburg. It was a rugged life, with few rewards, and after two years sweating in the desert heat, the straight life's minimal attractions had begun to fade.

On February 9, 1954, Wickenburg's night marshal, Clarence Dotson, surprised Hopkins in the act of burglarizing a drug store. Shots were exchanged, and both men were wounded. Dotson survived long enough to name his assailant, and Hopkins was convicted of murder, packed off in May to the state penitentiary at Florence.

While incarcerated, John was one of ten Florence inmates convicted of filing false tax returns in order to obtain fraudulent refunds from the government. It was a minor setback for a convict serving life, and Hopkins funneled his attentions toward the prison machine shop, where, incredibly, he was allowed to build a jeep with parts he scavenged from the junk yard. On November 30, 1953, with another inmate riding shotgun, Hopkins used the jeep to make his getaway. Pursuers found it on a street in Phoenix, where the fugitives had stolen more conventional transportation.

Splitting with his comrade, Hopkins drove to Watsonville, in California, hiding there until his name was posted to the "Ten Most Wanted" list on May 8, 1954. The fresh appearance of his mug shot in the local post office put Hopkins in motion. The authorities in Reno posted flyers, too, but Hopkins thought he might be safe at tiny Beowawe, in the northern wasteland of Eureka County.

Hopkins tried his hand at mining once again, obtaining employment at the Gold Acre Mine, on the fringe of the rugged Cortez Mountains, thirty miles south of Beowawe. Federal agents, acting on a tip, surprised him at the mine June 7, 1954. Despite the three knives which he carried on his person, Hopkins offered no resistance to arrest.

77 ■ OTTO AUSTIN LOEL

Dubbed a "social reject" by court psychiatrists, Loel sought refuge in the navy, but was ousted with a bad conduct discharge. He bummed around the Far East for several years, working odd jobs and accumulating strange experiences. Boastful in his cups, he had a knack for entertaining audiences with his tales of dealing opium in China, farming minks and working as a lumberjack in Oregon. His reputation as a con man may have been exaggerated, but in 1948 he talked himself into a job as police chief in the small town of Sandy, Oregon, due east of Portland in Clackamas County. Five-times married—once, allegedly, to a Chinese woman he purchased from her parents—Loel frequently complained that he had "nothing but trouble" with his wives. As it turned out, he could have said the same about his other lady friends.

In January 1954, Loel started east from Compton, California, traveling with housewife Elizabeth Henderson, whom he had picked up in a tavern, afterward persuading her to leave her husband for a jaunt across the country. Back in Compton, her abandoned spouse professed to think that Loel and his wife were merely "sharing expenses" for a visit to her relatives, back east. The dubious illusion was destroyed on January 10, when Henderson was found, half nude, her body torn by thirteen stab wounds, in an Oklahoma City motel room. Otto Loel had disappeared, but he had left his butcher knife —and fingerprints—behind. His name was added to the "Ten Most Wanted" list May 21.

Police in Sanford, Florida, arrested Loel on January 17, 1955. Returned to Oklahoma city for his trial, he first pled insanity, giving it up when psychiatrists examined him and found him sane. He was an "odd ball," they declared, but clearly capable of differentiating right from wrong, the legal test of sanity in court. Unable to defend himself on grounds of mental illness, Otto switched his plea to self-defense! In the revised edition of his alibi, Elizabeth Henderson became the aggressor, forcing Loel into an act of sexual perversion, during which he "went haywire," unaware that he was stabbing her until he "came around" and found her dead. A jury was unimpressed. Convicted on October 22, 1955, Loel was condemned to death and subsequently executed for his crime.

78 ■ DAVID DANIEL KEEGAN

Born in Iowa, September 1918, David Keegan served his country in the navy through the closing months of World War II. Returning to civilian life in late November 1945, he spent the next eight years as owner-operator of successive restaurants and taverns. As an alcoholic, he became his own best customer where liquor was concerned. Described, at one point, as a "silent partner" in a house of prostitution, Keegan had begun the drift from law-abiding business to the shady side of life which would eventually land him on the Bureau's "Ten Most Wanted" list.

On February 22, 1954, three gunmen invaded the farm-house of William Edwards, near Mondamin, Iowa. Also present at the time were Edwards's sister and a female guest. The late arrivals brandished weapons, driving Edwards toward the bedroom, where he kept a safe. Edwards scuffled with the leader of the trio—subsequently named as David Keegan—and was shot down in his tracks, two bullets snuffing out his life. The stolen safe was found next morning, outside North Sioux City, South Dakota. Nine thousand dollars in cash was missing; another $8,300 in bonds lay scattered around the scene.

The gang's getaway car, registered to Keegan, was recovered in Sioux City that same afternoon, and his accomplices were taken by police on February 24. Dave Keegan and the cash were still at large when he was added to the "Top Ten" list, June 21. Nine years and six months later, there was still no trace of Keegan, and his federal process was dismissed December 22, 1963. Although the FBI would venture no opinion, such procedures often indicate a felon is believed to be deceased.

79 ■ WALTER JAMES WILKINSON

In early 1954, Wilkinson led a ruthless gang which kidnapped a supermarket manager in Corinth, New York, robbed him of $2,000, and left him locked inside the freezer at his store. Discovered by employees still alive, the victim managed to identify his various assailants. Other charges of burglary and armed robbery were later filed against Wilkinson for crimes committed in Troy, New York. The other members of his team were all in custody when Walter's name was posted to the "Ten Most Wanted" list on August 17.

Publicity drove Wilkinson across the continent, to Southern California, where—as "Walter Rogers"—he obtained the job of busboy at the Fox Hills Country Club, in Los Angeles. He held the post three months before a member of the club identified his published photograph and called the FBI. Surrounded at his job, the fugitive was carrying a loaded automatic pistol, but he offered no resistance. Ruefully, he shook his head and told arresting officers, "It didn't take you long."

80 ■ JOHN HARRY ALLEN

Born November 10, 1909, in Carroll County, Tennessee, slow-talking John Allen was first arrested at age eighteen, in Pocatello, Idaho, when local officers picked him up on charges of highway robbery and auto theft. He escaped from the Pocatello jail prior to trial, thus laying the foundation for his life-long reputation as an escape artist.

Nabbed for highway robbery in Pawhuska, Oklahoma, on April 18, 1932, Allen was delivered to Tennessee authorities, who had issued warrants in a series of armed robberies. Conviction on three counts earned him a fifteen-year stretch in Nashville's penitentiary, and Allen served eight of those years before making his escape on May 28, 1940. Moving on to Kansas, he was arrested on first-degree robbery charges in September 1940, sentenced to a term of ten to twenty-one years in prison. Upon parole, in February 1947, he was returned to Tennessee and earned parole on his sentences there in June 1949.

On December 16, 1950, Allen and a male accomplice robbed a grocery store in Birmingham, Alabama, escaping in a stolen car. They shot it out with Mississippi Highway Patrol officers the next day, near Amory, but were captured and returned to Alabama, where Allen was sentenced to thirty-five years on conviction. He escaped from Kilby Prison, near Montgomery, on April 19, 1952.

Moving fast, Allen held up a gas station in Fargo, North Dakota, on June 25, and was arrested at Grand Forks the next day, driving a car he had stolen in Topeka, Kansas, a week earlier. Conviction of armed robbery earned him a sentence of fifteen to twenty-five years in the state prison at Bismarck —from which he escaped on September 26, 1952. Back in Kansas, he robbed a Pittsburg market on December 24, and was arrested by local officers at Iola on January 19, 1953. Another term of twenty-one years was added to his growing list of sentences, and Allen was packed off to the state penitentiary at Lansing. On March 25, 1954, he scaled the outer wall and made good on his latest break for freedom.

From that point on, Allen's travels were followed through the testimony of robbery victims who identified his mug shots after the fact. He struck a market in Coffeyville, Kansas, on April 24, 1954, raided a Springdale, Arkansas, grocery on May 22, and returned to Coffeyville for a drive-in theater robbery on July 29. His name was added to the Bureau's "Top Ten" list on September 7, 1954.

Fifteen weeks later, on December 21, 1954, police officers in Fort Smith, Arkansas, recognized Allen from photographs and descriptions provided on his FBI Wanted flyers, collaring the fugitive before he had a chance to flee or shoot it out. Returned to Kansas for the latest in his epic string of trials, John Allen could be certain that security precautions had been tightened in anticipation of his homecoming.

81 ■ GEORGE LESTER BELEW

A would-be bad check artist, George Belew was noticeably short on luck and talent. Picking up his first arrest on May 6, 1953, in Fargo, North Dakota, when he tried to write a check on his account in a fictitious South Dakota bank, George served a little time but failed to learn his lesson from the bungled crime. On July 30, 1954, he was arrested in Hays, Kansas, on another charge of passing worthless checks. Afraid his sentence might be more severe the second time around, Belew attacked a jailer and escaped on August 3. A federal warrant was issued four days later, charging George with interstate transportation of stolen property. His name was added to the Bureau's "Ten Most Wanted" list on January 4, 1955.

On January 24, the clerk at a motel five miles from Champaign, Illinois, became suspicious of his latest guests. Two couples had been registered by "Dr. Clyde C. Hoyt," but there was something odd about the doctor. He had acted nervous, and his face had been familiar to the clerk, somehow. A scan of recent Wanted flyers told the story; "Dr. Hoyt" was George Belew, and his companions might be fugitives as well, for all the startled clerk could tell.

In fact, George was accompanied by his wife, a brother- and sister-in-law. They were together when federal agents crashed the party, first identifying George Belew, then charging his companions with the crime of harboring a fugitive. A tackle box recovered from the motel room contained a kit for printing phony payroll checks, plus various ID cards used in cashing same. Belew was returned to Kansas for his trial and ultimate conviction on a list of counts including forgery, assault, and breaking jail.

82 ■ KENNETH DARRELL CARPENTER

Born in Ohio in 1912, Carpenter logged his first arrest at Upper Sandusky, for contributing to the delinquency of a minor. Convicted of car theft in November 1937, he drew a term of one to twenty years in the state reformatory. He escaped on September 5, 1938, and was recaptured four days later, winning parole in January 1940. By June 10, linked with a series of gas station robberies in northwest Ohio, he was declared a parole violator. Carpenter and an accomplice, both heavily armed, were arrested near Toledo on December 5, 1940, with subsequent conviction adding another sentence of one to twenty-five years. Carpenter escaped once more, in early February 1945, and was recaptured eleven months later by police in Oklahoma City. Paroled on August 17, 1949, he was declared in violation of parole four months later.

By January 13, 1950, Carpenter had graduated from gas station holdups to bank robbery, threatening tellers in a Mount Blanchard, Ohio, bank with a simulated bottle of nitroglycerine and escaping with the princely sum of $395. Arrested the same day, while driving a car stolen in Texas, Carpenter was hit with federal charges and packed off to serve a maximum of seven years at Leavenworth. Conditionally released on October 8, 1954, he lasted a month before new charges were filed, citing Carpenter's failure to keep appointments with his probation officer.

On November 15, 1954, Carpenter and accomplice Leroy Adolph robbed a liquor store and a gas station in Independence, Kansas. Twelve days later, they invaded a bank at Oswego, carelessly leaving fingerprints behind as they escaped with $9,300. Adolph was picked up in Webb City, Missouri, on December 11, and ultimately drew a sentence of fifteen years in prison. Carpenter, still at large, was added to the "Ten Most Wanted" list on January 31, 1955.

Four days after his addition to the list, Bureau agents traced the fugitive to East Arlington, Tennessee, where his identity was confirmed and he was taken into custody without incident. Carpenter was returned to Kansas for trial and conviction on outstanding charges.

83 ■ FLENOY PAYNE

Born July 18, 1909, at Scott, Mississippi, Flenoy Payne was remembered as a "bad boy" by neighbors and relatives alike. Habitually armed with at least one pistol, Payne threatened to kill his mother and half-sister on several occasions, but his first actual victim was a stranger. On February 7, 1933, Payne and an accomplice shot and killed a grocer in Greenville, Mississippi, during an attempted robbery of the victim's store. Arrested the next day, both gunmen confessed; Payne drew a term of life imprisonment, while his companion was hanged in December. Considering the racial climate of the times, it came as a surprise when Payne—a black—received an indefinite suspension of his sentence and was released from prison in December 1942.

By early 1949, Payne was residing with a married woman in Toledo, Ohio, keeping her lawful husband at bay with death threats. On May 4, 1949, the three met on a Toledo street-corner and an argument erupted, with Payne whipping out a revolver, wounding the couple before he fled the scene.

Earning pocket money through gambling and occasional work as a laborer, Payne drifted home to Mississippi and further trouble. On August 2, 1953, he shot and killed a man with whom he had been quarreling, leaving town before he could be apprehended. Federal charges of unlawful flight to avoid prosecution for murder were filed on September 22, and Payne was added to the "Top Ten" list on February 2, 1955. He lasted three years on the run, before Bureau agents traced him to Crittenden County, Arkansas, and took him into custody without resistance on March 11, 1958. Returned to Mississippi, Payne was once again tried and convicted of murder.

84 ■ PALMER JULIUS MORSET

Arrested for the first time on a charge of horse theft, in Nebraska, during 1922, Morset drew a term of one to two years in the penitentiary. In 1928, the charge was robbery in Illinois; one year to life in Joliet was Morset's sentence. Paroled in 1935, a violation sent him back to jail in 1938. He was released again in May of 1940, but the horse thief turned armed robber showed no signs of going straight.

In early 1950, Morset was connected with a string of holdups in Chicago, victimizing finance companies. With an accomplice, he was captured on March 20, attempting to escape their latest job. With officers in close pursuit, the bandits wrecked their car and were arrested when they tried to flee on foot. Indicted four days later on three counts of robbery, Morset was released on bail. In March of 1951, his bond was forfeited when he did not appear for trial. Unlawful flight would be the federal charge, and Morset's name was added to the "Top Ten" list on February 7, 1955.

By that time, Palmer had been hiding out in Indianapolis for nearly four years, and he had another year to go. Living as "Thomas Rooney," joined by his wife, the fugitive found work as a salesman for a local manufacturer of water softeners. From all appearances, he swore off crime and settled down to be a model of domestic mediocrity.

It almost worked.

The FBI would not explain precisely how it traced the fugitive at last. Leonard Blaylock, special agent in charge for Indianapolis, credited "investigative procedures" when Morset was seized at his home, March 2, 1956. For his part, Palmer Morset seemed relieved. "I knew it was going to happen," he said. "I am tired of running. I'm glad it's over."

85 ■ PATRICK EUGENE McDERMOTT

Born September 13, 1898, at Dunlo, Pennsylvania, Patrick
McDermott was perhaps unique in the world of organized
crime, as a professional hit man with an interest in astrology.
As a hobby, he was known to design crossword puzzles which,
when completed, gave the player predictions from his or her
horoscope. On the side, despite the limitation of an eighth-
grade education, McDermott acquired self-taught expertise in
the fields of chemistry, bacteriology and hematology, developing a new medical stain technique useful in swift diagnosis of
tuberculosis.

For all his near-genius potential, McDermott was a nervous
man, given to compulsive behavior and outbursts of violence.
Convicted of grand larceny by a military court-martial, while
serving in the army, Patrick escaped from the stockade in 1922
and wound up serving his time in the Atlanta federal penitentiary.

Emerging from confinement with a full set of dentures and
a grudge against society, McDermott found employment as a
gunner for Ohio's bootleg barons in the Roaring Twenties.
When Don Mellett, crusading editor of the Canton *Daily
News,* exposed the link between organized criminals and local
police officials, McDermott was assigned to eliminate the nui-
sance. On July 16, 1926, Mellett was ambushed and shot to
death while parking his car in the garage at home, with suspicion quickly falling on McDermott and his cronies; McDermott was convicted of first-degree murder in a trial which also
jailed his bootleg employer and the Canton chief of detectives
as co-conspirators. Sentenced to life, McDermott escaped
from the state prison at Columbus, Ohio, on November 28,
1954. Abducting a cab driver, he made his way to Chicago and
vanished there; charged with unlawful flight to avoid confinement on December 3, 1954, McDermott made the "Ten Most
Wanted" list on February 9, 1955.

Underworld connections in Chicago and points east were
responsible for hiding McDermott in flight, but the federal
heat was too much for old time's sake, and life "on the lam"
quickly took its toll on the fugitive. On July 20, 1955, he was

spotted by policemen in New York, identified from his federal wanted flyers, and taken into custody without resistance.

86 ■ GARLAND WILLIAM DANIELS

Known as "Flash," for his technique of stealing cars in record time, Garland Daniels was also a notorious "paper hanger," adept in passing bad checks. Employing better than a dozen pseudonyms in his career, by 1950 he had racked up prison terms in California, Maryland, the District of Columbia, Connecticut, and Kansas, serving time for auto theft, bad checks and forgery, concealed weapons, and violations of the federal Stolen Property Act. Arrested on the latter charge in Florida, and sentenced to a term of seven years in mid-October 1951, Daniels was soon transferred to the U. S. Public Health Service Hospital at Lexington, Kentucky, for treatment of narcotics addiction. He escaped from the hospital in November, picking up further charges of transporting stolen property in Chicago and Los Angeles before his name was posted to the "Ten Most Wanted" list on February 18, 1955.

On March 29, a subscriber of the *Herald & Express* recognized Garland's published mug shot as the likeness of a neighbor in Los Angeles. The FBI was notified, and he was captured at his home, cut off by agents as he tried to scale a backyard fence and make his getaway. Returned to Florida, "Flash" served his time and was eventually released. He died in Dallas, Texas, of a heart attack, in 1965.

87 ■ DANIEL WILLIAM O'CONNOR

When Dan O'Connor joined the army during 1946, at age eighteen, he had the foresight to consider that he might not take to military discipline. Enlisting as "Clarence O'Connor," he soon tired of the regimen and deserted on May 6, 1946, leaving military police to search for a nonexistent suspect. Drifting to Canada, already a haven for military fugitives,

O'Connor was convicted of burglarizing a hotel in July 1948 and sentenced to two years imprisonment.

Upon his release from jail, O'Connor, his wife and two children began an aimless odyssey through the United States and Canada, leaving a trail of bad checks across British Columbia, Oregon, Montana and North Dakota. Stopped for questioning by an officer of the Royal Canadian Mounted Police, on May 14, 1953, O'Connor pistol-whipped his interrogator and left the officer bound in a roadside ditch. A week later, his "paper-hanging" resulted in charges of transporting stolen property interstate, filed at Great Falls, Montana; a similar federal indictment was filed at Butte on November 9, and O'Connor's name was added to the "Ten Most Wanted" list on April 11, 1955.

The day after Christmas 1958, police in El Cajon, California, received a complaint from local residents concerning the theft of a two-wheeled trailer, valued at approximately $15. The suspect was a neighbor of the victims, Arthur Nelson, and it took a routine check of "Nelson's" fingerprints to finally identify fugitive Daniel O'Connor. In hiding, the bad check artist had altered his appearance by dying his hair bright red and cutting it short, growing a heavy mustache and putting on some sixty pounds, with a large, new tattoo on one arm. Confronted with the undeniable evidence of his fingerprints, O'Connor broke down and confessed his identity, returning for trial on pending charges.

88 ■ JACK HARVEY RAYMOND

Sentenced to life in Washington state as an habitual criminal, Raymond escaped from his guards on February 26, 1954, en route to the penitentiary at Walla Walla. Raymond's penchant for forging U. S. government checks put the Secret Service on his track, and by the time his name was posted to the FBI's "Most Wanted" list, August 5, 1955, the fugitive was sought by federal officers for interstate transportation of stolen property in San Diego and in Butte, Montana.

Raymond's normal dodge involved blank checks, resembling those put out by federal agencies, which he filled out with rubber stamps, made payable to "Lou J. Ames." A circular distributed by agents of the Secret Service warned proprietors of stores across the continent to watch for "Ames," and on October 14, 1955, the tips paid off.

A string of Raymond's worthless checks had surfaced lately, in the Denver area, and merchants were advised to be on guard. Dan Chaney, manager of a grocery store in suburban Englewood, was waiting when the fugitive laid out a check to cover purchases, and it was instantly refused. Disgruntled, Raymond left the store, but not before employees got a good look at his car.

Descriptions of the vehicle were broadcast, and patrolmen on the beat gave chase. Their suspect struck a traffic island, lost control, and swerved his car into a ditch. Jack Raymond tried to flee on foot, but warning shots persuaded him to think again. With the arrest of Daniel Everhart (#89), five days before, his seizure marked the second capture of a "Top Ten" fugitive in Denver for the week.

89 ■ DANIEL ABRAM EVERHART

It came as no surprise to anyone when Daniel Everhart was first arrested at the tender age of twelve. At least eight members of his family had records, including two brothers then serving long prison terms; and a third brother had committed suicide in jail. It may be said that Everhart was doomed from birth, and yet, he chose the course of action which would bring him into lifelong conflict with the law. By the beginning of 1955, Dan Everhart was sought by the authorities in Akron for at least two burglaries, three robberies, and charges of attempted murder, stemming from a shootout with police. Considered desperate and dangerous, his name was added to the Bureau's "Ten Most Wanted" list on August 17.

Approximately eight weeks later, on October 9, police in Denver stopped a vagrant on the street and asked him to identify himself. His attitude had roused suspicion, instantly confirmed when he attempted to escape. The beat patrolmen ran him down and cuffed him, unaware that they had seized a federal fugitive who often boasted he would not be taken in alive. A fingerprint comparison identified their man as Daniel Everhart, and he was subsequently handed over to the FBI, returned to Akron for his trial and ultimate conviction on a string of charges that would place him permanently out of circulation.

90 ■ CHARLES EDWARD RANELS

A native of Conroe, Texas, Ranels logged his first arrest at age fifteen, in 1937, for an auto theft at Waco. Confined to a state institution for deliquent boys, he escaped but was swiftly recaptured. By 1954, he had served fifteen years in various state prisons on convictions for kidnapping, car theft, robbery with firearms, and aiding a prisoner to escape. From all appearances, his latest prison term—resulting from a Fort Worth robbery, in 1943—had taught him nothing of the risks inherent in a criminal career . . . but it encouraged him to find new hunting grounds.

On October 8, 1954, Ranels and another gunman robbed a Louisville, Kentucky, supermarket of $3,000. Nineteen days elapsed before the bandits struck again in Louisville, looting a bank of $34,860. Ranels could afford a vacation after that score, but he turned up alone in Lonoke, Kentucky, on May 27, 1955, taking another bank for $9,760 in cash and $15,000 in unsigned traveler's checks. He had the federal government's attention now; his name was added to the "Ten Most Wanted" list September 2, 1955.

Celebrity did not slow Charlie Ranels down. On January 9, 1956, he robbed a bank in Monticello, Arkansas, of $11,000. He wore no mask, and tellers at the bank were able to identify his mug shots four days later. Some of them had also seen the words "HARD LUCK" tattooed across his fingers.

A few days shy of Christmas 1956, federal agents traced Ranels to the minuscule community of Dew Drop, Arkansas, near Pine Bluff, twenty miles southeast of Little Rock. A lady friend of Ranels, Opal May, had bought the local grocery store a few months earlier, and neighbors grew suspicious of her male companion, finally putting two and two together from a wanted flyer. Agents armed with Tommy guns and pistols caught the couple sitting down to supper on the sixteenth of December, taking Ranels by surprise and granting him no opportunity to reach the loaded pistol in his pickup truck, outside. In custody, the fugitive was philosophical about his fateful choice of sanctuaries. "I knew you'd get me," he informed arresting officers, "so I decided to hide out."

91 ■ THURMAN ARTHUR GREEN

The file on Thurman Green dates back to age thirteen, when he was first committed to a correctional institution for truancy. His subsequent arrests included counts of burglary, robbery, carrying a concealed weapon, and assault with intent to commit murder. Once, in a bid to escape from Chicago's House of Corrections, Thurman slugged a guard to make his getaway. By May of 1954, he had completed nearly five years of a six-year term for robbery, in Washington. Jailed for a heist involving "less than $100," Green chafed at confinement, deciding he could not afford to sit still in the hope of parole.

On May 21, Green—with fellow inmates Virgil Dillon and Paul Grimm—escaped from a new minimum-security barracks at the Washington state penitentiary in Walla Walla. Removing several bolts which linked the sections of a steel mesh fence, the convicts wriggled through and fled on foot, thereafter picking up a car to give themselves a better chance. Police in Creston, Iowa, arrested Grimm and Dillon in the stolen car, May 24, but Thurman Green remained at large. His name was added to the FBI's "Most Wanted" list on October 24, 1955, charging violations of the Dyer Act and unlawful flight to avoid confinement.

By the time of his promotion, Green had managed to construct a brand-new life. As "Frank DuMonte," he had settled down in Nashville, Tennessee, in mid-December 1954. By February, he had found employment at a local foundry, working steadily, with only one day off for illness in a nine-month period. In April he was married, and the residents of neighboring apartments thought of the "DuMontes" as a couple "very much in love." Granted, the newlyweds were "quiet and hard to get acquainted with," but slowly they made friends, and therein lay Green's downfall.

By the early days of 1956, at least two neighbor couples realized that "Frank DuMonte" was a wanted fugitive. They argued, off and on, about reporting him to federal officers, deciding to proceed in early February. Green, for his part, had begun to pick up bad vibrations, sensing that his run was almost at an end. On February 12, he sent his wife to stay with relatives in Knoxville. When a raiding party crashed his small apartment four days later, they discovered Green alone, in bed, recuperating from a toothache. "I was expecting you yesterday," he said. "I had a feeling. . . ."

92 ■ JOHN ALLEN KENDRICK

An inveterate felon, Kendrick was first arrested in Baltimore, during May 1923, on charges of larceny and murder. Convicted of larceny and a reduced assault charge, he drew five years in prison, discharging his sentence on December 4, 1928. An arrest on concealed weapons charges earned him two and a half years in February 1930. Kendrick escaped on September 2, 1931, but his freedom was short-lived; indicted in March 1932 for shooting a police officer in Washington, D.C., he was sentenced to ten years in the federal reformatory at Lorton, Virginia, from which he escaped on July 3, 1933.

In flight, Kendrick allied himself with the notorious (and misnamed) "Tri-State Gang," a collection of holdup artists active in Pennsylvania, Maryland, the District of Columbia, Virginia and North Carolina. Arrested at Johnson City, Tennessee, in June 1934, he was returned briefly to Lorton before a transfer to "the Rock" at Alcatraz. Another transfer, in July 1941, landed Kendrick in Leavenworth, where he finished his federal sentence. Instead of being set free, he was returned to New Jersey for completion of his interrupted sentence there, on concealed weapons charges, finally winning parole in June 1943.

Always quick on the trigger, Kendrick was arrested in June 1947 for shooting an underworld associate in Washington, D. C. Conviction, on December 10, earned him a term of three to ten years in Leavenworth, from which he was paroled in March 1954. Nine months later, on December 14, he was identified as the gunman who shot another Washington resident in the throat, leaving his victim critically wounded. Indicted during August 1955, he was charged with unlawful flight to avoid prosecution a month later, and his name was added to the FBI's "Most Wanted" list on November 2.

It took federal agents a month to trace their man, catching him in Chicago on December 5, 1955, and taking Kendrick into custody without resistance. Returned to Washington for yet another trial, the vicious triggerman was looking at a sentence which would finally remove him from the streets.

93 ■ JOSEPH JAMES BAGNOLA

A native of Chicago, born in 1916, Joe Bagnola was arrested for the first time in September 1932, on charges of petty larceny, and sentenced to six months in prison. Three years later, almost to the day, he was committed to the Illinois state prison on conviction for robbery. Paroled two days before Christmas 1940, Bagnola made his way home to Chicago and reportedly found work as a hired gun for the local syndicate, pulling off free-lance robberies and murders on the side.

In June of 1950, three New Orleans hoodlums planned to rob a local used-car dealer, calling in Bagnola as an "outside man" to shave the odds of recognition in a face-off. On the night of June 16, Bagnola and a male accomplice entered the victim's combined business and living quarters, bagging some $50,000 in cash and several diamond rings. When the victim physically resisted, he was pistol-whipped and dragged along a flight of stairs, sustaining lethal injuries. FBI investigation led to arrest of the original conspirators; they, in turn were quick to name the actual gunmen, with state charges filed on May

11, 1951, and federal fugitive warrants issued twelve days later.

One of Bagnola's companions was arrested by G-men in Milwaukee, on May 8, 1952; the other was seized in Oak Park, Illinois, on April 2, 1953. The sole conspirator at large, Bagnola was formally indicted for unlawful flight to avoid prosecution on November 3, 1955. His name was added to the "Ten Most Wanted" list on December 14, and two weeks later he was seized by Bureau agents in Chicago, wrapping up the case. Conviction on outstanding murder charges brought life sentences all around, and the plotters were consigned to Louisiana's state prison to serve the terms.

94 ■ NICK GEORGE MONTOS

The first of several fugitives to make the "Top Ten" list on two occasions, Montos won the dubious distinction by escaping from the Mississippi prison farm, at Parchman, on January 10, 1956. With inmate Robert Jones, Nick used a hacksaw to cut through the staple securing a door latch, tossing blankets over a barbed wire fence to make his getaway. A federal warrant was issued next day, and Montos was posted to the "Ten Most Wanted" list for the second time on March 9, 1956.

Additional publicity attendant on his two-time status numbered Montos' days of freedom. On March 29, an alert citizen of Memphis, Tennessee, recognized Montos and Jones as the same "James Harmon and party" who had recently checked in at a local motel. G-men established a command post at the motel, closing in before 3:00 A.M. on March 30. Blocking the driveway with cars, fourteen agents ringed the suspects' room before a telephone demand was made for their surrender. Thirty seconds later, tear gas shells were blasted through the windows, flushing out both fugitives. Inside their room, the raiders confiscated seven guns, three bottles of narcotics, body armor, and $4,300 in cash. The weapons included a sawed-off shotgun and a small-caliber weapon disguised as a pen, both held in violation of prevailing federal law.

On June 25, 1956, the fugitives appeared in federal court, in

Memphis. Montos entered guilty pleas to firearms and narcotics charges, drawing an eight-year prison term. His sidekick, Jones, earned six years for possession of illegal weapons. One month later, Montos went to trial in Georgia, for the brutal August 1952 robbery of an elderly couple which had put him on the "Top Ten" list the first time. Sentenced to death, he won an appeal on legal technicalities and was retried in May 1957. At his second trial, Nick drew a term of ten to twenty years.

95 ■ JAMES IGNATIUS FAHERTY
96 ■ THOMAS FRANCIS RICHARDSON

The great Brinks robbery of January 1950 was a year in the making. For twelve months prior to the event, eleven middle-aged Bostonians—including seven men with records of arrests for other crimes—planned every detail of a raid against the Brinks North Terminal garage. They slipped past guards to enter the garage by night, in stocking feet, and "cased" the floor plan, measured distances, determined which way doors swung open in an effort to avoid confusion at a crucial moment. Members of the team broke into a burglar alarm company, making off with samples of the model used by Brinks, to study its mechanism in detail. A full-scale dress rehearsal in December 1949 convinced the bandits they were ready for the score.

On January 17, the raiders entered the garage in broad daylight, decked out in simulated Brinks uniforms and rubber Halloween masks. Making their way to the counting room, they held startled employees at gunpoint and looted the vault of $1,218,211 in cash, plus another $1,557,183 in checks and securities. The total haul—well over $2.7 million—was a record for its time. In less than fifteen minutes, it was over.

The conspirators had planned to keep low profiles, sitting on their loot for six years, waiting for the statute of limitations to expire, but one of the team—James "Specs" O'Keefe— began to grumble that his share had not been large enough. Demanding another $63,000, he was angrily rejected by his comrades. Specs began to brood about injustice, while the gang faced problems on another front.

On May 14, 1952, convict Alfred Gagnon fingered Carlton O'Brien, of West Warwick, Rhode Island, as a planner of the Brinks job. Three days later, O'Brien was murdered by persons unknown, but his death, while plugging one leak, also opened another. On December 1, Specs O'Keefe was called before a special grand jury investigating the holdup. Two weeks later, five uncooperative witnesses, named by O'Keefe as participants to the robbery, were cited for contempt when they refused to testify.

It was apparent that O'Keefe would have to go. On June 10, 1954, the contract was assigned to Elmer "Trigger" Burke, the leading free-lance hit man of the 1950s. Burke caught up with Specs on June 16, spraying him with machine gun fire in a wild, nocturnal chase through the streets of Boston's Dorchester district. Wounded in the arm and chest, O'Keefe feigned death and Burke was satisfied, escaping from the scene as squad cars closed with sirens screaming.

(Arrested on June 24, Burke escaped from jail the next day. A year passed before his arrest by FBI agents in South Carolina. Hoping for extradition to Massachusetts, for trial on relatively minor charges of possessing a machine gun, Burke was instead returned to New York, on a pending murder case. Convicted on December 2, 1955, he was sentenced to death two weeks later. Burke died in Sing Sing's electric chair on January 9, 1958.)

The FBI had invested $25 million in its Brinks investigation by the time O'Keefe started talking in earnest. Arrested in Leicester, Massachusetts, on weapons charges August 1, 1954, Specs was sentenced to twenty-seven months in jail. Determined not to take the fall alone, he confessed his role in the heist and named his co-conspirators in late 1955. By that time, one—Joe Banfield—was deceased. Another, Stanley Gusciora, was incarcerated in the state of Pennsylvania, serving five to twenty years for pulling off a robbery in Pittsburgh. Still at large were Vincent Costa, Michael Geagan, Anthony Pino, Henry Baker, Joseph McGinnis, Adolph Maffie, Thomas Richardson, and James Faherty.

A grand jury hit the surviving suspects with forty-six indictments, including 148 separate counts of armed robbery, entering with felonious intent, conspiracy to steal, and putting a person in fear with felonious intent. On January 12, 1956, the FBI tried for a clean sweep of eight outstanding fugitives around the Boston area, but agents came up two men short. James Faherty had evaded authorities beforehand, and his longtime partner, Thomas Richardson, enjoyed an even narrower escape. When federal agents cornered Michael Geagan, in a bank where Richardson was presently employed, their second suspect managed to escape, unseen, in the confusion. Faherty was posted to the "Ten Most Wanted" list on March 19; his partner, Richardson, was added to the roster April 12.

In spite of massive heat, the fugitives would not desert their Boston stamping grounds. They had been hanging out together since their first arrest, in 1934, and togetherness had become a habit. On May 16, a squad of twenty-five heavily-armed FBI agents surprised the pair at an apartment in Dorchester, seizing three guns and $5,009 in cash. The lion's share of loot was never found, but there were indications that it might be working for the robbers. Ex-con William Cameron had sheltered Faherty, for pay, and it was rumored that he may have tipped authorities when he did not receive his pay on time. By June 10, Cameron was dead, shot down by unknown gunmen near his Boston home.

Eight members of the holdup gang, excluding Gusciora and O'Keefe (who turned state's evidence against his "friends"), were brought to trial in late September 1956. Convicted, they were sentenced to life terms on October 9, serving an average fourteen years each before winning parole. When an $18 million movie on the case began production, during 1980, Richardson and Adolph Maffie were invited to the set, amused to see their heist presented as a tongue-in-cheek affair. "I'm glad they made something light out of it," Richardson quipped. "People need a few laughs these days."

97 ■ EUGENE FRANCIS NEWMAN

Brooklyn-born, in 1928, Gene Newman was a wild, ungovernable youth who often stole from members of his family. His first arrest, for petty larceny, was logged at age fifteen, and he was sent to the reformatory at New Hampton, New York, for an indeterminate period. Drafted into the navy, as "Daniel Lyons," in April 1943, Newman went AWOL in August 1945. Court-martialed a month later, he was sentenced to twelve months in a disciplinary barracks, with completion of his term followed by a bad-conduct discharge in 1946. Arrested by New York City police for third-degree burglary in April 1947, he was convicted six months later and sentenced to ten years in the state reformatory. Parole put him back on the streets in December 1949, but he was not reformed. Arrested for the theft of a government vehicle on February 27, 1951, he gave his name as "Elvin Hall," pleading guilty to theft of government property and violation of the Dyer Act, prohibiting transport of stolen cars across state lines. On April 2, Newman was sentenced to eighteen months in prison, with an additional five years probation. Released in June, he was returned to the authorities in New York state, on violation of parole.

A free man once again by summer 1955, Gene Newman spared no time or energy in plotting out another heist. On August 3, with two accomplices, he tried to rob an armored truck in Buffalo, New York—and the result was a fiasco. The bandits—wearing stocking masks, with Newman brandishing a submachine gun—sprang their trap with the arrival of a truck in the security company's garage. Inside the armored van lay nearly half a million dollars in American and Canadian currency, lately retrieved from a race track at Fort Erie, Ontario. Bursting into the garage, Newman fired and wounded one of the guards, holding the others at bay while his allies collected the loot.

Unfortunately for the outlaws, Newman's wounded victim was alive and on the move. Unseen by his assailants, the injured officer managed to reach a tower overlooking the garage area, there sounding an alarm which brought employees and patrolmen on the run. The startled bandits dropped their loot and took off empty-handed. Newman commandeered a car at gunpoint, but a fault in the ignition left them stranded. Picking up a second car, the gunmen led police on a wild chase, spraying their pursuers with automatic fire before they dumped their latest car in a residential neighborhood. Splitting up, they took refuge in two separate houses, and were soon surrounded by police.

A new battle erupted, shattering the normal calm of tree-lined streets, and tear gas was employed to flush a pair of outlaws from their riddled sanctuary. Newman managed to escape in the confusion, while his two accomplices were being cuffed and bundled into waiting squad cars. Posted to the FBI's "Most Wanted" list on May 28, 1956, Eugene—and his machine gun—had already disappeared without a trace. A few days short of nine years later, federal process was dismissed on May 11, 1965. Gene Newman was another one of those who got away.

98 ■ CARMINE DI BIASE

A member of the Vito Genovese Mafia "family" in New York City, Carmine Di Biase earned his daily bread from gambling and extortion in Manhattan, sometimes taking on a murder contract if the target was important or the bounty high enough. Ironically, his placement on the "Ten Most Wanted" list came six full years before FBI Director J. Edgar Hoover's first grudging admission that an organized crime syndicate existed in America.

A few days before Christmas, in 1951, Di Biase was playing cards with business partner Michael Errichiello, at a social club in New York's Little Italy. They quarreled, and Carmine left, returning shortly after 5:00 A.M. to find his partner dozing, head down on the table. Creeping up on Errichiello, Di Biase drew a gun and pumped three shots into his skull. Turning to leave, he saw club member Rocco Tisi staring at him, horrified, and fired another shot that toppled Tisi in his tracks. Rocco survived to testify against Di Biase—marking one of the few occasions when one mafioso has publicly "ratted" on another—but by then Di Biase had vanished, going underground. His name was posted to the "Ten Most Wanted" list five years later, on May 28, 1956.

Considering his underworld connections, it is possible that Di Biase might have hidden out forever, baffling investigators with his disappearance, but the strain of living "on the lam" began to grate on Carmine's nerves. On August 28, 1958, he voluntarily surrendered to the FBI, disgusted with his years of hiding out. Convicted of murder and sentenced to die, Di Biase filed a successful appeal and was granted a second trial. The second time around, selected witnesses began to change their tune, and Carmine was acquitted by a jury.

By 1971, New York's Mafia was engaged in one of its periodic fratricidal wars. "Crazy Joe" Gallo, a renegade who triggered internecine violence in the 1960s with an underworld revolt against the Joe Profaci "family," walked out of Attica to take up where his former insurrection had been cut short by conviction on extortion charges. Gallo's nemesis, Profaci, had been claimed by cancer in the meantime, leaving Joe Colombo, Sr., in his place. On June 28, 1971, Colombo staged his second annual Italian-American "civil rights" protest, sponsored by his Mafia clan in an effort to throw FBI agents off his trail with bogus charges of "discrimination." During the festivities, an ex-convict, Jerome Johnson, crept up behind Colombo and shot him in the head, turning him into a vegetable.

Despite the trigger man's identity, Colombo's followers had little doubt that Joey Gallo was behind the shooting. Carmine Di Biase—having shifted his allegiance to Colombo's family in the intervening years—was chosen as a member of the hit team that would even up the score. On April 6, 1972, they overtook their target at Umberto's Clam House, a block and a half from the scene of the 1951 Errichiello murder. Witnesses named Carmine as the gunman who killed Gallo in the restaurant, wounding one of his bodyguards for good measure before he fled. Indictments were eventually filed, but Di Biase never surfaced, and authorities suspect he was eliminated in a move to guarantee his silence.

99 ■ BEN GOLDEN McCOLLUM

Born in Macum, Kentucky, Ben McCollum moved to Oklahoma with his family at the age of four. An unremarkable childhood provides no clue to his selection of a criminal career, but the choice was not auspicious. In 1929, he robbed banks in Prague and Checotah, Oklahoma, of $7,000 total, but the take would scarcely compensate McCollum for the prison term of forty years he earned upon conviction. Inside he quarreled with fellow inmates cutting two of them "to ribbons" with a homemade knife. Both died, and the brutality of the assault earned McCollum a death sentence. Three times he faced the chair, and three times stays of execution saved his life. McCollum's sentence was commuted to a term of life in 1935, but Ben did not intend to finish out his days behind gray walls.

It took a while to find an opening, but Ben McCollum finally made his break, escaping from the Oklahoma prison at McAlester on May 1, 1954. His name was added to the FBI's "Most Wanted" list on January 4, 1957, but another fourteen months would pass before he was caught.

Upon escaping from McAlester, McCollum drifted aimlessly for over two years, working odd jobs around the country, before finally settling in Indianapolis, during September 1956. As "George Napier," he rented a room and found work at Sunnyside Sanatorium, a county hospital serving tuberculosis victims. From all appearances, McCollum had gone straight, content to work and lead a normal life.

In fact, it was an effort to improve his situation honestly which ended Ben's charade. On March 7, 1958, McCollum applied for—and received—a new job, at Indiana's state school for the blind. He was scheduled to start work next Monday, March 10, but an employee of the school recalled a published photo lineup of the FBI's "Most Wanted" fugitives and tipped the Bureau off to "Napier's" address. Ben McCollum was arrested that same evening; three days later, waiving extradition, he was carried back to Oklahoma to complete his sentence.

A so-called "specialist" in burglary, Al White was not averse to trying other felonies when times were lean. His record spanned three decades, with arrests on charges that included auto theft, grand larceny, bank robbery, and violation of parole. Ohio locked him up for fourteen years, upon conviction for a bank job. Freed in 1940, he was hauled back three years later, after violating terms of his parole.

In summer 1954, policemen in West Hamlin, West Virginia, surprised White in the act of burglarizing a lumber yard. He answered their challenge with bullets, ducking return fire and plunging into a nearby river, scrambling to freedom in the darkness of the opposite bank. Identified from fingerprints, he proved more difficult to capture. More than two years passed before his name was added to the FBI's "Most Wanted" list, on January 14, 1957.

White had thus far managed to elude detection by adherence to a policy of isolation from his fellow man. Avoiding human contact when he could, White worked odd jobs and passed his leisure time alone. For relaxation, he would visit airports, sometimes watching planes take off and land for hours on end.

Addition to the "Top Ten" list, with its attendant fanfare of publicity, made it impossible for White to stay anonymous. On January 24, two citizens of Memphis saw his published photographs and recognized "Frank Shaw," a tenant of the local George Vincent Hotel. The FBI was notified, and agents bagged him as White emerged from the elevator, headed for his room. Unarmed, he offered no resistance, but a shakedown of his car and trailer, parked downstairs, revealed three pistols, an illegal sawed-off shotgun, ammunition, and a quantity of burglar's tools.

In custody, White told his captors he had nearly opted for surrender two months earlier, when he was injured in an accident and found that, as a fugitive, he could not use his paid-up health insurance. "I shouldn't have been on the FBI list in the first place," he groused. "It must have been the insistence of the West Virginia officers that got me on the list." As it would be their testimony, at his trial, which packed White off to prison on conviction for assault and burglary.

101 ■ ROBERT L. GREEN

Arrested several times for juvenile offenses, Robert Green made one attempt to change his luck by signing up for military service, but in vain. Dishonorably discharged, Green struck off for California and was briefly married there, but the domestic life was not his style. He drifted into Utah, where assorted felony convictions earned him one to twenty years for burglary and five to life for robbery. Committed to the penitentiary at Draper, Green and an associate escaped September 7, 1954, evading heavy gunfire from the guards to make their getaway.

In May 1955, Green made his way to Minneapolis and settled down. As "Floyd Baker," he found employment with a wholesale liquor dealer, loading box cars. A similar job opened up with the Minneapolis Barrel & Drum Company, in July, and Green made the move, hanging on through the end of September. Green's employer knew him as "one of the most cooperative men I've seen, and a fine worker." It was a different story, though, when Green resigned to take a job in the shipping department of a local plumbing supply house. There, he became known for his surly attitude and "goldbricking." As Green's supervisor recalled, "He was sulky and wouldn't look you in the eye. When he left here, he saved me the trouble of firing him."

The problem may have been a second fling at wedded bliss. In 1956, Green was a married man once more, this time the father of a child. The strain was showing by December, when he quit his job and burglarized a local service station, making off with a pistol and petty cash. In January 1957, "Baker" dropped his wife and child off with her family in Wisconsin, driving back to Minneapolis to launch a small-time crime spree. On February 4, he burglarized the office of his last employer, stealing three dictation machines, moving on to an apartment in the building where he lived, there picking up a camera and electric razor for himself. A week later, on February 11, he stole several typewriters from a local office building, afterward raiding another neighbor's apartment for a clock and radio.

It was an undistinguished climax for Green's criminal career. That afternoon, on the eleventh, he was added to the FBI's "Most Wanted" list, his photo published in the local press next day. Subscribers recognized "Floyd Baker," and the FBI received a tip their man was in the area. Intent on blowing town, Green did not reckon on the Bureau manning every airport, railroad station, and bus depot in the Twin Cities. On February 13, G-men bagged him at the Greyhound depot in St. Paul. His pockets held a loaded pistol and a one-way ticket to Milwaukee, neither of which he was able to use.

102 ■ GEORGE EDWARD COLE

A native of Philadelphia, Cole served time on theft convictions in Missouri, later moving on to California, where arrests for robbery brought time in Folsom and San Quentin. It was clear, in Cole's case, that a change of scene did not produce an automatic shift in fortune, but the small-time hoodlum never seemed to learn.

In San Francisco, Cole and sidekick Thomas Hamrick tried to rob a tavern on December 30, 1956. One of the patrons was an off-duty policeman, Sgt. Frank Lacey, who attempted to arrest the thieves. Two bullets laid him out, with mortal wounds, before the bandits fled, abandoning their loot in the confusion. Witnesses identified the triggerman as Cole, and Hamrick confirmed it from his cell a short time later. (A conviction as accessory to murder earned him life in prison, all the same.)

Cole fled the city hours after shooting Lacey, leaving most of his belongings in a rented room for the police to find. His mistress, Yvonne Conley, opted to join him in flight, despite the fact that her condition—advanced cirrhosis of the liver—called for constant, and expensive, medication. In the end, her loyalty to Cole would bring him down.

Cole's name was added to the "Top Ten" list on February 25, 1927. Federal agents traced the fugitives across Wyoming, to Nebraska, where their car was found in June. From there, the trail was lost. As "Mr. and Mrs. James Walker," Cole and Conley settled in Des Moines, Iowa, with Cole working two jobs until February 1959, when he opened his own filling station. His "wife" tended house in the meantime, taking her medicine, while agents of the FBI examined records of prescription sales from coast to coast, identifying those who bought the medication, weeding out potential suspects by the thousands.

The search paid off July 6, 1959, when G-men paid a call at "Walker's" station, recognized their man, and took him into custody. Cole stubbornly denied his name until a fingerprint comparison removed all doubt, and "Mrs. Walker" was arrested on the charge of harboring a fugitive. Returned to San Francisco for his trial, Cole pleaded faulty memory in Lacey's murder. "It's possible I did it," he insisted, "but I don't remember." Thomas Hamrick did his bit, with a refusal to incriminate his partner on the witness stand, but jurors were unimpressed with the sideshow, finding Cole guilty of second-degree murder. On November 2, 1959, he drew a term of five years to life in San Quentin. For Cole, it was like going home.

103 ■ EUGENE RUSSELL McCRACKEN

Confinement never suited Gene McCracken. Locked up on a minor charge in Bristol, Tennessee, in 1940, he immediately joined another prisoner in breaking jail. John Mills, an officer at Kingsport, found them hiding in a thicket two days later, and McCracken shot him dead. Convicted on a murder charge this time, he drew a term of life imprisonment. It took him fifteen years, but in October 1955 he staged another breakout, this time from the penitentiary at Nashville. His name was posted to the federal "Top Ten" list March 26, 1958.

In the interim, McCracken—traveling as "Richard Kirkman"—had already resettled in Baltimore, marrying a local woman and obtaining employment as a male nurse for an invalid physician. One day after his addition to the list, a resident of Baltimore alerted federal agents and they called on "Kirkman" at his home, arresting him without a fight. He was returned to Tennessee for the completion of his sentence.

104 ■ FRANK AUBREY LEFTWICH

Born in Surry County, North Carolina, in February 1922, Frank Leftwich grew up with a brooding hatred of authority. State police at Richmond, Virginia, arrested him for housebreaking in June 1941, and he was sentenced to a year in jail. Conscripted by the U.S. Army during World War II, he "served" from June 1943 to July 1945, including five prosecutions for absence without official leave between March 1944 and April 1945. On another occasion, his rowdy behavior led a female tavern proprietor in Mount Airy, North Carolina, to shoot Leftwich through the arm in self-defense. In April 1945, Leftwich and two companions wrecked a stolen army truck after a wild ride through Mount Airy, and his conviction for theft of government property earned him three years imprisonment. He was conditionally released from custody in August 1947.

On May 21, 1950, Leftwich was arrested as a common drunk in Lumberton, North Carolina, but the experience was hardly routine. While being booked, he drew a hidden pistol and opened fire on the arresting officers, wounding one before a police bullet ripped into his stomach. Surviving his wound, Leftwich was convicted of assault with intent to kill in September 1950, drawing a sentence of six to ten years in prison.

A violent and troublesome inmate, Leftwich seemed to seek out quarrels with his fellow prisoners, and one of them fractured his skull in a prison brawl, leaving Frank a legacy of dizzy spells and blinding headaches. He escaped from the state prison camp on October 30, 1952, and was recaptured at a Bay City, Michigan, saloon in January 1953. His second escape attempt, on October 19, 1954, was more successful, and no trace of Leftwich was found until April 14, 1957, when he paid a $200 fine for drunk driving in Georgetown, Delaware. Nine days later, a federal warrant was issued charging Leftwich with unlawful flight to avoid confinement, and his name was added to the "Ten Most Wanted" list on April 4, 1958.

Two weeks later, on April 18, FBI agents caught up with Leftwich in Chicago, where he had been living as "Ralph Calvin McDonald," employed as a welder since May 1957. Despite his stated plans to shoot it out with any officers who tried to bring him in alive, Leftwich was unarmed and offered no resistance when G-men arrived at his home to make the arrest.

105 ■ QUAY CLEON KILBURN

As a career criminal, Kilburn was mediocre at best. By age thirty-four, he had spent fourteen years behind bars, beginning with conviction for unauthorized sale of GI clothing while he was enlisted in the army. Later busts, as a civilian, earned more time for auto theft, bad checks, and violation of the Dyer Act. Convicted of a bank robbery in Orem, Utah, he was sent to Leavenworth on federal charges, earning a conditional release in 1956. A violation of those terms put Kilburn on the "Ten Most Wanted" list on April 16, 1958.

Six weeks later, agents in Los Angeles received an urgent tip from Long Beach, where a citizen was certain he had spotted Kilburn in the neighborhood of Sanborn Street. Investigation proved him right; the fugitive—who called himself "Clay Kilborn" now—had rented lodgings there, and agents found him home when they went calling on June 2. They were not deceived by Kilburn's false mustache or bogus ID cards, including "thumbprints" which, in fact, were taken from his toe! The suspect wore a loaded pistol underneath his jacket, with another in his briefcase, but the agents took him in without a struggle. Once his true identity had been confirmed, he was returned to Leavenworth to finish out his sentence.

106 ■ DOMINICK SCIALO
107 ■ ANGELO PERO

On March 16, 1958, police discovered seventeen-year-old Alexander Menditto lying in a Brooklyn gutter, leaking blood from several bullet wounds. They rushed him to a local hospital, where doctors gave him no hope of recovery, but he would live for nine more days, and in the meantime he was talking to police.

Menditto had been "taken for a ride," he said, along with sometime criminal accomplice "Bugsy" Garofalo. The subject of contention was a bungled arson job in Massachusetts. Garofalo and Menditto had been paid to torch a dance pavilion in the town of Framingham; they botched the job, but stubbornly refused to pay back some $500 which they had been paid beforehand. Punishment for welshing on the deal was swift and deadly.

Officers had turned up Garofalo's riddled body on a Brooklyn street March 17. When Al Menditto died March 25, the charge was double murder, and indictments were obtained against four suspects fingered by Menditto in his deathbed statement. Louis Esposito and Thomas Caizzo were arrested, briefly held for questioning, and then released for lack of evidence. The triggermen, police agreed, had been Dominick Scialo and Angelo Pero, both of whom had disappeared from their usual haunts when indictments were issued. Scialo's name was added to the "Ten Most Wanted" list on May 9, 1958; his cohort, Pero, made the list on June 16.

Some fourteen months elapsed before Scialo voluntarily surrendered to the FBI in Brooklyn, on July 27, 1959. The federal warrant against Angelo Pero was dismissed December 2, 1960, by the United States attorney for the eastern district of New York.

108 ■ FREDERICK GRANT DUNN

Frederick Dunn logged his first conviction in 1919, at age fourteen, when he was sent to the Iowa State Training School for Boys, at Eldora, on charges of breaking and entering and larceny. Paroled in 1921, he was finally discharged in 1924 and was next arrested two months later, for the burglary of a general store at Gayville, South Dakota. The proprietor had opened fire on Dunn and two accomplices, striking one of them in the eye. Dunn and his wounded companion were convicted of burglary in November 1924 and sentenced to five years in prison, with Dunn securing parole once more in 1927. Arrested for parole violation in Omaha, during May 1928, Dunn was returned to South Dakota's state prison, where he remained until August 1929.

A few weeks later, he was linked with the robbery of a bank in Salix, Iowa. Three weeks later, with a masked accomplice, he held up a store in Sioux City, firing his pistol into the ceiling before he waltzed out with $67 in cash. In early 1930, Dunn and an accomplice robbed a suburban bank near Sioux City. Arrested in Chicago during February, he was returned to Iowa for trial.

Ten days later, Dunn obtained a smuggled weapon in the jail and led another inmate in a bold escape, shooting one jailer in the thigh when his captor resisted. Dunn managed to elude pursuit, but briefly; later in the day, he was surprised by sheriff's deputies in a nearby alley and surrendered after a brisk exchange of gunfire. Sentenced to forty years for bank robbery and another thirty years for assault with intent to kill, Dunn entered the state prison at Fort Madison, Iowa, in March 1930. He was paroled, again, in June of 1941.

By this time, Dunn had begun to think of himself as a latter-day Dillinger, boasting of his prowess at blowing safes with nitroglycerine. On July 2, 1942, he joined two accomplices in looting a Portis, Kansas, bank of $2,861. Although locked inside the vault, a teller freed himself and grabbed a rifle, wounding one of Dunn's companions as they sped away. Outside of town, the bandits' vehicle swerved out of control, rolling over several times, but a second getaway car was waiting in the wings and the outlaws eluded pursuers.

On July 21, Dunn and his companions were arrested by the FBI in Denver, Colorado, ultimately sentenced to fifteen years on federal charges. (Two women, involved in the case as accessories, each drew sentences of six years.) Prior to sentencing, hacksaw blades were recovered from Dunn's cell, and he confessed to planning a jail break. Consigned to Leavenworth, he was paroled in November 1952, and arrest warrants charging parole violation were issued seven months later. Traced to Kansas City in January 1954, he was found in possession of firearms and ammunition, returning to finish his time in Leavenworth. Dunn was discharged from federal custody on August 16, 1957.

Two months later, in Westphalia, Iowa, he was accused of burglarizing a store. On November 14, he was arrested in Russell, Kansas, suspected of another burglary in nearby Palco, and an indictment on that charge was issued six days later. Dunn was subsequently transferred to the county jail at Lincoln, awaiting trial in the burglary of a grocery store at Sylvan Grove, Kansas, and he escaped from custody on January 11, 1958. Federal warrants charging him with unlawful flight to avoid prosecution were issued on January 16, and his name was added to the FBI's "Most Wanted" list on July 29.

As it developed, Dunn apparently had never fled from Kansas, after all. His skeletal remains were found near Ellsworth on September 7, 1959, and finally identified via post mortem examination on September 18. The cause of death was flexible —a homicide or suicide, with murder listed as the safer bet— but either way the rampage of a "modern Dillinger" was over.

109 ■ FRANK LAWRENCE SPRENZ

At fifteen years of age, Sprenz lied about his birth date and enlisted in the army. Honorably discharged in February 1947, he stole a car in Akron, Ohio, three months later, reenlisting with police one step behind him. Back in uniform, he stole a pistol and a submachine gun from the local armory. Both weapons were recovered when authorities detained him on a charge of auto theft, and Sprenz was sent to the Ohio State Reformatory, marking time until he reached adulthood.

Serving time did not change Frank's tendency toward crime. By April 1958, he was incarcerated in the Summit County jail, at Akron, facing trial on charges of burglary and armed robbery. On April 16, he persuaded a trusty to "forget" about securing the double-locking device on the cell block, opening his cell door with a key fashioned from a metal piece of his bunk. Releasing four other inmates, Sprenz led an assault on three deputies, dousing them with hot coffee before seizing two revolvers and a shotgun.

The inmates fled in two county cars, crashing through a garage door to reach the street. Within hours, one fugitive was captured and another killed by Akron officers. With his surviving comrades, Sprenz drove on to a gambling hall in Stark County, fifteen miles away, and there obtained another car. On April 18, police in Norfolk, Virginia, sighted the fugitives, chasing their vehicle into a dead-end street. One man was captured at the scene, while Sprenz and Richard Hoskinson escaped by dashing off in opposite directions. Entering an unattended house, nearby, Sprenz calmly showered, found himself a change of clothes, and left the area. Sought by federal agents for interstate transportation of a stolen car, Hoskinson surrendered in Detroit a short time later. Sprenz remained elusive, and his name was added to the "Ten Most Wanted" list on September 10, 1958.

On October 14, police in Spokane, Washington, reported that a pistol stolen by Sprenz had been pawned in their city, during April, by a man who called himself "Harold Scali." The alias, combined with Sprenz's habit of dispatching birthday cards to friends and relatives, enabled agents of the FBI to trace his moves around the country. In the next six months, Sprenz would employ thirty-five aliases, stealing twenty-nine cars and three airplanes as he covered an estimated 25,000 miles.

Nor was he simply running from the law. On March 29, 1959, Sprenz looted a bank in Hamilton, Ohio, of $29,955. He worked alone on the job, thanking employees and customers for their "cooperation" as he left. From the bank, Sprenz drove to Middleton, Ohio, in a stolen car, picking out an airplane at random and flying to an airport near Coshocton, Ohio, where a second set of wheels was waiting.

Sometimes, Sprenz bought planes instead of stealing them. One such was landed at Raymondsville, Texas, on March 31, 1959, where the airport manager recognized Frank from the

FBI poster. A description of the plane was broadcast, and on April 9, a pilot returning from Honduras reported a sighting at Tecolutla, near Vera Cruz. Mexican authorities, investigating the report on April 11, discovered that the plane was damaged. Five days later, on the anniversary of his escape from Akron, Sprenz was picked up by police who found him walking along a dirt road on the island of Cozumel, off the southeastern coast of Mexico.

"Wherever I went," Sprenz told his captors, "I felt the pressure of the FBI. The pressure confused me so that I used to run in all directions without knowing why. I just wanted to get somewhere where there was no FBI men. There's no such place."

The courts provided a solution for his problem. Speedily convicted on a list of state and federal charges, Sprenz accumulated prison terms amounting to 180 years.

110 ■ DAVID LYNN THURSTON

Another fugitive whose legal problems surfaced during military service, David Thurston joined the Army Air Corps during April 1946, at age eighteen. He fled the world of uniforms and discipline October 1, remaining at large until May 29, 1947, when he was arrested in Kansas City. A general court-martial in July resulted in his dishonorable discharge and a sentence in the guardhouse at Fort Leavenworth, Kansas, from which he was released on November 25, 1947.

In January 1948, Thurston was arrested as a vagrant in San Bernardino, California, receiving a sixty-day suspended sentence. Moving on, he joined two accomplices in a car theft at Laramie, Wyoming, followed by a bungled burglary attempt in nearby Lamont. Surprised in the act of breaking into a gas station, they fled empty-handed, later stealing canned goods and clothing from a store in Baggs, Wyoming. The hoodlums were arrested on July 24, near Rock Springs, after rolling their stolen car, and Thurston received a sentence of twelve to eighteen months in prison. All three were paroled on September 18, 1948, with the stipulation that they compensate the owner of the stolen car for damages sustained, but Thurston reneged on his part of the bargain and was declared a parole violator.

On the last day of 1948, Thurston and an accomplice were arrested in Inglewood, California, charged with robbing a store the previous day. Thurston pled guilty to stealing $300 worth of clothing and was referred to the California Youth Authority for detention until his twenty-fifth birthday, in March 1954. Transferred to a forestry camp near Whitmore on July 14, 1949, Thurston and a fellow inmate escaped three days later. Both were recaptured the following day, while attempting to steal a car in Redding.

After communication with authorities in Wyoming, Thurston was returned to face charges of parole violation on July 17, 1950, winning release from state prison a year later. Aware that his name was well-known to police, Thurston began calling himself "James L. Moore." He was using that name in Los Angeles, on January 13, 1952, when another robbery resulted in a high-speed chase and collision with a police vehicle. Though handcuffed, Thurston tried to seize a shotgun from the dashboard rack of a patrol car, but the rack was locked and he was quickly subdued by arresting officers. Convicted of robbery, Thurston was sentenced to one year in county jail and five years probation.

Honest work held no attraction for Dave Thurston, and he was picked up again on January 25, 1954, in Long Beach, following the robbery of a liquor store. Irrational and violent in custody, Thurston tried to dive through a window while handcuffed, afterward beating his head on the walls and floor. Pleading guilty on two counts of second-degree robbery, the wild man drew a sentence of one year to life in San Quentin.

Paroled in December 1957, Thurston worked briefly as a dishwasher, in Sacramento, during January 1958. But he soon stole a pistol and picked up an accomplice for the drive to San Francisco, where they stole a newer car and made their way to Portland, Oregon. On February 25 they robbed a Portland grocery store of $1,155, Thurston's sidekick nearly shooting himself when the pistol went off in his pocket. Arrested the same day, after witnesses memorized their license number, the outlaws were jailed pending trial on robbery charges.

In March 1958, while traveling to a courtroom appearance, Thurston wriggled free of his handcuffs and led police on a wild chase over several blocks, before he was recaptured. The next time, April 29, he used a makeshift key to free himself and this time managed to escape. A federal fugitive warrant was filed on May 26, and Thurston's name was added to the FBI's "Most Wanted" list on January 8, 1959.

A month later, on February 6, Thurston was spotted by local police officers in New York City. Unarmed at the time of his arrest, he was taken into custody without serious resistance and returned to Oregon for trial on charges of robbery and escape.

111 ■ JOHN THOMAS FREEMAN

A fast-moving gunman with multiple charges of robbery behind him, John Freeman was added to the FBI's "Ten Most Wanted" list on February 17, 1959, charged with unlawful flight to avoid prosecution in Missouri. Replacing David Thurston on the roster, Freeman lasted one full day before a sharp-eyed citizen in Hillside, Maryland, recognized his face from published photographs and telephoned the Bureau. Agents bagged him without a struggle, relieving him of his snub-nosed .38 revolver before he had an opportunity to resist arrest. The civilian informant's identity was protected in accordance with standing FBI policy.

112 ■ EDWARD SANFORD GARRISON

Another "Ten Most Wanted" list alumnus, Edward Garrison was serving life in Alabama when he staged another breakout on August 23, 1958. His name was posted to the roster for a second time on March 4, 1959, but eighteen months would pass before the perennial escape artist was apprehended by federal agents.

In the meantime, Garrison had settled in St. Louis, employing his fabled skills as a "human adding machine" to find work as a bookkeeper in nearby Eureka, Missouri. Local friends of Garrison were placed under surveillance, and on September 9, 1960, one of them finally led G-men to the fugitive's apartment on Nottingham Avenue. Described by Alabama lawmen as being "as dangerous as a rattlesnake," Garrison surrendered without resistance. "I won't give you boys any trouble," he said. "I guess the hunt for me is over."

En route to the federal building, Garrison expressed relief. "I'm glad it's over with," he told arresting agents. "I know the FBI. You can't fool the FBI very long." Entering the lockup, Garrison spotted his poster on a bulletin board, smiled, and said, "You can take my picture down."

113 ■ EMMETT BERNARD KERVAN

A victim of tuberculosis, Emmett Kervan's illness did not stop him from compiling an impressive record of arrests and felony convictions, coast-to-coast. At one time or another, charges filed against him ran the gamut from possession of a deadly weapon, burglary, and grand theft to the relatively sophisticated crime of counterfeiting. Kervan never had much luck at crime, but his expensive tastes prevented him from going straight.

On February 5, 1959, a lone bandit entered the Merchants Bank and Trust Company in Norwalk, Connecticut. Drawing a pistol from one pocket of his coat, he produced a sack from the other and ordered a startled teller to "Fill it up." An estimated $30,000 went into the bag before he departed, eluding local roadblocks to make his getaway.

That afternoon, police received a phone call from a trucker who had nearly been forced off Route 136, south of Norwalk, a few minutes after the holdup. The car that nearly clipped him was a large, black sedan, bearing license plates with white numbers displayed on a green background. Federal agents, answering the holdup call, were cautiously encouraged as they realized that only three states—Washington, New Hampshire, Michigan—might fit the bill. (A fourth state, Florida, used white-on-green, but only single plates were issued, while the suspect vehicle had license plates in front and back.)

The bandit's car was found, abandoned, on a street in Buffalo, New York. The plates were stolen, but a registration slip led agents back to Norwalk, where the suspect had allegedly resided. Sketches of the bandit were immediately recognized by workers at a Norwalk hospital, where Kervan was employed before he turned his hand to robbery. Kervan's name was added to the "Ten Most Wanted" list on April 29, 1959.

By that time, Kervan had already moved to Texas. Arriving in El Paso, during February, he had passed a month in various hotels before acquiring an apartment. Known locally as a big spender, laying out some $500 a week on living expenses, Kervan impressed his landlady as "a nice gentleman." A local woman who began to date the fugitive knew nothing of his record; she was told that he had come to Texas for his health, beset by chronic asthma.

Agents of the FBI, meanwhile, pursued their man through grim, methodical examination of hotel registers and used-car sales receipts across the nation, finally homing in on Texas and El Paso. Kervan was traced to his apartment and surprised there, in pajamas, on May 13, 1959. He surrendered without resistance, and agents recovered $20,000 of the Norwalk loot on May 15, when they cleaned out his safe deposit box. Returning to Connecticut for trial, Kervan pled guilty on a robbery charge and was sentenced to prison.

114 ■ RICHARD ALLEN HUNT

The product of a broken home, Hunt spent his early years in an orphan's home maintained by the Women's Christian Temperance Union at Corvallis, Oregon. He joined the army in 1950, and was wounded by live ammunition during a practice parachute jump, later serving with the military police during the Korean War. On balance, though, MPs saw Hunt more often as a prisoner than as a colleague. Stationed in California during 1952, he was arrested for stealing a truck but got off with a term of probation. Convicted on a second grand theft charge a short time later, Hunt served six months in the county jail at Rocky Butte, Oregon. Released to military authorities, he went AWOL twice. The first time, he tried to evade MPs by diving into an icy river, taunting his pursuers until the cold forced him ashore; later, hiding out at the Corvallis orphan's home, he threatened military policemen with a pitchfork, and was taken prisoner at gunpoint. In October 1954, a grand larceny conviction at Big Timber, Montana, earned him eighteen months in prison, plus a dishonorable discharge from the army. Hunt escaped from the state prison, at Deer Lodge, in November 1955, but was recaptured next day, with another eighteen months added on to his sentence. He was paroled to relatives at Riddle, Oregon, in January 1957.

Freedom and civilian life appeared to make a difference to Richard Hunt, but any change was purely superficial. Drifting aimlessly from one job to another, working chiefly as a ranch hand, he avoided trouble with the law until the early part of April 1958, when he began to pass bad checks in Idaho. The next eleven months found Richard stealing cars and working dead-end rural jobs in Oregon, Nevada, and Wyoming.

On March 24, 1958, Police Chief Ernest McPhee, of Harrisburg, Oregon, was abducted at gunpoint after he sought to question Hunt about a stolen car. Driving through Brownsville, ten miles to the north, he was spotted by Chief Robert Kemnow. Pulling over on command, Hunt burst from the car with a pistol, firing one shot which struck Kemnow in the head and left him critically injured. McPhee was left unharmed as Hunt escaped, eluding trackers in the rugged country he had known from childhood.

Federal agents joined the hunt on a presumption that their man was fleeing interstate. A warrant charging Hunt with interstate transportation of a stolen car was issued on September 22, with a secondary charge of unlawful flight appended on April 13, 1959. Hunt's name was added to the Bureau's "Top Ten" list on May 27, 1959.

By that time, the elusive gunman had left tracks in California, Arizona, Nevada, and New Mexico, crossing the border for a brief stay in Tijuana before moving north again. He settled in Wyoming, working at a ranch outside Thermopolis, in Hot Springs County. Sheriff Eddie Todorovich met the new hand, in passing, a couple of weeks before Hunt made the "Most Wanted" list, and publicity sparked the sheriff's memory. On June 2, 1959, Todorovich arrested Hunt and turned him over to the FBI for extradition. Returning to Oregon, Hunt pled guilty to shooting Chief Kemnow, and was immediately sentenced to a term of life imprisonment.

115 ■ WALTER BERNARD O'DONNELL

Launching his criminal career in 1922, with the theft of a collection box from a New Orleans church, Walter O'Donnell used a score of aliases in the next three decades, racking up convictions for burglary, breaking and entering, petty larceny, grand larceny, second-degree burglary, and impersonating a federal officer. The 1950s saw his usual approach refined to something of an art form: sporting a toupee and posing as a doctor, he would prey on older women, offering to help them trim unsightly fat with "weight-loss" capsules which, in fact, immediately rendered them unconscious, leaving Walter free to loot their homes of cash and jewelry, furs and firearms—anything, in short, which caught his eye. An "educated talker," fluent in Spanish, he was frequently invited to address small gatherings of older people on a range of topics dealing with their health.

By early 1959, O'Donnell was a fugitive from local warrants filed in California, Illinois, Ohio, Pennsylvania, Florida, and Washington, D.C.; the charges ranged from auto theft and larceny to the administration of a stupefying drug. The transportation of a stolen car from Detroit to Toledo, Ohio, put federal agents on O'Donnell's trail, for violation of the Dyer Act, and he was also sought on charges of unlawful flight. His name was posted to the Bureau's "Top Ten" list on June 17, 1959.

Two days earlier, the fugitive had checked into a Norfolk, Virginia, hotel, signing the register as "A. J. Rossi." He had come from New York City, scheduled to address a meeting of Alcoholics Anonymous on Friday evening, June 19, but his

addition to the "Ten Most Wanted" list upset O'Donnell's
plan. His photograph was printed in the local paper June 18,
identified by a subscriber, and the FBI was notified. A squad
of agents found him in his room and took him into custody
without resistance. "I knew you'd get me eventually,"
O'Donnell said. "I'm glad it's over." Throwing himself on the
mercy of the court, he received a ten-year sentence for transporting stolen goods between New York and Norfolk, with
five years tacked on to cover the Detroit auto theft.

116 ■ BILLY OWENS WILLIAMS

Born in Tampa in 1927, Billy Williams was accused of stealing
chickens at his first arrest, in 1941, but juvenile authorities
released him on the basis of his tender years. In January 1947,
while serving with the army in Korea as "Owens Williams,"
Williams was charged with burglarizing the home of a Korean
national. Conviction earned him a dishonorable discharge,
forfeiture of all pay, and a sentence of ten years hard labor,
but he escaped with only the dishonorable discharge after the
rest of his sentence was remitted.

Failing to learn from experience, Williams reenlisted with
the army in July 1947—this time as "Gene Williams"—and
was posted to a duty station in Japan. In December, he faced
charges of theft and depriving a person of liberty, after he
locked a fellow serviceman in the trunk of a car. Convicted in
his second court-martial, Williams was again dishonorably discharged, forfeiting all pay and allowances, with a sentence of
eighteen months hard labor. He was conditionally released
from the federal lockup at Danbury, Connecticut, on February 16, 1951.

In the interim, physicians had described Williams's behavior
as "delusional, alternating between ideas of grandeur and
ideas of extreme humility. He sometimes distorts reality to a
world of fantasy." He was known to have threatened family
members with a knife on several occasions, and a hometown
doctor stated that Williams should be considered a menace to
the public welfare.

On June 9, 1954, Williams and a male accomplice kidnapped a Tampa businessman on his way home from work, robbing him at gunpoint before they tied him with ropes and placed him in the trunk of their car, driving aimlessly around the city for five hours. Their victim was released after promising to pay his abductors $1,000, and Billy's companion was picked up by local officers the next day, eventually drawing a sentence of life imprisonment.

Williams, meanwhile, had fled the state, and federal charges of unlawful flight to avoid prosecution were filed in Tampa. On June 30, stopped for a routine traffic check in New Jersey, Williams bolted from his stolen car and escaped on foot, leaving a pistol and thirty rounds of ammunition behind. On August 10, 1954, New Jersey State Police arrested him in possession of another hot car, stolen that day in New York City.

In custody at Trenton and awaiting transfer back to Florida, Williams set fire to his cell and later attempted to strangle himself with a belt. He also made statements implicating himself in the infamous Sam Sheppard murder case, following his "confession" with demands for money from the Sheppard family. (Investigators found no evidence of his involvement in the case.) Upon his return to Florida, Williams was diagnosed as criminally insane and was confined to the state hospital at Chattahoochee on December 13, 1954. He escaped from the tuberculosis ward on March 21, 1958, and federal warrants charging Williams with unlawful flight were issued a week later. Billy made the FBI's "Most Wanted" list on July 10, 1959.

It took eight months for Bureau agents to locate Williams in New York City. Acting on a tip from an informant, G-men made the collar on March 4, 1960, taking Williams into custody without resistance. He was returned to the Florida hospital under guard, there to finish out his days as a ward of the state.

117 ■ JAMES FRANCIS JENKINS

Trained as a welder in the army, Jenkins seldom plied his trade, preferring the pursuit of "easy" money through assorted felonies. Inaugurating his career of crime in 1941, he spent a decade running up convictions for burglary, larceny, receiving stolen property, and violation of parole. Convicted, in 1948, of pulling off two dozen burglaries in Delaware County, Pennsylvania, Jenkins was paroled in 1950, but other offenses soon put him back behind bars. Conditionally released in 1958, he tried the straight life for a year, but found it tedious. An avid bettor on the ponies, Jenkins needed ready cash on hand, and honest labor seemed to offer no immediate reward.

On March 4, 1959, with sidekick Randall Nuss, James robbed a bank near Broomail, Pennsylvania, of $17,870. Both men were arrested by FBI agents a week later, in Providence, Rhode Island, and returned to Philadelphia for trial, but Jenkins had already seen enough of prison from the inside. Working cautiously for thirteen days, he used a smuggled screwdriver to gouge a hole in the wall of his cell, escaping from the Moyamensing County jail with two other inmates. Ropes made out of bedsheets were employed as the escapees scrambled to the street from their cell on the top floor, a two-hour gap between bed checks granting them a substantial headstart on their pursuers.

From the lockup, Jenkins went directly to the home of Henry Kiter, formerly a cellmate, free on bail and awaiting a trial on weapons charges. Federal agents traced their man to Kiter's home, too late, and Kiter's name was entered on a May 6 warrant charging him with aiding an escape. James Jenkins made the Bureau's "Ten Most Wanted" list on July 21.

On August 12, a tip from residents in Buffalo, New York, brought G-men to a small motel where Jenkins and Kiter were registered under assumed names. Jenkins was taking a shower when agents knocked on the door, engaged Kiter in small talk, then forced their way inside to take the fugitives without a struggle. Neither man was armed, although a sawed-off shotgun was recovered from their car, outside. Returned to Philadelphia, where he was eventually tried and convicted, James Jenkins heard his new bond set at $50,000. Chuckling ruefully, he asked the bailiff, "Will you take a check?"

118 ■ HARRY RAYMOND POPE

A veteran hoodlum in the neighborhood of Dallas, Texas, Harry Pope ran up a record of convictions for possession of narcotics, burglary, attempted burglary, and drunken driving by the age of thirty. Dubbed "the walking arsenal," after the shotgun and three pistols he habitually carried, Pope was not averse to violence. An associate of triggermen and contract killers, he possessed the reputation of a fast-gun artist who would shoot it out with officers in lieu of passively submitting to arrest.

On November 23, 1958, police in Phoenix, Arizona, surprised Pope in the act of burglarizing a drug store. Harry shot his way out of the trap, but lost his right eye to a bullet in the process and was quickly captured. Free on bond, he disappeared before his trial, and fugitive warrants were issued for his arrest. On August 11, 1959, his name was added to the FBI's "Most Wanted" list.

Two weeks later, on the twenty-fifth, police in Lubbock got a tip that Pope was hiding in a local trailer park. At 4:15 P.M., a team consisting of two federal agents, five patrolmen, and a Texas Ranger stormed the trailer, catching Pope unarmed, browsing through a newspaper. Arrested with him, on a charge of harboring a fugitive, were Clifton and Christine Thompson, of Los Angeles. Ironically, Pope had been ignorant of his addition to the "Ten Most Wanted" list.

For all his fearsome reputation, Harry opted to surrender in the face of overwhelming odds. "We saw them getting out of the cars," he said, "but I knew I didn't have a chance. There were too many of them, and they were armed too heavily. If there had been just three, that would have been good odds, but eight was too many. I'm not stupid."

119 ■ JAMES FRANCIS DUFFY

A violent, unstable felon, James Duffy had served several prison terms in Pennsylvania by the spring of 1958, with one stint in a hospital for the criminally insane. Nurturing his reputation as a gunman, Duffy boasted that he would never again be taken alive. "I'll fire all my bullets at the cops," he told acquaintances, "except one which I am saving for myself."

On March 28, with accomplices Harry Shank and William McGee, Duffy robbed the Drexelbrook Inn, in Upper Darby, Pennsylvania, of $4,500. The bandits escaped after a wild chase, in which they wrecked their car, but Shank and McGee were apprehended a short time later. Evidence of flight across state lines sent federal agents after Duffy, but invariably he returned to Pennsylvania, popping up in Philadelphia to rob a drug store on May 1. His name was added to the "Ten Most Wanted" list on August 29.

Investigation traced the fugitive to Newark, New Jersey, and G-men were tightening the noose when Duffy's homing instinct brought him back to Philadelphia. On September 2, 1959, he registered as "Allan Sullivan" at a hotel on 15th Street, but agents were hot on his heels. Mindful of Duffy's threat to shoot it out, they surrounded the hotel five hours after his arrival, armed and ready for battle. Approaching the fugitive's room, they were surprised to find their man unarmed, apparently anxious to surrender. "I knew you would get me," he said, as they led him away.

120 ■ ROBERT GARFIELD BROWN , JR.

On July 7, 1959, Canadian tourists Maurice and Lise Couture were accosted by two armed strangers in a picnic grove at Old Orchard Beach, Maine, south of Portland. The couple was robbed of $190 at gunpoint, after which one of the bandits shot Maurice in the chest, leaving him for dead as they drove away. Roadblocks failed to stop the gunmen, but their van was traced, the next day, to a local garage where its "owner" had dropped it off "for repairs"; items recovered from the vehicle were linked to several recent burglaries. Police tracked down a taxi driver who had driven the suspects from the garage to the Greyhound bus depot, where they bought tickets for Boston. A Greyhound driver recalled their frequent inquiries about stops, placing their departure in Chelsea, a Boston suburb.

While the manhunt shifted to Massachusetts, Lise Couture was busy with State Police officers, scouring mug books for a likeness of the bandits. The man who shot her husband was identified as Robert Brown, a three-time loser from New Hampshire with convictions which included grand larceny, breaking and entering, and two counts of breaking parole. A "John Doe" warrant was issued for the second, younger gunman, listing a description which enabled officers in Westwood, Massachusetts, to arrest ex-convict Kenneth Chenette on July 13. Identified by Mrs. Couture the next day, Chenette confessed his role in the robbery and was sentenced, two months later, to a term of fifty to 100 years in prison.

Robert Brown was added to the FBI's "Most Wanted" list on September 9, 1959. Four months later, on January 11, 1960, a tip led Cincinnati agents to a Salvation Army home, where Brown surrendered without resistance. Voicing a sentiment common among "Top Ten" alumni, he told arresting officers, "I'm glad it's over. I knew the FBI would get me."

At his trial, on February 2, Brown was sentenced to concurrent terms of twenty years, for assault with intent to kill, and forty to eighty years each on two counts of armed robbery. Six years later, in February 1966, the Maine Law Court reduced sentences for Brown and Chenette to a maximum of sixty years apiece.

By 1974, Brown was back on the street and up to his old tricks, joining accomplice Terrill Jewett in the robbery of a Portland bank. The bandits scooped $5,000 into their sack, unaware that tellers had added a "bonus." The anti-theft device exploded in their car, filling the vehicle with smoke and red dye which forced Brown and Jewett to abandon the car, fleeing on foot, empty-handed. Brought to trial in January 1976, Brown pled guilty to robbery and drew another twenty-five year sentence in the penitentiary.

121 ■ FREDERICK ANTHONY SENO

The holder of a criminal record dating from 1926, Seno once robbed his own mother, and later threatened to kill his ex-wife. By 1958, he was free on parole from a sentence of five to thirty years, resulting from a $20,000 robbery in Minnesota. Refusing to learn from experience, he robbed two markets in Chicago and was locked up pending trial. On December 11, 1958, he fled from a Cook County courtroom, eluding pursuers to make good his escape.

Seno's name was added to the "Top Ten" list on September 24, 1959, resulting in a tip the same day, from Miami, Florida, where he had been working the past nine months as a chef and caterer. Seno's job had taken him into some of Miami's most lavish homes, but he had thus far resisted the temptation to rob his clients. Surprised at his apartment by a team of federal agents, he shouted, "Don't shoot! Don't shoot!" Unable to produce $10,000 bond at his preliminary hearing Seno was jailed pending extradition to Illinois.

122 ■ SMITH GERALD HUDSON

Smith Hudson first clashed with the law at age sixteen, but his real trouble did not start until 1951. After his brother-in-law was killed in a car wreck, with Hudson at the wheel, a charge of involuntary manslaughter was filed by authorities in Scranton, Pennsylvania. Free on bond, Hudson went berserk, blasting acquaintance John Ferguson to death with a shotgun, leaving behind a note which expressed his intention to kill other persons before committing suicide. Captured by officers of the State Police four months later, at Smithfield, Hudson drew a term of ten to twenty years upon conviction for Ferguson's murder. He escaped from the Pennsylvania state prison in 1957, and his name was added to the Bureau's "Ten Most Wanted" list October 7, 1959.

In late July 1960, Glendon Maline, a merchant in Cozad, Nebraska, received a shipment of FBI flyers which included Hudson's photograph. Maline immediately recognized the fugitive as one "Gerald Bennett," an occasional patron who, since October 1958, had been locally employed as a ranch hand. After conferring with Cozad banker W. E. Young, Maline contacted the FBI, and samples of Hudson's handwriting were compared with the signatures on "Bennett's" checks. The writing matched, but agents took their time, avoiding any possible mistake.

On the night of July 30, Hudson visited Maline's store, dropping the offhand remark that he might be leaving Cozad in the near future. Maline took the opportunity to note prominent scars on Hudson's face, near one eye, and on his left thumb. Their confirmation assured, FBI agents surrounded the suspect's small house before dawn the next morning, taking him into custody without resistance. As the handcuffs closed around his wrists, Hudson remarked, "I feel suddenly like a man who has no future."

123 ■ JOSEPH LLOYD THOMAS

Twice imprisoned for auto theft in Indiana, once fined and jailed for possession of an illegal still, Joseph Thomas had apparently gone straight by the late 1950s. Married and the father of two children, he owned a restaurant in Terre Haute, supporting his family through honest labor. Still, the "easy" life of crime had its attractions, which Thomas seemed unable to resist.

According to the federal charges filed against him, Joseph was one of three men who invaded a Shreveport, Louisiana, bank on February 13, 1958, making off with $34,000 in a daring daylight robbery. His accomplices were swiftly captured, but Thomas remained at large, earning a spot on the Bureau's "Ten Most Wanted" list on October 21, 1959.

By that time, he had relocated to the town of Pelzer, South Carolina, traveling as "George Ashley," using his share of the Shreveport loot to open a used car agency. Joseph's wife swapped her name for an alias, and their daughters were enrolled at local schools, presenting the perfect image of a normal family.

At least one of their neighbors knew better, the truth revealed by Thomas's photograph hanging in a local post office. Tipped to the fugitive's whereabouts, agents surrounded him at a Pelzer filling station on December 10. Joseph surrendered without resistance, but arresting officers discovered he had come prepared: a gun was tucked behind the radio in his car, Thomas had two hacksaw blades strapped to one of his legs, and his shoes were stuffed with $125 in cash.

124 ■ KENNETH RAY LAWSON

Born at Esserville, Virginia, in November 1927, Lawson tried military service in the army and was honorably discharged, moving on to the air force a short time later. Things went sour on his second tour in uniform, resulting in a dishonorable discharge and two years in a disciplinary barracks after Lawson was convicted of desertion and escape.

As a civilian, Lawson tried his hand at several occupations, variously working as a mechanic, used-car salesman, dance instructor and coal miner, before trying his luck at burglary. On August 5, 1956, he was arrested for looting a hardware store at Limestone, Tennessee, sentenced on conviction to a term of three to five years in prison. Granted forty-five days in which to file an appeal, Lawson and an accomplice were trapped by officers in Greeneville, less than a month later, as they burglarized a supermarket. Tossing hams through a plate glass window, they fled in an exchange of gunfire but were captured later in the day.

Diagnosed as a psychopath, Lawson still had friends on the outside. One of them sent him a hacksaw blade, concealed in a large tube of toothpaste, but Lawson's escape plan was discovered before he could finish cutting through the bars of his cell. Convicted of burglary, larceny, and felonious assault, the defendant drew a sentence of twelve to thirty years in Brushy Mountain Prison, near the little town of Petros.

On January 31, 1958, tower guards at Brushy Mountain spotted Lawson struggling to scale the prison wall and opened fire with rifles. Sprinting back across the yard, with bullets whistling around his ears, he scaled a second wall and fled, but was arrested hours later in a stolen car. In March of 1958, the troublemaking convict was a ringleader and spokesman for rioting prisoners at Brushy Mountain, but his next escape attempt was postponed for thirteen months. On April 22, 1959, with four other inmates, Lawson hid behind a false partition in a railroad freight car parked inside the prison walls, and rode to freedom unobserved. His four accomplices were quickly captured, but Lawson remained at large, facing federal charges of unlawful flight to avoid confinement. His name was added to the "Ten Most Wanted" list on January 4, 1960.

Ten weeks later, on March 17, Lawson was identified and arrested by local authorities in Mexico City. Extradition procedures were swiftly completed, and he was delivered to the FBI three days later, returning to Tennessee for completion of his original sentence.

125 ■ TED JACOB RINEHART

An accomplished burglar and jewel thief, Ted Rinehart was born January 21, 1927, in Poplar Bluff, Missouri. Logging his first arrest in 1944, at age seventeen, Rinehart went on to compile a record of convictions for breaking and entering, grand larceny and armed robbery in several states. His modus operandi involved extensive travel, renting inconspicuous houses in middle-class neighborhoods, from which he proceeded to raid homes in more affluent areas.

Sentenced to ten years for a Florida robbery, Rinehart was paroled after serving five and a half years of his term, but his parole was revoked on June 17, 1959. Federal charges of unlawful flight to avoid confinement were filed on July 23, and Rinehart made the FBI's "Most Wanted" list on January 25, 1960. Additional counts charged him with interstate transportation of stolen property, alleged to be the loot from his most recent burglaries.

Fond of high society, Scotch whiskey and older women, Rinehart once boasted of plans to make bankrobber "Baby Face" Nelson "look like a piker." His opportunities ran out on March 6, 1960, when federal agents traced him to Los Angeles and took him into custody without a fight. In hiding, Rinehart had attempted to change his appearance by growing a mustache and gaining forty pounds, but the disguise proved ineffective and he was returned to Florida to serve his time.

126 ■ CHARLES CLYATT ROGERS

Sentenced to life imprisonment during November 1950, on his conviction for first-degree murder in Florida, Rogers was transferred to a Chattahoochee hospital for the criminally insane after he attempted suicide in prison. On March 29, 1959, he escaped from his second-floor hospital room by tying bedsheets together and lowering himself to the street below. A federal warrant, charging Rogers with unlawful flight to avoid confinement, was issued on April 3, 1959. His name was added to the FBI's "Most Wanted" list eleven months later, on March 18, 1960.

On May 11, Patrolman Donald Schilz was walking his beat in Minneapolis, making his last stop of the morning at a call box outside Salvation Army headquarters, on Marquette Avenue, when he noticed a familiar face in the breakfast line. Checking his FBI flyers, Schilz recognized Charles Rogers at a glance, making a closer pass to confirm a tell-tale scar on the fugitive's neck and a tattoo—"Mother"—on the back of his right hand. Under questioning, Rogers identified himself as "Charles Norris," one of five pseudonyms listed on his FBI Wanted flyer, and Schilz arrested him on the spot. Ironically, it was the second time in two years that Patrolman Schilz had collared an FBI fugitive on the basis of his sharp memory for faces, the prior arrest taking place in 1958.

127 ■ JOSEPH CORBETT , JR.

A criminal with a collegiate background, Joseph Corbett logged his first felony arrest shortly after withdrawing as a

physics major from the University of California. The corpse of
U.S. Air Force Sgt. A. L. Reed was found near San Francisco
on December 22, 1950, and the evidence recovered from a
stolen car connected Corbett with the slaying. Arrested on
January 4, 1951, with two loaded pistols in his possession,
twenty-two-year-old Corbett pled guilty to second-degree
murder, receiving a sentence of five years to life. His term was
fixed at ten years in San Quentin, and he was transferred to
the medium-security facility, at Chino, in the spring of 1955.
On August 1, 1955, Corbett removed the screen from a
shower room window and fled his Chino barracks, surfacing
eight days later in Los Angeles, as "Walter Osborne," a name
he borrowed from an uncle. For the next four-and-a-half
years, "Osborne" would bide his time, waiting for the perfect
crime to come along.

On February 9, 1960, Adolph Coors III, chairman of the
board for the Adolph Coors Company, disappeared en route
from his Morrison, Colorado, home to a business meeting in
Golden, five miles to the north. His station wagon was found
abandoned later that morning, its engine running and radio
playing, on a narrow bridge spanning Turkey Creek. Kidnapping was suspected, but in the absence of positive evidence,
FBI agents were prohibited from entering the case until
twenty-four hours had elapsed.

On February tenth, a letter arrived at the Coors home, demanding $500,000 ransom to be paid in ten- and twenty-dollar
bills. Mrs. Coors was instructed to signal compliance with the
demand by running a classified ad—"Tractor for Sale"—in a
Denver newspaper. The cash was collected, and the ad was
published on February 14; it ran for the next three weeks,
daily, but there was no response from the kidnapper.

Meanwhile, federal agents had been working hard to trace
their suspect. Local residents recalled descriptions and partial
license numbers of unfamiliar cars seen repeatedly around the
Turkey Creek bridge over several days prior to the kidnapping. Agents identified the stationery and typewriter—a
Royalite—used to prepare the ransom note, tracing both to a
Denver store where "William Chiffins," listing a phony address, had made the purchase on October 8, 1959. A suspect
vehicle was likewise traced to a used-car lot in Denver, where

"Walter Osborne" had paid cash for his wheels on January 8, 1960.

Suspecting that "Chiffins" and "Osborne" were one and the same, agents traced the car buyer to his listed address, a rented room abandoned on February 10. From information gathered at the rooming house, G-men learned that "Osborne" had purchased a mail-order pistol, from a firm in Bangor, Maine. They also traced him to a Denver paint company, where he had worked the past three-and-a-half years, spending most of his time on the night shift. On examination, his personnel file was found to be empty, stripped clean prior to "Osborne's" departure. The company did have his industrial insurance policy, however, listing the suspect's sole beneficiary as Joseph Corbett, Sr. Fingerprints obtained from "Osborne's" lodgings matched the Corbett file in Washington, and a fugitive warrant charging Corbett with unlawful flight to avoid confinement was issued on March 5, 1960. Twenty-five days later, he was added to the Bureau's "Ten Most Wanted" list.

By that time, Corbett's burned-out car had been recovered, turning up in Atlantic City, New Jersey, on March 14. Analysis of soil collected from beneath the fenders placed the vehicle at Turkey Creek; another sample, unidentified in March, would later match the area near Louviers, Colorado, where the skeletal remains of Adolph Coors III were found on September 11, 1960. The kidnapping became a murder case four days later, with positive identification of the remains.

November's issue of the *Reader's Digest*—published in October—ran an article on Corbett, with his mug shot, prompting a Toronto resident to contact the police. He recognized the fugitive as a former co-worker, once employed at a Toronto warehouse, and FBI agents were notified by local authorities. Corbett was tracked through several changes of vehicle, residence and identity, his latest car turning up in Vancouver, British Columbia, on October 29. Constable Jack Martin spotted the car on the street, outside a rooming house, and the landlady confirmed that its owner, tenant "Thomas Wainright," was upstairs in his room. G-men were summoned, and Corbett was taken into custody at 9:45 A.M., without offering resistance.

At Corbett's trial in Colorado, 93 witnesses were called by the prosecution, weaving an unbreakable net of circumstantial evidence around the defendant. Convicted of first-degree murder on March 29, 1961, Corbett was sentenced to a term of life imprisonment without parole.

128 ■ WILLIAM MASON

A native of Nashville, Tennessee, Mason there slashed the throat of a constable who ejected him from a dance hall, receiving a sentence of three to twenty-one years on conviction for attempted murder. Conditionally released on three occasions, he was hauled back twice for violations of parole before finally moving to Detroit in 1952.

On the night of March 10, 1959, Mason quarreled with James Quinney and Luther Johnson in a Detroit tavern. Taking their argument outside, Mason slashed Quinney with a knife, inflicting superficial injuries before he fled into the darkness. Hours later, he returned to find his enemies still drinking at the bar. This time, Mason drew a gun, shooting both men and leaving James Quinney dead on the floor. A fugitive from murder charges, he was added to the Bureau's "Top Ten" list on April 6, 1960.

In the wake of the shooting, Mason had fled to Chicago, drifting on from there to Milwaukee, where he settled during early 1960, finding employment as an arc welder. After his addition to the "Ten Most Wanted" roster, federal agents got a tip that Mason was residing in Milwaukee. They had traced him to his rented room and were deployed around the neighborhood when Mason showed himself on April 27. Taken into custody without a struggle, he informed his captors, "I knew it was only a matter of time until you got me. I saw the posters you had out on me."

129 ■ EDWARD REILEY

A father of four and former operator of an auto wrecking yard at Bourbonnais, Illinois, a suburb of Kankakee, Edward Reiley was not the typical family man. He had logged his first arrest at the age of ten, piling up a record of convictions for burglary, robbery, larceny, auto theft, and possession of burglar tools. By autumn 1958, he was prepared to crack the big time.

On November 4, Ed Reiley robbed a bank in Hamlet, Indiana, making off with $3,390. His next target was a bank in Onarka, Illinois, and he rebounded on January 29, 1959, with a raid against the Farmers and Merchants Bank in Logansport, Indiana, waltzing out with $19,827 in cash. Fleeing the scene, he crashed a state police roadblock, slightly injuring an officer who fired a shotgun blast at his retreating car. The vehicle was traced next day, to a garage where it had been dropped off for body work, new paint, and replacement of a shattered rear window. Vehicle registration identified Reiley as the owner, and his link to the series of heists was confirmed on April 25, when witnesses selected Reiley's mug shot as the likeness of a bandit who stole $16,000 from a bank in Des Moines, Iowa.

Reiley's name was added to the "Ten Most Wanted" list on May 10, 1960. Days later, a used-car dealer in Rockford, Illinois, was visiting the local sheriff's office on unrelated business when he recognized Reiley's poster, remarking that the fugitive had visited his lot a short time earlier, to price some cars. The dealer was advised to keep in touch if Reiley showed himself again.

On May 24, Ed Reiley paid another visit to the lot and bought himself a car. The dealer pocketed his money, made his call to the authorities, and settled back to wait. Six minutes after sheriff's officers received the all-points bulletin, their suspect's car was sighted at a drive-in restaurant. Blocked in by a patrol car, Reiley raised his hands without attempting to retrieve a pair of loaded pistols from the trunk. "I'm glad you got me," he remarked. "Now, maybe I'll be able to sleep nights."

130 ■ HAROLD EUGENE FIELDS

Described by federal agents as an expert safe cracker, Fields possessed a criminal record dating from 1938, including convictions for burglary and issuing fraudulent checks. In 1952, policemen in Champaign, Illinois, surprised him in the act of burglarizing the local Moose Club. Captured after a wild shootout, Fields fought a series of legal delaying actions which postponed his trial until 1956, escaping with a wrist-slap of two years probation. Soon rearrested for trying to rob a Cicero nightclub, Harold was returned to Champaign on charges of parole violation, where an unforgiving judge prescribed a term of ten to twenty years in state prison. Posting a $25,000 appeal bond, Fields immediately fled the state, becoming a federal fugitive on charges of unlawful flight to avoid confinement. His name was added to the Bureau's "Ten Most Wanted" list on May 25, 1960.

In the wake of his hasty departure from Illinois, Fields settled in Springfield, Missouri, until publicity surrounding his "Top Ten" status forced him out of town. He started drifting, living on the road and traveling in stolen cars which helped the FBI to chart his movements. On September 5, he was arrested by a team of federal agents at a restaurant in Schererville, Indiana. A search of his vehicle—stolen in Zionsville on July 30—turned up burglar's tools, dynamite and blasting caps, handcuffs, and lock-picking equipment. Though armed with a .38 revolver, Fields was taken into custody without a struggle.

131 ■ RICHARD PETER WAGNER

A veteran burglar who launched his career in Ashland County, Wisconsin, Richard Wagner spent more of his adult life in jail than on the street. Active in at least fifteen states, coast to coast, Wagner specialized in robbing wealthy homes, concentrating on furs, jewelry, and expensive luggage. His victims included a Hollywood actor, but for all his flair, it seemed impossible for him to give police the slip. His record showed convictions in Missouri, California, North Dakota, Kansas, Michigan, Montana, Minnesota, on a list of charges that included burglary, auto theft, and violation of parole. Authorities described him as "a confirmed thief who is said to be incapable of telling the truth."

In February 1947, Richard and his new bride, Betty, led police on a wild chase through Billings, Montana, finally crashing their stolen car into a drainage ditch. Originally stolen in Oklahoma City, transportation of the car across state lines added federal charges to Wagner's rap sheet, and both of the newlyweds filed guilty pleas. On July 18, 1954, Wagner and an accomplice were captured after burglarizing a church in Fargo, North Dakota, their guilty pleas bringing terms of five to ten years in prison. The summer of 1959 found Wagner serving time for parole violation, in Minneapolis, and by December federal authorities had him under lock and key, for violation of the Dyer Act. On December 17, with only thirty days of his sentence remaining, Wagner walked away from a wood-cutting detail at the federal prison in Sandstone, Minnesota, to become a fugitive. His name was added to the "Ten Most Wanted" list on June 23, 1960.

One month earlier, the wanted man had climaxed a nomadic trek through New York City, Cleveland, Pittsburgh, and Duluth, by settling at Ray, Minnesota. He found work as a combination chef and fishing guide at the Chippewa Lodge, dazzling management with his spurious claims of eighteen years experience as a professional cook. As Wagner's boss recalled, "He just didn't have any finesse. In fact, my mother said he cooked like he'd been in a lumber camp or a prison." Meals were habitually prepared an hour early or an hour late, while Wagner quarreled incessantly with his assistant chef. He got on better with the guests who sought his service as a guide, despite his seeming inability to find a decent fishing stream, and one of them remembered him when mass publicity attended Wagner's posting to the "Top Ten" list in June.

Attorney Philip Lusk had visited the lodge a week before the news broke, and he recognized the mug shots of his guide immediately, tipping agents of the FBI. A team descended on the lodge, including one special agent who had arrested Wagner on a previous occasion. At sight of his old adversary,

Wagner grinned sheepishly and followed his captors to their waiting car.

132 ■ JAMES JOHN WARJAC

Born Dale Harold Cline in October 1926, "James Warjac" logged his first arrest in Massillon, Ohio, during August 1941. Police found him behind the wheel of a car stolen in his hometown Fort Wayne, Indiana, and subsequent conviction of auto theft earned him two years probation. A second arrest, for burglary in 1942, landed Cline in the Indiana Boys School at Plainfield, sentenced to remain until he reached the age of twenty-one. Impatient, he recruited an accomplice to escape in August, fleeing in a stolen car to Gary, Indiana, where they looted several homes and stole another vehicle, heading west. Warjac subsequently confessed to robbing an Omaha gas station, along with burglaries of two homes in Denver and two in Salt Lake City as the fugitives migrated westward.

Arriving in Nevada, Cline and his companion quarreled, parting company. His former crony later shot and killed a sheriff in Carlin, Nevada, a crime for which he was subsequently put to death. Continuing his flight alone, Cline was captured at a roadblock near the state capital at Carson City, held for trial on federal charges in Reno. Conviction of Dyer Act and Juvenile Delinquency Act violations landed Cline in the Englewood, Colorado, lockup for the remainder of his minority—roughly five years, in all—but he was paroled in the summer of 1945.

Returning to Fort Wayne, Cline was implicated, with two accomplices, in a series of twenty-five local burglaries. Following his arrest on January 7, 1946, he was returned to federal custody, this time entering the correctional institution at Chillicothe, Ohio, where he remained until October 3, 1947. In January 1950, convicted of theft in Fort Wayne, Cline was fined and given a six-month suspended sentence.

He drifted southward, winding up in Texas, and his given name was lost along the way. By the mid-1950s, Cline was known throughout south Texas as "James John Warjac," a label he would carry through the rest of his career outside the law. On March 26, 1955, he was convicted of burglary in Corpus Christi and sentenced to twelve years in prison. Seven weeks later, while awaiting results of his appeal, Warjac escaped from the county jail and melted into the crowd of spectators viewing a rodeo parade. A federal fugitive warrant was filed on March 31, 1959, charging Warjac with unlawful flight to avoid confinement, and his name was added to the FBI's "Most Wanted" list on July 19, 1960.

Reputedly a "master of disguise," who had attended special classes to refine his skill at changing his appearance, Warjac had no luck at all in hiding from the FBI. Three days after he was added to the "Top Ten" roster, federal agents traced him to Los Angeles and took him into custody, returning him to Texas where a prison cell had been reserved.

133 ■ ERNEST TAIT

Another "Ten Most Wanted" list alumnus back for seconds, Ernest Tait apparently learned nothing from his two-to-five-year sentence in a 1951 burglary at New Castle, Indiana. In December 1958, police in Crawfordsville picked him up for the burglary of a local bottling plant. Free on bail, Tait failed to appear for his trial in April 1960, and on August 16 his name was added to the roster for the second time.

Federal agents traced him to the Denver area, where several weeks of intense investigation paid off on September 10. Tait was riding with Dale Wing, an Indiana barber, and Raymond Duvall, a convicted murderer and escapee from Indiana's state prison at Michigan City, when G-men cut them off and forced their car to the curb. "It happened too fast," Tait explained, "we didn't have a chance to speak." Neither did he have an opportunity to reach a pistol in the glove compartment as the three were taken into custody. Tait's vow that he would not be taken in alive had come to nothing, as he gave up meekly and was led away.

134 ■ CLARENCE LEON RABY

First arrested for purse snatching, by Atlanta police, at the age of fifteen, Clarence Raby had been in trouble ever since. His list of crimes included drunken driving, burglary, and auto theft, authorities describing him as dangerous, obsessive in his "mania" for shotguns. Often caged, he chafed against captivity and seized the slightest opportunity for flight.

On July 6, 1960, Raby and another inmate, Bill McCoy, escaped from a prison road gang in Knox County, Tennessee. They surfaced the next day in Andersonville, robbing Frank Keith's sports shop of $1,000, killing the elderly proprietor with a single shotgun blast. Murder warrants were issued on July 11, and McCoy, soon captured, named Clarence Raby as the trigger man.

On August 1, two Union County sheriff's deputies, brothers Ben and Lloyd Devault, were patrolling together in Big Ridge State Park when Raby passed them on the highway. Giving chase, they tailed their quarry to a farmhouse owned by Fred Rutherford. Taking Rutherford hostage at gunpoint, Raby stole a pickup truck, forcing Rutherford to lie in the back while Raby took the wheel. The fugitive was pulling out of Rutherford's driveway when Ben Devault blocked his path, on foot, and Raby opened fire without warning, killing the officer where he stood.

Furious deputies fanned out through the countryside, encountering surprise resistance from some local friends of Raby's. Kaley Cooper and his son, Dan, opened fire on officers from ambush when the searchers reached their farm. Returning fire, the officers killed Dan immediately, wounding his father and hauling the older man off to face charges of attempted murder. Raby, meanwhile, kidnapped Thomas Jones and Jones's wife outside a Knoxville tavern, forcing them to drive him into Heiskel, where his family resided. Nearing their destination, Raby clubbed Mrs. Jones with his pistol, forcing both hostages out of the car, which was later found by possemen, a few miles down the road.

Eluding bloodhounds, Raby vanished in the woods, living hand-to-mouth on roots and berries, squirrels and pilfered ears of corn. His name was added to the "Ten Most Wanted" list on August 19, but life in the forest was already taking its toll. A few days later, weary and unwashed, Raby surfaced at his parents' home, expressing a desire to surrender. Twice, his father led Sheriff E. B. Bowles to meet Clarence in the woods, and each time Raby was spooked by the approach of other manhunters. Finally, on August 28, Raby surrendered to the sheriff and was taken into custody.

Transferred to the jail at Anderson, Raby was indicted on two counts of first-degree murder on September 26. Each charge carried a possible death sentence, and it soon became apparent that his prosecutors had no thoughts of leniency in mind. Once more, the inmate turned his thoughts to flight, but this time, Raby needed outside help.

On the evening of October 24, Clarence hailed his warders with the information that he wanted to discuss the Cooper shootout. He had watched the action from a ringside seat, and might be able to provide some details for investigators. Ushered to a conference room where state police were waiting, Raby soon proved less informative than simply windy. Officers were escorting him back to his cell when Raby produced a .357 magnum, smuggled into jail by an accomplice, and informed them, "I ain't going to no damn electric chair."

The outlaw's planning may have been meticulous, but timing was a problem. Brandishing his pistol, Raby left the courthouse elevator as a shift was changing at the sheriff's office and the corridor was filled with deputies. One officer, Ken Milligan, drew down on Raby, wounded in a fierce exchange of gunfire as he followed the escapee toward his only exit. Clarence made it to the stairs, outside, before a bullet pierced his chest and knocked him sprawling, dead before his body settled on the lawn.

135 ■ NATHANIEL BEANS

A petty criminal of violent temperament, familiar to police in Oakland Park, Florida, Beans settled a lover's quarrel by shooting his girlfriend, Curley Raymond, to death on March 5, 1960. The crime was not unusual in an area which boasted frequent "Negro homicides," but it was most unusual for suspects to escape immediate arrest. When six months passed without a break, Nathaniel's name was added to the "Top Ten" list September 12, and federal agents were dispatched to hunt him down.

Informants told the Bureau Beans had relatives in Buffalo, New York, and local officers were notified. Two brothers and a sister of the fugitive were interviewed, but none had been in touch with Beans, whom they pronounced "too mean to have anything to do with." Local investigators traced Beans to a rented room, where they burst in to corner him on the night of September 30. Taken into custody for possession of a knife, the fugitive first identified himself as "Jim Hendley." Confronted with an FBI mug shot, Beans crumbled, telling detectives, "It's all over now."

136 ■ STANLEY WILLIAM FITZGERALD

An Oakland, California, native, Stan Fitzgerald earned the reputation of an avid gambler and accomplished con man, racking up convictions for passing fraudulent checks. In his cups, he enjoyed treating patrons of favorite saloons to a medley of Irish lullabies, rendered in a strong tenor voice. Ironically, it would be Stanley's love of music which betrayed him in the end.

On April 3, 1960, Fitzgerald drove two drinking buddies from San Francisco to Truckee, California, in a stolen station wagon. In Truckee, he wound up robbing them at gunpoint, wounding one victim twice, killing the other with five well-placed bullets. According to investigators, the last round was fired at point-blank range, while Stanley's target lay prone and helpless on the ground. Fitzgerald's name was added to the FBI's "Most Wanted" list September 20, on charges of unlawful flight to avoid prosecution.

Traveling as "Ralph Johnson," Fitzgerald drew attention to himself in Colorado Springs, with his spirited rendition of an Irish ballad in a local bar. The curious behavior, publicized on bureau flyers, brought a tip enabling the FBI to trace their man from Colorado, on to Portland, Oregon. Arrested at his rented lodgings on September 22, Fitzgerald surrendered without a struggle, making no effort to reach the automatic pistol hidden in his briefcase.

137 ■ DONALD LEROY PAYNE

Payne's history of violent sex offenses dated from July 1937, when, at the age of nineteen, he was charged with raping a fifteen-year-old girl in Albuquerque, New Mexico. A guilty plea earned Payne a term of three to five years in state prison, but he encountered further trouble before leaving the county lockup. On September 30, 1937, he attacked and beat a jailer during an escape attempt, drawing a further sentence of twenty-five years. The latter term was suspended due to "good behavior," and in September 1938, Payne's original sentence was commuted to a term of two to five years, making him eligible for parole in February 1939.

In November 1940, Payne was charged with sexual perversion on an adult woman, and his jail break sentence was invoked to put him back in prison. He escaped custody while working at a prison clay pit, on September 9, 1945, but was recaptured the next day. In August 1948, his sentence was reduced to fifteen years, and he was freed on November 1, 1949, with authorities providing a one-way bus ticket to Los Angeles.

California became his new hunting ground. On April 29, 1950, offering "a ride to the movies," Payne abducted a nine-year-old girl and her ten-year-old brother, driving his captives to a remote area of Monterey County. The girl was raped twice, and both children were subjected to acts of perversion before their release. Arrested days later, Payne filed a guilty plea and was sentenced to a maximum of fifty years in prison. He was paroled from San Quentin on July 23, 1957, with state supervision to continue through May 1962.

The new restrictions proved too much for Donald Payne. He disappeared in mid-November 1957, and was being sought for violation of parole when he attacked and raped a Houston dancer in July of 1959. Federal agents entered the case at the request of Texas authorities, seeking Payne on charges of unlawful flight to avoid prosecution for rape. His name was added to the "Ten Most Wanted" list on October 6, 1960.

Five years later, on November 26, 1965, the federal process in Payne's case was formally dismissed, again at the request of Houston prosecutors. Fading memories and disappearing witnesses had doomed the case against him, but the lifelong sex offender was not free and clear. On July 9, 1966, he was arrested by local police in Portland, Oregon, following a housewife's complaint that Payne had molested her child. Traveling with his pregnant common-law wife and their own seven-year-old, Payne told officers his latest crime had grown out of an urge to be arrested, thus escaping from domestic obligations. Oregon agreed to help him with his "problem," and he was committed to the penitentiary on charges of child molestation. If and when he won parole, Payne would be called upon to finish out his time in California.

138 ■ CHARLES FRANCIS HIGGINS

Born in 1906, Higgins first ran afoul of the law as a juvenile delinquent, at age ten. His first adult arrest was logged in November 1926, on charges of auto theft, carrying concealed weapons, and assault with intent to kill; a bargained guilty plea to reduced charges of grand larceny let him escape with a term of five years in prison. Back on the streets by 1929, Higgins tried to shoot a Detroit cab driver, then commandeered a car with three elderly passengers for his getaway. Convicted of assault with intent to rob in that case, he was sentenced to a term of twenty to twenty-five years in state prison. The stabbing of a fellow inmate notwithstanding, Higgins was paroled in May of 1945.

By 1946, Missouri had him under lock and key, in the state prison at Jefferson City, convicted of a robbery in St. Louis. Working in the prison power house, he joined two other inmates in construction of a ladder, overpowering their guards and blacking out the prison while they tried to scale the outer gate. So eager were the convicts to escape, however, that all three climbed on the ladder simultaneously, causing it to crack beneath their weight and dump them in the prison yard.

Eventually released by Missouri, Higgins moved on to Colorado and still more trouble. Convicted of aggravated robbery, he drew a sentence of thirty to fifty years in the state prison at Canyon City. Higgins escaped on October 28, 1954, and in November pulled two one-man holdups in St. Louis. Arrested for petty theft at Colton, California, in January 1955, he drew a term of sixty days, but escaped from the county road gang six days later, vanishing before authorities connected him with the escape in Colorado. In May 1955, he was arrested by police in New Smyrna Beach, Florida, while working as a fry cook. Back in Colorado's prison two months later, Higgins managed to escape a second time, on July 28, 1959. A federal fugitive warrant was issued in September, and his name was added to the "Ten Most Wanted" list on October 10, 1960.

One week later, in Kirkwood, Missouri, Patrolman Robert May observed the fugitive staggering, drunk, down the sidewalk, and recognized his face from the flurry of recent publicity. Taken into custody for public drunkenness, Higgins refused to admit his identity, but a fingerprint comparison removed all doubt. He was returned to Colorado to complete his sentence, with additional time for his latest escape.

139 ■ ROBERT WILLIAM SCHULTZ , JR.

A hard-luck thief with prior convictions for military desertion, bank robbery, and transporting stolen cars across state lines, Robert Schultz was in no mood to face another prison term by 1958. Convicted as the "mastermind" of an abortive bank job in Knowles, Wisconsin, Schultz took his eight-year prison sentence badly, threatening to kill the presiding judge and a United States marshal involved in his arrest.

Described by federal agents as a "revenge-crazed robber," Schultz seemed to mellow in custody, earning a transfer from Leavenworth to the softer penitentiary at Sandstone, Minnesota, in October 1959. Eleven months later, on September 6, 1960, he was working alone and unsupervised, grading a road near the prison, when he made his break for freedom. Based on a report of suspect vehicles near the scene, authorities believed that Schultz had outside help in his escape. On the basis of his prior threats, Schultz was added to the FBI's "Most Wanted" list on October 12, 1960.

Sighted in New Orleans on October 17, Schultz surfaced five days later at Bonifay, Florida, where highway patrol officers stopped his car at a routine checkpoint and discovered he had no driver's license. Arrested on the spot, Schultz gave his correct name—emblazoned along his left forearm in a tattoo—and was released after posting a $25 cash bond. Local officers failed to recognize his name at the time, but word got around, and FBI agents apprehended Schultz in Orlando on November 4, surrounding the motel where he had registered as "Frank Shelton." Arrested with him was a local man, Willie Cannon, charged with harboring a fugitive. Schultz offered no resistance, and was not allowed to reach the loaded shotgun waiting in his car.

140 ■ MERLE LYLE GALL

Gall's record of arrests began in February 1942, at age eighteen, when he served ninety days in Utah on conviction for assault and battery. Successive charges would include public drunkenness and disorderly conduct, burglary, robbery, and interstate transportation of stolen property. A narcotics addict and heavy drinker with a violent temper, Gall was fond of firing shots at close friends during drunken arguments, and he was sometimes fired on in return, sustaining bullet wounds which left a scar beside his nose. Familiar with houses of prostitution from Montana to Mexico, Gall hated policemen as much as he liked whores; in his cups he liked to boast that he "would not die happy" until he had killed a lawman.

On August 7, 1957, Gall and two associates—James Reynolds and Leo Bean—stole a wallet from a motel room in Great Falls, Montana. Arrested two months later, all three were convicted of burglary on November 19. Reynolds and Bean were sentenced to terms of twenty-five years, while Gall, somehow persuading the court that his crime was a first offense, escaped with a sentence of fifteen years. While Bean went off to serve his time, Reynolds and Gall filed appeals, remaining at large after posting $15,000 appeal bonds. On learning that his sentence was affirmed by higher courts, Gall forfeited his bond and vanished, thereby being elevated to the status of a federal fugitive. His name was added to the Bureau's "Ten Most Wanted" list on October 17, 1960.

Three months later, on January 18, 1961, FBI agents cornered Gall and two companions in a Scottsdale, Arizona, parking lot. Despite his boast to "kill anyone who got in his way," Gall surrendered without a fight. The three men—including Albert Hepley, who had a record dating back to 1926—were traced through the investigation of a floating crap game they had organized in Arizona.

Gall went back to serve his pending sentence in Montana, but eventual release brought no relief from rotten luck. In December 1967, he was wounded in a shooting that killed his female companion, in Sioux City, Iowa, climaxing a violent argument over money. Gunman Floyd Peterson was charged with murder in the case, and Gall made his next courtroom appearance on the witness stand, a change of scene which must have seemed unusual, considering his background.

141 ■ JAMES GEORGE ECONOMOU

By the age of forty, Economou had compiled a record of arrests and criminal convictions covering a quarter-century. A brandy-drinking horse player, he moved in "fast" circles, associating with criminals known for their involvement in robbery, prostitution, and the narcotics trade. Consigned to San Quentin on conviction of armed robbery, Economou was working with an inmate forest crew in Northern California when he escaped from custody on April 23, 1958. Sought on federal charges of unlawful flight, he was linked with another robbery, in San Francisco, while still at large.

Economou's name was added to the FBI's "Most Wanted" list on October 31, 1960. Less than five months later, on March 22, 1961, a tip led federal agents to a rented room in Los Angeles, where Economou was living under the alias of "Louis Rasko." Bursting in to take James by surprise, the agents had him manacled before he could retrieve his loaded .45 and offer armed resistance.

142 ■ RAY DELANO TATE

Launching his criminal career with a long record of juvenile delinquency arrests, Ray Tate went on to collect adult convictions for armed robbery and parole violation. In 1956, he received an indeterminate sentence, with fifteen years maximum, for the robbery of a clothing store in Trenton, New Jersey. At the time of his arrest in Trenton, Tate was sought by authorities in Hudson, North Carolina, as a fugitive escapee from the prison work camp there.

On June 23, 1960, two gunmen entered the offices of the Yorke Savings and Loan Company, in Newark, New Jersey, one brandishing a shotgun and the other wielding a pistol as they raided the cash drawers for $2,704. Retreating to a car outside, where an accomplice waited at the wheel, they made their getaway, but two were snared by local officers within the next three days. The missing bandit was identified as Ray Delano Tate from photographs and through interrogation of his partners in the crime. Tate's name was added to the "Ten Most Wanted" list on November 18, 1960.

One week later, on November 25, Tate telephoned the New York *Daily Mirror* and expressed his wish to end the chase. That day, the fugitive surrendered to a reporter and photographer in Vancouver, British Columbia. With an exclusive interview in hand, the newsmen turned him over to authorities, for subsequent delivery to the FBI.

143 ■ JOHN B. EVERHART

Passion seemed to be the root of John Everhart's clash with the law. Sentenced to life, in Georgia, for the 1956 slaying of a rival for his girlfriend's affections, Everhart also shot and seriously wounded an Atlanta detective before he was captured and brought in for trial. Two years after his conviction, during 1958, he fled a prison road crew working near the town of Lexington and vanished in a nearby swamp. Evading local deputies and prison guards, he was declared a federal fugitive on charges of unlawful flight to avoid confinement. His name was added to the Bureau's "Top Ten" list on November 22, 1960.

Believing safety lay in distance, Everhart had run to California, hoping to lose himself in San Francisco, where he settled down as "Walter Williams," picking up his income from odd jobs. The FBI's painstaking search put agents on his trail in 1963, and G-men caught up with him the morning of November 6, as he prepared to paint a house. Surrounded in the small garage where he was mixing paint, Everhart surrendered without resistance, stubbornly clinging to the "Williams" alias. A favorite lodge ring and a hasty fingerprint comparison confirmed his true identity.

"I've been here about five years," Everhart told his captors, "and I've stayed out of trouble to keep from coming in contact with the FBI." Preparing for his extradition, Everhart was grim. "I just hate going back [to Georgia]," he explained. "It would be going to my death."

144 ■ HERBERT HOOVER HUFFMAN

A North Carolina native with a penchant for brutal violence, Herbert Huffman ran afoul of the FBI on his first foray into homicide. On July 1, 1959, a woman's lifeless body was discovered in a cheap Chicago motel room. The victim of a savage beating, she had also suffered burns from cigarettes and what appeared to be a makeshift torch, created out of rolled-up paper.

With identification of the victim as Virginia Edwards, homicide detectives traced her back to Fayetteville, North Carolina, whence she had departed on June 30. According to her friends and neighbors, Edwards had received one hundred dollars from her common-law husband, Herbert Huffman, and had gone at once to join him in Chicago. They had found a room that night, as man and wife, but check-out time found Huffman gone, his "wife" discarded in the wake of what appeared to be a homicidal frenzy.

Sought on murder charges in Chicago, with a federal warrant for unlawful flight, Huffman made the Bureau's "Ten Most Wanted" list on December 19, 1960. By that time, the fugitive had already settled in Euclid, Ohio, and a local resident was quick to recognize the mug shots on his WANTED poster. On December 29, a squad of federal agents found Huffman at work, on the loading dock of a warehouse, and arrested him without a struggle. Huffman seemed relieved that his long flight was over, and he waived extradition to Chicago, returning voluntarily for trial on murder charges.

145 ■ KENNETH EUGENE CINDLE

Born in Oklahoma in April 1912, Cindle logged his first arrest in March of 1930, charged with forgery at Anadarko. Conviction earned him a six-month sentence in a state reformatory, but his subsequent activities suggested that he had not been reformed. Arrested in Oklahoma City as a vagrant, during July 1932, Cindle was released when he could not be linked to any local crimes. Two years later, in Enid, he paid a twenty dollar fine upon conviction for a liquor violation. In May 1935, following the holdup of a gas station and a running shootout with police, Cindle pled guilty to a charge of robbery with firearms, drawing a thirty-year sentence in the state penitentiary. Paroled in January 1948, he was returned to prison in February 1949 for violating terms of his release. He was eventually discharged from custody in June 1950.

Twice arrested for drunk driving in California, during 1954 and 1955, Cindle was also picked up for theft, in Bakersfield, on November 13, 1957. A guilty plea brought him six months in jail, but Cindle escaped from custody in February 1958, earning additional time upon his recapture the following day. He was discharged in September 1958 and drifted east, toward Kansas.

On October 12, 1959, Cindle and a male accomplice raided a Wichita restaurant, looting the register of $236 while covering customers and employees with a sawed-off shotgun. Cindle was arrested in Tulsa, Oklahoma, two days later, charged with failing to register as an ex-convict, but he was released on bond and fled the area before authorities learned of his latest robbery in Kansas. His accomplice was later arrested in Amarillo, Texas, but Cindle remained at large when federal fugitive warrants were issued on May 10, 1960. His name was added to the "Ten Most Wanted" list on December 23.

On March 11, 1961, police in Abilene, Texas, arrested "Gus Anderson" as a participant in a drunken brawl. "Anderson" was released hours later, after paying a twenty-five-dollar fine, and he was nowhere to be found when G-men had a chance to scrutinize his fingerprints nine days later.

At 3 P.M. on April 1, 1961, the sheriff at Brownfield, Texas, received a call from a local farmer, advising him that one of the FBI's "Top Ten" fugitives—recently shown on television—was employed on a neighboring ranch. A deputy sheriff and two federal agents drove to the spread, where they recognized Cindle driving a tractor. The fugitive identified himself as "William Merchant," producing a Social Security card in that name, but gave up the pretense after an examination of his fingerprints. Convicted of his latest robbery in Kansas, Cindle was sentenced to fifteen years in prison as an habitual offender.

146 ■ THOMAS VIOLA

A hardened felon with convictions for armed robbery, counterfeiting, grand larceny and assault with intent to kill, by the late 1930s Thomas Viola had a reputation as a hit-man for the tough Ohio mob. Efficient, ruthless, he was the natural choice when a major "contract" was issued by the syndicate in spring of 1941.

In Youngstown, numbers banker Jim Munsene had lately fallen out of favor with the syndicate, then bent upon absorbing independent operators. When he balked at signing on as an employee of the larger mob, Munsene began to suffer "accidents": two close associates were lost in a suspicious auto crash, and arson fires began to raze his several properties. On March 24, 1941, two gunmen cornered Munsene in his Youngstown steakhouse, pumping a half-dozen shots into his body at close range. When Munsene's nephew, Felix Monfino, came running to help, a bullet through the heart dropped him in his tracks.

A three-year search for evidence produced indictments of Viola and another gunman, Charles Monazym, during 1944. By that time, Monazym was safely tucked away in Leavenworth, serving 25 years on a bank robbery conviction. It took another year to trace Viola, but the FBI arrested him in Tucson, Arizona, during August 1945. Returned for trial, he was convicted of premeditated homicide in April 1946 and sentenced to a term of life in the Ohio penitentiary.

By 1960, after fourteen years inside, Viola was considered a model prisoner. Despite rejection of his various appeals by the United States Supreme Court, he appeared to feel no bitterness at his predicament. Promoted to the honors program, he was working in the prison business office on September 22, trusted by his keepers and regarded as a classic case of prison's rehabilitative powers.

After work that day, Viola was allowed to pass the prison gates, ostensibly returning to the honor barracks, just outside the walls. He never made it to his bunk, and federal warrants were immediately issued, charging him with unlawful flight to avoid confinement. Viola's name was added to the "Top Ten" list on January 17, 1961.

Two months later, in the early days of March, a Detroit resident recognized Viola's mug shot in a magazine. Viola called himself "Jim Sloan" during those days, his transformation aided by a new mustache and hair dyed glossy black. Intent on making no mistakes, a team of G-men stalked Viola for three weeks, staking out the small apartment which he shared with manicurist Gertrude Sloan, before they picked him up on March 27. A search of his apartment yielded up two guns and some $4,000 cash.

Viola's live-in girlfriend was convicted on a charge of harboring a fugitive, along with local mafioso James Maccagnone, a syndicate captain charged with helping Viola find an apartment after his escape from prison. Their trial, in April 1965, served notice that the FBI meant business in its search for federal fugitives.

Returned to the Ohio prison, stripped of his accumulated "honors," Tom Viola sat out five more years before his nagging cough attracted the attention of a prison doctor. Diagnosed as a terminal victim of lung cancer, he was paroled in March 1966 and died shortly thereafter.

147 ■ WILLIAM CHESTER COLE

A hard-luck bandit, William Cole began accumulating felony convictions during 1954, with charges ranging from auto theft, breaking and entering an automobile, through grand larceny and several armed robberies. For holdups, he preferred to wear a stocking mask, but no disguise prevented him from being frequently arrested and convicted. Serving time most recently in Florida, he fled a prison camp on August 6, 1960, thereafter kidnapping and robbing a couple near Venice, Florida. Within the week, he was linked to robberies in New Orleans and Lake Charles, Louisiana. Police in New Orleans gave chase after a grocery store heist, on August 16, but Cole eluded his pursuers in a maze of narrow streets and alleys.

Added to the Bureau's "Ten Most Wanted" list on February 2, 1961, the fugitive had just four days of freedom left. A team of federal agents visited his grandfather, in Gulf Breeze, Florida, on February 6, and learned that Cole was visiting an uncle's home nearby. Surprised when G-men crashed the family reunion, Cole surrendered peacefully and was returned to prison for completion of his sentence.

148　■　WILLIE HUGHES

Betrayed by an explosive temper, Willie Hughes was quick to quarrel with friends or strangers, and his arguments were prone to end in violence. Boasting convictions for murder, manslaughter, and assault with a deadly weapon, he sometimes supported himself through theft, racking up further charges of breaking and entering. Detroit police were seeking Hughes for violation of parole on June 12, 1960, when he settled a dispute by gunning down his closest friend and fled the state one step ahead of murder warrants. Armed and dangerous, he joined the FBI's "Most Wanted" fugitives on March 15, 1961.

Intent on staying out of prison, Hughes led federal agents on a hectic chase through Arizona, Utah, Colorado, California, Oregon, Nebraska and Wyoming, working briefly at a string of ranches, changing names each time he shifted jobs. For all his efforts, G-men had a fix on Hughes within a few days of his finding work in Pocatello, Idaho. On August 8, as Willie left his rented room, a team of agents dressed as farm hands made their collar, taking him without resistance. Hughes waived extradition to Detroit, and was returned to prison as a violator of parole, awaiting trial on murder charges.

149　■　WILLIAM TERRY NICHOLS

The file on William Nichols spanned a criminal career of fourteen years' duration, with convictions registered for burglary, armed robbery, grand larceny and transportation of illegal whiskey. Nervous in confinement, he had also broken out of lockups in Atlanta and several other Georgia communities.

On December 1, 1960, Nichols led three other convicts in overpowering their guard on a prison work gang, seizing a shotgun and pistol before locking the guard—with other inmates—in the prison van. Proceeding to a nearby farm, the outlaws locked a man and wife inside the crowded truck and stole their car to make a getaway. While his companions were recaptured swiftly, Nichols managed to elude pursuers, and his name was posted to the FBI's "Most Wanted" list on April 6, 1961.

A list of previous associations led the FBI to concentrate its search along the southeast coast of Florida, and agents found their man on April 30. As "Luther Smith," the fugitive had bought himself a boat and entered the commercial fishing business, north of Homestead, at the Rock Harbor Fishing Camp. Disgruntled at the scuttling of his new career, Nichols demanded to know how the agents had traced him, but G-men declined to explain. With their man in custody, they headed back to Georgia, where Nichols completed his prison term.

150 ■ GEORGE MARTIN BRADLEY, JR.

A felon whose record dated back to 1946, including convictions for counterfeiting, fraudulent checks, armed robbery and confidence games, George Bradley showed a fondness for deception in his holdups. During 1950, he used a toy pistol to rob the box office of a Cincinnati theater, but plastic weapons did not help his case in court. Sentenced to a term of one to twenty-five years in prison, Bradley was paroled in March of 1952.

There was nothing fake about the shotgun Bradley carried when he robbed a bank in Stuart, Florida, on January 16, 1961. His two accomplices were captured swiftly, but elusive George was added to the FBI's "Most Wanted" list on April 17. His capture, two weeks later, could be traced directly to another bluff that blew up in his face.

On May 2, 1961, Bradley entered the First Federal Savings and Loan Association, in Davenport, Iowa, carrying a simulated bomb inside a paper bag. Giving employees a glimpse of his "weapon," Bradley demanded $60,000 cash. Instead of paying up, loan officer Paul Josinger snatched the bag from Bradley's grasp, risking death as he hurled the "bomb" across the room. Unarmed, the would-be bandit fled on foot, with customers and bank employees in pursuit. Attracted by the chase, Patrolman Ray Musselman cornered Bradley in a nearby alley and held him at gunpoint. Once in jail, George was identified and soon delivered to the hands of waiting federal agents.

151 ■ PHILIP ALFRED LANORMANDIN

Philip Lanormandin got an early start in crime, repeatedly committed to juvenile homes on charges of truancy, auto theft, and possession of burglar's tools. In January 1924, at seventeen, he was committed to the Massachusetts state reformatory for breaking and entering. Paroled in June 1925, Lanormandin was back three months later, his parole revoked in the face of new breaking and entering charges. By August 1927, he was serving a five-year-maximum term for a new conviction on the same offense. Along the way, he had acquired a reputation as an expert trumpeter, and often played with prison bands to pass the time.

In 1930, Philip was paroled again, with permission to join the army. By January 1931, still fresh in uniform, he was declared a fugitive by New York state authorities, on charges of grand larceny. Arrested with a concealed weapon in Hartford, Connecticut, Lanormandin was returned to New York for trial, and his guilty plea earned him ten years in Sing Sing prison. Paroled after five years, in January 1936, he was shot in the leg that November, while fleeing the scene of a holdup in Philadelphia. Again Lanormandin pled guilty, drawing a sentence of twenty to forty years. Released in June of 1958, he was paroled to Massachusetts, but Lanormandin could not stay out of Pennsylvania—or out of trouble—very long.

On June 5, 1959, he joined another gunman in the bungled holdup of a grocery manager in Reading, Pennsylvania. Fleeing empty-handed, Philip and his sidekick led pursuers through the woods and finally evaded capture in a blazing shootout with police. Now sought for violation of parole, as well as charges of attempted robbery, Lanormandin was traced to Wauwatosa, Wisconsin, in early July. Residing there as "Samuel Stewart," he once more eluded searchers and was added to the FBI's "Most Wanted" list on April 17, 1961.

A few short hours after the announcement of his elevation to the list, New Jersey agents of the FBI received a call from Hackensack. A local resident immediately recognized the published photographs, directing federal officers to Jersey City, where Lanormandin had been residing—as "John Callan"—for the past six months, employed as an oil burner serviceman. Arrested on the job, Lanormandin offered no resistance and was soon returned to Pennsylvania for trial.

152 ■ KENNETH HOLLECK SHARP

An explosive, mentally unstable personality, Ken Sharp was fond of firing pistols at his girlfriend during arguments. His record listed charges ranging from vagrancy to armed robbery, the latter incidents made doubly dangerous by Sharp's own mental instability.

In 1952, with accomplice Lloyd Gherriault, Sharp robbed a service station in Chicago. On a whim, he shot and killed the lone attendant, adding murder to his list of dubious achievements. Soon arrested, Gherriault was quick to finger Sharp as the trigger man; for Lloyd's participation in the heist—and several others—he received a term of ten to twenty-five years in prison.

Kenneth Sharp, despite his mental quirks, evaded the authorities for nine long years. His name was added to the FBI's "Most Wanted" list on May 1, 1961, and by the time his photograph was published in the press, Sharp's days were numbered.

Two months later, responding to a tip from sources wishing to remain anonymous, the Bureau traced Sharp to Philadelphia, where he had spent the past five years as "Bryan Benton," renting quarters in a private home. They learned that Sharp had, ironically, been working at a service station in the neighborhood. Unarmed, the killer offered no resistance when a squad of agents crashed his door the morning of July 3, 1961. He was returned to Illinois for trial and sentencing.

153 ■ VINCENT ANTHONY FEDE

Convicted of burglarizing a candy store at age fourteen, Vincent Fede was briefly confined to a "boys' farm" at Hudson, Ohio. A second conviction at fifteen—for the same offense—landed him in the state-run industrial school for delinquent boys. A compulsive gambler, he sought to raise a stake by pulling off a string of holdups in Cleveland, during June of 1935. The victims recalled Vincent's face and his wisecracks; at trial, in July, he pled guilty on three counts of robbery, drawing a sentence of eleven years. Paroled after two, Fede was back behind bars a year later, charged with carrying a concealed weapon.

Upon his ultimate release, in December 1949, Fede tried his hand at barbering, a trade he learned in prison. He avoided conflict with the law for several years, but signs of mental instability were surfacing. Among his stranger quirks, Fede started carrying a hand grenade, which he would sometimes use to threaten people who annoyed him. During 1959, he served a Cleveland workhouse term of ninety days for larceny.

On September 9, 1960, Fede entered a Cleveland tavern with gun in hand, raiding the cash drawer for $1,500. Leaving the scene, he kidnapped the manager, William Grouse, and a barmaid, Phyllis Rose, presumably as hostages to aid in his escape. When Grouse escaped and armed himself, the bandit fled on foot. He was identified from mug shots in the Cleveland files, and indictments were issued for kidnapping and robbery. Fede's name was added to the "Ten Most Wanted" list on May 22, 1961.

Feeling the heat, Vince ran westward, stopping only when he reached the coastline. Lingering a while around Los Angeles, he caught a bus to San Francisco, but the Southern California climate seemed to suit him better. Fede had seen enough of cold back home, in Cleveland.

Agents of the FBI in California got a tip, in late October 1961, that Fede was moving back from San Francisco to Los Angeles. His bus arrived October 28, and G-men trailed him to a cheap hotel, arriving on his threshold as he tried to settle in. No hand grenades were found, but agents seized a plastic pistol and a toy "detective" badge, with which the fugitive had hoped to bluff his way through any confrontations with police. Returned to Cleveland and convicted on the waiting charges, Fede was sentenced to a term of fifteen to fifty-five years in prison.

154 ■ RICHARD LAURENCE MARQUETTE

A native Oregonian, from Portland, Marquette logged his first arrest in June 1956, on a charge of attempted rape. His victim failed to press the charge, and so her twenty-one-year-old assailant was released. A few months later, he was held a second time, for disorderly conduct. In August 1957, Marquette tried to rob a Portland service station, clubbing the attendant with a sack full of wrenches. His guilty plea earned Richard eighteen months in jail, but he was turned out after twelve—for good behavior—and returned at once to Portland.

On June 5, 1961, a Portland housewife, Joan Rae Caudle, was reported missing by her husband when she failed to come home after shopping. Three days later, parts of a dismembered woman's body were discovered, scattered over several vacant lots around the southeast side of Portland. Fingerprints identified Joan Caudle as the victim on June 14. Eyewitnesses had seen the murdered woman in a tavern on the night she disappeared; she had been killing time with Dick Marquette, a regular, and they had left the bar together.

A murder charge was filed against Marquette on June 19, and one day later he was named a federal fugitive, on charges of unlawful flight. His name was added to the Bureau's "Ten Most Wanted" list June 29—the first time that the list had been expanded to include eleven names. The extraordinary step was warranted, the FBI decided, based on Marquette's demonstrated tendency toward violence and the threat he posed to women.

On June 30, one day after the release of Marquette's WANTED flyers, the manager of an employment agency in Santa Maria, California, recognized his newest client in the mug shots. Agents of the FBI were notified, and they surprised Marquette at work, repairing furniture for resale in a thrift shop. Seemingly relieved, the killer offered no resistance. "I knew the FBI would get me sooner or later," he told his captors.

According to Marquette, his victim had been picked up in a bar, and they had argued after having sex. He strangled her and then, impulsively, cut up her body to facilitate disposal. On July 2, Marquette led authorities to the missing remains. Convicted of first-degree murder in December, sentenced to a term of life imprisonment, his parting words to the court were a heartfelt "Thank God."

155 ■ ROBERT WILLIAM SCHUETTE

Born in Baltimore on May 2, 1922, Schuette's conflict with lawful authority began after he was drafted into the army in World War II. He went AWOL on several occasions, and in early 1944, following a lengthy absence from duty, he was dishonorably discharged, sentenced to three years at hard labor. Hometown police picked him up for larceny in November 1953, resulting in a minor jail term, but Schuette was only warming up, preparing himself for a one-man crime wave.

Beginning in November 1955, he pulled a string of burglaries and daylight robberies in Baltimore which ultimately led to his arrest in June of 1957. Convicted on five counts of armed robbery with a deadly weapon, he was sentenced to twenty years in the state penitentiary at Baltimore. He escaped from prison on October 24, 1960, and a federal warrant charging him with unlawful flight to avoid confinement was issued four days later. Schuette's name was added to the "Ten Most Wanted" list on July 19, 1961.

Two weeks later, on the afternoon of August 2, federal agents traced Schuette to Chicago, making the arrest without resistance. Schuette was returned to Maryland to finish out his sentence, with new time added on for the escape.

156 ■ CHESTER ANDERSON McGONIGAL

Statistics demonstrate that three of every four American murder victims die at the hands of a relative or "friend." A prime example of the individual who keeps his violence in the family, Chester McGonigal had a long history of mayhem directed toward relatives. In 1948, he was sent to the Missouri state prison for shooting his brother in the stomach. Back on the street two years later, McGonigal stabbed his wife, and was sent back to jail on a charge of attempted murder. He would be paroled again, in time, but the experience had taught him nothing.

Married to his second wife in January 1961, McGonigal restrained his lurking rage until the second week of April. On the afternoon of April 12, the newlyweds were quarreling in an Aspen, Colorado, bar when Chester pulled a pocket knife and slashed his bride across the throat. He fled in haste, abandoning his hat and coat, perhaps believing she was dead, but doctors saved her life, and once again the charge would be attempted murder. Chester's name was added to the Bureau's "Top Ten" list on August 14, 1961.

By that time, federal agents had already traced McGonigal to an isolated ranch near Elk Mountain, Wyoming, where he worked briefly as a hired hand before heading back to Colorado. McGonigal reached Denver the night of August 11, unaware that he was about to make nationwide headlines. Tipped to his presence in the mile-high city, G-men were waiting for him at a local employment agency when he turned up, looking for work, on the morning of August 17. Arrested without a struggle, he was returned to Aspen for trial and ultimate conviction on the waiting charges.

157 ■ HUGH BION MORSE

Born in Kansas City during January 1930, Hugh Morse was the product of a forced marriage, abandoned by his father in infancy. He grew up in a harsh, abusive home, completely dominated by a grandmother who brutalized her daughter and grandson with complete impartiality. When Hugh was four years old, a hammer blow from grandma scarred his face for life; another time, she slaughtered his pet mice after Morse went to a movie without her permission. It comes as no surprise that he informed police in later years, "I can't remember being happy at any time since I was born." In adolescence and adulthood, Morse was tortured by a mix of awe and hatred for the women who had ruled his early life. The end result was sexual ambivalence and violence, the trademarks of a classic serial murderer.

Escaping from his home environment, Morse enlisted in the Marine Corps, but he soon ran into conflict with the law. Arrested the first time in May 1951, for indecent exposure and assaulting a woman in Wilmington, North Carolina, he left the service seven months later with a dishonorable discharge. More arrests followed, in Los Angeles, during 1953 and 1954, with Morse serving six months on a burglary conviction. In 1955, charged with trying to molest two eight-year-old girls in Fairfield, California, he was committed to Atascadero state hospital for therapy. Released as "cured" in January 1957, he was picked up for sex crimes in Burbank four months later.

A pattern had begun to form in Morse's criminal behavior. Prowling residential neighborhoods by night, he entered houses and apartments, creeping up on girls and women in their beds. Briefly settled in Spokane, Washington, Morse tried his hand at marriage, but it didn't take. On November 7, 1959, he raped and murdered Glorie Brie, age 28, in her Spokane home. His second known victim, on September 26, 1960, was sixty-nine-year-old Blanche Boggs. Two weeks later, on October 10, Beverly Myers was attacked in her home, but managed to survive her wounds.

On October 28, 1960, Morse broke into the home of his estranged wife, attempting to strangle her before he was interrupted and forced to flee. A federal warrant was issued, charging unlawful flight to avoid prosecution for burglary and attempted murder. Morse was added to the FBI's "Most Wanted" list on August 29, 1961.

By that time, there were other victims, all unknown to federal agents who were stalking Morse. He raped at least two women in Atlanta, Georgia, in the spring of 1961; arrested on a charge of voyeurism there, he paid $200 bail and walked away, amused that officers had failed to recognize his WANTED poster hanging in the jailhouse.

On July 11, 1961, Morse entered Bobbi Ann Landini's home in Birmingham, choking her unconscious and beating her to death with a length of pipe. Moving north, he attacked Mildred Chasteen in her Dayton apartment on August 2, stabbing her several times and leaving her for dead.

Morse drifted into St. Paul, Minnesota, on August 15, posing as "Darwin Corman" when he rented a room, acquiring odd jobs at a car wash, a gas station, a hotel kitchen. On September 18, he raped and strangled Carol Ronan in her home, five blocks from his rooming house. A few days later, Morse lured a six-year-old girl into an alley, where she was molested.

Published photographs of Morse, meanwhile, were turning heads around St. Paul, and phones were ringing at the local office of the FBI. On August 29, agents called on Morse at home, arresting him without a struggle. Searchers found a knife, a straight-edged razor, and a loaded pistol in his room.

Pleading guilty in the Ronan case, Morse received a double life sentence in December 1961, on charges of second-degree murder and first-degree burglary. As late as January 1964, he was attempting suicide in jail, without success. In the event he is paroled, the states of Washington and Alabama are prepared to level other murder charges, guaranteeing Morse will never be at liberty to kill again.

158 ■ JOHN GIBSON DILLON

Nicknamed "Matt," after the Western marshal portrayed by James Arness on the long-running "Gunsmoke" television series, Dillon was a dealer in narcotics, operating from his rural home outside Coweta, Oklahoma. Convicted on eleven counts of dealing drugs in early 1961, Dillon faced 190 years in jail but was released on $35,000 bond prior to sentencing. In February, on the night before his final Tulsa court appearance, Dillon vanished, forfeiting his bail. A federal warrant was issued, charging the fugitive with unlawful flight to avoid confinement, and his name was added to the "Top Ten" list on September 1, 1961.

Near the end of February 1964, the FBI received a message at its Tulsa office. Speaking in a voice which had been carefully disguised, the caller said that Dillon's body could be found by checking out a well eight miles due west of Chelsea, Oklahoma. Federal agents scoured the area, with local deputies assisting them as guides, and singled out a cistern at an old, abandoned home site on the first of March. Next morning, pumps evacuated sixteen feet of water from the shaft, and grappling hooks retrieved "Matt" Dillon's decomposed remains. Identified from dental records, Dillon had been knocked unconscious by a blow that cracked his skull; the water in his lungs revealed that he had been alive when thrown into the well. His murderers—presumably associates in the narcotics trade—have never been discovered.

159 ■ JOHN ROBERT SAWYER

In August 1961, with accomplice John Vito Moise, Sawyer invaded the home of a bank manager in Omaha, Nebraska. Keeping the manager and his wife tied up overnight, Sawyer and Moise battered their captive until he provided the vault's combination, with a description of various bank alarm systems. Next morning, the hostages were driven downtown, forced to open the bank and the vault for their captors, who made off with $72,599. The manager and his wife were dropped off at home, bound and gagged, while their tormentors fled with the loot.

Identified from mug shots, Moise was captured two months later, in New York, confirming the identity of his accomplice. Charged with violation of the federal statute on bank robbery, John Sawyer was added to the "Ten Most Wanted" list October 30, 1961. With help from Moise, the FBI broadcast descriptions of his last known vehicle, complete with license plates from Florida.

A pair of Arizona highway patrolmen spotted the car near

Wickenburg, on November 3, stopping Sawyer and a female companion. "What's the trouble, officer?" the bandit asked. "I can't think of anything I might have done."

A loaded pistol on the car's back seat provided grounds for an arrest, and fingerprint comparisons identified the fugitive. None of the missing loot was found with Sawyer. "I didn't get any of it," he told federal agents, "and I haven't got any of it." Arraigned in Phoenix, with his bond set at $50,000, Sawyer seemed resigned to jail. "I haven't got thirty cents in my pockets," he told the court, before he was led away.

160 ■ EDWARD WAYNE EDWARDS

An avid bowler and weight lifter, Ed Edwards also took pains to exercise his criminal talents, racking up convictions for robbery, armed robbery, interstate transportation of stolen cars, and the illegal wearing of a United States Marine Corps uniform. Still on probation for a robbery conviction, Edwards was arrested in Portland, Oregon, for impersonating a federal officer in April 1961. He managed to arrange a phone call to the jail, from an accomplice posing as his probation officer. A careless jailer willingly accepted verbal orders for the prisoner's release, and Edwards walked away. A federal warrant, charging unlawful flight to avoid confinement, was issued on April 11, and Edwards made the Bureau's "Top Ten" list November 10.

Undaunted by his recent elevation to the "Ten Most Wanted" roster, Edwards robbed a bank in Akron, Ohio, of $7,707 on January 17, 1962. Three days later, he was painting the town in Atlanta, Georgia, when suspicious calls about a lavish spender brought detectives to his rented room. Surprising Edwards and his "wife" in bed, the lawmen took both suspects into custody. Ed's wallet and an overnight bag yielded $2,859 in loot from the bank; the rest had been spent on boxes of new clothes and the flashy automobile parked downstairs, complete with a loaded .32 pistol in the glove compartment. Delivered to FBI agents, Edwards was held on $60,000 bond pending extradition to Ohio; his lady friend was

charged as an accomplice in the Akron heist, and held on
$50,000 bond.

161 ■ FRANKLIN EUGENE ALLTOP

If asked, Frank Alltop gave his place of birth as Given, West
Virginia, and the year as 1933. No records can be found to
verify those facts, but it would scarcely matter in the long run.
Lawmen who encountered Alltop in his decade-long career of
crime were more concerned about his present and his future
than about his past.

By early 1952, Alltop's was a well-known face throughout
the underworld of Canton, Ohio, where he was involved in
various illegal enterprises. In February of that year, convictions for assault with intent to rob and breaking and entering
earned Alltop two concurrent one-to-fifteen-year terms in the
Ohio State Reformatory at Mansfield. Fellow inmates called
him "Top" or "Stub," the latter nickname so appealing that he
had it tattooed on his arm.

Paroled in May of 1954, Alltop was arrested for another
armed robbery, in Hamilton, Ohio, three months later. The
arrest reportedly wrapped up a crime spree involving the robberies of several area gas stations, and Alltop was packed off
to state prison, winning parole in October 1959. Freedom remained elusive, however, as he was immediately delivered to
West Virginia authorities, pending trial in a robbery committed at Kenova, back in August 1954.

Five days after his arrival in Wayne County, West Virginia,
Alltop managed to escape from jail. Investigation proved that
he had fled across state lines, and federal warrants charging
him with unlawful flight to avoid prosecution were issued on
February 19, 1960.

Alltop's name was added to the "Ten Most Wanted" list on
November 22, 1961. Ten weeks later, on March 2, 1962, a
team of Bureau agents apprehended him in Kansas City, making the arrest without resistance. Alltop was returned to finish
out his sentence in West Virginia, with time added for his
escape.

162 ■ FRANCIS LAVERNE BRANNAN

A native of Frederick, Illinois, born in 1925, Brannan was first arrested for petty theft at age eleven. Later, in December 1957, while serving in the military, Brannan was arrested by Long Beach, California, police officers on charges of sex perversion. Upon conviction, Brannan paid a fine and was sentenced to a term of two years' probation. In April 1960, he was charged with public drunkenness and drunken driving, once again in California; four months later, he was sentenced to eleven months in jail for auto theft and forgery, completing less than half his sentence prior to parole in January 1961.

On October 23, 1961, an elderly widow was shotgunned to death in her home, at Rushville, Illinois, the victim's auto stolen and subsequently recovered in Springfield. Evidence demonstrated that Brannan, drifting through the area and suspected of stealing a shotgun, had disappeared from Rushville shortly before the crime was discovered. He was also linked with the theft of a car in Springfield, from the same city block where the dead woman's car was recovered. A federal fugitive warrant for Brannan was issued October 27, and his name was added to the "Top Ten" list exactly two months later.

Publicity about the crime and Brannan's new addition to the list was massive, fanning out across the continent. In Florida, the fugitive maintained his "cool" for twenty days before surrendering to agents of the FBI on January 17, 1962. The pressure had become too much, and Brannan waived the normal extradition process, voluntarily returning for his murder trial in Illinois.

163 ■ DELBERT HENRY LINAWEAVER

With prior convictions for forgery and assault with a deadly weapon, Delbert Linaweaver was jailed at Salina, Kansas, in July 1960, awaiting transfer to state prison on his latest conviction for burglary. Facing a sentence of five to ten years, Linaweaver opted for a shortcut. On July 8, he led two other inmates in overpowering the sheriff and a jailer, beating both officers over the head with a sackful of broken glass.

Following his escape, Linaweaver joined a harvest combine crew in Nevada, traveling into Canada as they followed the crops. By November 1960 he was in Texas, working at a cotton gin near Lockney. A month later, traveling as "James Edward Thomas," he settled at Floydada, finding employment at a ranch seventeen miles north of town. In 1961, a whirlwind courtship culminated in his marriage to a local restaurant proprietess.

A federal fugitive since his escape from Kansas, Linaweaver made the FBI's "Most Wanted" list on January 30, 1962. A few days later, two Floydada residents dropped by the offices of Floyd County Sheriff Walter Hollums, checking out his copy of the poster bearing Linaweaver's mug shots. They had seen his flyer in the post office, remarking on the fugitive's resemblance to "James Thomas," and now they were certain; the two men were one and the same.

Sheriff Hollums telephoned the FBI in Lubbock, and a team of agents caught their man at work on February 5. Despite a pledge that he would not be taken in alive, Linaweaver surrendered peaceably, confessing his identity. Tattoos—"In God We Trust," a flower, "Joy," and "Mother"—indicated there was no mistake. The fugitive's employer, watching Linaweaver led away in handcuffs, was amazed. "I thought he was one of the nicest men I'd ever known," the rancher declared. "I had no trouble out of him whatsoever."

164 ■ WATSON YOUNG , JR.

Born in Jefferson County, Kentucky, during June 1932, Watson Young carried 200 pounds on his squat five-foot-five frame. The high-pitched cackling laugh belied his size, and it took a bit of conversation to unearth his fascination with the undertaker's art. So high on death was Watson Young that he enrolled in an embalming school to be around the corpses, later holding jobs in funeral homes and once impersonating a mortician.

Young served in the Marine Corps from January 1952 until September 1953, and was finally discharged when his mental aberrations made themselves apparent. Over the next four years, he was treated in mental hospitals at Charleston, South Carolina; Philadelphia, Pennsylvania; Louisville, Kentucky; Dayton, Ohio; and Kansas City, Missouri. In 1958 and 1959, he spent nearly a year at St. Elizabeth's Hospital, in Washington, D.C., on four separate visits. Late in 1959, he spent nine days in a federal hospital at Marion, Indiana, finally checking out against the advice of his physicians. In 1960, tired of psychiatric tests and questions, he escaped from a mental institution in Lakeland, Kentucky.

Diagnosed as a paranoid schizophrenic and sexual deviant, Young was suspected of dabbling in arson and other crimes of violence. Between commitments, he was variously charged with forgery, impersonation of a federal officer, and interstate transportation of a stolen car, but his mental condition helped him avoid prosecution in each case. A black man who hated other blacks—and people in general—he was bitter, friendless, unpredictable. As Christmas 1961 approached, Young was a walking time bomb, waiting to explode.

On December 13, Young invaded the home of an elderly Indianapolis couple, shooting both in the head before escaping with eighty dollars in cash. Moments after the double slaying, a young housewife admitted Young to her home on the pretext of calling a taxi. Once inside, he drew a knife and razor blade, declaring, "I'm a maniac!" before he ordered her to strip and started choking her. When the woman's two-year-old daughter rushed into the room, Young choked the girl unconscious, then raped the housewife repeatedly before fleeing with her husband's clothing and the family car.

Police traced Young to a local bordello, and from there to Chicago, where he consorted with other known prostitutes. Federal warrants were issued on December 14, charging Young with unlawful flight to avoid prosecution for murder, and his name was added to the FBI's "Most Wanted" list on February 5, 1962. He lasted a week after making the roster, swiftly identified and arrested by local police in Salina, Kansas. He was returned to Indiana for his trial on rape and murder charges.

165 ■ LYNDAL RAY SMITH

Born at Drakesboro, Kentucky, on March 31, 1924, Lyndal Smith launched his criminal career at age eighteen, rolling on from there to accumulate convictions for larceny, burglary, first-degree robbery and interstate transportation of a stolen car. Dishonorably discharged from the army and diagnosed as emotionally unstable, Smith still wore his patriotism for all to see, with flags and eagles tattooed on his arms.

While serving time for robbery in California, Smith overpowered a prison camp guard on the night of February 21, 1960, leaving the officer in shackles as he fled with $168 and a stolen car. Federal warrants charging Smith with unlawful flight to avoid confinement were issued on March 3; his name was added to the "Top Ten" list on February 14, 1962. (Out of 165 fugitives listed so far, he was the only "Smith.")

Settling briefly in Milwaukee, Smith was startled by his addition to the "Most Wanted" roster. Publicity led him to panic, running from Milwaukee to Cleveland, on from there to Chicago, finally reaching the end of his personal road in Baltimore, where he found work as a bartender under an alias. There was no escaping the heat, however, and Smith's fears were rekindled after two local papers carried his picture on March 22. Disgusted with life "on the lam," he surrendered to federal agents that day, explaining that, "I'm tired of running from the FBI."

166 ■ HARRY ROBERT GROVE

A seasoned veteran of crime, Grove was first arrested in 1940, as a juvenile. The next two decades saw him locked away on multiple convictions for theft of currency, unlawful firearms possession, burglary, possession of burglar's tools, and larceny of a motor vehicle. On December 30, 1960, with accomplice Daniel Garczynski, Grove robbed businessman John Pappas of $3,700 in Toledo, Ohio. One month later, agents of the Secret Service charged him with spending some $15,000 in counterfeit money at an Indianapolis shopping center.

Facing separate trials in Indiana and Ohio, Grove was free on bail that totalled $40,000. Vanishing in May 1961, he forfeited the money and was named as a federal fugitive, charged with unlawful flight to avoid prosecution. (Dan Garczynski appeared for his trial in Toledo, was convicted, and drew a sentence of ten to twenty-five years in state prison.) On February 19, 1962, Grove's name was added to the list of "Ten Most Wanted" fugitives.

Eleven months slipped by, while agents hunted Grove without result. On January 26, 1963, Donald Hostetler, a resident of Philadelphia, noticed two strangers "casing" the market across from his home. He telephoned police, but by the time a cruiser made the scene, the would-be thieves had driven off toward Uhricsville. Highway patrol officers stopped them there, discovering two loaded automatics under the front seat, a satchel of burglar's tools in the back. At the station, Grove told arresting officers, "I may as well save you some trouble. I'm on the ten most wanted list."

Grove's companion at the time of his arrest was Alfred Conti, forty-eight, a recent parolee from the Ohio state prison. Both men were charged with possession of burglar's tools and concealed weapons. Both pled guilty: Grove to both charges and Conti to possession of burglar's tools only.

167 ■ BOBBY RANDELL WILCOXSON
168 ■ ALBERT FREDERICK NUSSBAUM

Wilcoxson and Nussbaum resembled each other closely enough to be mistaken for brothers, but there were crucial differences, as well. One-eyed Bobby was the muscle of the team, quick on the trigger, volatile and brutal. Albert was the brains, a bookworm with a taste for criminology and chemistry, firearms and explosives. Nussbaum studied makeup and disguises, poring over the biographies of famous criminals to learn from their achievements and mistakes. He loved to work with guns, but when the chips were down, it would be Wilcoxson who pulled the trigger.

Launching his criminal career in 1952, with a charge of auto theft at age eighteen, Nussbaum was placed on probation and joined the army. Honorably discharged in 1957, he went into gun-running, picking up arrests over the next two years on charges of robbery and burglary, possession of a deadly weapon, and interstate transportation of a Thompson submachine gun. The latter charge landed Albert in the federal reformatory at Chillicothe, Ohio, where he met Bobby Wilcoxson, then serving time for interstate transportation of a vehicle purchased with a fraudulent check. (Another inmate, Peter Columbus Curry, became friendly with Nussbaum and Wilcoxson, returning in later years to play a pivotal role in their downfall.)

Paroled in 1959, Wilcoxson headed south and waited for his pal's release, in 1960. They regrouped at Nussbaum's home, in Buffalo, New York, in mid-September, raising cash by pulling off a string of local burglaries in weeks to come. The money went for guns and rented cars, as they prepared to hit the big time with a string of daring daylight robberies.

On December 5, 1960, the duo struck a savings and loan company in Schiller Park, New York, just before closing time, walking out with $5,709 in cash. Their next take, on January 12, was bigger, as they made a clean getaway from the M & T Trust Company, carrying $87,288 in their satchel.

The partners split up and invested their loot, Wilcoxson visiting Florida, buying into a jewelry store, a lettuce farm, and an automobile dealership. Nussbaum, meanwhile, used an alias to rent a storefront in Buffalo, stockpiling firearms and ammunition, building an arsenal that grew to include machine guns, grenades, and anti-tank weapons.

In June 1961, the bandits planned a series of random bombings in Washington, D.C., designed to generate fear of a "mad bomber" at large, distracting police on the day of a scheduled bank robbery. Trash cans and phone booths were demolished, with Nussbaum placing anonymous calls to the authorities, posing as a fanatic white supremacist, claiming credit for the blasts. Their final bomb, planted in an office building on June 30, turned out to be a dud, but the partners went ahead with their robbery on schedule, bagging another $19,862.

A short time later, agents of the IRS Alcohol, Tobacco and Firearms division arrested Wilcoxson's father for illegally receiving anti-tank guns and ammunition. The arrest would ultimately lead them back to Nussbaum's arsenal, in Buffalo, but in the meantime there were other targets to be looted.

Staking out a trust company in Rochester, New York, Nussbaum and Wilcoxson raided the office after a Brinks truck had dropped off a shipment of cash. The bandits made off with $57,197, but in their haste they missed another $81,700, lying behind the counter in bags.

Come winter, Pete Curry was fresh out of jail and itching for action. On December 15, 1961, Curry and Wilcoxson entered a bank in Brooklyn, leaving Nussbaum outside at the wheel of their getaway car. When security guard Henry Kraus went for his pistol, Wilcoxson unleashed a burst of submachine gun fire, killing Kraus instantly. Outside, a patrolman responded to the sound of shots and tried to shoot Wilcoxson, but a heavy plate glass door deflected bullets from his .38. Returning fire, Wilcoxson had a little better luck; the officer was wounded, but a slug that would have pierced his heart was stopped on impact with his badge. The robbers escaped with $32,763, dumping their car and Wilcoxson's weapon nearby. Serial numbers led ATF agents to Nussbaum's gun shop in Buffalo, and the separate bits of a baffling puzzle began to mesh.

On January 30, 1962, federal warrants were issued charging Wilcoxson with two counts of bank robbery. Nussbaum was named in the warrants as a material witness. Reports of a black bandit in Brooklyn led investigators back to Chillicothe, where officials at the federal lockup remembered Peter Curry's friendship with the wanted fugitives. Arrested on February 13, by FBI agents staking out his mother's home in Brooklyn, Curry soon began to sing.

Infuriated, Nussbaum and Wilcoxson plotted to murder their "friend," but they never got the chance. Federal agents uncovered Albert's arsenal, near Buffalo, and slugs removed from nearby trees were found to be identical with those employed to murder Henry Kraus. New warrants were prepared, upgrading Nussbaum from a material witness to the status of a full participant in the lethal Brooklyn holdup.

On June 26, 1962, the bandits raided a savings and loan company in Philadelphia, but a teller sent to empty the vault locked herself inside, leaving them with a pitiful $160 in singles. Driving on to Pittsburgh, they struck at a branch bank in a shopping mall, netting $4,373 and overlooking another $10,000.

It seemed apparent that the famous Nussbaum strategy was failing. Quarreling bitterly through summer, Bobby and Albert agreed on one more job together; Nussbaum stubbornly insisted he would only drive the car, a cop-out which led Wilcoxson to offer him a flat $500 fee. On September 19, Wilcoxson looted a Pennsylvania bank of $28,901, later "splitting" the take as agreed—$500 for Albert, $28,401 for Bobby. Enraged, Nussbaum stormed out with his handful of cash and the partnership ended; the outlaws would not see each other again until both were arrested.

On November 3, 1962, Nussbaum's wife returned from a secret meeting with her husband to find FBI agents waiting at her home. With some coaxing from her mother, she was finally persuaded to describe Al's car, his new disguise and probable location. Spotted close to 2 A.M., November 4, Nussbaum was captured after a brief high-speed chase.

Five days later, acting on a "tip" that may have come from Nussbaum, G-men dropped the net on Wilcoxson, in Baltimore. Thirty agents ringed the outlaw's home on November 9, armed in expectation of a battle, waiting through the night, until his girlfriend left the house the next morning. Bobby followed on her heels, a baby in his arms, and offered no resistance when he found himself surrounded.

Convicted for the robbery which led to Henry Kraus's death, Bobby Wilcoxson and Peter Curry were sentenced to life imprisonment. For his participation in the crime, Al Nussbaum drew a term of twenty years.

169 ■ THOMAS WELTON HOLLAND

Baltimore-born in November 1931, Holland was first arrested in Jacksonville, Florida, during January 1949, drawing a six-month sentence on a guilty plea to charges of larceny and breaking and entering. That December, while serving in the army, he was arrested for auto theft in Maryland; conviction earned him a dishonorable discharge and a suspended jail sentence. Dyer Act charges were filed against him in Pennsylvania, during February 1950, with another guilty plea bringing Holland a two-year suspended sentence and five years of federal probation. An August arrest in Maryland—again for auto theft—landed Holland in a state reformatory for one year, during which he failed in his single escape attempt. Upon release, in July 1951, his federal probation was revoked and Holland was confined to the United States penitentiary at Lewisburg, Pennsylvania, there earning a reputation as a serious discipline problem.

Released from custody in October 1952, Holland ran home to Baltimore, avoiding further arrests until he was picked up for disorderly conduct in July 1953. In February 1954, he stole $125 from a Baltimore woman at knifepoint, evading arrest when she failed to identify her assailant. Arrested for indecent exposure in November 1954, he was finally connected with that robbery, along with the following crimes: burglary, with theft of cash and pistols from the home of friends; the attempted rape of a Baltimore woman at gunpoint; sexual assault on one young boy and the lug-wrench beating of another who rejected his advances; and lewd advances to underage girls on at least two occasions, seeking sexual favors. Conviction on the list of heavy charges landed Holland ten more years in prison, and he was paroled in early 1960, on condition that he look for psychiatric help.

Instead, the sex offender found a warehouse job, from which he disappeared on February 2, 1961. Returning twenty-five days later, with a claim that he had joined the Cubans fighting Fidel Castro, Holland vanished for a second time in May. By June, he was declared in violation of parole, and federal warrants charging him with unlawful flight to avoid confinement were issued on August 29. His name was added to the FBI's "Most Wanted" list on May 11, 1962.

Whatever Holland's theoretical involvement with the Cuban struggle, there was little to be done about the cause in Kansas, where highway patrol officers picked him up on June 2, 1962. Arrested near La Harpe, he was returned to Maryland to finish out his ten-year prison term.

A Marine Corps veteran with combat service during World War II, Edward Maps was considered an expert with firearms. He was also a college graduate, majoring in psychology and art, who developed his talents to become an accomplished artist and sculptor. In the late 1950s, he cultivated a reputation as a "nonconformist," sporting a beard, sloppy clothing and unconventional footwear. At the same time, he endeavored to cast himself in the role of a ladies' man, and was known for "sponging" in the company of older women. A psychiatric examination, performed in February 1961, diagnosed Maps as suffering from schizophrenic reactions.

A complex man, beset by contradictions, Maps eventually turned to violence in his private life. On January 21, 1962, firefighters battling a blaze at his Stroudsburg, Pennsylvania, home found Maps's wife unconscious in the house; their daughter, four months old, had suffocated from inhaling smoke.

At the hospital, doctors tried in vain to save Maps's wife, but a heavy blow had fractured her skull, producing cerebral hemorrhage. Nor was the fire a simple accident: ten separate blazes had been set inside the house, with the gas oven left on.

The search for Edward Maps began and intensified when other local residents began receiving calls, allegedly from Maps, to warn them they were "next." A federal warrant charging Maps with unlawful flight to avoid prosecution for arson and murder was issued on January 23, 1962; five months later, on June 15, his name was added to the Bureau's "Top Ten" list.

No trace of Edward Maps was ever found, and federal process was dismissed on December 1, 1967, at the request of the district attorney in Stroudsburg. Passing time, in the D.A.'s opinion, had eliminated any possibility of a successful prosecution in the case.

171 ■ DAVID STANLEY JAĊUBANIS

Born at Baku, Russia, in July of 1910, David Jacubanis was a rootless drifter, characterized by federal agents as "a man without a country." His thirty-seven-year criminal record included convictions for breaking and entering, larceny, auto theft, armed robbery, bank robbery, and carrying a gun without a license. Considered an escape risk at the several prisons where he served his time—including Alcatraz—Jacubanis was rejected for deportation by his native Russia, along with the nations Canada, England, and France.

On March 27, 1962, Jacubanis looted a bank in Dedham, Massachusetts, of $6,004 at gunpoint. Because the bank was not federally insured, the FBI had no jurisdiction over the robbery proper, but warrants were issued charging Jacubanis with unlawful flight to avoid prosecution, along with charges stemming from violation of his federal parole. A second bank robbery in North Smithfield, Rhode Island, on April 5, 1962, brought further charges, and his name was added to the "Ten Most Wanted" list on November 21, 1962. Eight days later, G-men cornered Jacubanis in Arlington, Vermont, arresting him without incident and returning him to Massachusetts for trial.

172 ■ JOHN KINCHLOE DeJARNETTE

A native of Hardinsburg, Kentucky, DeJarnette was first incarcerated at age fifteen, growing up to spend most of his adult life in various prisons. During one escape attempt, he threw explosives at a prison guard, inflicting painful burns. Most of DeJarnette's arrests were logged in the vicinity of Louisville, but during January 1955 he was picked up in Washington, D.C., after bungling the robbery of a jewelry store. A frequent violator of parole, he spent substantial portions of his holdup loot on drugs.

In the summer of 1962, DeJarnette and his girlfriend, Doris Nelson, were sought by Kentucky authorities for obtaining narcotics by fraud. A federal warrant named them both as fugitives, charged with unlawful flight to avoid prosecution, and they were still at large when John was implicated in a string of bank heists, adding further charges to the list.

On September 10, 1962, DeJarnette entered a Louisville bank with gun in hand, and walked out moments later with $23,773 in cash. For the convenience of investigators, he left behind a perfect likeness, captured by surveillance cameras, and was instantly identified. Exactly one month later, he knocked over another branch of the same bank, escaping with $36,471. On October 22, 1962, he robbed a Cincinnati bank for another $38,000 and change.

By the time DeJarnette was added to the "Top Ten" roster, on November 30, his luck was running out. Robert Eugene Johnson, DeJarnette's accomplice in one of the October robberies, was arrested near Covington, Kentucky, on December 2, and he started talking to authorities. The next day, DeJarnette and Doris Nelson were surprised by federal raiders in their Hollywood, California, apartment, rented under the names of "Mr. and Mrs. John Nelson." The fugitives were playing Monopoly when G-men crashed through their door, giving DeJarnette no opportunity to reach his three loaded pistols, lying nearby.

173 ■ MICHAEL JOSEPH O'CONNOR

Nicknamed "Moon Mullins," Michael O'Connor liked the nickname enough to have the word "Moon" and the initials "MM" tattooed on his left arm. An eccentric stickup artist given to wearing mascara on occasion, O'Connor was also possessed of an explosive temper, manifested in unpredictable outbursts of violence. One such occurred on August 27, 1962, when he shot and killed a drinking partner, Michael "Knobby" Walsh, in a Jersey City tavern, leaving himself open to charges of second-degree murder.

At the time of the shooting, O'Connor was free on bond pending trial for theft of twenty-two cartons of clothing, valued at $2,300, from a truck he was driving in interstate commerce. New Jersey authorities also suspected him of several armed robberies, including the October 24, 1962 holdup which netted $5,844 from a savings and loan office in Fairlawn. Added to the "Top Ten" roster on December 13, 1962, O'Connor was picked up by federal agents three days after Christmas, in New York, and he was returned to New Jersey for trial on outstanding charges.

174 ■ JOHN LEE TAYLOR

Born December 7, 1933, in Tutwiler, Mississippi, Taylor logged his first arrest at age twelve. Growing up a belligerent, violence-prone misfit, he boasted adult convictions for robbery, rape, and auto theft. Distinguished by his posture, habitually walking with his shoulders stooped, head down, and one hand clenched in a fist, he was considered armed and dangerous by the police officers from whom he escaped on several occasions. Compensating for his soft voice and slender build, he was said to carry a pistol and knife at all times.

On July 8, 1961, Taylor invaded the Champaign, Illinois, apartment occupied by a middle-aged schoolteacher, binding her hands, beating his victim unconscious and raping her before he looted the dwelling of jewelry and cash. Federal warrants charging Taylor with unlawful flight to avoid prosecution were issued on July 21, and his name was added to the "Ten Most Wanted" list on December 14, 1962. Six days later, federal agents tracked their man to a Chicago hideout, making the arrest without resistance. Taylor was returned to Champaign, for trial on charges of robbery, rape and assault.

175 ■ HAROLD THOMAS O'BRIEN

Chicago-born in February 1905, Harold O'Brien was possessed of a violent temper, prone to drunken displays of his favorite .22-caliber "equalizer." During 1930 and 1931, Chicago police arrested him three times on armed robbery charges, but the cases were dropped without prosecution. In

August 1932, O'Brien and a male accomplice were arrested at the scene of an armed robbery which netted them $1,500 worth of new tires. Convicted of grand larceny, Harold was sentenced to ten years imprisonment, winning parole in 1936.

A self-styled ladies' man, O'Brien tried going straight on release from "the joint," holding down various jobs as a bartender, chauffeur, taxi driver and deliveryman. Thrice married and divorced, he liked to talk about his plans for opening a rooming house in California, Florida or Arizona—someplace where the sun would keep him warm.

On August 12, 1960, O'Brien quarreled with a drinking buddy in a small Fox Lake, Illinois saloon. Producing a pistol to threaten his "friend," Harold was swiftly disarmed by the bartender. Undaunted, he whipped out a second gun, firing three shots into his companion at close range, leaving the other man dead on the floor as he fled. A federal warrant charging O'Brien with unlawful flight to avoid prosecution for murder was issued on August 18, and his name was added to the Bureau's "Ten Most Wanted" list on January 4, 1963.

Two years later, on January 14, 1965, O'Brien's warrants were dismissed at the request of local prosecutors, who decided passing time had dimmed their hopes for a successful prosecution. At this writing, no solution to the case has been recorded. Harold O'Brien joins the lists as one of those who got away.

176 ■ JERRY CLARENCE RUSH

A stickup artist with a penchant for escaping from confinement, Jerry Rush was sought by Maryland authorities for breaking out of prison at the time he made the FBI's "Most Wanted" list. His latest crime involved the robbery of a bank in Perth Amboy, New Jersey, from which he obtained $100,000 in cash. The money was used to finance a free-wheeling, cross-country honeymoon, but Rush was already running out of time. Federal warrants listing charges of unlawful flight to avoid confinement and bank robbery were issued in his name, and he made it to the Bureau's "Top Ten" roster on January 14, 1963. Ten weeks later, on March 25, FBI agents caught him in Miami, closing their net as Rush slid behind the wheel of a brand-new luxury car. Upon conviction of bank robbery charges, he was sentenced to twenty-nine years in a federal penitentiary.

177 ■ MARSHALL FRANK CHRISMAN

Born in Denver, Colorado, on August 22, 1925, Chrisman logged his first arrest at age eleven, proceeding from there to compile a record of adult convictions for burglary, larceny, mail robbery, assault, and receiving stolen goods. Sporting a total of fifteen tattoos, he ranked as one of the FBI's most "decorated" fugitives, easily distinguished by his art work, a missing front tooth, and his vicious temper.

On July 10, 1962, Chrisman and two male accomplices raided a bank in Toledo, Ohio, bagging $12,264 at gunpoint before they escaped in a stolen getaway car. Upon arrest, Chrisman's partners pled guilty to the robbery and were consigned to Ohio's state prison, leaving only their leader at large. Federal warrants charging Chrisman with bank robbery were issued on July 11, and his name was added to the "Ten Most Wanted" list on February 7, 1963. Identified by local officers from his FBI wanted flyers, Chrisman was arrested in Los Angeles on May 21, 1963 and returned to Ohio for trial.

178 ■ HOWARD JAY BARNARD

Barnard's record dated from 1943, when he was first arrested by police in Pasadena, California, on charges of auto theft and desertion from the army. Later discharged from the service on grounds of mental instability, he went on to spend fifteen years in various prisons on felony convictions. Arrested twice by the FBI—in Memphis, during 1946, and at Huntington Beach, California, in 1955—Barnard was described by federal agents as "a robbery specialist, disguise expert and highly skilled escape artist." In 1962, he was arrested in Seattle after bungling a robbery attempt; his strange disguise included heavy makeup, cotton padding in his mouth, and rubber bands to help distort his ears.

In lieu of spending money on a trial, authorities in Washington returned Barnard to California, where he was sought for violation of parole. In transit on November first, chained hand and foot inside a locked compartment, Howard somehow shed his bonds and leaped to freedom from a moving train near Orland. His name was added to the "Ten Most Wanted" list on April 12, 1963.

A year later, on April 5, 1964, a bizarre-looking gunman entered the Hotel El Dorado, in Sacramento, California. Wearing two sets of clothing, the robber had bleached hair, with heavy theatrical makeup on his face; rubber bands were wrapped around his ears, and cotton wadding filled his cheeks. Absconding with $1,057, the thief fled on foot but was cornered by police in a nearby alley. Wounded in a brief exchange of gunfire, he surrendered. After layers of glue had been removed from Barnard's fingertips, his prints confirmed the fugitive's identity.

In custody, Barnard confessed to several robberies around the San Francisco Bay, including one in Contra Costa County where an officer was held at gunpoint, locked inside the trunk of a stolen car. Mug shots further linked Barnard to the robbery of a Sacramento tavern in July 1963, and the holdup of a local market eight months later. By the time he finished serving time on all his pending charges, there would be no need of a disguise to simulate old age.

179 ■ LEROY AMBROSIA FRAZIER

Alleged to suffer from violent mental disorders, known to associate with drug addicts and female impersonators, Leroy Frazier boasted a record of convictions for white slavery, larceny, and assault with a deadly weapon. On January 14, 1962, while serving a federal narcotics sentence, he was under treatment in the secure ward of St. Elizabeth's Hospital, in Washington, D.C. That evening, Frazier unlocked his door with a homemade key, fashioned from the plastic handle of a toothbrush, and escaped. His name was added to the FBI's "Most Wanted" list on June 4, 1963.

Intent on hiding out, the fugitive had run directly west, to Cleveland, where he stopped on January 27, 1962. As "Johnny Gray," he purchased two old trucks, acquired employees, and made use of certain building skills to launch a small contracting business, labeled "Johnny Gray & Sons." (In fact, none of his five employees were related, nor were they aware of Frazier's true identity.) Between September 1962 and his arrest, the business put an estimated $16,000 into Frazier's pocket.

Federal trackers focused their attention on the Cleveland area, when Frazier was reportedly observed—in women's clothing—on September 10. The bulletin led local papers to reprint his photograph, and that in turn brought other, more substantial tips. A team of agents seized the fugitive at his apartment on September 12, eliciting a curt denial to the charge that Leroy sometimes dressed in drag. "That's not true," Frazier insisted. "I dressed as a woman only once in my life. That was in prison, once, when I was in a play."

180 ■ CARL CLOSE

Born in West Virginia during 1915, Close served with the navy for six months in 1945, before receiving a medical discharge as a psycho-neurotic. From those humble beginnings, he went on to accumulate felony convictions for embezzlement, bank robbery, and interstate transportation of stolen funds. On April 21, 1949, Close was arrested in West Virginia with two brothers-in-law, charged with the robbery of two banks in Maryland. A submachine gun and two pistols were confiscated at the time of his arrest.

During their trial on the Maryland charges, Close and kin escaped from their detention cell but were recaptured moments later. On conviction, each received a $15,000 fine, together with a term of thirty-five years in prison. Carl started his time at the federal lockup in Atlanta, where he joined two other inmates in attempting to escape by helicopter from a cell block roof. Deterred by prison personnel, Close was transferred to Alcatraz, where he remained until September 1954. Shipped on to Leavenworth, he was paroled to Nokomis, Florida, in July 1961. On March 3, 1963, Carl skipped town with his brother, Harold, to launch another crime spree on the eastern seaboard.

On March 8, the brothers raided a Baltimore bank for $21,078, dropping some $4,141 en route to their getaway car. Both were charged with bank robbery in a federal complaint issued on May 31, and Harold Close was picked up the next day, in Roanoke, Virginia, on a charge of vagrancy.

Undeterred by his brother's arrest, Carl hit a bank in Roanoke on June 4, waltzing out with $6,330 in cash. A second federal warrant for bank robbery was issued in his name two days later, and he made the FBI's "Most Wanted" list September 25.

One day after joining the "Top Ten," Close held up a bank in Anderson, South Carolina, stuffing his satchel with $28,262. Unknown to the bandit, a silent alarm had been sounded, and local patrolmen were waiting with shotguns as Close left the bank. Carl surrendered quietly, dropping the loot on command, and officers relieved him of two loaded pistols. Held on $100,000 bond, Close entered a plea of guilty to the Anderson robbery on October 7, 1963, and was sentenced to another twenty-five years in Leavenworth.

181 ■ THOMAS ASBURY HADDAR

A petty criminal from all appearances, Tom Haddar logged his first arrest at Richmond, Virginia, during October 1959, on suspicion of purse snatching. Later, in the navy, he was charged with insubordination at Portsmouth, New Hampshire. A few months later, in December, Portsmouth officers detained him on a misdemeanor charge.

The incident which put the FBI on Haddar's trail seemed likewise insignificant, in the beginning. On May 2, 1963, he was accused of failing to pay for a tire, at a gas station in Prince George's County, Maryland. It was a misdemeanor charge, at most, but Haddar panicked when his car was stopped by Pvt. Alfred Steinat on a rural highway. Whipping out a pistol, Haddar fired a single bullet into Steinat's chest and killed him instantly.

The misdemeanor charge was murder, now. Next day, the fugitive approached an isolated home and told the owner he was ill, in need of medical attention. When the ambulance arrived, attendants were amazed to hear their passenger confess the shooting of a local officer.

Incarcerated at the Clifton T. Perkins State Hospital, in Jessup, Maryland, pending trial, Haddar and another inmate staged a breakout in September. Sawing through bars on their second-floor window with a smuggled hacksaw blade, the shoeless prisoners descended ropes made out of knotted bedsheets. Haddar's sidekick was recaptured swiftly, but the petty thief turned killer managed to escape. A federal warrant charging him with unlawful flight to avoid prosecution was issued on September 14; on October 9, 1963, Haddar's name was added to the list of "Ten Most Wanted" fugitives.

In January 1964, the sighting of a Haddar look-alike in Texas focused FBI attention on southwestern states. A search of every cheap hotel and flophouse in the region ended on January 13, when Haddar was discovered at a Salvation Army mission in Oklahoma City. Registered as "Thomas Longstreet," he was watching a group sing-along when agents made the collar. Surrendering without resistance, he was held for extradition on $100,000 bond.

182 ■ ALFRED OPONOWICZ

The criminal record on Alfred Oponowicz dates from 1943, when, at age sixteen, he pulled a string of robberies and burglaries in Cleveland. Sentenced to the Mansfield Reformatory, he escaped that same year. While at large, in the company of another escaped inmate, he participated in other robberies and safecracking raids. On arrest, Oponowicz confessed his crimes and was committed to the Lima State Hospital for the criminally insane under an Ohio law, the Ascherman Act, designed to take mental defectives off the streets. In October 1944, Oponowicz and four other Lima inmates staged a break, pulling the steel grill off a supply room door, but Alfred was wounded by guards and recaptured. At age eighteen, he was transferred to a state prison to complete the remainder of his sentence, and was eventually paroled.

On September 2, 1962, Oponowicz and two accomplices were seized in the act of trying to burglarize the Cleveland Trust Company. Released under $25,000 bond, Alfred was awaiting trial in March 1963, when he walked out of a Cleveland courtroom and disappeared. A federal warrant charged Oponowicz with unlawful flight to avoid prosecution, but agents had trouble locating their man as he drifted back and forth, between Ohio and Pennsylvania. By October 1963, Alfred had settled in Painesville, northeast of Cleveland in Lake County, and set up housekeeping with Ina Marie Cook, then pregnant from a previous failed marriage. They lived together as "Mr. and Mrs. Robert Bennett," with the child arriving on December 17. By that time, Oponowicz was sought on looting charges in Pittsburgh, and was a prime suspect in the murder of a Pittsburgh vending machine salesman. His name was added to the "Top Ten" list on November 27, 1963.

Three days prior to Christmas, agents of the Secret Service acting on a tip from an informant raided the "Bennett" home in Painesville. They swept up $50,000 worth of counterfeit $100 and $20 bills, along with some $22,000 worth of printing and camera equipment. Oponowicz—still unidentified by his captors—was clad in underwear and handcuffs when his "wife" drew a .357 magnum revolver from the blanket swaddling her baby, passing the weapon to Alfred.

Covering his captors with the pistol, Oponowicz leaped through a living room window and ran across the lawn, but there was nowhere to go. Bullets in the hip and shoulder brought him down, and he was carted off to the hospital under guard.

Next day, December 23, Oponowicz managed to escape from his hospital room, securing a gun in the process. That evening, he was spotted by a group of boys, aged nine to twelve, who recognized the fugitive and started chasing him, ignoring Alfred's threats to shoot. The youthful posse lost him in a railroad yard, but police had already been summoned, and officers found Oponowicz huddled in a nearby ditch, bleeding profusely from his newly-opened wounds. Returned to the hospital prison ward, he faced charges of assaulting a federal officer, bank burglary, and possession of counterfeiting equipment.

183 ■ ARTHUR WILLIAM COUTS

Arthur Couts worked hard at crime, but practice never seemed to bring perfection. His long police record included convictions for armed robbery, aggravated robbery, atrocious assault and battery, burglary, narcotics violations and auto theft. In June 1955, surrounded by police in a motel at Mays Landing, New Jersey, Couts and accomplice John Feeny chose to shoot it out, surrendering as soon as Feeny stopped a bullet. By mid-summer 1963, Couts was once more on parole, this time from a five-to-fifteen-year term in Pennsylvania, resulting from conviction in two holdups and an assault on a sixteen-year-old girl.

On July 17, Couts and an accomplice entered a combination grocery store and check cashing service in Philadelphia. He brandished a pistol at grocer George Combs, threatening violence if cash was not tendered at once. Thinking fast, Combs ducked behind a steel counter, robbing Couts of his target. The bandit fired several shots, all the same, before departing empty-handed. Tipsters informed the FBI that Couts had left town, prompting issuance of a federal warrant for unlawful flight to avoid prosecution on charges of robbery with intent to murder.

Six months later, still in Philadelphia, Couts—sporting a new mustache and dyed hair—was spotted by informants who saw through the frail disguise. The FBI was notified, and they surprised the outlaw at his rooming house on January 30, 1964. Arrested without a struggle, Couts was delivered to local authorities for prosecution, the federal charges against him dismissed.

184 ■ JESSE JAMES GILBERT

No studies have been made of the relationship between a subject's name and ultimate selection of adult career, but it would seem that any infant christened for America's most famous outlaw has a head start on the road to crime. Such was the case of Jesse James Gilbert, convicted on various charges of burglary, interstate transportation of stolen cars, and parole violation. While confined in a California state prison, Gilbert stabbed a fellow inmate to death and had more time tacked onto his sentence.

On July 20, 1963, Jesse James escaped from San Quentin, where he was serving fifteen years on a burglary conviction. A federal fugitive warrant was issued on September 24, by which time Gilbert had been linked with California robberies in Los Angeles, Compton, Culver City, Torrance, and Long Beach.

On January 3, 1964, Gilbert and accomplice Edgar Ball Weaver raided an Alhambra savings and loan office for $11,492. Leaving the crime scene, they abducted a female employee for use as a shield, but police gave chase anyway, and shots were exchanged. Sgt. George Davis, struck in the head by a .45-caliber round, was killed instantly, and Ed Weaver was fatally wounded by return fire. In the confusion, Jesse Gilbert managed to escape, and a federal warrant charging him with bank robbery was issued three days later. Gilbert's name was posted to the Bureau's "Ten Most Wanted" list on January 27, 1964.

A month later, on February 26, G-men acting on a tip surprised Gilbert in Philadelphia, surrounding him on the street outside the building where he had rented an apartment under the name "Donald Masters." Disguised with a black wig, sunglasses, and an adhesive bandage covering a tattoo on his left arm, Gilbert was armed with a .45 automatic but offered no resistance. A half-hour later, agents dropped by the apartment to arrest Gilbert's traveling companion, Billie Jo Carder, sought by California authorities for violation of parole on an armed robbery conviction.

185 ■ SAMMIE EARL AMMONS

A native of Knoxville, Tennessee, with three hometown arrests on his record, Sammie Ammons loved to travel with his wife, Barbara Sue, and their six children. Frequent jaunts through Dixie were financed by printing bogus personal and payroll checks, which Ammons cashed while wearing various identities. At times, to make himself seem more reliable, he posed as a policeman. Authorities in Nashville got wise to the scheme, but Sammie was one jump ahead of them, and a fugitive warrant was issued on February 8, 1963, charging Ammons with unlawful flight to avoid prosecution for forgery.

Traveling with six children can be an ordeal, but Ammons found the perfect babysitter. Alma Reed Matthews was Barbara Sue's half-sister; with two kids of her own, she was seeking refuge from bitter divorce proceedings, and travel with the Ammons family seemed ideal.

But on September 2, 1963, the decomposing bodies of her two small children were retrieved from an abandoned septic tank twenty-two miles east of Crossville, Tennessee. One, a three-year-old girl, had been crammed into a suitcase for disposal. The other, a two-year-old boy, was found with a diaper around his neck; the medical examiner's report confirmed strangulation as the cause of death. From scraps of clothing and the footprints taken after birth, the bodies were identified as those of Rose and Johnny Reed.

No trace of Alma Matthews could be found in the vicinity, despite the fact that searchers drained a nearby lake and beat the brush for days. In any case, detectives knew the missing woman and her children had been traveling with Sammie Ammons and his brood. The footloose forger's name was added to the FBI's "Most Wanted" list on February 10.

Since May of 1963, the Ammons family had been living quietly in Rome, Georgia, ten miles east of the Alabama line. Posing as "John and Barbara Nixon," Sammie and Barbara

Sue cleaned up their act for a while, but when their cash ran short they reverted to type. Two bogus checks were passed in Rome and a third in nearby Cedartown before they fled in mid-May 1964.

Authorities were waiting on the Alabama side, at Farrell, when the fugitives appeared on May 15. Sammie crashed through a roadblock under fire, collided with an oncoming vehicle, and somehow kept going, leading his pursuers on a chase with speeds topping 100 mph, until both his rear tires were shredded by gunfire. Abandoning the car and Barbara Sue, Ammons fled into a nearby field, where he was quickly routed by bloodhounds. Waiving extradition, the fugitives were returned to Rome, facing new forgery charges.

Bad checks were the least of their problems, however, when detectives located Alma Matthews, living quietly in Gadsden, Alabama. Under questioning, the woman said her son had been hospitalized in Atlanta during February 1963, after suffering "a fall" which left him "ill." A month later, terrorized by Ammons's assertion that the state would keep her child, Alma said she smuggled John out of the hospital, rejoining Sammie and Barbara Sue on the road. As time passed, little John "kept losing weight," while Ammons refused to summon a doctor. The boy reportedly died "of convulsions" while riding in the car near Marietta, Georgia. Alma herself had selected the dump site, helping Sammie weight the small body with stones. In May 1963, Alma continued, the tribe had moved from Marietta to Gadsden, and a month later Rose "got sick" because she "missed her brother." Once again, no doctor was consulted, and upon her death one night, the girl was sent to join her brother in the septic tank.

The story told by Alma Matthews failed to mesh with evidence that Johnny Reed was strangled, and renewed interrogation changed the woman's tale to one of murder. Barbara Sue and Sammie were responsible for killing off her children, she decided in a second version of her story, prompting murder charges to be filed against the couple. On the basis of her contradictory statements and admitted complicity in disposal of the bodies, Alma Matthews was also charged and held for trial.

186 ■ FRANK B. DUMONT

The rap sheet on Frank Dumont dated from 1936, with six convictions on charges ranging from burglary to auto theft. A perennial escape artist, he also broke out of jail several times during his criminal career, but Dumont's real problems grew out of an apparent sexual problem. On October 30, 1963, he abducted a fourteen-year-old girl in Pocatello, Idaho, subsequently beating her unconscious and tossing her out of his moving car. Believing his victim was dead, Dumont fled the state while authorities moved to indict him for the "brutal and motiveless" crime. A federal warrant charged him with unlawful flight to avoid prosecution for assault, and Dumont was added to the "Ten Most Wanted" list on March 10, 1964.

On April 27, Melvyn Marcus, a tenant of the Arroyo Chico apartments in Tucson, Arizona, noticed a stranger loitering around the complex. Suspecting a burglary in progress, Marcus alerted the manager, Mark Ellis, who in turn summoned tenants Robert Wilson and Richard Milne—both Tucson policemen. Ordered to halt, the suspect took off at a dead run, Milne in pursuit, while Wilson went to fetch his gun and car. The chase—soon joined by college wrestler Dennis Favero—continued for a mile along some railroad tracks, until the suspect turned to make his stand.

Milne was twice knocked to the ground by his assailant before Favero tackled the stranger and pinned him with an armlock. Exhausted by the chase and battle, Frank Dumont—his hair and mustache now dyed red—pleaded with his captors to "Give me a break."

Allegedly armed with a .38 revolver and known for his threats to "shoot it out," Dumont carried only a package of razor blades at the time of his capture. Lodged in jail at Tucson, he was held on $10,000 bond pending extradition to Idaho for trial on assault charges.

187 ■ WILLIAM BEVERLY HUGHES

On June 3, 1961, while serving time for the 1958 shotgun robbery of a Baldwin County, Alabama, beverage company, William Hughes escaped from Kilby Prison, at Montgomery. A federal fugitive warrant was issued, charging Hughes with unlawful flight to avoid confinement, and his criminal record, listing several prior convictions, qualified him for a posting on the "Ten Most Wanted" list. His name was added to the roster on March 18, 1964.

FBI agents traced Hughes to Bel Aire, Texas, where he had worked briefly as a carpenter, but the fugitive was gone when they arrived. Informants offered information that the convict was bound for Southern California, and on April 11 descriptions of his car were broadcast to law enforcement agencies along the route of travel.

That night, Sgt. William Chewing, of the Arizona highway patrol, sighted the suspect vehicle near Geronimo, in Graham County. Highway 70 crosses the San Carlos Indian reservation, and Chewing radioed ahead for assistance from reservation police. Responding to the call, Sgt. Roy Kitcheyan and Patrolman Kennedy Johnson forced the suspect vehicle off the road near the town of Bylas.

William Hughes, behind the wheel, presented officers with a driver's license and draft card in the name of "Robert Holloway," from Houston, but confessed his true identity when he was taken into custody. His traveling companions—Edna Voyles and her three children by a previous marriage—were not charged.

188 ■ QUAY CLEON KILBURN

The fourth man to earn a second posting on the "Top Ten" list, Quay Kilburn had passed the time since his last arrest as editor of the inmate newspaper at Utah's state prison. Paroled on November 12, 1963, he returned to his hometown Salt Lake City, where he liked to call himself an "editor at large." A short time after his release from prison, Kilburn was accused of cashing worthless checks in Salt Lake City. When he dropped from sight, a federal warrant was issued charging him with unlawful flight to avoid confinement for robbery and embezzlement. Quay made the bureau's roster for a second time in March 23, 1964.

Three months later, on June 25, Kilburn was surprised by federal agents in the parking lot behind a bank in Ogden, Utah. Presumably intent on robbery, he carried a revolver but was not allowed to reach it as the G-men took him into custody. Returned to Salt Lake City, Kilburn faced a charge of violating his parole, along with brand-new counts of fraud and forgery.

189 ■ JOSEPH FRANCIS BRYAN , JR.

A native of Camden, New Jersey, Joseph Bryan first ran afoul of the law in 1958, at age nineteen, when he abducted two small boys, tied them to a tree, and sexually molested them. Committed to a Camden County mental hospital, Bryan was diagnosed as schizophrenic, once informing doctors that he liked to see little boys "tied up and screaming." Upon release from the hospital, Bryan enlisted in the navy, but was discharged after further psychiatric tests and treatment. Convicted of burglary and auto theft in Nevada, he served time in the state prison and was paroled on January 20, 1964. By that time, Bryan's twisted sexual desires had blossomed into something dark and dangerous.

On February 27, John Robinson, age seven, disappeared in Mount Pleasant, South Carolina, while riding his bicycle near home. FBI agents discovered that Joe Bryan had spent the night in a local motel, and they looked up his record of crimes against children. Two farmers reported pulling a car from a mud hole on the morning of February 28; the driver had been traveling with a boy and the license number was traced back to Bryan. The clincher was John Robinson's abandoned bike, discovered in some weeds not far from where the car bogged down.

On March 23, 1964, seven-year old Lewis Wilson, Jr., vanished from his school in St. Petersburg, Florida. Searchers were beating the bushes, in vain, when three youths on vacation discovered the remains of a child in a marsh near Hallandale. Stripped clean, except for shoes and socks, the skeletal remains were finally identified by reference to the footwear. The search for Johnny Robinson was over.

A fugitive from charges of kidnapping and murder, Joseph Bryan was declared a federal fugitive from justice. On April 14, 1964, his name was added to the FBI's "Most Wanted" list, with photographs displayed from coast to coast.

By that time, David Wulff, age eight, was missing from his home in Willingboro, New Jersey. Snatched on April 4, his fate was still a mystery when eight-year-old Dennis Burke disappeared from Humboldt, Tennessee, on April 23.

Five days later, a pair of off-duty FBI agents spotted Bryan's car—a distinctive white Cadillac—outside a shopping mall in New Orleans. They staked out the vehicle, pouncing when Bryan emerged from the mall with Dennis Burke in tow. Held on $15,000 bond, Bryan denied kidnapping anyone. Asked how he came to be traveling with a child, he seemed bewildered. "I don't know how it happened," he said. "I don't know." Dennis Burke, for his part, described Bryan as "a nice man" who fed him well and rented comfortable motel rooms during their three days together.

190 ■ JOHN ROBERT BAILEY

A self-styled "ladies' man" who sometimes liked his romance on the violent side, John Bailey had a criminal record dating from 1944, with convictions for petty larceny, robbery, rape, and carnal abuse. Sentenced to life imprisonment for an Arkansas rape, he wangled parole in November 1961, but Bailey had never been any good at staying out of trouble.

On February 22, 1962, Bailey and three companions held up a motel in Hot Springs, Arkansas. His accomplices were soon captured, but Bailey fled westward to California, settling in Hayward as "Charles Robert Carpenter." Finding work as a plumber, he tried to "go straight," and married a local widow in December. Bailey's bride and her two daughters had no idea that the new man in their life was a fugitive from justice, sought by the FBI on charges of unlawful flight to avoid prosecution for robbery and parole violation.

Bailey's name was added to the "Ten Most Wanted" list on April 22, 1964. Twelve days later, on May 4, agents responding to a tip descended on his Hayward home, surprising him as he sat watching television. Stunned by the revelation of Bailey's secret past, his wife could only lament the loss of a second husband. "Death one can almost take," she declared, "but this . . . I don't know what to think."

191 ■ GEORGE ZAVADA

Jailed for the first time in March 1933, at age seventeen, Zavada spent four years in the Ohio state reformatory before his release in January 1937. Fourteen months later, on March 21, 1938, he was sentenced to twenty-five years on conviction for three armed robberies in Cleveland. Between 1938 and 1961, Zavada logged time in the Tennessee state prison, along with federal lockups at Alcatraz, Atlanta, and Leavenworth. Released from the latter prison on October 24, 1961, George drove west to renew his acquaintance with hoodlum Howard Jensen, a crony from his days at Alcatraz, in the 1950s.

In the early spring of 1963, Zavada and Jensen teamed up to rob a supermarket in Whittier, California, making off with $2,633. In May, they were joined by ex-convict Clarence Kostich in robbing a motel and another supermarket. Zavada was emerging as the brains of the gang, plotting their raids, and his partners soon dubbed George "The King." Zavada grew so fond of the nickname that he had it embroidered on his underwear.

On June 4, 1963, the King led his subjects into a Culver City savings and loan office, bagging $3,034 at gunpoint. A month later, on July 9, they relieved a Los Angeles firm of $10,049, making a clean getaway. Zavada was developing a certain style along the way. Raiding the United California Bank, in

Canoga Park, on July 26, he vaulted over the teller's cage to retrieve $33,771 in cash.

Throughout the crime spree, Zavada resided in San Francisco, traveling south when a holdup was scheduled. Jensen and Kostich were less security-conscious, and their negligence backfired on August 8, when they were seized—with guns and stolen money—at a Hollywood motel. The outlaws tried to bluff their way through questioning, but a phone number found in Jensen's room led police to Zavada. Arrested in San Francisco, the King was returned to Los Angeles, and there confessed his role in the holdups.

On December 23, 1963, Zavada failed to put in an appearance at his trial. The King was otherwise engaged, with an abortive bank heist in Reno, Nevada. Working with ex-convicts Joseph Anderson and Thomas Lombardi, Zavada was frustrated by a bank manager who declined to open the vault. Fleeing with small change, the outlaws sideswiped an oil truck in their haste to get away.

Zavada and Lombardi fared a little better in their next outing, on January 20, lifting $7,696 from a savings and loan office in Los Angeles. On March 13, they tapped an L.A. bank for $4,478, rebounding a week later with another bank job, netting $13,000 for their trouble. By this time, the FBI was hot on Zavada's trail, and agents nearly bagged him on April 17, settling for Tom Lombardi when they missed their prey by minutes. Lombardi and Zavada were indicted for three counts of bank robbery on May 6, 1964, and George made the Bureau's "Top Ten" list the same day.

On June 12, following a Sacramento bank heist which had netted $73,000, Zavada's car was spotted in San Jose. Agents surrounded the house, closing in as Zavada emerged, but the King chose to fight for his freedom. Producing a pistol, Zavada had no time to fire before one well-placed shot laid him out on the grass. Pleading guilty to all counts in federal court, on October 26, 1964, the King was sentenced to another twenty-five years in Leavenworth. He died in prison, of natural causes, during June 1965.

192 ■ GEORGE PATRICK McLAUGHLIN

As members of a family born to crime, McLaughlin and his brothers led a rugged Irish gang in Boston, hiring out their services as "muscle" to assorted loan sharks, bookies, even members of the Mafia. Hot-tempered, prone to sudden violence, they became involved in bloody internecine warfare that would kill one brother, wound another, and eventually land George Patrick on the FBI's "Most Wanted" list.

The trouble started in July 1961, at a Salisbury beach. The McLaughlin brothers were boozing it up and feeling no pain when a rival gang boss—James MacLean, from Somerville—turned up with his entourage. One of the McLaughlins, variously named as George or brother Edward in conflicting stories, threw his arms around MacLean's bikini-clad girlfriend and demonstrated his passion by trying to bite off her ear. A brawl erupted, with minor injuries on both sides, but neither faction was inclined to let the matter rest. That afternoon, George Patrick was abducted by his rivals, beaten bloody, and unceremoniously dumped outside a local hospital.

The war was on. On October 30, a McLaughlin loyalist was spotted rigging a bomb to MacLean's car and was driven off by pistol fire. Next day, a mobile firing squad cornered Bernie McLaughlin in Charlestown, leaving him dead on the sidewalk. Edward was subsequently wounded by gunshots, and George was beaten a second time, once more escaping with his life. By early 1965, an estimated forty hoodlums had been slain, and "bosses" of the Mafia had found themselves unable to control the carnage.

Ironically, the crime that brought McLaughlin to the FBI's attention during 1964 was unrelated to his war with the MacLeans. On March 15, a bank employee, William Sheridan, was leaving a party in Roxbury when a sniper shot him once, between the eyes. The gunman's getaway car was traced to McLaughlin, with police attributing the murder to a personal quarrel or a case of mistaken identity. (McLaughlin's car had been abandoned near the home of a woman friendly with both George and his victim.)

A glance at McLaughlin's rap sheet—including arrests for larceny, armed robbery, assault, carrying a revolver, possession of firearms, possession of burglar's tools, and assault with intent to kill—convinced the Bureau that he rated a spot on the "Most Wanted" list. His name was added to the roster on May 8, 1964, with a charge of unlawful flight to avoid prosecution for murder.

Eleven months later, on February 24, 1965, a tip led agents to a third-floor apartment in Dorchester, where McLaughlin was hiding out under the alias of "John O'Connor." The fugitive had three .38s within reach as G-men and Boston police officers crashed through his door, but the odds were against him, and he raised his hands, crying, "Please don't shoot." A mob associate, one James O'Toole, was charged with harboring a federal fugitive.

193 ■ CHESTER COLLINS

Born December 1, 1913, at Dothan, Alabama, Chester Collins was a study in contradictions. Fond of poetry and dream interpretations, Collins also had a taste for liquor which provoked him into bouts of unpredictable, explosive violence, leading friends to shun his company when he was drinking. On the evening of December 7, 1956, he argued with his girlfriend at a dance in Winter Haven, Florida, and was ejected from the building after threatening her life. Next morning, Collins used a hatchet to assault the woman and her female roommate, leaving both victims critically injured.

Pleading guilty shortly after his arrest, Collins was sentenced to ten years imprisonment, escaping from the prison camp at Fort Pierce in June 1957. Two months later, a federal warrant was issued charging Collins with unlawful flight to avoid confinement for attempted murder. His name was added to the FBI's "Most Wanted" list on May 14, 1963, but agents had no luck in finding him. At the request of local prosecutors, federal warrants against Collins were dismissed on March 30, 1967, leaving him at large, the case unsolved.

194 ■ EDWARD NEWTON NIVENS

A one-time firearms instructor for the United States Army, rated an excellent shot, Ed Nivens had no luck adjusting to civilian life. At forty-two, he had compiled a record of convictions for armed robbery, forgery, and interstate transportation of stolen cars. The latter charge landed him in federal prison, with parole coming early in 1963. He was free only a short time before the lure of easy money got him into trouble once again.

On March 1, 1963, Nivens held up a tavern in Toledo, Ohio, pocketing $375 at gunpoint. Pursued by the bartender and one of his patrons, Nivens shot the customer once, in the stomach, and then commandeered a passing car, forcing the driver to help him escape. Dumping his hostage a few miles away, Nivens abandoned the car nearby and made his escape on foot. Charged with unlawful flight to avoid prosecution for robbery and assault with intent to kill, he was added to the FBI's "Most Wanted" list on May 28, 1964.

Five days later, on June 2, agents in Tampa, Florida, were contacted by citizens who recognized the published photographs of Nivens. Using the name of "George Ferguson," Nivens had gone to work at a local warehouse, loading trucks, and federal officers found him there that afternoon, taking him into custody without resistance. Held under $10,000 bond, his identity confirmed by fingerprints, Nivens waived extradition and was transported back to Ohio for trial.

195 ■ LEWIS FREDERICK VASSELLI

A native of Chicago, born in August 1930, Lew Vasselli chalked up numerous arrests around the Windy City, including convictions for carrying a concealed weapon and violating narcotics laws. In July 1959, he was accused of shooting his brother-in-law and killing the wounded man's brother, but jurors acquitted him of murder charges. (Vasselli was convicted of assault with intent to kill the survivor.) A member of the local gang commanded by hoodlums Nick Guido and Frank

Yonder, Vasselli was part of the team which invaded the Winnetka home of G. Laury Botthoff, a business executive, on May 28, 1961. Botthoff, his wife and two maids were beaten and tortured with lit cigarettes as the bandits attempted to locate their valuables, finally settling for $130 in cash and some minor pieces of jewelry.

Indicted on robbery and narcotics charges by a Chicago grand jury during October 1962, Vasselli posted a total of $55,000 bail before skipping town, a move which did not block the court from convicting him in absentia, imposing a sentence of twenty-five to fifty years imprisonment. Sought by federal agents on a charge of unlawful flight to avoid prosecution, Vasselli was added to the FBI's "Most Wanted" list on June 15, 1964.

By that time, Lew had been arrested on a charge of public drunkenness in San Francisco, but he gave his name as "Theodopholus Riordan," paying a $65 fine before a fingerprint check was completed by local authorities. On the afternoon of September 1, 1964, FBI agents traced their man to a motel in Calumet City, Illinois, where he had resided for several weeks as "Tom Polito." Though armed with a .38-caliber revolver, Vasselli offered no resistance and was taken into custody for transportation to the Illinois state prison.

196 ■ THOMAS EDWARD GALLOWAY

Nine times married, Thomas Galloway occasionally interrupted his pursuit of matrimony with a stay in jail. His record listed prior convictions for assault and battery, petty larceny, aggravated assault, and violations of the Mann Act—transportation of women across state lines for immoral purposes. The latter charge was strictly business, and FBI spokesmen characterized Galloway as "a luxury-loving pimp with an IQ of about 124." For all of his alleged intelligence, however, Galloway seemed bent on living out his life in prison.

On the afternoon of January 29, 1963, St. Louis mobster Paul J. Martorelli was discovered, shot to death, in his convertible. The victim had been partying with Thomas Galloway

the night before, when he was last seen alive, and a fugitive
warrant was issued on charges of murder. Arrested in Spokane, Washington, on February 18, Galloway was returned to
St. Louis for trial, but he forfeited bond and failed to appear
in court on October 28. Charged with unlawful flight to avoid
prosecution, Galloway was added to the "Ten Most Wanted"
list on June 24, 1964.

In Danville, Virginia, newspaper photos of Galloway were
published on July 1, and a resident identified the likeness of
"Roger McNally," a new face at the local golf course. "Mc-
Nally" had been turning up around the club house for a week
or so, shooting games in the seventies and offering tips to
other, less accomplished players. On the morning of July 17,
FBI agents surrounded Galloway on the putting green and
took him into custody without resistance. Held in lieu of
$35,000 bond, he was returned to St. Louis for trial in the
Martorelli slaying.

197 ■ ALSON THOMAS WAHRLICH

In 1957, a Phoenix, Arizona, jury convicted Alson Wahrlich of
aggravated assault and child molesting, sending him up for a
sentence of two to five years in the state penitentiary. Similar
charges consigned him to the Oklahoma state prison a few
years later, but he was paroled in October 1963. It soon became apparent that incarceration had not tamed his hunger in
the least.

On April 15, 1964, Wahrlich was cruising the streets of Tucson in his Renault, when he spotted a six-year-old girl walking
to her neighborhood school. The child declined his offer of a
ride, so Wahrlich forcibly abducted her, driving the girl to a
point several miles from her home. Alson tried to molest the
child, bloodied her nose when she resisted him, and finally
choked her into semi-consciousness, shoving her out of the
moving vehicle. The Renault was found on April 17, forty
miles north of Phoenix, with telltale bloodstains on the passenger's seat. Wahrlich's victim fingered a 1957 mug shot, and
warrants were issued charging him with unlawful flight to

avoid prosecution for kidnapping. On July 9, 1964, his name was added to the "Ten Most Wanted" list.

Three and a half years later, in October 1967, Wahrlich's photograph was published in *Argosy* magazine, with an article covering the "Top Ten" fugitives at large. On Treasure Island, Florida, a seafood company employee recognized the likeness of a truck driver, employed by the firm for approximately three years. The man called his brother-in-law—Treasure Island police officer George Austin—and reported his suspicions. On October 28, Austin, accompanied by an FBI agent and two other policemen, surprised Wahrlich on the job and took him into custody without resistance. Ironically, the fugitive explained that he had managed to elude the FBI with tips provided in a 1964 *Argosy* article, entitled "81 Ways to Hide."

198 ■ KENNETH MALCOLM CHRISTIANSEN

Twice honorably discharged from the Navy, the second time in 1948—at age seventeen—Kenneth Christiansen was arrested that same year, charged with armed robbery and assault following a series of hotel robberies in Portland, Oregon. Extradited to California on similar charges, Christiansen was imprisoned from 1949 to 1951. Two months after being released on parole, he was picked up again, convicted on two counts of first-degree robbery, and returned to prison on two consecutive sentences of five years to life. Paroled again in May 1956, he was seized by Los Angeles police officers in April 1957, on charges of armed robbery and parole violation. A conviction for first-degree robbery, in July 1958, put him back behind bars, a new five-to-life sentence running concurrently with his previous terms. Described by authorities as a heavy narcotics user, Christiansen typically employed masks, theatrical makeup, or fake mustaches as a disguise in his holdups.

On Christmas Eve, 1963, Christiansen and another inmate escaped from the California state prison at Chino. His companion was soon recaptured, in Seattle, but Christiansen remained at large, embarking on a series of "lone wolf" robberies, knocking over a jewelry store in Phoenix, a tavern in

Glendale, California, restaurants and markets in San Gabriel, Santa Monica, La Habra, West Covina, Daly City, San Jose, and San Francisco. A warrant charging him with unlawful flight to avoid confinement was issued on February 11, 1964, and his name was added to the "Top Ten" list July 27.

On September 8, 1964, Christiansen held up a seafood restaurant in Silver Springs, Maryland, stuffing his satchel with $6,000 in cash. The job went sour when the owner's wife ran out of the restaurant, screaming, with Christiansen in pursuit, giving the chef time to telephone police. Outside, a pair of milkmen started chasing Christiansen, joined shortly by Patrolman Charles Kriss. In flight, the outlaw traded gunshots with police, but no one suffered any injuries. Disoriented, running in the wrong direction, Christiansen was collared a block from the police station, as he tried to commandeer a passing car.

The Maryland fiasco carried sentences totaling 107 years, but Christiansen had no intention of doing the time. On May 18, 1967, while returning from a court appearance in a prison vehicle, Christiansen and fellow inmate Harry McClellan pulled a gun on their guards, handcuffing both to a tree before making their getaway. They dumped the stolen car at Dundalk, there abducting motorist Richard Ruger, forcing him to drive them to Baltimore. Nearing their destination, Christiansen shot Ruger in the chest and pushed him from the car, but he survived his wounds to testify against the kidnappers. Soon recaptured, Christiansen had earned himself another block of time, insuring he would never walk the streets again.

199 ■ WILLIAM HUTTON CABLE

Launching his criminal career with a stint in reform school, at age twelve, Cable went on to serve nineteen years of his adult life in various penal institutions. His convictions included robbery, forgery, larceny, housebreaking, and violations of the Dyer Act, with several jail breaks thrown in for good measure. On May 15, 1964, Cable escaped from the city jail in Nashville, Tennessee, where he was confined following conviction for a $34,000 bank robbery at Ardmore. Federal warrants were issued on charges of robbery and prison escape, earning Cable a spot on the "Ten Most Wanted" list on September 11, 1964.

By that time, the fugitive had already settled in Charlotte, North Carolina, arriving in June and renting an apartment under the name of "Marvin Ikard." With a touch of humor, Cable told his landlady he was an FBI agent on secret assignment, swearing her to silence in the interests of national security.

In fact, his business was the same as always. On September 30, as if to celebrate his posting on the "Top Ten" list, Cable looted a small bank in Charlotte of $7,226. Five months later, on March 1, 1965, he tried again at the First Citizens Bank, also in Charlotte, but the caper blew up in his face.

Patrolman Jack Bruce, passing the bank on his rounds, witnessed the holdup in progress and summoned assistance. Shots were exchanged as Cable left the bank, carrying a sack filled with $8,869. Fleeing on foot, the bandit approached a station wagon, occupied by Mrs. E. B. Vosburgh and her two children. Firing as he approached, wounding the woman in both legs, Cable forced everyone out of the car and took off with a screech of the tires.

Patrolman Bruce, arriving seconds too late, flagged down a vehicle driven by Duane Bruch, ordering the startled motorist to "follow that car." Cable led his pursuers on a winding course, over fifteen blocks, before he chose a dead-end street by accident and found himself cut off. He refused to get out of the car until Bruce fired four shots through the windows, at which point the bandit emerged, his hands raised in surrender.

Local conviction on two counts of bank robbery earned Cable 25 years in the state penitentiary. In the event of his parole, he owed another fifteen years to the federal government, for violation of national bank robbery statutes.

200 ■ LLOYD DONALD GREESON , JR.

Lloyd Greeson liked to see himself in uniform, but he could never get the hang of military discipline. During World War II, as a volunteer member of the Canadian army, he was convicted of several crimes while stationed in England. Between 1946 and 1950, he was dishonorably discharged from both the United States Army and the Marine Corps on charges of desertion. Returning to civilian life, he logged arrests for auto theft, aggravated robbery, vagrancy, carrying a weapon, unlawful entry, and theft. Somewhere along the way, perhaps while serving time, he graduated into homicide.

Lola Cotton, age forty-four, of Miami, Florida, was last seen alive—in Lloyd Greeson's company—on the night of May 16, 1964. Her naked, lifeless body was discovered nine days later, at her home. In the meantime, her car had been recovered at Bonita Springs, on May 18. The coroner's report attributed her death to alcohol and barbiturate poisoning, but further investigation revealed that the woman had never voluntarily used drugs. On learning that a valuable ring was missing, homicide investigators obtained warrants charging Lloyd Greeson with grand larceny and auto theft.

On June 16, thirty-seven-year-old Margaret Ayoub, of Wilkes-Barre, Pennsylvania, was found dead in a ditch outside Bloomsburg. Investigation revealed that she had last been seen alive on the night of June 13, when she left a local tavern on Lloyd Greeson's arm. Suspected in two murders and charged with unlawful flight to avoid prosecution, Greeson was added to the FBI's "Ten Most Wanted" list on September 18, 1964.

Four days later, at Perris, California, in Riverside County, an alert citizen recognized Greeson from his photograph, published in a local newspaper. As "Don Francis Merrow," Greeson had been living in nearby Elsinore for the past six weeks, employed as a house painter. Arrested on September 23, the fugitive was held under $25,000 bond on each of the two federal charges against him.

201 ■ RAYMOND LAWRENCE WYNGAARD

By the summer of 1961, Raymond Wyngaard had already spent most of his adult life in prison, confined on a series of convictions for burglary and larceny. On July 24, 1961, he escaped from police custody en route to a Detroit courtroom, where his arraignment was scheduled on new charges of armed robbery. Immediately after his escape, Wyngaard joined an accomplice for a three-day crime spree in Detroit, looting a gun store for weapons and a supermarket for cash, wounding a police officer, robbing ten occupants of a downtown office building, stealing three cars and abducting two motorists. Proclaimed a federal fugitive on charges of unlawful flight to avoid prosecution, Wyngaard was still at large three years later, and his name was added to the FBI's "Most Wanted" list on October 5, 1964.

In late November, federal agents learned that Wyngaard had recently settled in Madison, Wisconsin, renting a small East Side apartment under the alias of "Fred Rogers." On November 28, they were informed, his girlfriend from Chicago, Judith Bocklus, would be coming in by train to stay with Wyngaard for a time.

Recruiting cab driver Richard Green, FBI agents arranged for him to pick up Wyngaard and Bocklus as they emerged from Madison's North Western Station. Driving to a pizzeria designated by his fare, Green was tailed all the way by carloads of G-men, keeping in touch with each other via two-way radios. As they reached their destination, the taxi was surrounded by armed federal officers, who took Wyngaard and Bocklus into custody without resistance. Raymond Wyngaard was held on $15,000 bond pending his return to Michigan; Judith Bocklus was held on $1,500, charged with harboring a federal fugitive. Asked how he felt about making the Bureau's "Top Ten," Wyngaard smiled and said, "I felt sorta hemmed in."

202 ■ NORMAN BELYEA GORHAM

Born in Boston on the first of February 1919, Gorham was a loner with a lengthy record of convictions for armed robbery, auto theft, assault with intent to kill, making a false affidavit, carrying a weapon without authority, assault by means of a dangerous weapon, larceny, possession of burglary tools, and interstate transportation of a stolen car. A veteran of several prisons in New Hampshire and his native Massachusetts, by the early 1960s he had spent most of his adult life behind bars.

On June 18, 1963, Gorham and a male accomplice entered a branch bank in Beverly, Massachusetts, wearing full-face masks and waving pistols at the startled tellers. They escaped in a stolen car after bagging $6,111 in cash, but Gorham's sidekick was swiftly arrested and sentenced to prison for his role in the crime.

Picked up by Boston FBI agents on August 26, following his indictment on federal bank robbery charges, Gorham posted $25,000 bail and promptly skipped town. When he failed to appear for his scheduled trial on November 19, 1963, a federal fugitive warrant was issued for his arrest. His name was added to the FBI's "Most Wanted" list on December 10, 1964. Gorham was traced to Los Angeles on May 27, 1965, and there surrounded by a combined raiding party of federal agents and local police. Surrendering without resistance, he was returned to Massachusetts for trial.

203 ■ JOHN WILLIAM CLOUSER

Chicago-born in 1932, John Clouser became a police officer in Orlando, Florida, and rose swiftly through the ranks, earning his sergeant's stripes after less than five years of service on the force. Along the way, he also became friends with one George Fogel, a local hustler and ex-convict in charge of a major abortion ring. Clouser professed surprise when Fogel was arrested, after long surveillance, but his fellow officers were skeptical, believing Clouser to be "dirty." When Clouser refused to confess participation in the abortion racket, high-ranking members of the force allegedly retaliated by procuring false statements from local prostitutes, claiming sexual relationships with Clouser, and furnished these to Clouser's wife. Following the break-up of his marriage, Clouser resigned from the force in disgust.

Another ex-policeman, Mike Trestlee, introduced civilian Clouser to some local hoodlums and gamblers, including Donald Marshall, Allie Brown, Tim Peterman, Toby Thomas, and Kenny Diamond. Arrested for burglary, Thomas implicated Peterman as an accomplice; Peterman, in turn, gave information on the recent holdup of a theater. Detectives "urged" Peterman to identify Clouser as one of the robbers, and Clouser fled to Tampa, where he was soon arrested and returned for trial. Rejecting a plea bargain, Clouser was convicted by a jury; he was sentenced to thirty years for armed robbery, ten years for kidnapping a theater employee, and five years each on charges of conspiracy and aggravated assault.

After two years in prison, Clouser's verdict was overturned by an appeals court, citing irregular conduct on the part of his prosecutor. Released pending retrial, Clouser began firing off angry letters to the district attorney and the FBI, signing some with a self-chosen nickname, "The Florida Fox." The D.A., meanwhile, was busy filing new charges against Clouser charging him with the robberies of a gas station and liquor store, along with efforts to intimidate his former wife and thereby keep her silent on the witness stand. Acquitted of the robberies, satisfied with a mistrial when his jury failed to reach a decision on the extortion charges, Clouser still faced retrial on the original robbery charge.

Grasping at straws, Clouser tried to ride out the final six months of a hostile prosecutor's term in office by faking insanity, having himself sent to the Chattahoochee state hospital for observation. There, confronted with a diagnosis of psychosis which threatened him with long-term confinement, Clouser escaped on April 6, 1964. A month later, he was detained in Myrtle Beach, South Carolina, as the alleged accomplice of a burglar killed by police. Released after questioning, he was not recognized as a fugitive. When Clouser began mailing threats to Orlando's chief of police, his name was added to the "Ten Most Wanted" list as a special eleventh addition, on January 7, 1965.

By August 1965, Clouser had settled in Los Angeles, living as "John Ripley." Picked up by local police in a routine sweep of "new faces," he was released once again without being identified. Later, two FBI agents visited Clouser at work, in a Goodyear plant, but he refused to volunteer his fingerprints and bluffed the agents down by shouting about his constitutional rights. (Both agents subsequently received one-month suspensions for losing their man.) Still under surveillance, Clouser was prepared for arrest on August 12, when the Watts riot disrupted a stakeout and gave him time to flee the city.

As a fugitive, Clouser remained at large for ten years, four months, and nineteen days, traveling through forty-four states and fourteen other nations in his flight. Federal process was dismissed against him on August 1, 1972, but he still faced problems with the law. On June 8, 1974, he was accused of attempted rape by a "friend" who withdrew her charges the next day; in the meantime, Clouser fled to Chicago before a check could be run on his fingerprints. Collaborating with author Dave Fisher, Clouser agreed to a private mental examination, conducted at Mt. Sinai Hospital, and then surrendered to authorities, at Tallahassee, Florida, on August 21, 1974.

Denied a change of venue by the court, Clouser was faced with the prospect of another conviction—and thirty-year sentence—or a plea bargain, with a guaranteed maximum sentence of five years for time served and became eligible for parole after fourteen months in jail.

204 ■ WALTER LEE PARMAN

A native of the Philippines, Parman came to the United States early in life, logging his first juvenile arrests—for unauthorized use of an auto—at Washington, D.C., during 1949 and 1951. Occasionally working as an aircraft mechanic or business machine repairman, he was later arrested in California, Texas, Colorado, Kansas, Missouri and Minnesota. Most of his crimes involved false pretenses, and Parman—married and the father of two children—had no history of violent crime before the early days of 1965.

At 7 A.M., January 9, 1965, the body of Shirley Ann Cary, a thirty-two-year-old secretary at the Department of State, was found in a Washington alley. Nude upon discovery, she had been strangled and molested; local officers reported that "the body bore markings that indicated the murderer is a sex pervert." The victim was last seen alive, by a co-worker, around 3:30 that morning. She had been drinking in an after-hours club with Walter Parman.

A local warrant charging Parman with first-degree murder was issued on January 11. Confronted with evidence that their suspect had fled the District of Columbia, federal agents sought a warrant charging him with unlawful flight to avoid prosecution for murder. Parman's name was added to the Bureau's "Top Ten" list on January 15, 1965.

On January 31, a tip led G-men to the small Los Angeles apartment where Parman had been hiding out as "George Farr." He offered no resistance, but the agents confiscated a .25-caliber pistol, along with a note apparently meant for use in a future bank robbery. Safely in custody, Parman declared, "I'm glad it's over. I'm tired of running from the FBI."

205 ■ GENE THOMAS WEBB

On September 29, 1964—with accomplices Robert Cody, Frank Macias, and Richard Riccio—Gene Webb robbed a Chicago jewelry store of $10,000 in cash. Leaving the scene, the outlaws were surprised by police officers, and shots were exchanged. The thieves finally escaped after taking the proprietor and two other persons hostage, using them as human shields to make their getaway.

Cody, Macias, and Riccio were soon captured, but Gene Webb was still at large four months later, and his name was added to the FBI's "Most Wanted" list on February 11, 1965. One day later, he was spotted by a team of federal agents patrolling the streets of his native Lemont, Illinois, not far from Chicago, and was taken into custody without incident.

206 ■ SAMUEL JEFFERSON VENEY
207 ■ EARL VENEY

The first "family act" to win inclusion on the FBI's "Most Wanted" list, Samuel Veney and his baby brother Earl ran afoul of the law with a 1964 Christmas Eve crime spree in Baltimore, Maryland. With three male accomplices, the brothers had knocked over two liquor stores without difficulty, but they ran into trouble on number three. Emerging with $2,379 in cash, Samuel shot and wounded Lieutenant Joseph Maskell, the first policeman to arrive in answer to the store's silent alarm. Hours later, at 4 A.M. Christmas morning, police Sgt. Jack Cooper was found, shot to death near his cruiser, on a Baltimore street. Samuel Veney's driver's license lay on the front seat of the patrol car, and other pieces of ID were scattered at the scene.

On December 28, 1964, Samuel Veney was indicted on charges of first-degree murder, assault with intent to kill, and three counts of armed robbery. Brother Earl was likewise charged with everything except the death of Sgt. Cooper. Federal warrants, charging unlawful flight to avoid prosecution, were issued against the brothers on December 29. While their accomplices were soon arrested, Sam and Earl remained elusive. Added to the Bureau's "Ten Most Wanted" list on February 25, 1965, Samuel was joined by his brother eight days later, on March 5.

On March 11, 1965, an agent with the Federal Bureau of Narcotics recognized one of the brothers on a street in Garden City, New York. Keeping the fugitive under close surveillance, he managed to notify the FBI, and agents swept the brothers up together, moments later. The Veneys were held without bond, pending extradition to Maryland for trial and sentencing.

208 ■ DONALD STEWART HEIEN

Minneapolis-born in June 1937, Donald Heien was a heroin addict and trigger-happy holdup artist primarily active in California. On January 31, 1956, he robbed and murdered a Whittier gas station attendant, making off with the victim's .38 revolver for use in future robberies. On March 12, attempting to rob another service station in Lomita, he panicked and shot the attendant once in the chest, leaving him critically wounded. On arrest, Heien confessed to a series of similar robberies in the Los Angeles area, aimed at supporting his drug habit.

Convicted of the robbery-murder in Whittier, Heien was sentenced to life in San Quentin. He escaped from the prison on May 4, 1964, and a federal warrant charging him with unlawful flight to avoid confinement was issued on August 17. His name was added to the bureau's "Top Ten" list on March 11, 1965.

Eleven months later, on February 3, 1966, FBI agents found Heien on the opposite side of the continent. Hiding out in Newton, Massachusetts, he was traced by federal investigators and surrendered to arrest without resistance. Heien was returned to California for completion of his sentence, with additional time added for the escape.

209 ■ ARTHUR PIERCE , JR.

At age twenty-eight, Arthur Pierce had a record of nine felony arrests, with three resulting in convictions for burglary and auto banditry. The latter charge had earned him ten years in the Indiana State Reformatory, but Pierce served only three before his release, in February 1964. Settling in Indianapolis, he registered as a parolee and soon began dating Mabel Toney, age forty-two, a mother of three whose husband was also serving time. As the relationship progressed, Pierce moved in with Mabel and her fifteen-year-old daughter, Norma Jean, in their apartment on the city's east side.

On June 13, 1964, mother and daughter were found dead in their home, stretched out side-by-side on Mabel Toney's bed. As homicide detectives reconstructed the event, Mabel had been strangled where she lay; her killer then went on to rape and strangle Norma Jean, depositing her naked body on the bed, beside her mother's corpse. Both victims had been covered to their shoulders with a blanket.

Surviving members of the Toney clan immediately fingered Arthur Pierce, reporting that he carried an illegal pistol in his car from time to time. Indicted on a charge of double murder, Pierce was named a federal fugitive on charges of unlawful flight to avoid prosecution. His name was added to the "Ten Most Wanted" list on March 24, 1965.

The killer's flight had carried him to New York state, where he secured employment at a hotel in the Catskills. There, Pierce met and wed a twenty-year-old waitress; in September 1964, they rented an apartment in Spring Valley, New York, shelling out fifteen dollars a week while Pierce went to work as a painting and wallpaper contractor.

On March 25, one day after his addition to the "Top Ten" list, Pierce was fingered by a neighbor who recognized his published photograph. FBI agents arrested him at home, without resistance, and drove him to New York City, where he was held in lieu of $25,000 bond pending extradition.

210 ■ DONALD DEAN RAINEY

Convicted of auto theft in 1948 and armed robbery in 1951, Don Rainey never seemed to learn from his mistakes. On May 25, 1956, he entered the Del Rey branch of the Bank of America, in Fresno, California, firing a pistol slug into the wall before he raided the cash drawers for $5,147. Arrested in Mexico and returned to California for trial, he was convicted on federal bank robbery charges and packed off to Leavenworth, serving nearly eight years before his conditional release in April 1964.

Still on parole eight months later, on December 8, Rainey returned to the same Fresno bank with his sixteen-year-old son, Gerald. Waving a pistol while Gerald brandished a sawed-off shotgun, the father-son team netted $19,995 for their efforts. Unfortunately for the bandits, witnesses secured the license number of their car, which Donald had rented in Fresno, using his own name. Federal warrants were issued immediately, charging both Raineys with bank robbery, and Donald made the "Ten Most Wanted" list on March 26, 1965.

Less than three months later, on June 18, Gerald Rainey was arrested by federal agents in Brownsville, Texas. Faced with the prospect of serious jail time, the boy started talking. One June 22, G-men were waiting in Nogales, Arizona, when Don Rainey crossed the border out of Mexico. Bearded, wearing a cowboy hat pulled down to cover his eyes, Rainey carried $11,000 cash and a loaded .38, but he had no chance to use either as agents took him into custody. He was held in lieu of $35,000 bond, pending trial on new federal charges.

211 ■ LESLIE DOUGLAS ASHLEY

A native of Houston, Texas, Ashley logged his first arrest in Los Angeles, during 1955. A heavy smoker who wore gaudy jewelry and carried a Bible, frequently quoting snatches of scripture, he also had a history of working as a female impersonator in clubs catering to homosexuals. In February 1961, with accomplice Carolyn Lima, Leslie interrupted a sex party at the office of Houston real estate broker Fred Tomes by shooting his host six times, later cremating the body in a ditch. Ashley was dressed as a woman when New York police bagged the killers three weeks later; his confession brought a death sentence, later overturned on appeal. Before his retrial, Ashley was declared insane, committed to the maximum-security ward of the San Antonio Mental Hospital until he was deemed fit for trial. (Carolyn Lima, convicted in her second trial, received a five-year sentence; with credit for time served since her arrest, she was released in April 1965.)

On October 6, 1964, Ashley took advantage of lax security at the Texas hospital to make his escape. The resultant scandal led to the dismissal of several staff members, and Ashley was declared a federal fugitive, charged with unlawful flight to avoid confinement. On April 6, 1965, his name was added to the FBI's "Most Wanted" list.

Two weeks later, on April 20, Ashley found work with a traveling carnival as "Bobo the Clown." The show was playing

Atlanta on April 23, when co-worker Jerry Auten noticed a brunette woman's wig and an FBI "Wanted" poster in Ashley's open suitcase. After a quick consultation with his fellow carnies, Auten called the FBI.

"Bobo the Clown" was dozing in his trailer when federal agents reached the grounds of the Carver Boys Club. Arrested without resistance, the fugitive was held on $50,000 bond pending extradition to Texas. In San Antonio, directors of the mental hospital announced their decision that Ashley had been feigning insanity all along. Accordingly, they recommended that he be immediately tried upon return.

212 ■ CHARLES BRYAN HARRIS

Reputedly a member of a widespread moonshine syndicate, "Black Charlie" Harris was no stranger to the inside of a jail. Accused of murdering a neighbor during 1961, he managed to persuade a jury of his innocence, but prosecutors felt he had been something less than honest on the witness stand. They were considering a charge of perjury, when Harris let his rampant jealousy explode in violence and sudden death.

Betty Shockley-Newton had been dating Harris through the early spring of 1964, but she had found herself another beau by summer. Betty's new intended, William Jerry Meritt, lived near Fairfield, Illinois, in a wooded area, the Pine Creek bottoms. Charlie Harris found them there on August 16, 1964, and riddled both with bullets, setting fire to Meritt's home before he fled.

As homicide detectives put the facts together, Harris was indicted on a double charge of murder, with a single count of arson; perjury, relating to his trial in 1961, was added almost as an afterthought. The FBI began to search for Charlie, acting on a federal warrant charging him with unlawful flight to avoid prosecution for arson and murder. On May 6, 1965, his name was added to the Bureau's "Ten Most Wanted" list.

Six weeks later, on the seventeenth of June, a resident of Fairfield tipped the FBI that Harris had been hiding in a house outside of town. Surrounded by a flying squad of federal officers, the murder suspect grinned and told them, "I'm your man."

Held in lieu of $50,000 bond, Harris pled not guilty to the several charges. Arsonists destroyed his Fairfield hideaway September 30, but it was far too late to cover Charlie's tracks. Convicted by a jury on November 3, he drew a term of sixty years in prison.

213 ■ WILLIAM ALBERT AUTUR TAHL

From the age of three, William Tahl was frequently arrested for a variety of petty crimes. But in the spring of 1965, when he was twenty-seven Tahl's law-breaking became violent.

On April Fool's Day, Tahl approached his husband-and-wife employers, Mr. and Mrs. Victor Bowen, at the Mission Bay Yacht Club in San Diego, California. Brandishing a shotgun, he demanded cash, and was indignantly refused. Impulsively, Tahl shot both victims, killing Mrs. Bowen instantly; her husband would survive just long enough to name the gunman for police.

Mere hours later, still on April 1, Tahl invaded a nearby apartment, threatening to stab a two-year-old child if the boy's teenaged mother did not submit to intercourse. Following the rape, he fled from California, giving San Diego officers the slip, and set his sights on Texas. In El Paso, Tahl acquired a bogus driver's license, draft card, and Social Security number in the name of "Arthur Spencer," moving on to Dallas as he searched for work.

In Dallas, Tahl made friends with Allen Wright, age 24, and shortly moved his few belongings into Wright's apartment. There, on April 26, a neighbor found Wright's body—naked, torn by knife wounds—and police began a search for "Arthur Spencer," on another count of murder.

Tahl, meanwhile, was hiding in Fort Worth. While there, he "found" a Social Security card in the name of "J. D. Baxter," usurping that identity as he evacuated Texas, homing on St. Louis. Back in Dallas, "Arthur Spencer" had been made as William Tahl, and federal warrants had begun to multiply on charges of unlawful flight. Tahl's name was added to the FBI's "Most Wanted" list on June 10, 1965.

Tahl's latest buddy, in St. Louis, was a teacher by the name of Marvin Thomas. After several meetings, Tahl moved into Thomas's apartment, watching from a distance as the FBI continued their pursuit across the great Southwest. Come autumn, William's cash and self-control evaporated simultaneously; on November 5 he bound his roommate, battered Thomas with a sock containing buckshot, and coerced the teacher into signing four $100 checks, made out to "J. D. Baxter." Leaving the apartment shortly after 1 A.M., Tahl had no way of knowing that a neighbor had already called police.

St. Louis officers arrived to rescue Thomas, listening as he related details of his ordeal. They were still on hand when Tahl returned, but they proved careless in allowing him to use the bathroom prior to making the arrest. Emerging with a pistol pointed at himself, Tahl threatened suicide, revealing his identity and startling police with details of his several homicides. An hour and twenty minutes passed before he finally surrendered and was carted off to jail, awaiting the arrival of the FBI.

214 ■ DUANE EARL POPE

A mild-mannered Kansas farm boy, widely admired and respected in his home community, Duane Pope was every parent's dream. Respectful of his elders, regular in church and school, the young man clearly had potential. Captain of the varsity football team during his senior year at MacPherson College, Pope graduated on May 30, 1965, at the age of twenty-two.

Five days later, his world exploded.

At a quarter past eleven in the morning, June 4, 1965, Duane Pope parked his green rental car outside the Farmers State Bank in Big Springs, Nebraska. He cut a dashing figure as he entered, dressed in suit and tie, the briefcase that he carried making him resemble a young lawyer or executive.

Inside the bank, Pope spoke with the president, elderly Andreas Kjelgaard, about a farm loan. Informed that the bank did not engage in such transactions, Duane opened his briefcase, extracting an automatic pistol with a silencer attached. Moving swiftly into the cashier's cage, Pope scooped $1,598 into his valise, but the vault was secured with a time lock, and he could not afford to wait.

Andreas Kjelgaard, age seventy-seven, was forced to lie face-down on the floor, beside his nephew Frank, cashier Glenn Hendrickson, and bookkeeper Lois Hothan. Moving down the line, Pope shot each hostage twice—once in the nape of the neck, once in the back—before casually leaving the bank. Of the four, only Frank Kjelgaard would survive his wounds, paralyzed from the waist down by a bullet in his spine.

FBI agents were immediately involved in the case, investigating the federal offenses of bank robbery and murder of a bank employee. Pope had rented the getaway car in his own name, and snapshots of the smiling murderer were readily identified by witnesses. His name was added to the Bureau's "Ten Most Wanted" list on June 11, 1965.

That day, a short time after the announcement was released, Pope telephoned police in Kansas City. Convicted in Nebraska, months later, on a triple charge of murder, he was sentenced to die.

215 ■ ALLEN WADE HAUGSTED

A native of Minneapolis, born in January 1931, Haugsted chalked up a lengthy record of juvenile arrests for theft before a 1950 conviction on charges of grand larceny sent him to the Minnesota State Reformatory. On release, he put his mind to going straight, holding down jobs as a cook, handyman, janitor, and motion picture projectionist before settling on a career as a baker. By the mid-1960s he was recognized as an accomplished baker, successful in business, but his marriage had foundered on the rocks of Haugsted's violent temper, setting the stage for a homicidal rampage.

On the night of February 19, 1965, Haugsted invaded the

home of his mother-in-law near Willmar, Minnesota, killing his estranged wife with gunshots to the head and chest. Clubbing his mother-in-law to the floor, Allen finished her off with three bullets and turned on the other occupants of the house. He shot his own seven-year-old daughter in the head, leaving her critically wounded, and also inflicted a superficial gunshot wound on his brother-in-law before fleeing the scene.

Indicted locally for murder and attempted murder, Haugsted was also named in federal warrants charging him with unlawful flight to avoid prosecution. His name was added to the FBI's "Most Wanted" list on June 24, 1965, but the homicidal baker had six months of freedom remaining. Federal agents tracked him to Houston, Texas, in December, making the arrest on December 23, and Haugsted was returned to Minnesota for trial on outstanding charges.

216 ■ THEODORE MATTHEW BRECHTEL

Convicted of armed robbery in Louisiana, during 1956, Brechtel was on parole when he was picked up with a sawed-off shotgun and packed off to prison for violation of the National Firearms Act. Held for observation at a federal hospital in New Orleans, he escaped from the second floor window of his room on May 7, 1964, and was declared a fugitive on charges of unlawful flight to avoid confinement. Still at large thirteen months later, he was added to the "Ten Most Wanted" list on June 30, 1965.

By that time, Brechtel had been residing in Chicago for eleven months, as "Roy Channing," employed at the local Ekco Products Company. Fingered by a co-worker who recognized his published photograph, the fugitive was taken into custody at work, without resistance, on August 16, 1965.

217 ■ ROBERT ALLEN WOODFORD

A hard-luck bandit, Woodford had been recently paroled from an armed robbery conviction, in the state of California, when he was arrested and charged with violation of the federal bank robbery statute. After some discussion, federal indictments were withdrawn, and Woodford was scheduled for release to California authorities in San Francisco, as a parole violator, to finish the remainder of his standing sentence.

Suddenly, his luck began to change.

Instead of being handed over to the state authorities, as planned, Woodford was inadvertently released in December 1964. Never one to look a gift horse in the mouth, he took to his heels, and a federal warrant was issued charging him with unlawful flight to avoid confinement. On July 2, 1965, his name was added to the FBI's "Most Wanted" list.

Two months later, in the early-morning hours of August 5, a squad of FBI men, acting on a tip, surprised Woodford in his Seattle hotel room. Though armed with a .22-caliber revolver, he made no attempt to resist. In custody, he voiced relief that he had been arrested by the FBI, instead of local officers, because "You're such nice guys." Woodford was held in lieu of $20,000 bond in Seattle, pending extradition to California for completion of his prison term.

218 ■ WARREN CLEVELAND OSBORNE

Osborne's prison record dated from 1936, with a list of convictions for auto theft, grand larceny and robbery. While most of his offenses had the "normal" economic motives, Warren also suffered from a violent temper, aggravated by his morbid jealousy, producing fits of rage. In July 1964, briefly at liberty, he invaded a Nashville, Tennessee, beauty salon, bent on shooting his estranged wife. When beautician Anna Corlew tried to stop him, Osborne shot her dead on the spot, pausing to wound cab driver Homer Lee Hannah in his flight from the scene.

Indicted on murder charges, Osborne was declared a fugitive from justice, charged in federal warrants with unlawful flight to avoid prosecution. His name was added to the "Ten Most Wanted" list on August 12, 1965.

Meanwhile, tragedy continued to stalk the Osborne family. On August 1, 1965, Charles Osborne—Warren's brother— sold the combination motel and trailer park which he had operated with his wife, in Charlotte, North Carolina. The asking price was $250,000, and the Osbornes would have been well-off . . . if they had lived. A short month later, on September 7, Warren's brother and sister-in-law were found dead in their home, slain in a grim murder/suicide.

Unknown to Warren Osborne, his luck had turned again. On September 9, he checked into a Louisville, Kentucky, motel where he had stayed on previous occasions, registered as a businessman from Florence, Alabama. That evening, Police Chief Frank Judd was observing highway traffic near Mt. Washington, Kentucky, when a vehicle flashed past him, easily exceeding posted speeds. Giving chase, Chief Judd hit speeds of 115 miles an hour before he backed off, using his radio to arrange for a roadblock in front of the speeder.

Officers would never get their chance to block the car, however. Three miles out of town, Osborne's car left the pavement, crashed and rolled. Behind the wheel, Warren Osborne was killed on impact, deprived of any opportunity to explain the large amount of cash in his possession. In all, police counted out $22,000, neatly divided into four bundles of $100 bills. Its source remains a mystery, but Osborne scarcely reached his grave before his two ex-wives filed suit to claim the money for themselves.

219 ■ HOLICE PAUL BLACK

Shortly after 9 o'clock, on the morning of August 4, 1965, Holice Black and his younger brother, Richard, entered Chicago's Treasure Island Food Mart with pistols in hand. Holding the manager and cashier at bay, they scooped $3,000 into a tattered paper bag—unaware that the sack had a rip in the bottom.

Outside, Sgt. Charles Eichorst of the Chicago Police Department was checking complaints of a broken parking meter when a citizen informed him of the market robbery in progress. Sending his informant off to hail a passing squad car, Eichorst hastened to the store, arriving just as Richard Black emerged. Believing there had only been one robber, Eichorst was about to frisk his suspect when Holice Black came out shooting, drilling the policeman with a fatal bullet through the forehead.

The brothers fled, dropping their loot in the process and making off with an empty sack. Behind them, they left perfect sets of fingerprints throughout the market, easily compared to records from their juvenile arrests. As if to cinch the case, one brother paused to leave his shirt nearby, an unpaid traffic ticket in the pocket serving as his calling card.

Murder indictments were filed against both brothers, and federal warrants charged them with unlawful flight to avoid prosecution. On August 25, Holice Black—identified as the triggerman in Eichorst's death—was added to the list of "Ten Most Wanted" fugitives.

The brothers hung together for a while. On September 14, they were linked with the murder of a St. Louis liquor store proprietor, shot down in the course of another robbery. In early October, FBI agents obtained evidence that Holice and Richard had gone their separate ways, and on December 14, 1965, a tipster reported that Holice had moved to Miami.

In fact, the fugitive had surfaced in Dade County by November 20, traveling and renting accommodations as "Fred Perkins." A round-the-clock search of Miami bore fruit at 4:30 A.M., December 15, when landlord Joe Smalley identified Black's photograph as one of his tenants. Agents were waiting when Holice came downstairs at seven o'clock, and they found him unarmed, confirming his identity by means of a unique scar on his left hand. In custody, the killer said, "I'm quite relieved. I was tired of looking over my shoulder."

220 ■ EDWARD OWEN WATKINS

Pittsburgh-born in April 1919, Watkins logged his first felony conviction at age twenty and thereafter spent most of his adult life in prison or on the run. A specialist in bank heists, he was dubbed "Fast Eddy" after his technique—a quick entry, melodramatic display of a firearm or bomb, followed by rapid looting of the till and a hasty exit. In the course of his career, Ed Watkins robbed sixty-one banks, broke out of federal lockups on three occasions, and staged several other escapes from local jails.

In the summer of 1965, Fast Eddy was up to his old tricks, staging a series of bank jobs throughout Ohio. Federal warrants were issued against him in Cleveland, on July 12 and 13, with another released at Columbus on September 1. One of the Cleveland warrants named his wife, fourteen years Eddy's junior, as an accomplice to the crime. Already on parole when he began his latest spree, Watkins netted some $103,000 from the holdups. In one of the robberies, in Cleveland, he threatened to use the employees for "target practice" after one of them tried to sound an alarm.

Watkins was added to the Bureau's "Top Ten" list on September 21, 1965, but there seemed to be no stopping him. The larcenous couple pulled several bank jobs in Arizona and New Mexico during the summer of 1966, gravitating toward Montana in August. As "Robert and Dee Johnson," they rented a small house at Sweeney Creek, a few miles from Florence, embarking on sporadic "business trips" to hit banks as far away as Minneapolis and Spokane.

On December 2, 1966, Veda Dietzman, a local cafe owner, recognized Eddy's mug shot in a detective magazine, reporting her information to local authorities. Sheriff Dale Dye and FBI Special Agent John Moe collared Watkins that afternoon, outside the Florence post office, relieving him of an automatic pistol as they took him into custody. Eddy groused that he would have "shot it out," if they had come for him at home, where he maintained his arsenal. An hour later, with his wife in jail, the round-up was complete.

Convicted of six robberies, Watkins was sentenced to forty-five years in prison, but his story was far from complete. Back on the street in 1975, he staged another bank heist in Cleveland, taking seven hostages before a heart attack compelled him to surrender. During 1980, he escaped from the federal prison in Atlanta, robbing seven more banks during five weeks of freedom. Captured at a roadblock in Ohio, slightly wounded in a brief exchange of gunfire, Watkins was returned to prison—in a more secure Wisconsin lockup.

221 ■ JOEL SINGER

Assisted by his uncle, Jack Frank, Canadian Joel Singer staged a criminal coup on October 24, 1965, using an anti-tank cannon to blast open the vault in a Brink's office, at Syracuse, New York. The bandits escaped with $161,000 in cash and $292,587 in non-negotiable securities.

By November 1, Frank was in custody, spilling everything he knew about the crime in return for a grant of total immunity from prosecution. According to his statement, he had purchased two 20-mm anti-tank guns in Alexandria, Virginia, along with 200 rounds of armor-piercing ammunition. The purchase was Singer's idea, and his nephew had fronted the money. Ironically, FBI agents and officers of the Royal Canadian Mounted Police had been aware of the purchase, tracking the weapons on suspicion of a link to terrorist activity, but Singer was alerted to the surveillance, and he "stole" the shipment in a warehouse burglary, at Plattsburg, New York, on the night of April 7, 1965. To prove himself, Frank led a team of agents to a bridge, near Jones Beach, New York, where the cannon was discarded following the burglary.

On November 17, 1965, Joel Singer was indicted on a charge of third-degree burglary. Further charges of first-degree larceny were subsequently filed, and his name was added to the FBI's "Most Wanted" list on November 19.

Twelve days later, on the evening of December 1, Joel Singer was arrested by detectives in his native Montreal. A vial of nitroglycerine was found inside his auto, parked nearby. In his possession the arresting officers found $188.35; no other loot from the Brink's job was ever recovered.

Singer battled extradition, but in vain. Convicted during 1966, he drew a term of five to ten years in prison. On July 27, 1972, Singer was transferred from the state penitentiary at Clinton, New York, to a mental hospital, where he received therapy for an apparent breakdown. On parole in early 1973, he returned to Montreal, and was found dead in his apartment there, on February 9. An autopsy discovered traces of cyanide in his system, and his death was ruled a suicide.

222 ■ JAMES EDWARD KENNEDY

James Kennedy launched his criminal career during 1954, in Massachusetts, with brief incarceration on a charge of breaking and entering. In 1955, he was sent to the Ohio State Reformatory for a period of one to fifteen years, convicted in a string of burglaries and housebreakings. Kennedy escaped, but was recaptured in 1956, when police raided a Massachusetts roadhouse. Paroled in October of that year, he was jailed a month later for bank robbery, earning a twenty-year stretch on conviction. In January 1961—once more on parole—he was convicted of breaking into a dairy and returned to prison as a parole violator; his new sentence of ten to twenty years was suspended. In November 1963, conviction of a bank robbery in Columbus, Ohio, returned him to prison for another twenty years.

While serving out that sentence, Kennedy was driven from the federal penitentiary to Cleveland, pending trial in a holdup he pulled before the Columbus bank robbery. On November 10, 1964, he sawed through the bars of his fourth-floor cell, employing smuggled hacksaw blades, and broke out of the Cuyahoga County jail. Federal warrants were issued, on a charge of unlawful flight to avoid confinement, and Kennedy was added to the FBI's "Most Wanted" list on December 8, 1965.

The fugitive then returned to Massachusetts. FBI agents received a tip that Kennedy and a companion, parole violator Paul Davis, had flown into Boston's Logan Airport on December 23, rented a car, and proceeded toward Worcester. G-men had no trouble recognizing Kennedy, as he drove past one of their stakeouts, and a brief pursuit ended with Kennedy's vehicle rammed to the curb beneath a highway overpass. Cornered, he opened fire, but quickly dropped his weapon after suffering a superficial wound.

223 ■ LAWRENCE JOHN HIGGINS

The holder of a felony record spanning thirty years, Higgins was released from his latest confinement—five years for burglary and grand larceny in Arkansas—on January 28, 1965. Eighteen days later, on February 15, he held up the Crocker-Citizens National Bank in Covina, California, and was declared a federal fugitive. His name was added to the FBI's "Most Wanted" list on December 14, 1965.

Following the Covina robbery, Higgins had traveled to northern California, finding work as a chef at a Sacramento rest home. On January 3, 1966, a highway patrolman saw Higgins driving erratically near Emigrant Gap, and he was taken into custody on a charge of drunken driving. Examination of records for the California Department of Motor Vehicles and the State Bureau of Criminal Identification and Investigation confirmed his identity, at which point the FBI was notified of his arrest.

224 ■ HOYT BUD COBB

An alcoholic and narcotics addict, Cobb financed his expensive habits through robbery, eventually turning to murder. Convicted in the fatal beating of a Georgia holdup victim, Cobb was serving life when he escaped from the state prison, at Jessup, in April 1965. A federal warrant was routinely issued, charging him with unlawful flight to avoid confinement.

On July 20, 1965, fifty-eight-year-old Frances Johnson, a door-to-door cosmetics saleswoman, vanished from her home in Tampa, Florida. One day later, Joe Cross, a gas station attendant in Dade County, noticed blood dripping from the trunk of a customer's car. Cross made note of the license number, which matched that of Frances Johnson's missing vehicle. Upon recovery, the car yielded fingerprints, and Joe Cross identified Cobb's mug shot as a likeness of the nervous driver.

Frances Johnson's decomposing body was discovered on September 26, beneath a quilt, on a deserted path northeast of Tampa. An indictment for first-degree murder was returned against Hoyt Cobb, and his name was added to the FBI's "Most Wanted" list on January 6, 1966.

Five months later, to the day, a tip led federal officers to the address in Hialeah, where their man—as "Robert Jones" —had been residing. Cobb was taken into custody without resistance and returned to Tampa for his murder trial.

225 ■ JAMES ROBERT BISHOP

A native of Greenville, South Carolina, Bishop boasted a long record of felony convictions by the time he reached Arizona, late in the summer of 1963. On September 28, he confronted Bud Hamish, manager of a Phoenix Safeway store, holding one hand inside a paper bag and demanding that Hamish fill a second bag with money. Hamish complied, handing over $500, and the thief fled. Upon his identification, from mug shots, Bishop was indicted on a charge of armed robbery, simultaneously declared a federal fugitive on charges of unlawful flight to avoid prosecution. With his record in mind, Bishop's name was added to the "Top Ten" list on January 10, 1966.

Nine days later, the fugitive found employment at an Aspen, Colorado, restaurant, as a kitchen helper. Co-workers soon identified his published photographs, and the FBI was notified on January 21. That afternoon, two agents visited the restaurant and took their man without resistance. Held for extradition to the state of Arizona, he was subsequently sent to prison on the robbery charge.

226 ■ ROBERT VAN LEWING

Born in 1922, Robert Van Lewing chalked up an impressive record of arrests and convictions for robbery before he was named to the "Ten Most Wanted" list on January 12, 1966. Two months later, on March 29, he was identified as the lone gunman who entered a St. Louis savings and loan office, displaying a pistol as he handed the teller a note demanding large bills. Van Lewing fled with $2,456 in cash, but his mug shots were identified by three witnesses at the scene. Wise enough to leave St. Louis in the face of mounting heat, he still refused to leave Missouri. Traced to Kansas City on February 6, 1967, Van Lewing was arrested without incident by agents of the FBI.

227 ■ EARL ELLERY WRIGHT

Chalking up his first arrest at age fourteen, in November 1942, for stealing a bicycle at Kingsport, Tennessee, Earl Wright eventually logged convictions in eleven states and the District of Columbia, on felony counts including auto theft, breaking and entering, grand theft, and interstate theft. By summer 1964, Earl thought that he was ready for the big time.

On June 17, 1964, the ex-convict raided a bank at Greenup, Kentucky, for $173,989. Emboldened by instant success, he moved on to other jobs. On January 8, 1965, he tried to knock over a bank in Washington, D.C., but finally fled empty-handed. Five months later, on June 21, he was luckier with the robbery of a trust company in Coral Hills, Maryland. On November 17, Wright looted another bank in Ashland, Ohio.

Along the way, there had been scattered clues enough for FBI agents to identify their man. Charged with violations of the federal bank robbery statutes, Wright was listed as a fugitive, his name appended to the "Ten Most Wanted" list on January 14, 1966.

Traced to a downtown motel in Cleveland, Ohio, Wright was captured by the FBI on June 20, 1966. A guilty plea in federal court earned him a sentence of thirty-five years; he was paroled in 1978, after serving slightly more than one-third of his sentence.

Upon release from prison, Wright settled in Parma, Ohio, remaining there until his eviction, in September 1979, for nonpayment of rent. By that time, local authorities were already probing his involvement in cases of fraud and the illegal use of a credit card. On September 1, he robbed a bank in North Olmstead, Ohio, making off with $14,619 in cash.

Warrants were issued on November 14, but Wright had already moved on to Huntington, West Virginia. On December 4, 1979, he raided a bank in nearby Kenova, dumping $37,900 into a plastic bag before he locked employees in the vault, leaving one outside to telephone authorities. While FBI agents tried to pick up his trail, Wright was already casing his next job.

On February 23, 1980, he invaded a bank at Berea, Ohio, taking four hostages when police surrounded the building. The siege dragged on for twenty-two hours, during which time Wright incinerated $11,000 in currency, finally surrendering when authorities agreed that he would not be sent to any one of several prisons which he deemed objectionable. Convicted in federal court on two counts of bank robbery, in April 1980, Wright was sentenced to another prison term of fifty years.

228 ■ JESSIE JAMES ROBERTS , JR.

A native of Sylvester, Georgia, born on November 13, 1920, Roberts early displayed a fondness for concealed weapons and armed robbery. His adult convictions listed counts on larceny, assault with intent to commit armed robbery, attempted escape, interstate transportation of stolen motor vehicles and fraudulent checks, and post office burglary.

On December 21, 1965, while free on appeal bond after conviction for burglarizing a Tennessee post office, Roberts looted a bank at Quapaw, Oklahoma, of $34,144. Three weeks later, on January 10, 1966, he robbed a bank in Lenox, Georgia, of $38,322, rebounding minutes later with a failed attempt to raid another bank in nearby Alapaha. In that incident,

Roberts fled under fire from a bank officer, speeding away after one of the clerks tried to grab his pistol. Return fire from the getaway car grazed the banker's head, wounding him slightly.

Roberts, in his flight, was also charged with burglarizing a Modoc, South Carolina, post office in December 1965, stealing and subsequently cashing numerous postal money orders. His name was added to the Bureau's "Top Ten" list on February 3, 1966, and G-men traced him to Laredo, Texas, five days later, making the arrest without resistance from the fugitive.

229 ■ CHARLES LORIN GOVE
230 ■ RALPH DWAYNE OWEN

In the fall of 1965, while serving terms of five years to life on matching convictions for armed robbery, Gove and Owen managed to escape from the California state medical facility at Vacaville. Prying open a steel-frame window, they cut through three chain-link fences, overpowered two deputies, and escaped in the deputies' jeep. Five days later, the pair looted a ranch near Napa, California, holding three women and a boy hostage for two hours before fleeing in another stolen vehicle.

Already sought by the FBI on charges of unlawful flight to avoid confinement, Gove and Owen seemed bent on calling attention to themselves. On November 23, they robbed a bank in Cold Springs, Kentucky, making off with $6,800. Returning to the same bank on December 13, they improved their score, netting $14,500 in cash. Gove was alone on the afternoon of February 10, 1966, when he raided the Whitney National Bank in New Orleans, making an unscheduled withdrawal of $4,500.

Both fugitives were posted to the FBI's "Most Wanted" list on February 16, 1966. That very afternoon, New Orleans officers arrested Gove on Bourbon Street, before he had a chance to unload any of his latest loot at Mardi Gras. Identified in a police lineup by victims of the recent holdup, Gove began talking, and his outpouring led FBI agents to Ralph

Owen. On March 11, 1966, the second fugitive was seized in Kansas City, yielding to arrest without resistance.

231 ■ JIMMY LEWIS PARKER

A native of Iredell County, North Carolina, born in April 1935, Parker went berserk in April 1961, shooting to death the parents of his estranged wife and kidnapping a family of four, from Statesville, in his bid to escape. Convicted on all counts, Parker was sentenced to life for the murders, with an additional twenty to twenty-five year sentence applied for the kidnapping charges. In December 1964, while being transferred to Central Prison in Raleigh, he cut through the window bars on the prison bus and escaped from his captors on foot.

Federal warrants were issued on December 29, 1964, charging Parker with unlawful flight to avoid confinement for murder and kidnapping. His name was added to the FBI's "Most Wanted" list on February 25, 1966, and the widespread publicity paid off at once. On March 4, agents traced Parker to the Detroit apartment house where he had resided—as "Joe Lee Young"—for the past six months, while holding down a job in a furniture upholstery plant. Confronted with superior force, Parker surrendered without resistance and was returned to North Carolina for completion of his sentence.

232 ■ JACK DANIEL SAYADOFF

A veteran of crime with convictions for bank robbery in California and Georgia, Jack Sayadoff wasted none of his jail time on rehabilitation, preferring to think of prison as a kind of vocational school. By learning from his own mistakes and those of others, he surmised, he could become a better, more efficient robber.

Testing out his theory on October 21, 1965, Sayadoff—acting alone—raided a Chicago savings and loan association for $1,549. The take was average, at best, and there were countless risks involved in working solo. Determined to better himself, he began shopping around for an accomplice.

He found one, in the person of Patsy Janakos, while traveling in California. Patsy was having custody problems with her three-year-old daughter, and Sayadoff had the solution. Abducting an elderly babysitter, the couple left her bound and gagged in a Newark, California, home, making off with the child. Their actions brought FBI agents into the case, pursuing charges of kidnapping and interstate transportation of a stolen vehicle.

On December 8, 1965, Jack and Patsy looted a San Francisco bank for $3,131. A month later, on January 6, 1966, they struck a Lakewood savings and loan office, netting another $2,186. On March 14, a bank job in Hampton Township, Pennsylvania, yielded $11,113. Three days later, Sayadoff's name was added to the FBI's "Most Wanted" list.

Sayadoff and his adopted "family" had settled in Indianapolis on January 18, renting an apartment as "Mr. and Mrs. Jack F. Delano." Tipped to their location in March, FBI agents staked out the dwelling, following Jack and Patsy on their daily rounds until positive identification was confirmed. On March 24, 1966, Sayadoff was arrested at a local shopping center; Patsy Janakos was taken at home, a short time later, and her daughter was placed in a Marion County children's shelter. In custody, Sayadoff was identified by a tattoo on his right forearm, reading "Born to Love." Glancing down at the mark, he offered agents a rueful grin and said, "So true."

233 ■ ROBERT CLAYTON BUICK

A part-time bullfighter, sought by federal agents in connection with a series of California bank robberies, Buick confessed to certain apprehensive thoughts about the FBI's technique of publicizing wanted fugitives. After viewing a television program on the "Ten Most Wanted" fugitives, Buick worried that he might someday receive similar attention. His nightmare came true on March 24, 1966, with his nomination to the "Top Ten" roster, and he was picked up by local authorities in Pecos, Texas, five days later, identified from mug shots and descriptions on his wanted flyers. Buick was returned to California for trial and subsequent conviction on outstanding charges of armed robbery.

234 ■ JAMES VERNON TAYLOR

A native of Baltimore, born in November 1922, Taylor chalked up convictions for assault and robbery, burglary, larceny, disorderly conduct and discharging firearms, with several involuntary confinements to mental hospitals around his home town. On the night of January 22, 1966, Taylor beat his young wife brutally, then slashed her throat and stabbed her several times to finish off the job. His three children—ages five, three, and eighteen months—were also murdered as the family home became a slaughter pen, the violence apparently provoked by Taylor's mental instability.

Indicted on four counts of murder, Taylor was named in federal warrants charging him with unlawful flight to avoid prosecution, issued on January 26. Ten weeks later, on April 4, his name was added to the Bureau's "Ten Most Wanted" list, and the attendant publicity produced immediate results. Arrested the same day by Baltimore police officers, Taylor was held for trial and ultimate conviction in the murders of his wife and children.

235 ■ LYNWOOD IRWIN MEARES

An expert safecracker who liked to call himself "the old master," Lynwood Meares had a thirty-five year record of convictions for breaking and entering, bank burglary, larceny, storebreaking, housebreaking, receiving stolen goods, grand larceny, auto larceny, and escape. In 1952, Meares was arrested at Elizabeth City, North Carolina, for a series of crimes he staunchly denied committing. Convicted in Pasquotank County on charges of larceny, breaking and entering, he re-

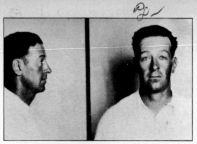

1 ■ THOMAS JAMES HOLDEN

8 ■ GLEN ROY WRIGHT

11 ■ WILLIAM FRANCIS SUTTON

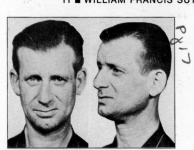

15 ■ THOMAS KLING

19 ■ HARRY H. BURTON

22 ■ FREDERICK EMERSON PETERS

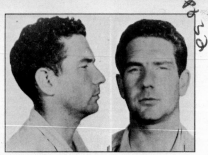

29 ■ SYDNEY GORDON MARTIN

36 ■ JAMES EDDIE DIGGS

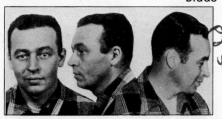

31 ■ THOMAS EDWARD YOUNG

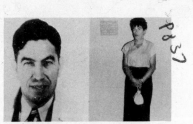

33 ■ ISAIE ALDY BEAUSOLEIL

45 ■ PERLIE MILLER

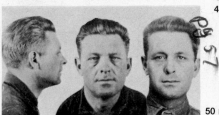

50 ■ ARNOLD HINSON

56 ■ ALEX RICHARD BRYANT

52 ■ FLEET ROBERT CURRENT

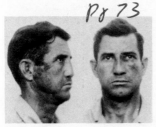

66 ■ ALEX WHITMORE

59 ■ EDWIN SANFORD GARRISON

69 ■ NELSON ROBERT DUNCAN

65 ■ CHESTER LEE DAVENPORT

83 ■ FLENOY PAYNE

71 ■ BASIN KINGSLEY BECK

105 ■ QUAY CLEON
KILBURN

79 ■ WALTER JAMES
WILKINSON

93 ■ JOSEPH JAMES BAGNOLA

73 ■ CLARENCE DYE

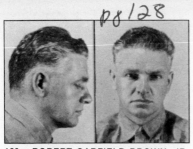

120 ■ ROBERT GARFIELD BROWN, JR.

109 ■ FRANK
LAWRENCE
SPRENZ

101 ■ ROBERT L.
GREEN

85 ■ PATRICK EUGENE McDERMOTT

113 ■ EMMETT
BERNARD KERVAN

97 ■ EUGENE
FRANCIS
NEWMAN

pg 128 pg 115 pg 108 pg 91 pg 120 pg 103

117 ■ JAMES
FRANCIS
JENKINS

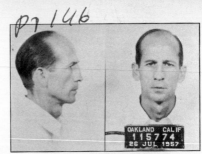

137 ■ DONALD LEROY PAYNE

144 ■ HERBERT
HOOVER
HUFFMAN

131 ■ RICHARD
PETER WAGNER

127 ■ JOSEPH
CORBETT, JR.

146 ■ THOMAS VIOLA

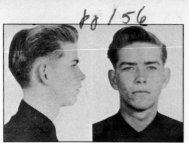

_pg 156_

147 ■ WILLIAM CHESTER COLE

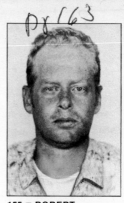

_pg 163_

155 ■ ROBERT WILLIAM SCHUETTE

_pg 167_

159 ■ JOHN ROBERT SAWYER

_pg 182_

174 ■ JOHN LEE TAYLOR

_pg 170_

163 ■ DELBERT HENRY LINAWEAVER

168 ■ ALBERT FREDERICK NUSSBAUM _pg 174_

181 ■ THOMAS ASBURY HADDAR

186 ■ FRANK B.
DUMONT

191 ■ GEORGE ZAVADA

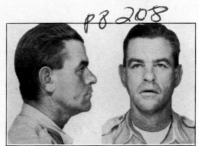

200 ■ LLOYD DONALD GREESON, JR.

196 ■ THOMAS EDWARD GALLOWAY

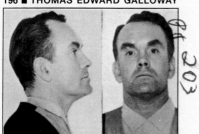

206 ■ SAMUEL JEFFERSON VENEY

208 ■ DONALD
STEWART HEIEN

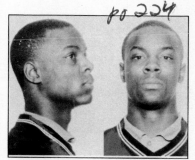

219 ■ HOLICE PAUL BLACK

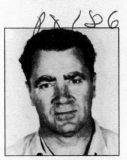

180 ■ CARL CLOSE

211 ■ LESLIE DOUGLAS ASHLEY

pp 238

pp 285

292 ■ GARY STEVEN KRIST

236 ■ JAMES ROBERT
RINGROSE

pp 230

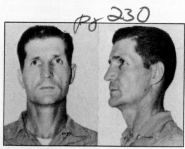

225 ■ JAMES ROBERT BISHOP

pp 219

213 ■ WILLIAM
ALBERT
AUTUR TAHL

262 ■ RONALD
EUGENE
STORCK *pp 259*

pp 266

271 ■ MICHAEL JOHN SANDERS

Pg 226
pg 246

220 ■ EDWARD OWEN WATKINS

245 ■ CHARLES
EDWARD ERVIN

pg 262

266 ■ LEONARD
DANIEL SPEARS

295 ■ BILLY AUSTIN BRYANT *pg 289*

290 ■ RICHARD LEE
TINGLER, JR.

Pg 283

301 ■ MARIE DEAN ARRINGTON *Pg 295*

318 ■ HERMAN BELL

309 ■ ANGELA YVONNE DAVIS

315 ■ KATHERINE ANN POWER

347 ■ BENJAMIN GEORGE PAVAN

316 ■ SUSAN EDITH SAXE

322 ■ RUDOLPH ALONZA TURNER

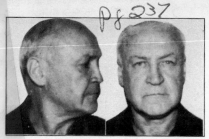

339 ■ JOSEPH MAURICE McDONALD

335 ■ LEONARD PELTIER

349 ■ ROY ELLSWORTH SMITH

353 ■ LARRY SMITH

330 ■ ROBERT GERALD DAVIS

325 ■ LENDELL HUNTER

pg 385

pg 370

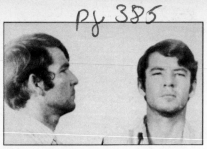

391 ■ LOHMAN RAY MAYS, JR.

385 ■ CHRISTOPHER
BERNARD
WILDER

pg 350

pg 354

363 ■ MICHAEL
GEORGE
THEVIS

368 ■ MELVIN BAY GUYON

pg 344

370 ■ EARL EDWIN AUSTIN   pg 356

360 ■ THEODORE
ROBERT BUNDY

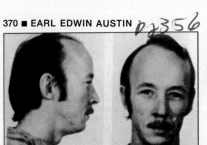

388 ■ ALTON
COLEMAN

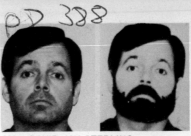

395 ■ DAVID JAY STERLING

405 ■ DANNY
MICHAEL
WEEKS

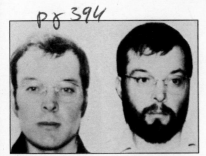

400 ■ CLAUDE LAFAYETTE DALLAS, JR.

398 ■ BRIAN PATRICK
MALVERTY

pg 411

pg 412

418 ■ JACK
DARRELL
FARMER

420 ■ TERRY LEE JOHNSON

pg 406

413 ■ DARREN DEE
O'NEALL

pg 401

407 ■ THOMAS GEORGE HARRELSON

pg 408

414 ■ LOUIS RAY BEAM

ceived three concurrent terms of eight to ten years in prison; charges of prison escape earned him six months in Currituck County; in Camden County, convictions for larceny and storebreaking brought two consecutive terms of five to seven years.

By January 1963, Meares had discharged all but the second of his Camden County sentences, with a year and a half remaining before he was eligible for parole. Tired of waiting, he escaped from the state prison at Cary, North Carolina, on January 16. On March 8, 1963, Meares was declared a federal fugitive on charges of unlawful flight to avoid confinement. His name was added to the "Top Ten" list on April 11, 1966.

On May 1, 1967, the *Twin City Sentinel*, in Winston-Salem, ran a photograph of Meares, together with a retrospective story on his case. Unknown to the reporter, Meares had lived in nearby Wallburg for the past four years, as "Howard Jackson," and the publication of his photograph unleashed a startling chain reaction.

Meares reviewed the story, realized his time was running out, and penned a letter to the FBI, preparing to surrender. Meanwhile, a neighbor had already phoned the Bureau, and agents were descending on the convict's rural home. Another local saw the agents coming and warned Meares in advance, but Meares was tired of running. As G-men staked out his property on May 2, the fugitive asked himself, "Why make them wait?" Empty-handed, he walked to the gate and surrendered.

In the wake of "Jackson's" arrest, his elderly employer and adoring neighbors began circulating petitions, writing letters urging an early parole. Convicted of prison escape, Meares received an additional twelve months in jail, but the sentence was ordered to run concurrently with his existing terms. After 178 days in prison, he was released and immediately returned to his quiet life in Wallburg.

236 ■ JAMES ROBERT RINGROSE

Born April 19, 1942, in Iowa City, Iowa, Ringrose was a narcotics user with a taste for Ivy League fashions and large ci-
gars. Fluent in Spanish and quick on the trigger, he was
charged with joining accomplices in circulating fraudulent
checks worth several hundred thousand dollars across the
United States. Members of the ring cashed counterfeit traveler's checks, also drawing upon fictitious checking accounts
maintained under assumed names.

On September 2, 1964, Ringrose collected $3,000 from a
fraudulent check scheme in Minneapolis, Minnesota, but his
luck turned sour the following day, in Seattle. Caught in the
act of writing a worthless check, he shot it out with bank
guards but was captured at the scene. En route to jail, he
slipped away from the arresting officers and fought another
running battle with police before he was recaptured. Posting
bail on September 11, he purchased another gun in Tacoma
and vanished, forfeiting bond when he failed to appear for
arraignment following his indictment on federal charges. Following his disappearance, Ringrose was linked with armed
robberies and the passing of further fraudulent checks
throughout the country.

Added to the FBI's "Most Wanted" list on April 15, 1966,
Ringrose survived another eleven months on the run. On
March 29, 1967, he was arrested by local police in Osaka,
Japan, facing extradition to the United States for trial on a
long list of outstanding charges.

237 ■ WALTER LEONARD LESCZYNSKI

An ex-convict with larceny in his blood, Lesczynski had his
last fling on August 20, 1965. Working with an unknown accomplice, he robbed Chicago's Kiddieland amusement park of
more than $20,000, fleeing with the loot in canvas bags as
squads of uniformed police began arriving at the scene. It
took nine bullets to bring Lesczynski down, and even then he
refused to name his accomplice.

On December 17, 1965, while recovering from his wounds, Lesczynski astounded police by escaping from Cook County Hospital. Examined at 5 A.M., he had been tucked in bed, secured with handcuffs and leg irons, in a sixth-floor ward. Less than thirty minutes later, a nurse found his bed empty; Lesczynski had apparently broken the chain on his shackles, picked the lock on his handcuffs with the filler from a ballpoint pen, and fled down the fire escape. Declared a federal fugitive on charges of unlawful flight to avoid prosecution, his name was added to the "Ten Most Wanted" list on June 16, 1966.

Three months later, on September 6, a tip led federal agents to Lesczynski's hideout in Chicago. Recovered from his wounds by now, he had no further taste for gunplay and surrendered peacefully. He was delivered to Cook County authorities for trial on the outstanding charges.

238 ■ DONALD ROGERS SMELLEY

Born in Oklahoma City, Don Smelley found the desert more to his taste, relocating in New Mexico. The climate was good for his health, but it could not keep him out of trouble, and he soon compiled a list of criminal convictions around Albuquerque. In February and March of 1964, he was accused of robbing the same market twice, firing a shot at employees who chased him the second time. His loot—$350—was recovered from his abandoned getaway car.

Facing life imprisonment as an habitual offender if convicted, Smelley failed to appear for his robbery trial on March 15, 1965. Ten days later, federal warrants were issued, charging him with unlawful flight to avoid prosecution. Based on his reputation for violence—and rumors that Smelley had sworn he would "never be taken alive"—his name was added to the "Ten Most Wanted" list on June 30, 1966.

On November 7, G-men acting on a tip trailed Smelley to a restaurant in Hollywood, California. Unarmed at his arrest, the desperado offered no resistance. "I'm glad it's over," he told his captors. "You guys are too hot for me."

239 ■ GEORGE BEN EDMONDSON

In 1955, as a seventeen-year-old navy recruit, George Edmondson robbed a bank in Republic, Missouri, of $4,146. After bagging the loot, he forced employees to lie facedown on the floor, then bound their hands with adhesive tape before fleeing the scene. The exploit cost him five years in prison and a dishonorable discharge, but in the long run it taught him nothing.

On December 23, 1961, Edmondson ambushed two department store employees in Springfield, Missouri, relieving them of $5,000 at gunpoint. Convicted in 1962, he was sentenced to thirty years in prison, but the verdict was overturned on appeal; pleading guilty to lesser charges at his retrial, in 1965, George got off with a term of ten years. But on August 3, 1965, he escaped from the state prison at Jefferson City. A federal warrant was issued, charging Edmondson with unlawful flight to avoid confinement, and his name was added to the Bureau's "Ten Most Wanted" list on September 21, 1966.

By that time, the fugitive had settled in Quebec, where he lived as "Alex Peter Bormann." Married to a teacher in 1966, he fathered a child and launched a successful career as a self-taught engineer. With Expo '67 looming large on the horizon, "Bormann" was largely responsible for design and construction of the West German pavilion.

In June 1967, a resident of Shawville, Quebec—fifty miles northwest of Ottawa—recognized Edmondson's photograph in a magazine article dealing with American fugitives. Officers of the Royal Canadian Mounted Police were notified, and they arrested Edmondson without incident on June 28.

In custody, the fugitive began a five-year journey through the courts and prison system. Convicted of escape, in September 1967, Edmondson received another two-year term. Three months later, his original robbery conviction was overturned on appeal, but the escape sentence kept him behind bars. Posting $5,000 bail in March 1969, he was briefly united with his family in Canada, pending a new trial; arrested two weeks later on illegal entry charges, he was ordered out of Canada, but appeals delayed deportation through late summer. Convicted of robbery a third time, in October 1969, he drew another ten-year sentence and was finally paroled in September 1972.

240 ■ EVERETT LEROY BIGGS

A hard-luck bandit, Everett Biggs was readily identified when he raided a bank in Springfield, Illinois, for $17,560 on September 13, 1966. The following day, federal warrants were issued charging him with unlawful flight to avoid prosecution, and his name was added to the FBI's "Most Wanted" list September 21.

Undaunted by his sudden notoriety, Biggs came back strong a month later, in Tulsa, Oklahoma. On October 21, he raided a local bank with accomplices John Frank Larson and Willard McClanahan. The bandits netted $77,606, but the robbery was not without problems. Witnesses described Biggs as "careless and apologetic," after his pistol discharged in a scuffle with a bank cashier.

On December 1, 1966, FBI agents traced John Larson to a rented house in Denver, Colorado. Unarmed at his arrest that afternoon, Larson offered no resistance and was given no opportunity to reach the five guns hidden in adjoining rooms. Three hours later, G-men captured Everett Biggs at a second rented home. Surrounded, Biggs did not attempt to use his .38 revolver. Six other guns and a large amount of cash were recovered by agents in a search of his hideout.

241 ■ GENE ROBERT JENNINGS

Born in Penns Grove, New Jersey, during 1927, Gene Jennings was a study in contradictions, using narcotics while he exercised religiously and professed an abiding concern with physical fitness. Sentenced to life imprisonment for armed robbery in Kentucky, Jennings escaped four times from the state penitentiary at Eddyville. His escapes—in 1958, 1960, 1962 and 1966, were marked by chaotic violence, kidnapping of hostages, and the display of guns or knives as Gene attempted to avoid confinement. After one of his early breakouts, Jennings kidnapped two motorists and left them locked in the trunk of their car, an offense which added 20 years of federal time to his existing sentence.

In his final jailbreak, on September 4, 1966, Jennings once more commandeered a passing car, this time occupied by a man and five children. Driving to the Tennessee-Kentucky border, Jennings' hostages were ejected after he stole the driver's cash and shirt, fleeing in the car which was later recovered from a patch of Tennessee woods.

Named in federal warrants charging him with Dyer Act violations and unlawful flight to avoid confinement, Jennings was added to the FBI's "Most Wanted" list on December 13, 1966. Two months later, on February 14, 1967, federal agents found him in Atlantic City, New Jersey, arresting him without incident and returning him to Kentucky for completion of his ever-lengthening sentence.

242 ◼ CLARENCE WILBERT McFARLAND

A resident of Washington, D.C., McFarland joined accomplice John Thomas Crawford in robbing a local bank on the morning of March 13, 1966. Waiting behind the wheel of their getaway car, while Crawford bagged $5,900 in mutilated bills scheduled for exchange with the Treasury Department for new money, McFarland watched his companion emerge from the bank with manager Drapher Pagan and a customer in close pursuit. Crawford dropped his gun while scrambling for the car, and clamoring bells brought police cars to the scene, touching off a wild chase through the streets of Washington.

FBI agents had joined the chase by the time McFarland crashed into a taxi, both bandits breaking for safety on foot. Leaving a trail of loose bills behind them, the robbers dodged police bullets—one of them grazing Crawford's leg—until they crashed through a glass door to invade a private residence on 21st Street. Hiding in the basement, they were swiftly flushed from cover and arrested with the balance of their mangled loot.

Crawford pled guilty to bank robbery in September 1963, but McFarland refused to confess, staking his hopes on a full-blown jury trial. While free on bond, in October 1963, McFarland was shot by police officers during a burglary in Prince Georges County, Maryland. (Hospitalized for his wounds, he was never prosecuted for the abortive burglary.) In February 1964, when McFarland indicated he might plead insanity, he was committed to St. Elizabeth's Hospital for observation and diagnosis. Withdrawing the insanity plea, he was convicted on federal bank robbery charges in April, but his bond was continued pending appeal of the verdict and sentence.

On November 6, 1964, McFarland was arrested in Washington on charges of unlawful receiving and possession of a firearm. Convicted in March 1966, he was sentenced to a term of sixteen months to four years in prison, said term to run concurrently with his sentence for bank robbery. Alleged threats from fellow prisoners in Washington prompted his transfer to the Montgomery County Detention Center, in Rockville, Maryland, from which he managed to escape a few weeks later.

Posted to the FBI's "Most Wanted" list December 22, 1966, McFarland remained at large until April 4, 1967, when he was identified and arrested by local police in Baltimore. Never ranging very far from home, he was captured without incident and returned to Washington for completion of his outstanding federal sentences.

 ■ MONROE HICKSON

A native of South Carolina, Hickson logged his first arrest there in 1931; convicted of assault with intent to kill, he was sentenced to five years in prison and paroled after two, in 1933. In 1942 he was sentenced to serve eighteen months on a larceny conviction. Five years later, a robbery at New Holland, South Carolina, earned him twenty years. With time off for good behavior, he was paroled in April 1957.

Through the years, Hickson's pattern of crimes had run toward petty robberies accompanied by violence; in his last known job, the "loot" had been some clothing and a pistol. No one in authority suspected that this black man—nicknamed "Blue Boy"—was in fact the slayer of at least four persons, sought for crimes that terrorized the neighborhood of Aiken during 1946.

On August 7, 1957, Hickson entered Lucy Parker's dry goods store, in Graniteville, and beat her up before escaping with the petty cash. Arrested August 8, he sat in jail nine days before astounding officers with his confession to a string of unsolved crimes.

According to his affidavit, Hickson was responsible for the ax murder of David Garrett, an Aiken storekeeper bludgeoned and robbed on April 17, 1946; the crime had netted Hickson a pistol and $22 in cash. Eleven days later, he used the stolen gun to murder Mr. and Mrs. Edward Bennett in their grocery store, making off with seven or eight dollars and another gun. Questioned by a posse on that occasion, Hickson had not been detained. On September 28, 1946, he invaded Annie Wiseberg's home, in Aiken, stealing five dollars after he beat her to death with a piece of firewood. The sole survivor of his spree was Christine Cholakis, employed at a local liquor store. Hickson knocked her out with a brick on December 4, 1946, escaping with seven dollars, but his final victim lived to tell the tale.

While Hickson was at large or doing time on other charges, L. D. Harris was convicted of the Bennett homicides, condemned to die in the electric chair. An appeal to the United States Supreme Court saved his life, but he remained in prison until Hickson's confession finally cleared his name in 1957.

Convicted on four counts of murder, Hickson was sentenced to a term of life plus twenty years. On March 10, 1966, he escaped from the state prison at Columbia, South Carolina, and was declared a federal fugitive on charges of unlawful flight to avoid confinement. His name was added to the FBI's "Most Wanted" list on February 17, 1967.

By that time, unknown to the FBI, their man was already dead. While hiding in New Bern, North Carolina, under the alias "Willie Tyler," Hickson had fallen ill in early December. Transferred from New Bern's hospital to a larger facility in Chapel Hill, he died of natural causes on December 29. Federal agents traced him there a year later, and his remains were finally identified, from fingerprints, on January 30, 1968.

244 ■ CLYDE EDWARD LAWS

A native of Crocker, Missouri, Laws was born in 1927, logging his first arrest, for theft, in Omaha at age eighteen. While free on bond, he was drafted into the army and prosecution was deferred until his release from service on medical grounds, in April 1946. Convicted of two Dyer Act violations in June 1947, Laws received matching concurrent sentences of three years probation. In November 1951, Laws was sentenced to two years imprisonment for forgery, in Missouri, winning parole in December 1953. A few months later, he received a term of fifteen to twenty-five years for forgery, in Kansas, with an equal concurrent term for grand larceny and escape. Eventual commutation of his sentence put Laws on the street in December 1959, but he was arrested again for forgery and Dyer Act violations in May 1961, at Norfolk, Nebraska. Returned to Kansas as a parole violator in February 1962, he was released again two years later, discharging his time in May 1966. In mid-January 1967, he abruptly left Missouri, telling friends that he was looking for a warmer climate.

With accomplice Thomas Dorman (#247), Laws robbed a supermarket in Wheaton, Maryland, of $1,500 on February 8, 1967. Fleeing the scene, they engaged police officers in a wild shootout before abducting a motorist and using their hostage to effect an escape. Behind them, they left a Montgomery County police officer critically wounded.

Indicted on a list of felonies including armed robbery, kidnapping, and attempted murder, Laws was declared a federal fugitive on charges of unlawful flight to avoid prosecution. On February 28, 1967, he was added to the FBI's "Most Wanted" roster.

Fresh publicity surrounding his addition to the list produced results in May. A tip led federal agents to Raytown, Missouri, where Laws had gone to ground. Recalling the fugitive's shootout with Maryland officers, G-men were ready for trouble when they cornered their man on May 18. Drawing a weapon, Laws suffered a flesh wound before he surrendered and was taken into custody.

245 ■ CHARLES EDWARD ERVIN
246 ■ GORDON DALE ERVIN

Hard-nosed twins made up the Bureau's second "Top Ten" family act. Boasting four convictions since 1949—one for larceny, three for breaking and entering—Gordon Ervin set a standard for his brother to follow. In 1954, the twins were convicted together in the armed robbery of a Michigan supermarket. Making their first bid for escape in the courthouse, they failed miserably: Gordon was wounded in the shoulder by a policeman, while Charles hurt his back in a forty-foot fall. Called back for sentencing the next day, both received terms of fifty to sixty years in state prison. On his way to the lockup, Gordon made public threats against the prosecutor and presiding judge in his case.

By 1965, the Ervins were considered model prisoners, assigned to the state penitentiary at Jackson. As trusties, they were allowed to work outside the prison walls, and on October 8 they disappeared together. Federal warrants charged the twins with unlawful flight to avoid confinement, and they were still at large eighteen months later. On April 13, 1967, they were posted on the "Top Ten" roster simultaneously.

Canada had lured the brothers, with its reputation as a fugitive's paradise. On July 25, 1967, Charles Ervin was arrested by officers of the Royal Canadian Mounted Police at Hawkesbury, Ontario. Residing under an alias, he also sported facial scars indicative of plastic surgery. Returned to Michigan with extra time appended to his sentence for the breakout, Ervin waited anxiously for word about his brother.

Nearly two years later, on June 7, 1969, a flying squad of Mounties routed Gordon from his third-floor rented room in

Winnipeg. Registered as "David Anderson," he was sleeping when detectives, acting on a tip, barged into the apartment. Unarmed, he offered no resistance and readily confessed his identity.

In Michigan, authorities had learned their lesson where the Ervins were concerned. In the future, it was publicly announced, the brothers would be separated, one locked up at Jackson, while the other served his time in prison in Marquette. Nor would they soon regain their trusty status. As a prison spokesman summarized the situation, "They'll never see outside again."

247 ■ THOMAS FRANKLIN DORMAN

An Indiana native, born in 1931, Tom Dorman's life and criminal record were summarized by the tattoo on his left arm: "Born to Lose." As the accomplice of Clyde Edward Laws in a February 1967 holdup, Dorman participated in the wounding of a Montgomery County, Maryland, police officer and the abduction of a hostage used in their escape. Indicted on charges of armed robbery, kidnapping, and attempted murder, Dorman was also listed as a federal fugitive. FBI agents sought him on charges of unlawful flight to avoid prosecution, and his name was added to the "Ten Most Wanted" list on April 20, 1967.

Exactly one month later—two days after Laws was apprehended in Missouri—federal agents traced Dorman to a rural cabin near Grantsburg, Indiana. Joined by sheriff's deputies and state police, G-men surrounded and captured him without resistance. Dorman was held under $25,000 bond pending extradition to Maryland for trial.

248 ■ JERRY LYNN YOUNG

Born in Alabama in October 1942, Jerry Young joined the Marine Corps in February 1961, but he found military discipline too rigorous. Convicted of robbing a Richlands, North Carolina, bank of $4,359, he received a dishonorable discharge in March 1962. The rap also carried a six-year federal prison sentence, but Young was paroled in August 1963. He was discharged as a free man on March 1, 1967, upon successful completion of his parole.

The next day, Young carried a shotgun into a bank in Asheville, North Carolina, looting the cages for $13,671 in cash. Threatening to kill any pursuers, he fled in a stolen car, firing pistol shots at an employee who briefly gave chase.

On April 14, he struck again, robbing a bank in Olive Branch, Mississippi, of $14,919. Identified from photographs, Young was declared a federal fugitive, on bank robbery charges, and his name was added to the "Ten Most Wanted" list in May 1967.

One month later, on June 15, FBI agents were waiting when Young and accomplice William Webb left their room at an Akron, Ohio, motel. Young was fond of boasting that he would "never be taken alive," and G-men were ready when he reached for a pistol. Confronted with superior firepower, he swiftly reconsidered and was taken into custody without incident.

249 ■ JOSEPH LEROY NEWMAN

At thirty-one, Joe Newman had compiled a record of involvement in burglaries and robberies spanning several years. His latest conviction, for burglarizing a home in Washington, D.C., earned him a sentence of two to six years in prison. On February 13, 1967, Newman escaped from the District of Columbia Reformatory, at Lorton, Virginia, by hiding himself in a laundry truck. Another inmate, dressed in a stolen guard's uniform, played chauffeur for the break-out, and both were charged with violation of the Dyer Act, plus unlawful flight to avoid confinement.

On May 13, a Washington detective spotted Newman on the street and tried to make the collar. Whipping out a pistol, Newman left the officer in serious condition from a bullet wound, racking up new charges of assault with intent to kill. On June 2, 1967, his name was added to the FBI's "Most Wanted" list.

Before the month was out, a tip led federal agents to the neighborhood of Journal Square, in Jersey City. Newman had been killing time in town the past two weeks, and on the twenty-eighth, informants leaked the word that he was fond of hanging out in Journal Square. A team of agents spotted him June 29, as he was window-shopping with an innocent companion, and they swept him up without resistance. Safe in custody, the gunman told his captors he had also been involved in several unsolved robberies around the District of Columbia.

250 ■ CARMEN RAYMOND GAGLIARDI

A Boston mobster active in loan sharking, extortion, and gun running, Gagliardi was also a prime suspect in several gangland slayings in the bloody 1960s. His downfall, when it came, owed more to luck and negligence than any great detective work by Boston's finest.

On April 18, 1967, two officers on routine patrol were startled when a dark sedan sped through a red traffic light, directly in front of their cruiser. Giving chase, they watched the speeding driver douse his lights, eventually pulling to the curb across the street from Carmen Gagliardi's house. Two men jumped from the car and ran in opposite directions. One, identified as Gagliardi, sprinted past his house and vanished in the darkness; his companion, finally identified as Benjamin De Christoforo, lost pursuers after several blocks.

Inside the car, police found Frank Otero, fresh blood soaking through his clothes. Frank wasn't hurt, however; all the blood belonged to Joseph Lanzi, shot four times, whose corpse lay huddled on the seat beside Otero. Searchers found two pistols and a baseball bat tucked underneath the auto's seat.

Held over for a murder trial, Otero cooled his heels while his accomplices remained at large, indicted on charges of murder and unlawful flight to avoid prosecution. Named as the primary triggerman in Lanzi's execution, Gagliardi was added to the FBI's "Most Wanted" list on June 9, 1967.

Relying on their underworld contacts for protection, the fugitives stayed close to home, and overconfidence was ultimately their undoing. Ben De Christoforo was arrested by FBI agents in November 1968, and by then Gagliardi had less than a month of freedom remaining. Two days before Christmas, G-men picked him up at his mother's home in Medford, Massachusetts, handing him over to local authorities for prosecution on murder charges.

251 ■ DONALD RICHARD BUSSMEYER

Heavily-tattooed, a known narcotics user, Donald Bussmeyer boasted a record of convictions for auto theft, attempted burglary, assault with intent to kill, and robbery with a deadly weapon. On March 2, 1967, with accomplices James Alaway and Russell Jones, he robbed a Los Angeles bank of $75,000, instantly becoming a federal fugitive. Arrested on March 9, Alaway was sentenced to seventeen years for his part in the holdup; wheelman Jones, picked up on March 10, received a sentence of ten years. Bussmeyer was indicted on federal bank robbery charges in April 1967, and his name was added to the "Ten Most Wanted" list on June 28.

Publicity and Bussmeyer's penchant for tattoos led federal agents to his Upland, California, hideout two months later. Closing the net on August 24, raiders captured Bussmeyer, his wife Hallie, and a companion named Gene Herrington. Two pistols were found in the house, but Don Bussmeyer—clad only in shorts—was in no position to resist arrest. A tattoo on his chest—"Don Bussmeyer Loves Joyce"—removed any doubt of the fugitive's identity.

Bussmeyer was held under $200,000 bond pending trial on the Los Angeles robbery. Gene Herrington and Hallie Bussmeyer—an addict like her husband—were held in custody on charges of harboring a federal fugitive.

252 ■ FLORENCIO LOPEZ MATIONG
253 ■ VICTOR GERALD BONO

Marijuana smugglers Mationg and Bono were notorious in Southern California long before their posting to the FBI's "Most Wanted" list. Identified as dealers and importers on an epic scale, they were the targets of investigation by the local, state, and federal governments, suspected as the masterminds of West Coast smuggling. Authorities were prone to speak of Bono as the Southland's "king of smugglers," but police were not prepared for the display of ruthless violence he put on in early summer 1967.

U.S. Border Patrolmen Theodore Newton and George Azrak were working a routine highway checkpoint, watching for illegal aliens in San Diego County, when they disappeared without a trace on June 18. Their jeep was found that afternoon, carelessly hidden in Riverside County, and searchers fanned out over the surrounding countryside, seeking any trace of the two missing officers.

They were discovered early in the afternoon of June 19, their lifeless bodies handcuffed to a stove inside a rural cabin. Newton had been murdered with a single gunshot to the head. His partner had been shot three times—once in the head, and then twice in the chest—as if his killers were determined to make certain he was dead.

The kidnapping and murder of two federal officers brought agents of the FBI into the case. For all their seeming efforts to avoid detection, the assassins had been careless at the crime scene, leaving fingerprints inside the cabin, clear-cut footprints in the mud outside. A scan of Bureau print files narrowed down the suspect search to Bono, Mationg, and two accomplices, drug-dealing brothers Alfred and Harold Montoya. Agents theorized the four were smuggling drugs from Mexico, through San Diego County, when their car was stopped routinely at the checkpoint manned by Newton and his partner, Azrak.

Victor Bono, as it happened, was a federal fugitive already, having failed to show for his arraignment in Los Angeles Superior Court, where he faced charges of possessing marijuana valued at $1.7 million. He had skipped $100,000 bail, and warrants had been issued for immediate arrest.

Local officers and federal agents swarmed Los Angeles and its environs, leaving no stone unturned in their hunt for the fugitives. Added to the Bureau's "Top Ten" list on July 1, Mationg and Bono became numbers 252 and 253, respectively, on the dishonor roll. The grapevine said both men were armed and dangerous, proclaiming they would not be taken in alive.

On July 13, 1967, federal agents raided a Los Angeles apartment, firing tear gas through windows before they crashed the front door. A neighbor had identified Mationg as new tenant "D. Pompa," but the agents found their suspects had fled in haste, abandoning an arsenal of weapons which included three submachine guns, numerous rifles and shotguns.

In Mexico, near Hermosillo, brothers Al and Harold Montoya were arrested on July 13. Both men waived extradition to Los Angeles and turned state's evidence against their comrades. According to the brothers' testimony, there had been 800 pounds of grass in Bono's car when they were stopped on June 18. The two patrolmen had been executed to protect their stash, and to prevent Bono's arrest as a fugitive from justice.

Mationg and Bono were surprised by G-men on July 16, a dawn raid on their new apartment catching both assassins fast asleep. They had no time to reach their loaded weapons, six in all, before they had been cuffed and dragged to waiting cars. Convicted of the murders and assorted other charges, both were sentenced to a term of life without parole.

254 ■ ALFRED JOHNSON COOPER , JR.

In 1966, with two accomplices, Al Cooper robbed a gas station in Cinnaminson Township, New Jersey. Police arrived in the midst of the holdup, and gunfire erupted, the outlaws escaping in a hail of bullets. A policeman was shot in the face, losing the sight in one eye, before Cooper and company seized a passing motorist, forcing her to drive them clear of the scene. Their hostage was dropped off in Camden—Cooper's home town—and charges of kidnapping were added to those of robbery, assault and battery. On July 27, 1967, Cooper's name was added to the "Ten Most Wanted" list.

Life on the lam did not seem to cramp Alfred's style. In January 1967, as "Joe Brady," he fought in the Holyoke Golden Gloves tournament, but FBI agents only learned of his outing after the fact. On September 8, 1967, acting on a tip, they traced Cooper to a Boston hideout and arrested him without resistance, holding him for extradition to New Jersey on a list of pending charges.

255 ■ JOHN D. SLATON

A petty criminal by all accounts, Slaton raised the ante on October 30, 1965, when officers sought to question him on a bad check charge in Oroville, Washington. In the face of probable arrest, Slaton grabbed a rifle and opened fire on the officers. No one was injured, but charges of first-degree assault were filed against him in absentia, and the Justice Department issued a warrant charging Slaton with unlawful flight to avoid prosecution. As a potential cop killer, he joined the Bureau's "Top Ten" list on August 2, 1967.

Four months later, on December 1, a team of agents apprehended Slaton in Harquahala Valley, Arizona, seventy-five miles west of Phoenix. Slaton was working at a labor camp when G-men arrived and took him into custody without resistance. Unarmed, he readily confessed his true identity and was returned to Washington for trial.

256 ■ JERRY RAY JAMES

A native of Electra, Texas, Jerry James was sought by the FBI for burglarizing a Mobeetie, Texas, bank on March 16, 1966. Arrested later that year and charged with the robbery of a nightclub in Biloxi, Mississippi, he was held in jail pending delivery to federal agents. Before they arrived, on December 26, James escaped from his cell in Biloxi and was named a federal fugitive, on charges of interstate flight to avoid prosecution. On August 16, 1967, his name was added to the Bureau's "Ten Most Wanted" list.

The search for Jerry James focused on Tucson, Arizona, in January 1968. On January 23, his wife, Joan, was arrested at the home which she had occupied for ninety days; simultaneously, another raiding party captured Wayne Padgett, a friend of James's, and charged him with harboring a federal fugitive. The rented house was filled with televisions, radios and other small appliances, along with stolen furs from stores in Texas, Illinois, and Indiana.

On the afternoon of January 24, G-men surprised Jerry James and another "Top Ten" fugitive, Donald Sparks, as they sat watching television in another rented house. Unarmed, the men were taken into custody without resistance and James was subsequently convicted on federal bank robbery charges.

Confined to Leavenworth in 1980, James made friends with convicted drug dealer Jamiel "Jimmy" Chagra, reporting conversations in which Chagra allegedly took credit for the 1979 ambush slaying of a federal judge in Texas. Promised his freedom and $250,000 in return for testimony leading to Chagra's conviction, James did his best on the witness stand, in 1983, but it wasn't good enough. Chagra was acquitted on the murder charge, and Jerry James remained in jail.

257 ■ RICHARD PAUL ANDERSON

Anderson logged the first of his eighteen arrests at Buffalo, New York, in 1957, on a charge of robbery. Most of his New York indictments were later dismissed, with the exception of a 1959 conviction for robbery in Elmira, and he moved to St. Louis County, Missouri, in the early 1960s. There, around Mattese, it was the same old story: charged with theft, burglary, and other crimes, Anderson saw most of his cases dismissed for lack of evidence. In March 1963, he was convicted of assault with intent to rob and sentenced to three years in state prison, but soon he was back on the streets and looking for action.

Love, or its equivalent, spelled doom for Anderson in 1967. Infatuated with a local girl, Richard broke into her home on July 1, forced her to join him at a nearby motel, and afterward threatened to kill her parents if they pressed charges. On July 15, denied entry to the family's home, he produced a shotgun, killing his "lover's" parents—Albert and Victoria Fisk—in a fit of rage.

Three days later, with murder charges already pending, Anderson kidnapped a gas station attendant in Biloxi, Mississippi, robbing his victim and leaving the hostage handcuffed to a tree. Federal agents, tracking Anderson on charges of unlawful flight to avoid prosecution, traced him to Long Beach, California, where he was linked with an assault on victim Charles Jordan. Kidnapping charges were filed on July 24, and Anderson's name was added to the FBI's "Most Wanted" list on September 7, 1967.

By mid-November, Anderson had settled in Toronto, posing as an American businessman. As it turned out, his "business" was confined to robbery. Anderson looted a Toronto department store of $10,000 on November 24, resurfacing on December 18 to rob a local bank. Despite the ready cash on hand, he grew increasingly unstable, seeming desperate for pocket money.

On January 16, 1968, Anderson abducted hockey player Sam Kimberley, 19, from the Don Mills Plaza, hitching a ride at gunpoint to the Thorncliffe Plaza shopping mall. Arriving at their destination, Anderson ordered Kimberley into the trunk of his car, but the hostage bolted, hurling his skates at Anderson, making good his escape. While Kimberley was flagging down police, Anderson hijacked an elderly salesman, Alfred Nobel, demanding $100 in cash. Nobel saved himself and secured his liberty with a trip to the bank, withdrawing fifty dollars which appeared to satisfy his abductor.

On January 19, Anderson was captured by a team of Toronto detectives who staked out his apartment. Asleep when they entered, he offered no resistance. Various felony courts earned him nine years in Canadian prisons, but the jackpot was waiting in Missouri, where conviction on murder charges brought him a sentence of sixty years. The conviction was overturned on appeal, in November 1974, but it did Anderson no good at the time.

Free on parole by November 1972, awaiting results of his appeal in the United States, Anderson tried to break up a bar fight between several bikers. One of the combatants knocked him down, and Richard came up shooting, wounding two assailants and squeezing off rounds at a constable who tried to restrain him. Convicted on two counts of attempted murder and one charge of possessing a dangerous weapon, he was sent back to prison for twelve years.

258 ■ HENRY THEODORE YOUNG

A native of Kansas City, born in June 1911, Young launched his criminal career with an armed robbery conviction in Montana, during 1932. Paroled in June 1933, he was convicted of second-degree burglary in Washington four months later, receiving a sentence of one to ten years in the state penitentiary. Released on parole in 1934, he lasted a month before robbing a Washington bank, earning twenty years in the federal prison at McNeil Island. While confined there, Young made an unsuccessful escape attempt, leading to his transfer in June 1935. Lodged at Alcatraz, he soon acquired a reputation as one of "the Rock's" most dangerous inmates.

In the predawn hours of January 13, 1939, Young joined Arthur "Dock" Barker (one of "Ma" Barker's notorious sons) and three other inmates in an attempted escape from Alcatraz. Pinned down by spotlights and machine gun fire, two of the convicts were wounded, two others surrendering before they were hit. Barker took his chances with the sea, but bullets found him there and he was dying when the guards fished him out. "I was a fool to try it," he muttered on his death bed. "I'm all shot to hell."

The following year, Young fatally stabbed another of the breakout participants, earning three more years on conviction for involuntary manslaughter. Along the way, he confessed to murdering another man, years earlier, during a bakery holdup in Everett, Washington, and was sentenced to life on that charge. Upon parole from Alcatraz, in 1955, he was delivered to Washington authorities to begin serving the latest in a long string of sentences.

Twelve years later, on June 8, 1967, Young escaped from the Washington state prison at Walla Walla. A federal warrant was filed on July 6, charging Young with unlawful flight to avoid prosecution for the crime of escape, and his name was added to the Bureau's "Ten Most Wanted" list on September 21, 1967. Federal agents traced him to Kansas City on January 9, 1968, and took Young into custody without resistance, returning him to Washington for completion of his outstanding sentence.

259 ■ DONALD EUGENE SPARKS

Linked with three armed robberies in Collinsville, Florida, and Payne, Alabama, Sparks was charged with unlawful flight to avoid prosecution in a federal warrant issued August 5, 1966. Fifteen months later, he was still at large, and his name was added to the Bureau's "Ten Most Wanted" list on November 13, 1967.

On January 24, 1968, FBI agents raided a home occupied by fugitive Jerry Ray James, in Tucson, Arizona, and were startled to discover Sparks on the premises. The outlaws were watching TV when the raiders arrived; neither was armed, but a search of the house turned up one .38, one .357 magnum, one .30-caliber carbine, and two .22-caliber pistols, along with large quantities of ammunition. Sparks was held under $100,000 bond, pending extradition and trial.

260 ■ ZELMA LAVONE KING

A Black Muslim known for his explosive temper, Zelma King was sought by Chicago authorities on triple murder charges, following the murder of his landlady and two other persons at King's apartment, on May 5, 1967. According to witnesses, the suspect drew a gun and started shooting in the middle of an argument concerning sale of a refrigerator. Named in federal warrants charging him with unlawful flight to avoid prosecution, King was added to the FBI's "Most Wanted" list on December 14, 1967.

On January 30, 1968, federal agents surprised King in Phoenix, Arizona, where he was employed as a porter for McGraw-Edison International Metal Products. Living in Phoenix as "Charles M. Bracey," King surrendered without resistance and confessed his true identity to arresting officers. His capture marked the fourth arrest of "Top Ten" fugitives in Arizona in the space of four months.

261 ■ JERRY REECE PEACOCK

Convicted in California of stealing $42,350 from a fellow armored car driver, Jerry Peacock was sentenced to a term of five years to life in the state penitentiary. While serving his time at Soledad prison, in October 1966, Peacock escaped and was declared a federal fugitive on charges of unlawful flight to avoid confinement. Still at large three months later, he was named by police as a suspect in the January 1967 beating death of a Los Angeles man. Peacock's name was added to the FBI's "Most Wanted" list on December 14, 1967.

Traveling as "Randy Kastor," Jerry Peacock sought to hide from the authorities by working on a series of remote alfalfa ranches in the tri-state area of Utah, Arizona, and Nevada. Unknown to the fugitive, FBI agents had already penetrated his disguise, and on March 3, 1968, he was arrested at a ranch five miles outside Mesquite, Nevada. Captured in the middle of a field, Peacock was driven directly to jail in Las Vegas, without being returned to the farm house where he kept a rifle hidden. He was extradited from Nevada to complete his prison term in California.

262 ■ RONALD EUGENE STORCK

A lifelong resident of Bucks County, Pennsylvania, Storck was first convicted there in 1958, at age nineteen, for burglary. By 1967, he was on parole, locally employed as a maintenance man, but the straight life offered few rewards in comparison to crime.

On November 22, 1967, a gunman invaded the Bucks County farm house of John Brickajlik, age seventy-two. Within the next few moments, Brickajlik was shot four times in the head with a .22-caliber weapon. Five bullets were fired into seventy-one-year-old Mary Brickajlik, John's wife; seven shots in the head ended the short life of grandson William Brickajlik, eleven years of age. Before he left the slaughter-house, their killer stole $6,000 William's father had collected to purchase Christmas trees for resale during the holidays.

The bodies were discovered next morning—Thanksgiving Day—by visiting relatives. From the beginning, there was no shortage of clues in the case. Neighbors had seen Ronald Storck walking toward the Brickajlik home on November 22; others had seen him drive away in a pickup truck owned by John Brickajlik, later found abandoned at Philadelphia's airport. Charged with three counts of murder, Storck was declared a federal fugitive on November 28, 1967. His name was added to the "Top Ten" list on January 19, 1968.

Six weeks later, agents following his trail traced Storck to Honolulu, where he gave his name as "Robert Berk." On February 29, Storck was arrested on his newly-purchased thirty-foot boat, moored in a Honolulu yacht harbor. Armed with a .22 rifle and two automatic pistols, he was given no opportunity to resist. Cash in the amount of $3,800 was recovered from the boat, and Storck was soon returned to Bucks County for trial on murder charges.

263 ■ ROBERT LEON McCAIN

A longtime felon, specializing in holdups, McCain's FBI dossier linked him with "hundreds of armed robberies in the

Texas area since 1964." On August 8, 1967, he crossed the line into federal jurisdiction by robbing a bank in Dallas, Texas, shooting a customer to death in the process. A federal warrant for bank robbery was issued on October 11, 1967, and McCain's name was posted to the Bureau's "Ten Most Wanted" list on January 31, 1968.

On February 23, a gunman wearing a rubber Halloween mask invaded a supermarket in Gulfport, Florida. Barging into the store's tiny office, he demanded money from manager Milburn Gallaher, but Gallaher bolted, his assailant in close pursuit. Outside the office, the gunman paused to loot one cash register and was moving on to a second, when customer Christopher Proper tackled him from behind, pinning his arms at his sides. Struggling to free himself, the robber fired a bullet which pierced his own knee before drilling Proper's thigh. A second shot struck Proper in the hip, but then another customer attacked the limping bandit, knocking him unconscious with a pop bottle. He was just coming around when police arrived on the scene.

In custody, the clumsy stickup artist gave his name as "Anthony Taylor," but his alias didn't work. Gulfport police Sgt. Herman Golliner had recently finished a training course at the FBI Academy in Quantico, Virginia, and he recognized Robert McCain from the "Top Ten" flyers displayed around FBI headquarters. A fingerprint comparison confirmed the fugitive's identity, and he was held for federal officers.

264 ■ WILLIAM GARRIN ALLEN , II
265 ■ CHARLES LEE HERRON

A native of Nashville, Tennessee, William Allen was active in militant "Black Power" circles around his home town, and in Cincinnati, Ohio, where he logged arrests for possession of marijuana and disorderly conduct by rioting. One of his Cincinnati acquaintances, Charles Herron, had reached adulthood without accumulating a record, but in early 1968 hometown authorities were seeking to question him on arson charges. Another black militant, Herron traveled with high-powered weapons and quantities of racist literature in his car.

On January 16, 1968, Allen, Herron, and three accomplices —John Alexander, Steve Parker, and Ralph Canady—attempted to pass stolen money orders in a Nashville liquor store. The proprietor called police, and the suspects' vehicle was stopped by two patrolmen a short time later. Approaching the car with no thought of imminent danger, the officers were caught in a withering barrage of rifle fire. Thomas Johnson was pronounced dead at the scene; his partner, Charles Thomasson, would survive to testify against the gunmen.

Soon identified from evidence in their abandoned car, the fugitives were targets of a sweeping manhunt. Parker surrendered a week after the shootings, and Ralph Canady was captured by police several days later. On February 9, 1968, William Allen and Charles Herron were posted to the FBI's "Most Wanted" list on charges of unlawful flight to avoid prosecution for murder.

On March 23, Allen was traced to Brooklyn and there arrested by FBI agents. At their murder trial in Nashville, Allen, Parker, and Canady were convicted and sentenced to ninety-nine years in the state penitentiary. In May 1974, all three escaped from prison at Nashville, and federal fugitive warrants were issued on May 13, charging the trio with unlawful flight to avoid confinement. (John Alexander was captured in East St. Louis during 1971, convicted of manslaughter, and sentenced to ten years in prison. He was paroled in 1974, the same year his cronies escaped from custody.)

Meanwhile, Charles Herron remained at large, months dragging into years as he eluded federal manhunters. He would set a record for the longest period of time a "Top Ten" fugitive has managed to evade pursuit—eighteen years, four months, nine days—and his eventual capture resulted directly from the carelessness of his associates.

In April 1986, fugitive Ralph Canady was arrested by Baltimore police, but he hanged himself in jail before FBI agents had an opportunity to question him. A month later, on June 18, William Allen applied for a driver's license in Jacksonville, Florida, using crudely-altered ID in the name of "William

Spencer." Arrested on the spot for fraud, he was not immediately identified as a federal fugitive.

Police believed they were pursuing a routine fraud investigation when they called at "Spencer's" address a few hours later. Charles Herron answered the door, evading their questions, but officers failed to recognize him. Returning to their office, where Herron's FBI poster adorned one wall, the red-faced detectives set up immediate surveillance of the suspect's dwelling. Playing it cool, Herron had remained in the house rather than taking flight. He was still there, unarmed, when members of an FBI SWAT team surrounded the house and took him into custody without resistance.

266 ∎ LEONARD DANIEL SPEARS

A native of Arkansas, born in 1935, Spears joined accomplices Carl Sims Pankey, Leonard Thomas Pope, and Verser Joseph Swaite in the September 1, 1967, armed robbery of a supermarket in Louisville, Kentucky. The bandits netted some $3,000 before fleeing the scene in a car rented by Pope for the getaway. Louisville police officer William Meyer, Sr., was shot to death by the thieves when he spotted their car and pursued them away from the scene.

Leonard Pope was arrested next morning, at a service station near Vincennes, Indiana, and $272 in rolled coins from the robbery was recovered from his car. A short time later, the rented car was found abandoned near Springfield, Illinois, complete with fingerprints identified as those of Leonard Spears. While Swaite and Pankey were arrested shortly, Spears remained at large, cited in federal warrants charging him with unlawful flight to avoid prosecution for robbery and murder. Added to the Bureau's "Ten Most Wanted" list on February 13, 1968, he was arrested seventeen days later, by FBI agents in Tampa, Florida. Returned to Louisville for trial, he joined his three confederates in court and was convicted of his crimes in June of 1968.

267　■　WILLIAM HOWARD BORNMAN

Born in Connecticut in May 1928, Bornman logged his first conviction, for theft, at age seventeen, earning a stretch in the state reformatory at Cheshire. In December 1948, he drew two years in Florida's state prison on conviction of grand larceny, with an additional count of breaking and entering. Back in Connecticut by November 1961, Bornman was convicted of receiving stolen goods, favored by the court with a suspended sentence. Nine months later, charges of theft and breaking and entering earned him a sentence of two to four years in Connecticut's state prison. In March 1963, he was confined to the Connecticut lockup at Wethersfield, serving two to nine years on six counts of statutory burglary.

Paroled in August 1964, Bornman was charged with parole violation three months later, after his arrest for writing worthless checks. Returned to prison, he attempted suicide and was committed to a mental hospital for observation. Twice escaping from the hospital, he was successful in his second bid for freedom, remaining at large after a breakout on April 22, 1965. Federal warrants charging him with unlawful flight to avoid confinement were issued on March 9, 1966.

On June 29, 1967, Bornman shot a Cleveland, Ohio, police officer during a bungled tavern robbery, leaving his victim to die at the scene. Arrested in Baltimore on July 5 and held for Ohio authorities, Bornman reportedly swallowed arsenic concealed in his clothing, escaping from the hospital on July 7. Recaptured the next day, he was hospitalized again after he "attempted suicide" with a razor blade. On July 19, although handcuffed to his bed, Bornman escaped from the hospital a second time.

On September 29, 1967, the fugitive was arrested for shoplifting and possession of a stolen auto in Pawtucket, Rhode Island, but he was released on bail before his true identity was learned by the arresting officers. By that time, new federal warrants had been issued, charging him with unlawful flight to avoid prosecution for robbery and attempted murder, along with interstate transportation of a stolen car. Bornman's name was added to the "Ten Most Wanted" list on February 13, 1968, with FBI agents bagging their man the same day, in

Covington, Kentucky. Bornman was returned to Ohio for trial and eventual conviction on the outstanding charges.

268 ■ JOHN CONWAY PATTERSON

In the early-morning hours of July 30, 1966, Patterson and an accomplice, LaCarettle Jones, held up a liquor store in East St. Louis, Illinois. As they were leaving, the proprietor set off a burglar alarm, attracting the attention of policemen on routine patrol. Confronted by two officers, the gunmen seized two hostages and a shootout erupted. Police Sgt. Frederick Hudson was killed outright, his partner critically wounded, as more squad cars arrived with sirens screaming. Jones was captured at the scene (and ultimately sentenced to ninety-nine years in prison), while Patterson ran to a waiting getaway car and made good his escape.

Identified with help from his embittered sidekick, Patterson was charged with murder, and a federal warrant cited him for unlawful flight to avoid prosecution. On February 26, 1968, after nineteen months at large, his name was added to the FBI's "Most Wanted" list.

The fugitive, meanwhile, had settled in a rundown Milwaukee apartment, residing with his wife and their four children. In the predawn hours of March 1, 1968, four officers on tactical patrol sighted a prowler lurking between two houses, pausing to ask him some questions. At sight of their patrol car, the suspect bolted for a car at curbside, roaring off with the police in close pursuit. Forced to the curb after several blocks, Patterson surrendered meekly, his identity confirmed by a comparison of fingerprints.

269 ■ TROY DENVER MARTIN

Born in Kentucky in January 1927, Martin racked up adult convictions for forgery, uttering forged U.S. Treasury checks, and being absent without leave from military service before he finally made the FBI's "Top Ten" on a kidnapping charge. Slow to anger in a quarrel, he was deadly when aroused, and had reportedly assaulted several "friends" with guns and knives.

On January 27, 1968, Martin swerved a stolen pickup truck into the yard of a farm outside Britton, Michigan, taking the farmer hostage at gunpoint. Taking off in the farmer's car, with his hostage at the wheel, Martin still allowed his captive time to spot a body lying facedown in the truck. By the time Martin released his hostage in Toledo, Ohio, the corpse had been identified as one of Martin's in-laws, owner of the stolen truck; he had been shot from behind, and Michigan authorities charged Martin with matching counts of kidnapping and murder.

A federal warrant was issued on January 29, 1968, charging Troy Martin with unlawful flight to avoid prosecution. His name was added to the FBI's "Most Wanted" list on March 8, and G-men caught him in Seattle, Washington, eleven days later. Surrendering without a struggle, Martin was returned to Michigan for trial and ultimate conviction on the charges lodged against him.

270 ■ GEORGE BENJAMIN WILLIAMS

A native of Malheur County, Oregon, George Williams spent most of his adult life in various prisons, confined for robbing banks. It was a specialty, of sorts, with criminal convictions dating back to 1931, and Williams could not seem to get the hang of "going straight." In December 1965, Williams set something of a record, looting $19,534 from the same New-castle, California, bank which he had previously robbed in 1946. On March 18, 1968, his name was added to the FBI's "Most Wanted" list.

Exactly two months later, on May 18, a man's skeletal re-mains were discovered near Lovelock, Nevada, in Pershing County. Unable to identify the victim, Lovelock's sheriff sent the bones to Washington, for examination by FBI forensic experts. On June 19, comparison of dental charts and other features "made" the corpse as that of George B. Williams, and his file was permanently closed.

271 ■ MICHAEL JOHN SANDERS

An amateur karate fan and member of an "outlaw" motorcycle gang, Sanders was born in Reno, Nevada, during July 1940. As a self-styled renegade, he often boasted of his conflicts with authority, including a dishonorable discharge from the military and conviction for armed robbery in Tennessee. His record also listed an attempt to flee from psychiatric treatment, ordered by the courts, and evidence suggests that Sanders drew no benefits from therapy he did receive.

On February 7, 1964, Sanders and two male companions were observed loitering near a store in Santa Cruz County, California, their appearances prompting the proprietor to call the sheriff's office. When a pair of deputies arrived to question Sanders and his friends, they were overpowered by the bikers, disarmed, and the radio microphone ripped from their squad car. As the outlaws sped away, they fired a parting shot in the direction of the officers to make their point.

A federal warrant was issued on February 14, 1964, charging Sanders with unlawful flight to avoid prosecution for armed robbery, and his name was added to the FBI's "Most Wanted" list after four years of searching, on March 21, 1968. Eighteen days later, G-men located the self-proclaimed outlaw in New York City, taking him into custody without resistance. Sanders was returned to California for his trial and ultimate conviction on outstanding charges.

272 ■ HOWARD CALLENS JOHNSON

A ruthless "lone wolf," born in Dallas County, Alabama, during April 1916, Johnson was notable for his violent personality, boasting criminal convictions dating back to 1935. Variously confined for arson, assault, and violation of state liquor laws, he drew ten years in Montgomery's Kilby Prison, during 1952, on charges of burning his estranged wife's home. Paroled in 1957, he was arrested for parole violation two years later, winning ultimate release from custody in 1961.

On May 3, 1966, Johnson visited the home of a female acquaintance in Summerfield, Alabama, quarreling with his hostess shortly after he arrived. Departing from the house in a rage, he vowed, "Sometime during the night, some member of this family will get sick and die." Within two hours, the woman's eighteen-year-old son had been killed by a shotgun blast in the front yard, and authorities charged Johnson with the murder.

A federal warrant charging Johnson with unlawful flight was issued on June 3, 1966. His name was added to the "Top Ten" list on March 21, 1968, and agents tracked him to Louisville, Kentucky, a month later, making the arrest on April 24. Surprised and cuffed before he could resist, Johnson was returned to Alabama for trial and conviction on charges of first-degree murder.

273 ■ GEORGE EDWARD WELLS

A native of Belmont County, Ohio, Wells was convicted of first-degree murder in the shooting of an Akron tavern owner. Sentenced to die, he won commutation of his sentence to life imprisonment in 1938, twelve hours before he was scheduled for electrocution. In 1961, Wells was paroled after Governor Michael DiSalle commuted his sentence again, to second-degree murder.

In October 1967, four gunmen invaded the home of coin collector Norman Kanserski, in Middleburg Heights, Ohio, pistol-whipping Kanserski and making off with coins valued at $50,000. A few days later, Wells was linked with the $40,000 robbery of a jewelry store in Brecksville, Ohio. Before the year was out, accomplice George Westrich, named as a participant in the Kanserski raid, was found shot to death in his car at Independence, Missouri.

Indicted on federal charges of transporting stolen property

across state lines, Wells was named to the FBI's "Most Wanted" list on March 28, 1968. Fourteen months later, he was captured by G-men outside a motel in South Point, Ohio. Accompanying Wells at the time of his arrest was Steve Gomori, Jr., recently indicted by a federal grand jury in Cleveland for distributing counterfeit $100 bills. Wells was held in lieu of $100,000 bail; Gomori's bond was set at $5,000, on new charges of harboring a fugitive. Convicted in November 1969 of transporting stolen property, Wells was sentenced to nine years in federal prison.

274 ■ DAVID EVANS

Born at York, Pennsylvania, in October 1944, Evans boasted adult convictions for assault and battery after throwing a young boy off a bridge without provocation. Questioned about his irrational crime, Evans told investigators that he simply "felt like killing someone," and his victim had been handy at the time. So fleet of foot that he outran police dogs on one occasion, Evans was regarded as unstable, violent, and extremely dangerous.

On December 28, 1967, Evans donned a ski mask to hold up the First National Bank and Trust Company in Bethlehem, Pennsylvania. Brandishing an automatic pistol, he looted the cages of $26,000, shouting "Happy New Year" to the cowed employees as he fled. At the time of the robbery, Evans was already being sought as a federal fugitive on charges of unlawful flight to avoid prosecution for burglary, larceny, and receiving stolen goods, those counts emerging from a string of Pennsylvania holdups during January and February 1967.

Added to the Bureau's "Top Ten" list on April 3, 1968, Evans lasted for twenty-three days before the roof fell in. Identified by local police in Philadelphia, on April 26, he was taken into custody without resistance and returned to Bethlehem for trial. Considering the list of charges lodged against him, there would be few happy years in the bandit's future.

275 ■ FRANKLIN ALLEN PARIS

Briefly jailed in 1966, for his alleged involvement in a string of safe burglaries in Shasta County, California, Franklin Paris was released for lack of evidence. The case seemed stronger on August 18, 1966, when he was arrested for burglary in Lamont, California; posting bail, Paris promptly fled town and embarked on a series of supermarket robberies which eventually placed him on the FBI's "Most Wanted" list.

According to police, the fugitive's standard M.O. included kidnapping the families of supermarket managers, holding them hostage until store officials delivered cash on demand. The technique was first applied in Santa Cruz, on January 22, 1967, leading to Paris's indictment on charges of armed robbery and kidnapping. Police in Santa Clara linked his name with several holdups in their jurisdiction over the next few months, with markets singled out for primary attention. On November 14, 1967, Paris pulled a carbon-copy heist in San Jose, and was indicted on further charges of kidnapping and robbery. The next day, in Santa Clara County, he rebounded with another supermarket raid, racking up charges of armed robbery and kidnapping with personal injury.

Federal warrants named Paris a fugitive, sought by the FBI on charges of unlawful flight to avoid prosecution, and his name was added to the "Top Ten" list on April 9, 1968. Six weeks later, on May 21, federal agents were advised that Paris, having spent some time in Medford, Oregon, was driving back to California, to resume his larcenous activities.

A deputy sheriff spotted the fugitive's car that morning, near Dog Creek, California, and a roadblock was hastily erected at the Pit River bridge. Spying the barricade, Paris swung his vehicle around and led pursuers on a high-speed chase, trading shots with police as he fled. Near Lakehead, Paris abandoned his car, wounded by police bullets as he ran toward a nearby grocery store. Seizing bystander Walter Klein as a human shield, the fugitive discarded his empty .357 revolver, drawing a .38 to continue the battle. Lawmen responded with a fusillade from shotguns and automatic rifles, inflicting multiple wounds on both Paris and his prisoner before the smoke cleared.

Incredibly, both men survived, Klein eventually settling his lawsuit out of court for $50,000. Searching the fugitive's car, authorities discovered two army rifles, two .45 automatics, several bayonets, two homemade pipe bombs, and plentiful ammunition for his several weapons. On June 21, 1968, Paris was sentenced to nine years in federal prison on conviction for unlawful flight; eleven days later, he was indicted on twenty-nine felony counts, including robbery, burglary, kidnapping, and assault with a deadly weapon.

276 ■ DAVID STUART NEFF

Born at Providence, Rhode Island, in December 1936, Neff was an accomplished car thief who frequently boasted of his convictions for forgery, uttering, breaking and entering, larceny, and possession of firearms. Convicted of forging U.S. Government War Bonds in November 1966, he jumped bond in Providence prior to sentencing and was sought by Secret Service agents as a federal fugitive when he made the FBI's "Most Wanted" list.

On October 4, 1967, Neff invaded a Lynn, Massachusetts, bank, brandishing a .45-caliber automatic pistol and wearing a mask which persisted in sliding off his face. Readily identified as the gunman who fled with $23,851, tearing away in a stolen car, Neff moved on to raid another bank in Beverly, Massachusetts, on March 27, 1968. That job netted him $28,500, along with formal listing as a fugitive on federal bank robbery charges.

Added to the Bureau's "Top Ten" list on April 18, 1968, Neff lasted one short week before a flying squad of Bureau agents cornered him in Brooklyn. Neff gave up without a fight, waiving extradition to Massachusetts and the open charges waiting for him there.

At 6:01 P.M. on April 4, 1968, America's leading spokesman for black civil rights, Rev. Martin Luther King, Jr., was cut down by a sniper's bullet on the balcony of the Lorraine Motel in Memphis, Tennessee. Embroiled in the midst of a bitter strike by city sanitation workers, most of whom were black, King had been the target of repeated threats in recent days. The night before his murder, in a speech which seemed to take impending death for granted, King had told his audience, "I'm not fearing any man. I've been to the mountain top, and I have seen the promised land."

King's murder sparked days of racial rioting in Memphis and other cities throughout America, but the first concern of homicide investigators was the swift location of his killer. Moments after Rev. King was shot, an unknown stranger dropped a rifle and assorted other personal belongings in the doorway of a nearby shop, fleeing the scene in a white Ford Mustang. The car was traced to Atlanta, Georgia, and recovered from the parking lot of an apartment complex; purchased in Birmingham, Alabama, six months earlier, it was registered in the name of "Eric Stavro Galt."

The same fictitious name had been employed in Birmingham, on March 30, 1968, to purchase the rifle dropped in Memphis. "Eric Galt" had told the salesman in the gun shop that he planned to do some hunting with his brother. Seizing on the possibility of a conspiracy to violate King's civil rights, the FBI began its search for "Galt," aware that it was working with an alias.

The items dropped in Memphis were examined for fingerprints, and on April 19, "Galt's" latent prints were matched with those of James Earl Ray, a fugitive escapee from the Missouri state prison at Jefferson City. The following day, April 20, Ray's name was posted to the FBI's "Most Wanted" list.

At a glance, Ray seemed an unlikely assassin. His career ran more toward petty crime, beginning with his first arrest in 1948, while serving with the army in Germany. Charged with being drunk in quarters, Ray was briefly held in the stockade and then discharged, on grounds of "ineptness and lack of adaptability to military service." In October 1949, he was sentenced to ninety days for burglarizing a Los Angeles cafeteria, released ahead of schedule on his promise to leave California forever. In April 1950, he was held as a vagrant in Cedar Rapids, Iowa; similar charges, along with one count of driving without a license, were lodged against Ray in Quincy, Illinois, on July 23, 1951.

In May 1952 he hit the "big time," robbing a Chicago cab driver at gunpoint. Wounded by police during a zany foot chase, Ray drew a sentence of one to two years in prison. Released in March 1954, he was arrested for burglary five months later, in East Alton, Illinois, and jumped bail before standing trial. In March 1955, he was picked up in Hannibal, Missouri, on federal charges of forging and cashing stolen money orders. That rap earned him 45 months in Leavenworth, and he emerged on April 15, 1958. A string of clumsy supermarket robberies climaxed with Ray's arrest, in St. Louis, on October 10, 1959. Sentenced to twenty years in state prison, he was successful in his third attempt to escape from Jefferson City, slipping out of prison in a bread truck on April 23, 1967.

With Ray's true identity in hand, FBI agents traced him north to Canada. Officers of the Royal Canadian Mounted Police discovered that Ray was traveling on a false passport, in the name of "Ramon George Sneyd." Officers visited his last known address, in Toronto, and learned that Ray had flown to London on May 6. British authorities were alerted, and Ray was captured at the passport desk of London's Heathrow Airport on June 8, as he returned from a side trip to Belgium.

On March 10, 1969—his birthday—James Earl Ray appeared in court at Memphis, pleading guilty to a murder charge. He was sentenced to ninety-nine years in prison, with more time added later, for repeated efforts to escape. Twenty years of speculation, including a congressional investigation of the case, has failed to resolve unanswered questions in the King assassination. In 1978, a House committee reported that King was "probably" the victim of an organized conspiracy, but no other participants were identified.

278 ■ JOHN WESLEY SHANNON , JR.

An ex-prize fighter and sometimes narcotics addict, Shannon was born at Pleasantville, New Jersey, on July 9, 1936. His pugilistic prowess won him a championship during military service, but in civilian life his violent temper made him an unstable contender. When not squaring off in the ring, he variously found employment as a caddy, dishwasher, hod carrier, construction worker and hospital orderly. None of the jobs supported his drug habit or his fondness for gambling, and by 1957 he had turned his hand to crime, logging arrests and convictions for larceny, robbery, possession of a weapon, and sodomy.

On May 26, 1967, Shannon joined four accomplices in robbing a Northfield, New Jersey, savings and loan office of $8,881. The take was less than fabulous, when split five ways, and three of the bandits were swiftly apprehended, sentenced to prison for their role in the heist. Federal warrants were issued on September 15, charging Shannon with bank robbery, and his name was added to the FBI's "Most Wanted" list on May 7, 1968. A month later, on June 5, he was cornered by federal agents and local authorities in Camden, New Jersey, flushed from his hideout and taken into custody without a fight. Held for trial on federal charges, Shannon was convicted and imprisoned for his crimes.

279 ■ TAYLOR MORRIS TEAFORD

Taylor Teaford launched his criminal career at age eighteen, with a conviction for burglarizing two cabins near Bass Lake, California. Free on parole after two years, he joined an accomplice in raping a fifteen-year-old girl on November 20, 1957. Conviction on that charge sent him back to prison until April 1967, when he was paroled a second time.

On July 18, 1977, Teaford settled a family argument by shooting his elderly grandmother dead in her home, between Bass Lake and North Fork, California. For good measure, he wounded his sister, Sherry McIntosh, and then shot a passing motorist—Charles Culpepper—who paused to investigate the sound of gunshots. Sheriff's deputies were summoned by a neighbor, and Teaford pinned them down with rifle fire, blasting the windows out of their cruiser before he made good his escape.

Indicted on charges of murder, assault to commit murder, and parole violation, Teaford became the subject of a widespread manhunt. Federal warrants raised the ante, charging him with unlawful flight to avoid prosecution for murder, and his name was added to the FBI's "Most Wanted" list on May 10, 1968.

Four years later, on May 24, 1972, federal process was dismissed against Teaford at the request of local prosecutors. Passing time had ruined any hope of a successful prosecution, and Teaford was dropped from the "Top Ten" list. Still at large as this is written, Taylor Teaford ranks as one of those who got away.

280 ■ PHILLIP MORRIS JONES

A Florida native with prior convictions for grand theft, Phillip Jones was known as an avid gambler, with a preference for blackjack and poker. Whenever possible, he liked to use marked cards, but cheating did not always pay, and Jones was constantly in need of cash. In 1968, he turned to robbery and bet the future on his own ability to outwit agents of the FBI.

On February 23, 1968, Jones raided a bank in Bakersfield, California, for $5,637, but luck was running against him, and all but $500 of the loot was recovered from his abandoned getaway car. On April 8, in Winter Haven, Florida, he locked eight bank employees in a vault, escaping with $79,874 to a nearby motel. When police arrived, Jones donned swim trunks, posing as a casual lounger by the pool, then stole a car and drove to a local lake; abandoning the vehicle, he swam fifty yards across the lake, stole a truck, and made good his escape. This time, all but $277 of the bank loot was recovered from Jones's motel room.

The bandit managed to keep his next score, in the amount

of $9,820, stolen from a bank in Wheaton, Maryland, on April 30, 1968. Four days later, in Phoenix, he raided a savings and loan association for $2,100, but his time was running out. Identified as the hit-and-run bandit, Jones was indicted on federal bank robbery charges. His name was added to the Bureau's "Ten Most Wanted" list on June 5, 1968.

Three weeks later, tired of running, Jones walked into an FBI office in San Mateo, California, calmly announcing, "You people want me." Special Agent John Breslin accepted a paper sack from Jones, discovering an automatic pistol inside, and the hard-luck fugitive was taken into custody.

281 ■ JOHNNY RAY SMITH

An ex-convict with time served for auto theft, armed robbery, and jailbreak, Smith pulled his last holdup on February 5, 1968, in Pensacola, Florida. Quickly captured, he faced additional charges of resisting arrest after scuffling with police officers. On April 16, while awaiting trial, Smith escaped from the Escambia County jail, in Pensacola, and was named a federal fugitive on charges of unlawful flight to avoid prosecution and interstate transportation of a stolen car. His name was added to the Bureau's "Top Ten" list on June 20, 1968.

Four days after his addition to the roster, Smith was captured by local police in Ocean Springs, Mississippi, not far from Biloxi. A traveling companion, hitchhiker Hyman Streiter, was booked on vagrancy charges until authorities determined that he knew nothing of Smith's criminal background. Picked up by Smith two weeks earlier, near Little Rock, Streiter had been chosen for his valid driver's license, but he played no conscious role in Smith's escape.

282 ■ BYRON JAMES RICE

Born in 1936, Byron Rice compiled the standard "Top Ten" record of arrests and convictions before he made the big time in early 1966. On February 21 of that year, acting with two male accomplices, Rice stopped an armored car in Mountain View, California, making off with $30,000 in cash after one of the guards was shot to death. Rice's companions were swiftly captured and sentenced to life imprisonment, but he remained at large when federal warrants were issued, charging him with unlawful flight to avoid prosecution for armed robbery and murder. Added to the FBI's "Most Wanted" list on July 5, 1968, he remained at large for over four years, moving constantly from city to city, holding down jobs as a carpenter, janitor, laborer, maintenance man, security guard and stock clerk. Finally, tired of running, he surrendered to Chicago agents on the afternoon of October 2, 1972, bringing the long hunt voluntarily to an end.

283 ■ ROBERT LEROY LINDBLAD

A San Francisco native, born in 1933, Robert Lindblad was the rugged outdoor type. An expert in judo and karate, he was also a skiing enthusiast and the author of a book on wilderness survival. In the Air Force, he had taught recruits the manly art of living off the land, but he had less success in civilized society. Variously employed as a waiter, busboy, card dealer and service station attendant, Lindblad realized that he was not fulfilling his potential, and in the late 1960s he decided on a new approach.

In October 1967, two male corpses were discovered in a shallow grave in Lyon County, Nevada, outside the town of Dayton. Both victims had been shot in the head at close range, then stripped of their clothing before they were dumped in the desert. Investigation revealed that the victims were Wyoming businessmen, missing since August 1967, when they flew to Reno to examine some alleged gold mining property. With a third man, the victims were partners in a motel located at Jackson Hole, Wyoming, each insured in the amount of $100,000. On the side, their jointly-owned motel had lately been destroyed by fire, a circumstance which brought the surviving partner another $125,000 in insurance payments.

Following intense police investigation, the remaining partner and two other men were charged with conspiracy in the double murder, and all three were arrested in Nevada. Lindblad, hired by the conspirators, remained at large, but federal agents knew he was supposed to kill the targets with a well-placed judo chop to each man's throat; when that plan failed, they had been shot to death and buried in the desert wasteland. Federal warrants charged Lindblad with unlawful flight to avoid prosecution on January 31, 1968, and his name was added to the "Top Ten" list July 11. Three months later, on October 7, he surrendered voluntarily to federal agents in the town of Yerrington, Nevada, and was held for trial.

284 ■ JAMES JOSEPH SCULLY

Born at Blackstone, Massachusetts, during August 1920, Scully was a moody gunman said to harbor suicidal tendencies. Paroled on his latest bank robbery conviction, he rebounded at once with a string of holdups in California between March 21 and June 14, 1968, knocking over banks in Torrance, San Jose, Santa Rosa, Covina, and Rowland Heights. The average take was small—a little over $10,000 total from all five jobs—and Scully's temper was displayed accordingly. In the Santa Rosa robbery he shot and critically wounded a newspaper delivery man who walked in on the holdup, unaware of what was happening.

With new federal bank robbery charges filed against him, as well as parole violation, Scully was added to the FBI's "Most Wanted" list on July 15, 1968. Eight days later federal agents and local police caught him in Arcadia, California, making the arrest without a shot fired in anger. The impressive list of charges filed against him guaranteed that Scully would be doing heavy time in state and federal prisons, effectively removed from circulation in the wake of his latest rampage.

285 ■ BILLY RAY WHITE

In September 1967, two gunmen held up a jewelry store in Metairie, Louisiana, escaping with $4,000 worth of diamond rings and other merchandise. In flight, they fired three shots at store employees who attempted to pursue them, vanishing before police arrived. One of the robbers was swiftly arrested by local police, and he named Billy White as his elusive accomplice.

A month later, in Albuquerque, New Mexico, White invaded the offices of a savings and loan association, herding employees into a back room and tying them up before looting the office of $1,650. In November 1967, witnesses identified White as one of two gunmen who robbed a trading post at Budsville, fifty miles west of Albuquerque. Netting a mere $300, the thieves went berserk, tying up two hostages and shooting both of them to death. The arrest of White's accomplice brought confirmation of his identity, and murder charges were added to several outstanding counts of armed robbery. On August 13, 1968, White's name was added to the "Ten Most Wanted" list.

Four days later, federal agents acting on a tip surrounded a rented home in Wood River, Illinois. The female occupant denied any knowledge of Billy White, granting permission for agents to search the house. White was discovered in a closet, trying to hold the door shut from inside, and he surrendered without resistance. Three pistols and a quantity of drugs were found inside the house, along with some 200 cartons of stolen cigarettes.

According to the landlord, White had described himself as a traveling "insurance agent," required to make long business trips at frequent intervals. Two maps of Illinois, recovered in the search, showed seventy towns marked with circles; White's girlfriend fingered the locations as the scenes of past—or future—robberies. In every case, the cash or stolen merchandise was driven back to Woods River, with various "hot" items unloaded through black market outlets. Held on federal charges, White was extradited to New Mexico for trial on two counts of murder.

286 ■ FREDERICK RUDOLPH YOKOM

A New York native, born in February 1946, Yokom liked to tell acquaintances that his occupation was armed robbery, no idle boast in view of his numerous arrests for that and other felonies. The conversation turned to crime most often when he had been using LSD or marijuana, but the prospect of an easy score was never far from Yokom's mind. The latter 1960s saw him put down roots in sunny Florida, where he commanded a disreputable team of jewel thieves dubbed the "Yokom Gang."

On January 4, 1968, Yokom and two masked accomplices invaded the home of a prominent Miami jeweler, leaving their victim, his wife and children bound with strips of bedding as they fled with some $6,000 in cash and jewelry. Three days later, a Miami socialite and tennis pro was shot to death when he resisted an attempted robbery, his wife seriously wounded in the exchange of gunfire which also injured their two assailants. Federal warrants were issued on January 29, charging the gang leader with unlawful flight to avoid prosecution for robbery. Yokom, scheduled to appear in court that day for trial on burglary, robbery, and assault charges, had already vanished, and his name was added to the "Top Ten" list on August 21, 1968.

He lasted sixteen days before a team of federal agents tagged him in Los Angeles, surprising Yokom on La Cienega Boulevard and taking him into custody without resistance. Living in L.A. as "Alfredo Rivas Loya," Yokom had believed himself secure, but as the handcuffs closed around his wrists he recognized the nature of his error.

287 ■ HAROLD JAMES EVANS

The jailbreak should have come as no surprise. By all accounts, Harold Evans was a desperate character, convicted in Norristown, Pennsylvania, of felony charges including burglary, armed robbery, assault and battery, rape, conspiracy, carrying a deadly weapon and violation of the National Firearms Act. On June 23, 1967, while walking from the court-room to his jail cell under guard, Evans and another inmate—to whom he was handcuffed—broke free of their escorts and vanished in traffic. Harold's companion was sighted that afternoon, on a trolley bridge spanning the Schuylkill River, and two days later his corpse was found bobbing in the stream, apparently the victim of an accidental fall. Evans, more sure-footed in his flight, remained at large.

A Chicago native, born in January 1945, Harold Evans had already racked up a criminal record spanning the continent, with arrests filed in California, Illinois, Pennsylvania, New York, and Ontario, Canada. Federal officers described him as a ranking member of a notorious burglary gang, considered habitually armed and dangerous by law enforcement personnel. A federal warrant was issued on June 27, charging Evans with unlawful flight to avoid confinement, and his name was added to the Bureau's "Top Ten" roster on September 19, 1968.

The lure of home was strong, and by the time he made the "Ten Most Wanted" list, Harold Evans was already rubbing elbows with his lifelong cronies in Chicago. Federal agents traced him there and made their collar on the second day of January 1969, surprising Evans and completing the arrest before he could resist or flee. He was returned to Pennsylvania and maximum security.

288 ■ ROBERT LEE CARR

A native of Sunbury, Pennsylvania, born on May 5, 1946, Carr launched his criminal career as a juvenile, with arrests for burglary and auto theft. In later years, he would compile a record of additional offenses, including parole violation, sometimes going straight as a bricklayer, roofer, or carpenter. The word "Love," tattooed across the knuckles of his left hand, reflected Carr's own image of himself as a ladies' man, but it bore no connection with his view of humankind in general. By autumn 1968, he was in jail again.

On September 16, 1968, while awaiting trial on robbery

charges, Robert Carr and inmate Michael Lynn Clark escaped from the Northumberland County jail, in Sunbury, Pennsylvania, after assaulting a deputy U.S. marshal and locking guards in a cell. During their flight, the fugitives invaded a home at Millersburg, handcuffing the female occupant to a chair and ransacking the house, fleeing with a rifle and $6,000 in cash. Other robberies were also charged against them in the next few days, and Carr was added to the FBI's "Most Wanted" list on October 16, 1968.

On November 4, federal agents followed the directions of a tipster, visiting a service station in South Gate, California. There, they found Carr employed under the alias of "Robert Daniels." Michael Clark, while not on the payroll, was visiting Carr on the job when G-men arrived, and the two fugitives were arrested simultaneously. Both were returned to Pennsylvania, for trial on outstanding charges related to their escape.

289 ■ LEVI WASHINGTON

A native of Alligator, Mississippi, Levi Washington was on parole from a narcotics conviction when police in New Orleans arrested him, filing charges in three local bank robberies, committed between July and November 1967. Before those cases came to trial, the FBI charged Washington with robbing a church in Chicago, and Louisiana surrendered him to Illinois authorities. On August 16, 1968, he escaped from the Cook County jail, in Chicago, and was declared a federal fugitive on charges of unlawful flight to avoid prosecution. Washington was added to the "Ten Most Wanted" list on November 15, 1968.

Three weeks later, on December 5, three gunmen entered a bank in Jackson, Michigan, scooping $37,000 into their satchels and spraying the room with a riot-control chemical as they fled. Witnesses described the outlaws and their vehicle, which was discovered by patrolling officers an hour later. Footprints in a snowbank led police to a nearby rooming house, where suspects "Paul Carter" and "Allen Rose" were taken into custody. A search of their room turned up loot from the bank heist, along with a sawed-off .30-caliber carbine and three pistols.

At midnight on December 5, a homemade bomb exploded at City Hall, in Jackson, wounding two policemen. Officers concluded that the bomb was meant to blow at noon, as a diversion for the bank job, but a faulty timer had delayed the blast twelve hours. Evidence recovered from the scene established that the suspects, "Rose" and "Carter," were responsible for the explosion.

On December 9, a fingerprint comparison revealed "Paul Carter's" true identity as that of Levi Washington. His cellmate, "Allen Rose," was Louis Carr. On the eleventh of December, the elusive third man, Delbert Beard, turned up to visit Carr in jail. Beard gave his name as "August Cerio," but officers were not deceived, and he was taken into custody on charges of attempting to arrange a jailbreak.

The federal trial of Carr and Beard began, in Detroit, on July 8, 1969. Levi Washington succeeded in severing his case from the others, and was placed on trial separately, but in the same building. On the morning of July 23, arriving for court in a prison van, the defendants made a desperate bid for freedom, fleeing under the guns of federal marshals. Louis Carr was seriously wounded, with a bullet in his chest, and three bystanders suffered minor injuries. Levi Washington, unharmed, was captured in the courthouse basement.

290 ■ RICHARD LEE TINGLER , JR.

Born out of wedlock in December 1940, Richard Tingler was raised by a mother who beat him regularly, interspersing punishment with frequent reminders that her son was "born in sin." Enlisting in the air force to escape from home, Tingler experienced his first run-in with police in June 1959, while stationed in Alaska. Going AWOL with a friend, he was arrested on a charge of burglary in Anchorage, and wound up pleading guilty to four break-ins. Transferred several times during his two-year federal sentence, Tingler was released at Chillicothe, Ohio, in February 1961. Six months later, with the same air force crony, he was busted in Portsmouth, Ohio, on thirteen counts of breaking and entering. Packed off to state prison for a term of one to fifteen years, Tingler was paroled in August 1964. More burglaries sent him back to prison, as a parole violator, but he was finally released in February 1968.

On September 16, early-morning joggers found four bodies laid out side-by-side in Cleveland's Rockefeller Park. The victims, slain by multiple gunshots from two different weapons, included tavern proprietor Joseph Zoldman, two of his part-time bartenders, and a young female prostitute. Authorities surmised that the four had been taken hostage in a tavern robbery, conveyed to the park at gunpoint, and murdered there to eliminate troublesome witnesses.

A month later, on October 20, a lone gunman entered a dairy bar in Columbus, Ohio, near closing time. Scooping $562 out of the register, he ordered manager Phyllis Crowe and two teenage employees—Susan Pack and Jimmy Stevens —into the back room. Binding their hands, the bandit was about to leave when he paused in the doorway, his face contorted by sudden rage, and snarled, "What the hell, I ain't got nothing to lose. I'm gonna kill you all."

Ripping the door of a safe from its mountings, the stranger advanced on Pack and Stevens, pounding their skulls in a frenzy. Turning on Phyllis Crowe, he twisted a coathanger around her neck, choking her into unconsciousness and leaving her for dead. When she woke and struggled free a half hour later, Crowe found that both her employees had also been shot in the back of their heads. Ballistics tests matched the bullets to one of the guns used in Cleveland and Mrs. Crowe identified a mug shot of Richard Tingler as her assailant.

Indicted on six counts of murder, Tingler was added to the FBI's "Ten Most Wanted" list on November 8, 1968. By that time, using the name of "Don Williams," he had secured employment on a farm owned by Alvin Hoffman, near Dill City, Oklahoma. Hoffman thought it strange that his employee packed a pistol everywhere he went, but "Williams" was a decent worker, and a love of firearms does not make a man stand out in Oklahoma.

On March 30, 1969, Tingler's photograph was broadcast

following an episode of "The FBI" television series. Viewing the program, "Don Williams" realized his time was running short. He became increasingly nervous on the job, and one morning he failed to report for work.

On April 27, forty-nine-year-old Brooks Hutchenson checked into a motel at Gilman, Illinois, accompanied by a new acquaintance, "D. L. Williams." Next morning, the maid found Hutchenson dead in his room, shot four times at close range, with his cash and late-model Ford LTD missing.

On April 29, "Don Williams" returned to the Hoffman farm, driving Hutchenson's car. He left again the next morning, but returned—minus the car—on May 2. By this time, his erratic behavior was drawing attention from neighbors, and Tingler's time was running out.

By mid-May, the Washita County sheriff's office was receiving complaints about "Williams" and his indiscriminate gunfire. A neighbor's dog had been killed without provocation, and the farm hand was fond of shooting glass insulators on high-tension poles lining the highway. Deputies investigating the complaints were warned by locals that the gunman bore a strong resemblance to a wanted fugitive.

On May 19, a team of federal agents joined sheriff's deputies on a second visit to the farm. They found Tingler working in a field, relieved him of an automatic pistol, and took him into custody without resistance. Tried on six counts of murder in Ohio, the fugitive was convicted and sentenced to die.

291 ■ GEORGE MICHAEL GENTILE

A New York native, born in April 1902, Gentile was a drifter with a taste for "easy" money. One of his favorite scams involved posing as a police officer, extorting money from homosexuals in various states via threats of arrest and exposure. Convicted of a Pennsylvania holdup-murder during 1923, Gentile logged other felony convictions for attempted grand larceny, impersonating a police officer, desertion, and various counts of extortion. Frequently paroled, he was as frequently arrested for violating the terms of his conditional release from prison.

On February 16, 1965, Gentile and two accomplices falsely identified themselves as police officers, extorting $2,500 from a gay victim in Denton, Texas. One month later, working with new companions, he pulled the same familiar scam in Alexandria, Virginia, pocketing $1,000 for his efforts. Federal warrants issued in Chicago and in Sherman, Texas, charged Gentile with interstate transportation in aid of racketeering—extortion, and his name was added to the Bureau's "Top Ten" list on June 28, 1968. He was arrested six months later, on December 17, by local officers in New York City, when they recognized his style and matched his face to mugshots on outstanding federal flyers. Safely under lock and key, Gentile could look forward to impersonating a convicted inmate for the next few years.

292 ■ GARY STEVEN KRIST
293 ■ RUTH EISEMANN-SCHIER

Gary Krist launched his criminal career at age fourteen, with the theft of a boat. A year later he stole a car, and at sixteen he was committed to the Utah State Industrial School, at Ogden, for a year. Krist entered confinement on June 2, 1961, but soon escaped; he was recaptured in Idaho on July 29, 1961. At age eighteen, he was sentenced to the state vocational school at Tracy, California, on conviction for two auto thefts in the vicinity of Oakland. Released on December 4, 1964, he was next arrested on January 6, 1966, after stealing two cars from a sales lot in San Mateo, California. Convicted of auto theft on May 20, 1966, he drew a term of six months to five years in state prison. Krist escaped from custody on November 11, 1966, and was still at large two years later, when he graduated to the big time.

Gary's accomplice for the fabled "big score" was Ruth Eisemann-Schier, a biology researcher and native of Honduras, attracted to Krist by his smooth talk and obvious self-confidence. If she had any doubts about his plan for instant wealth, they were suppressed as Krist spelled out the details of his scheme. Ruth's gullibility would earn her recognition as the first female addition to the FBI's "Most Wanted" list.

On December 17, 1968, twenty-year-old Barbara Jane Mackle, a student at Emory College in Atlanta, was spending the night with her mother in a suburban motel. Recovering from influenza, Barbara had left her dormitory in consideration of her roommates, and her mother had flown in from Florida to nurse her through the illness. While the treatment might have seemed extravagant, it fit the Mackle life-style; Barbara's father was a millionaire land developer and personal friend of President-elect Richard Nixon.

The women weren't expecting visitors that morning, in the predawn hours, when Krist and his companion forced their way inside the room at gunpoint. Barbara's mother, bound and chloroformed, was left behind; the ailing girl was driven twenty miles northeast of town and buried in a box which had been fitted with an air pump, food and water, and a battery-powered lamp. Their dirty work complete, the kidnappers drove back to Florida, waiting for the news to break.

A ransom note, buried in the Mackles' front yard at Coral Gables, Florida, demanded $500,000 ransom in old $20 bills. The family followed orders, running a specified ad in a Miami newspaper on December 18, waiting nervously for instructions on the ransom's delivery. The drop was arranged for December 19, on a causeway leading to uninhabited Fair Isle, in Biscayne Bay. Losing his way in the darkness, Robert Mackle arrived an hour late at the drop point, but Krist confirmed the payoff via telephone, circling back to pick up the suitcase. He barely had the bag in hand, when a policeman on routine patrol mistook Krist for a burglar, giving chase. The kidnapper escaped on foot, but clues from his abandoned vehicle identified both suspects for the FBI.

Meanwhile, at half-past midnight on December 20, a phone call to the Bureau's office in Atlanta gave directions to the site where Barbara Mackle had been buried. Exhumed after eighty-three hours, she was found alive and well. Arrest warrants for Gary Krist and Ruth Eisemann-Schier were issued the same day, and their names were simultaneously added to the "Ten Most Wanted" list.

In headlong flight, Krist had used some of the ransom money to purchase a boat, planning to escape by water. A Coast Guard helicopter spoiled his plan, trailing him until Krist abandoned his craft on Hog Island, in Charleston Harbor. Captured by Sheriff Richard McLeod on December 22, the fugitive was held in lieu of $500,000 bail.

On January 3, 1969, Krist and his female accomplice were indicted on state charges of kidnapping with ransom, a capital crime in the state of Georgia. On March 5, Ruth Eisemann-Schier was arrested in Norman, Oklahoma, where she had applied for a nursing job under the name of "Donna Sue Wills." A routine fingerprint check, required of all nursing applicants, revealed her identity and she was reported to the FBI by local authorities.

Convicted of state kidnapping charges on May 26, 1969, Gary Krist was sentenced to a term of life imprisonment. Three days later, his accomplice pled guilty on similar charges, receiving a sentence of seven years, with the condition that she be deported to Honduras on release.

In custody, awaiting trial, Krist startled jailers with confessions to a string of previously unsolved murders. According to the prisoner, his first victim was a sixty-five-year-old hermit, with whom Krist had a homosexual relationship at age fourteen, while living in Pelican, Alaska. He had killed the man, Krist said, by tripping him while they were walking on a bridge across a deep ravine. Investigators verified a case, identical to Krist's description, which had previously been described as death by accident.

At nineteen, Krist asserted, he had killed a girl near San Diego, strangling and beating her to death, concealing her body under a pile of rocks. Local officers confirmed the discovery of Helen Crow's body on October 3, 1964, with a coroner's estimate of death occurring six to eight weeks earlier. At that time, Krist was under lock and key at Tracy, California; his knowledge of the graphic details in the case remains a mystery.

A third homicide, reported by Krist, was committed in 1961, shortly after his escape from confinement in Utah. According to Gary's confession, he picked up a homosexual, described as a "sissy," and later killed his victim in a violent fit of rage. The body had been dumped near Wendover, Utah, where local officers confirmed discovery of a skeleton on July 27, 1967. The coroner's vague estimate of death, some three to five years earlier, roughly corresponds with Krist's period of freedom from custody.

Despite allusions to a fourth murder, Krist refrained from offering any details. At this writing, he remains confined in Georgia on kidnapping charges. There are no apparent plans to prosecute for murder in Alaska or Utah.

294 ■ BALTAZAR GARCIA ESTOLAS

A Filipino seaman turned to crime, Estolas held up a Stockton, California, clothing store in May 1968, bagging $2,203 before he shot two employees in the head, killing both instantly. Emerging from the shop, he came under fire from a neighboring storekeeper, wounding two bystanders in a fierce exchange of gunfire. Estolas escaped by flagging down an auto occupied by two young sisters, holding them hostage on a drive to San Francisco, where they were released hours later, unharmed. Indicted on charges of robbery and murder, Estolas became a federal fugitive with the issuance of warrants charging him with unlawful flight to avoid prosecution. His name was added to the Bureau's "Top Ten" list on January 3, 1969.

Eight months later, on September 3, the FBI received a tip from San Antonio, Texas, where a citizen had recognized the fugitive's picture on television. Posing as a Hawaiian, Estolas had found work at the Jersey Lily Dairy Bar in Langtry, a small town sixty miles west of Del Rio, Texas, on the Rio Grande. Arrested on the job by federal agents, Estolas offered no resistance. He was identified from fingerprints and extradited back to California for trial.

295 ■ BILLY AUSTIN BRYANT

A native of North Carolina, born in 1939, Bryant logged his first arrest at age twenty-seven, on charges of simple assault, following an altercation with his partner in a Washington, D.C., auto repair shop. Respected as a hard-working family man before that brush with the police, Bryant changed directions almost overnight, adopting the pursuit of "easy" money with a pistol in his hand.

On January 30, 1967, Billy Bryant robbed a Washington savings and loan office of $1,310, holding employees at gunpoint. A second robbery, on April 7, put $3,000 in his pocket, and he picked up another $2,686 in his third daylight heist, on April 30. Arrested by city detectives on May 6, 1967, Bryant was convicted on three counts of robbery, sentenced to the reformatory at Lorton, Virginia, for a period of eighteen to fifty-four years.

Bryant's talent with motors won him a job in the prison auto shop, where he began to hatch escape plans shortly after his arrival. On August 23, 1968, while working on a government vehicle, Bryant rolled the car downhill, toward a guard tower, gunning the engine as he reached level ground and smashing through the outer fence. On September 9, he was indicted by a federal grand jury on escape charges.

Four months later, on January 8, 1969, Bryant robbed a bank in Prince George's County, Maryland, of $1,800. One of the tellers recognized him as a former customer, and confirmation was obtained from photos on his federal Wanted flyers. Half an hour after the robbery, three FBI agents called on Bryant's wife, at her apartment, but the fugitive responded to their knock and opened fire without warning. Agents Anthony Palmissano and George Sullivan were mortally wounded, while Agent Edwin Woodriffe returned Bryant's fire, retreating to summon help. Bryant slipped out the back way while Woodriffe was calling for reinforcements, but a positive I.D. won him immediate posting to the Bureau's "Most Wanted" list.

That evening, news reports about the robbery and double murder alerted Robert Ross, a local resident who had been kept from work that day by illness. Ross recalled the sound of someone running up the stairs in his apartment building shortly after noon—around the time the agents had been shot, nearby—and someone had been rummaging around the crawlspace, over his apartment, through the afternoon. Around 6:45 P.M., Ross heard more sounds of movement from an attic, just above his living room, and called police. The officers, responding to a routine prowler call, were startled to discover Billy Bryant in the attic, but the killer dropped his weapon on command and offered no resistance to arrest.

Convicted of prison escape and the Maryland robbery on April 14, 1969, Bryant was sentenced to twenty years, the term to run consecutively with outstanding prison terms. On October 27, he was convicted on two counts of murder, addressing the court six days later with an absolute lack of remorse. "I can't say I'm sorry for what happened to the two men," he declared. "I feel they brought their death on their own self. To stand here and say I'm sorry would be a lie. I had a job to do, and I did it. If killing a man means surviving, I'm afraid I'd have to do it over." Bryant's unrepentant attitude earned him two consecutive life sentences, with the court's recommendation that he never be considered for parole.

296 ■ BILLY LEN SCHALES

Diagnosed by psychiatrists as a sexual deviate, Billy Schales was once convicted and confined in Michigan on charges of molesting a young girl. On April 4, 1967, giving his name as "Bill Miller," he answered a newspaper advertisement offering an apartment for rent in Houston, Texas. While touring the apartment with the owner's wife, Schales threw the woman to the floor and tried to rape her, punching her and drawing a knife when she resisted. After suffering two superficial wounds, the victim managed to disarm her attacker, slashing his neck and putting him to flight. Investigation led to identification of Schales, resulting in his indictment on charges of assault and attempted murder. A federal charge of unlawful flight to avoid prosecution was subsequently added, and Schales made the FBI's "Most Wanted" list on January 27, 1969.

Three days later, in Shreveport, Louisiana, resident Gerald Hawkins recognized Schales's photograph in the newspaper. Hawkins recalled seeing the fugitive at Plantation Park, in Bossier City, and notified police. A pair of detectives were dispatched to the park, and Schales was sighted within moments of their arrival. Ducking into an apartment building, Schales was cornered while the two detectives called for reinforcements and the building was surrounded. He surrendered under threat of tear gas, and police recovered a .22 magnum rifle from his apartment.

297 ■ THOMAS JAMES LUCAS

An ex-convict from Durham, North Carolina, Tom Lucas had already served time on a murder conviction before running afoul of federal agents. On February 22, 1968, he joined two other gunmen in looting a bank in West Baltimore, Maryland, of $22,398. By the time federal charges were filed in that case, Lucas was also suspected of involvement in several other Maryland bank robberies.

Lucas was added to the Bureau's "Ten Most Wanted" list on February 13, 1969. Hiding out in Washington, D.C., under the alias of "Anthony Lee," he killed time between bank jobs by working as a waiter at a private club. On February 26, while walking down a street in Northwest Washington, the fugitive was sighted by FBI agents and quietly taken into custody.

298 ■ WARREN DAVID REDDOCK

By age 42, Texas-born Reddock had compiled a record of fifteen felony arrests and five convictions, mainly in the field of bad checks and confidence games. Most recently sentenced in November 1963, he was paroled on May 18, 1967, with no serious intention of "going straight."

In July 1968, Chicago accountant Harvey Rosenzweig met Reddock while vacationing in Montreal. Rosenzweig answered a newspaper ad seeking investment partners in a real estate venture. He fell for Reddock's offer of a ranking position in the American branch of a nonexistent multinational firm called "European Arms Corporation." All it would take, Reddock promised, was a reasonable cash investment up front.

A few days later, Rosenzweig quit his job in Chicago, and on August 14 he joined Reddock for a tour of 1,050 undeveloped acres in Lake County, Illinois. "Tycoon" Reddock planned to buy the land and build a multi-million-dollar "recreation center." The property would cost him $1.5 million, but Reddock was confident, inviting Rosenzweig to join him in Monaco for final discussions with the "big boss" of European Arms.

Rosenzweig departed from Chicago on August 16, and worried relatives waited two days before calling the FBI. The trail went cold at a Waukegan motel, where Reddock and Rosenzweig had registered on the night of August 16. No other trace of the missing accountant was found, in Monaco or elsewhere, until his stolen credit card ran up bills of $1,165 in New York City a short time later. Rosenzweig's decomposing body, badly beaten, was discovered in rural Lake County on September 26, 1968, identified from dental records. Reddock was charged with his murder on October 10, and federal warrants issued on a charge of unlawful flight to avoid prosecution. On March 11, 1969, Reddock's name was added to the FBI's "Top Ten."

Federal agents learned that Reddock had rented a car in Peekskill, New York, during May 1968, dumping it two months later in Plattsburg. He rented a second car in Burlington, Vermont, on July 22, driving to Montreal, where he dropped out of sight on August 6—ten days before Rosenzweig disappeared. Three weeks after the murder, Reddock was sighted in Paris, traced on from there via credit card receipts to New Delhi, Hong Kong, Mexico City, and back to Los Angeles on September 19. From that point on, his aimless wanderings touched bases in Canada, Mexico and Jamaica, traipsing back and forth across America.

In early April 1971, *Life* magazine ran photos of the current

"Ten Most Wanted" fugitives, and agents based in San Francisco were rewarded with a phone call. Their informant fingered Reddock as a man who had been working at a ranch outside Pacifica, California, since April 1969. Three agents found him there on April 11, 1971, and took him into custody without resistance. In Chicago, Reddock waived a jury trial and was convicted of murder by the presiding judge, sentenced to a prison term of thirty to fifty years.

299 ■ GEORGE EDWARD BLUE

The straight life held a limited appeal for George E. Blue. A small-time robber, he was none the less consistent, never giving up the dream of easy money, one big score that would irrevocably change his life and set him up on easy street. It never seemed to dawn on Blue that he was spending the majority of his allotted time in prison. He no sooner hit the streets, released from one conviction, than he had another holdup in the works.

On July 11, 1968, less than a month after his parole from Indiana's state prison, Blue robbed a bank in Evansville of $5,670. Four months later, on November 26, he was identified as the gunman who took down another bank in Atwood, Indiana. Federal warrants were issued for his arrest on charges of bank robbery and unlawful flight to avoid prosecution, in addition to new counts of parole violation from his previous Indiana conviction.

Blue was added to the Bureau's "Ten Most Wanted" list on March 20, 1969. Eight days later, in Chicago, federal agents picked him up in the Chicago Greyhound terminal, relieving him of a pistol before he had a chance to resist arrest. Also bagged in the raid was Blue's female traveling companion, Mary Ann Downs, whom G-men detained as a material witness to the November robbery in Atwood, Indiana.

300 ■ CAMERON DAVID BISHOP

A militant member of Students for a Democratic Society (SDS), Cameron Bishop was the first "revolutionary" added to the Bureau's roster in a period of left-wing violence aimed at "The Establishment." In 1968, Bishop was charged with burglary after participating in the occupation of a building at Colorado State University. On February 14, 1969, he became the second American citizen ever indicted under a fifty-two-year-old sabotage law dating from World War I. Accused of bombing four utility towers which provided electric power to defense plants in Colorado, Bishop was added to the FBI's "Most Wanted" list on April 15, 1969. He promptly vanished into the radical underground.

On March 12, 1975, police in East Greenwich, Rhode Island, received a nervous call from the employees of a local bank. Two men were parked across the street, intently studying the bank, and it was feared a holdup might be in the making. Officers descended on the scene, arresting Bishop and another "Top Ten" fugitive, Raymond Luc Levasseur, with a small arsenal of guns in their car. Both were booked on charges of carrying concealed weapons and illegal possession of automatic weapons. On March 14, a federal judge ordered both suspects held on weapons charges, with an additional count of conspiracy to commit robbery.

Cameron Bishop was returned to Denver for his sabotage trial on May 2, 1975. The presiding judge announced that 1950's state of emergency, declared by President Truman over the Korean War, was technically still in effect, thus lending validity to the charges (normally applicable only in wartime). On September 19, Bishop was convicted on three counts, acquitted by jurors of bombing the fourth utility tower. Facing a possible sentence of 120 years, he was given two concurrent terms of seven years in prison.

301 ■ MARIE DEAN ARRINGTON

An habitual criminal, Marie Arrington boasted a record of arrests and convictions for assault and battery, robbery, grand larceny, issuing worthless checks, and escape. In July 1964, she shot and killed her husband, and received a twenty-year sentence on conviction of manslaughter. While free on appeal, during April 1968, she committed a second brutal murder. This time, the victim was Vivian Ritter, a legal secretary with the public defender's office in Lake County, Florida.

Arrington kidnapped her victim as a bargaining chip in a bizarre plan to free her two children from prison. Chips off the old block, Lloyd Arrington was serving life for armed robbery; Marie's daughter had been sentenced to two years on conviction of forgery. With Vivian Ritter in hand, Marie Arrington wrote to public defender Robert Pierce, threatening to return his secretary "piece by piece" unless her children were released at once. Of course, he had no such authority, and nothing was accomplished by her threats. Ritter's body was later found in a citrus grove, shot in the back, afterward run over several times by a car in a ghoulish effort to "make sure."

Convicted of first-degree murder this time, Marie Arrington was sentenced to die. On March 1, 1969, she escaped from the women's prison at Lowell, Florida, using a book of matches to burn through the mesh screen covering a window in her cell. Described by prosecutors as a "wild, cunning animal who will kill and laugh about it," she was charged with unlawful flight to avoid confinement on March 3. Shortly thereafter, the judge who sentenced her to die received a threatening letter from Arrington, accompanied by a voodoo doll with a pin through its chest. On May 29, 1969, Marie Arrington became the second woman ever added to the FBI's "Most Wanted" list.

Her luck ran out on December 22, 1971, in New Orleans, where she was employed—as "Lola Nero"—at a local drugstore. When she was apprehended by the FBI, Arrington at first claimed it was a case of mistaken identity, but she gave up the game when fingerprint comparisons checked out. Returned to Florida, she is awaiting execution of her sentence.

302 ■ BENJAMIN HOSKINS PADDOCK

Wisconsin-born, a veteran felon with a record of convictions, Paddock used no less than thirteen pseudonyms in his pursuit of easy money. "Big Daddy," "Chrome Dome," and "Old Baldy" were a few of the more colorful nicknames dreamed up by gangland cronies, emphasizing Paddock's shiny, hairless scalp.

On December 31, 1968, Paddock escaped from the federal penitentiary at La Tuna, Texas, while serving twenty years on his latest conviction for bank robbery. He made the Bureau's "Top Ten" list on June 10, 1969, and was removed eight years later, on May 5, 1977, when authorities decided space was needed for more recent offenders. Removal from the list, however, did not mean that "Chrome Dome" had it made.

In July 1977, posing as "Bruce Ericksen," Paddock surfaced in Springfield, Oregon, where he opened a large bingo hall, billing himself modestly as the "bingo king of the state." In early September 1978, federal agents were tipped that Paddock and Ericksen might be one and the same. On September 6, G-men and local officers staked out the Bingo Center, with one agent loitering near the door, playing the part of an irate customer, shouting complaints. When "Ericksen" emerged to pacify the hot-head, he was instantly identified and taken into custody on charges of unlawful flight to avoid confinement.

303 ■ FRANCIS LEROY HOHIMER

At 4 A.M. on August 17, 1967, two gunmen invaded the Denver home of wealthy architect Temple Buell, routing Buell and his wife from their beds. Buell's daughter, a female houseguest, and a maid were also locked up together in a closet while the hoodlums went about their task of looting the residence. In all, they escaped with $80,000 worth of jewelry, $2,000 in cash, and another $2,400 in traveler's checks.

Francis Hohimer was arrested in Alton, Illinois, September 8, on unrelated charges of possessing burglar's tools and illegal possession of firearms. Posting $25,000 bail in December, he promptly skipped town and disappeared. In February 1968, his name was linked with the Denver home invasion, and a federal fugitive warrant was issued. Hohimer's name was added to the FBI's "Most Wanted" list on June 20, 1969.

Exactly six months later, on December 20, the FBI alerted Greenwich, Connecticut, Police Chief Stephen Baran that Hohimer might be in town. Within the hour, Baran and two agents entered a restaurant which Hohimer, as "John Reynolds," had been managing since September 1969. Four special agents and two more policemen were covering various exits when "Reynolds" arrived, with his wife. Detained by federal agents, Hohimer stuck with his alias until photographs were produced, at which time he sighed and declared, "I'm tired of running away." In the wake of his arrest, it was revealed that agents had traced Hohimer across the continent through a series of jobs as a bartender and chef.

304 ■ JOSEPH LLOYD THOMAS

Another two-time entrant on the "Ten Most Wanted" roster, Thomas was paroled on federal bank robbery charges which originally placed him on the list in 1959. Unable to avoid temptation, Thomas soon held up another bank, in his native city of Terre Haute, Indiana, and was added to the "Top Ten" list a second time on September 2, 1969. Charged with bank robbery and violation of his federal parole, Thomas remained at large until March 8, 1970, when he was arrested in Peoria, Illinois, by FBI Special Agents Elias Williams, Jerome DiFranco, and John F. Leuck. Ironically, the same three agents would arrest another "Top Ten" fugitive—William Louis Herron—in Peoria five years later.

305 ■ JAMES JOHN BYRNES

A native of Los Angeles, born in February 1928, Byrnes logged his first arrest around 1950, moving on from there to collect prison sentences in Iowa, Oklahoma, and Kansas. An escape risk and habitual parole violator, prone to acts of violence, he occasionally supported himself as a musician between felonies, demonstrating talent on the saxophone. For all of its romantic trappings, though, a jazz musician's life held less attraction than the easy money promised by a criminal career.

On January 26, 1969, a Stafford, Kansas, police officer stopped a vehicle occupied by Byrnes and another man, sought in connection with a Wichita supermarket robbery the previous day. Overpowered and kidnapped by the suspects, the officer was driven to the Stafford airport, where Byrnes stole an airplane and escaped on his own. Armed with a revolver, he was arrested on touchdown in El Reno, Oklahoma, and conviction in Wichita eight months later brought him a sentence of fifteen years imprisonment.

A month after his trial, on September 26, 1969, Byrnes and inmate Ronald Archer escaped from the county jail at St. John, Kansas, overpowering a jailer to make their getaway. The fugitives stole a car in Wichita, October 3, leaving it wrecked and abandoned near Hardy, Arkansas, two days later. The same day, they kidnapped an Arkansas motorist, forcing their hostage to drive them to a West Plains, Missouri, airport, where they commandeered a private plane to Des Moines, Iowa. Releasing their hostages in Des Moines, the runners vanished.

Byrnes was charged in four federal warrants, issued between September 24 and October 9, on counts including kidnapping, interstate transportation of stolen cars and airplanes, plus interstate transportation of a firearm following a felony conviction. Archer, his accomplice, was included in one of the kidnapping charges. Byrnes was added to the FBI's "Most Wanted" list on January 6, 1970, remaining at large until agents tracked him to Huntington Beach, California, on April 17. Byrnes would be flying back to Kansas, where a cell in maximum-security was waiting, but he would not be at the controls.

306 ■ EDMUND JAMES DEVLIN

Edmund Devlin's criminal record dated from 1950, listing convictions on charges of theft and breaking and entering in his native Connecticut. Later, he served prison terms for attempted robbery with violence, armed robbery, assault, and parole violation. FBI files described him as "a reputed Connecticut organized crime gang leader" and a participant in gang warfare against underworld rivals. The Bureau also recognized Devlin as the "brains" of an efficient bank-robbing gang suspected of numerous raids.

On January 9, 1969, three gunmen entered a branch office of the Fairfield County Trust Company, in Norwalk, Connecticut, through a back door, brandishing weapons. Their take, an estimated $105,816, set a new record for Connecticut bank robberies. The abandoned getaway car, recovered on January 10, was traced to New York City, where it had been stolen four days earlier. Devlin's two accomplices, Edward Reed and Ralph Masselli, were soon arrested. Masselli made a deal with prosecutors, testifying for the state, and Reed drew twenty-five years in Leavenworth on conviction of bank robbery, with five years tacked on for transporting a firearm across state lines. Devlin's name was added to the "Ten Most Wanted" list on March 20, 1970, with Masselli remaining in custody pending Devlin's arrest and trial.

On August 15, 1970, FBI agents surrounded the fugitive on a streetcorner in downtown Manchester, New Hampshire. Unarmed, Devlin surrendered without resistance and was returned to Connecticut for trial. In addition to bank robbery, he also faced charges of interstate transportation of stolen property (related to the cashing of stolen money orders) and failure to appear at a hearing in September 1969, following his indictment on robbery charges.

307 ■ LAWRENCE ROBERT PLAMONDON

A native of Traverse City, Michigan, born in 1946, Plamondon came of age during the revolutionary 1960s, rising to hold a position as "Minister of Defense" in the radical White Panther Party. Lacking the apparent grievances of Black Panthers or the national reputation of fugitive Weathermen, members of the White Panther Party sought to put themselves on the map with a series of bombings aimed at government targets in Detroit and Ann Arbor, Michigan. Between August 30 and October 14, 1968, at least eight bombs were detonated by the radicals, damaging an army recruiting center, a school administration building and property of the Michigan state university system, a CIA office in Ann Arbor, and various private vehicles belonging to police officers or military personnel. Eleven conspirators were swept up in raids on November 11, 1968, but Plamondon and others remained at large, cited in federal warrants alleging conspiracy to damage government property and unlawful flight to avoid prosecution. Plamondon was added to the FBI's "Most Wanted" list on May 5, 1970, replacing James John Byrnes.

Two months later, on July 23, Plamondon was driving through Mackinac County, Michigan, with fellow Panthers John Forrest and Milton Taube, guzzling beers and pitching their empties out the windows (in clear violation of the Panther Ten-Point program, pledging an end to "pollution of the land"). Observed by Deputy Sheriff James Lietzow, they were stopped near Cheboygan and cautioned against further littering, allowed to proceed on their way while a quick check was run through the new National Crime Information Center. Two of the Panthers were immediately identified, and their van was stopped a second time, by state police, near Engadine. Plamondon was relieved of a .38-caliber derringer, adding concealed weapons charges to the various counts already pending against him in Detroit.

308 ■ HUBERT GEROID BROWN

The son of a maintenance worker, Hubert Brown became famous—or infamous—to a generation of Americans as H. "Rap" Brown, a leading spokesman for the militant fringe of the "Black Power" movement in the 1960s. A fixture of television news broadcasts during the long, hot summer of 1967, Brown rose from obscurity to stand at the right hand of Stokely Carmichael and other advocates of black revolution in the United States.

Brown's trouble with the federal government began in earnest on the night of July 24, 1967, after he delivered a speech in strife-torn Cambridge, Maryland. Advising his all-black audience to "get yourselves some guns" and "burn this town down," he singled out a local elementary school as his primary target, branding it a "firetrap," declaring that "You should have burned it down long ago." Early next morning, after a night of sporadic attacks on white motorists, someone took Brown's advice and burned the school to its foundation.

Within hours of the fire, Maryland authorities indicted Brown on charges of arson and inciting a riot. Federal charges of unlawful flight to avoid prosecution were filed on July 25, and Brown was seized at Washington National Airport the following day, as he prepared to board a plane for New York City. Delivered to local authorities in Alexandria, Virginia, he was released July 27, on $10,000 bond, with an extradition hearing set for August 22.

On August 19, Brown was arrested in New York City on charges of carrying a gun across state lines while under indictment. According to the charges, Brown had carried a firearm in his luggage when he flew from New Orleans to New York on August 16, and again on his return flight, two days later. He pled not guilty to firearms charges, in New Orleans, on September 8, and was jailed five days later in Alexandria, after Virginia's governor signed orders for his extradition to Maryland. On September 18, a federal judge ordered Brown not to leave the southern district of New York except for court appearances related to his case.

Court orders meant little to a man striving for violent revolution in the streets, and Brown flew to California in mid-February 1968, to address a series of "Black Power" rallies. On February 20, 1968, he was arrested again in New York, on a New Orleans bench warrant charging violation of his travel restrictions. The following day, after a hearing in New Orleans, Brown was charged with threatening the life and family of black FBI Agent William Smith, Jr. The California speeches cost Brown $15,000 as he was required to forfeit bail in New York City and New Orleans.

On May 4, 1970, Brown failed to appear for his arson trial in Maryland. Declared a federal fugitive on charges of unlawful flight to avoid prosecution, he made the Bureau's "Ten Most Wanted" list two days later.

On October 16, 1971, Brown and three accomplices—Sam Petty, Arthur Young, and Levi Velentine—invaded the Red Carpet Lounge in Manhattan, robbing twenty-five patrons at gunpoint. Two of the victims were pistol-whipped before the outlaws fled, emerging from the bar as a policeman passed by on routine patrol. They panicked, opened fire, and thus touched off a running battle in the streets. Fifty officers finally joined the chase, with two of them—Sal Rosato and Gary Hunt—suffering wounds in the exchange of fire.

The pursuit ended at a nearby apartment building, where one robber was captured on the street, two others inside. Brown was cornered on the roof by Officer Ralph Manetta, shot twice when he resisted arrest. Manetta carried his prisoner down thirteen flights of stairs, personally driving Brown to the hospital when an ambulance was slow in arriving. Taking stock of the outlaws' arsenal, police counted two shotguns, a carbine, three pistols, and 300 rounds of ammunition. Brown was arraigned, in his hospital bed, on additional charges of robbery and attempted murder.

309 ■ ANGELA YVONNE DAVIS

A native of Birmingham, Alabama, Angela Davis was a friend of the four girls who died when Ku Klux Klansmen bombed a black church in September 1963. Moving north with her affluent family, she finished high school in New York City, attending universities in Massachusetts, Paris, and Frankfurt. Returning from Europe an outspoken Marxist, Davis quickly immersed herself in the politics of black protest. In September 1969, she was dismissed from her position as an instructor at UCLA and plunged into "the struggle" full-time. Correspondence with black convict George Jackson, one of the so-called "Soledad Brothers," blossomed into a long-distance love affair, and Jackson's younger brother, Jonathan, became Angela's personal bodyguard.

On August 7, 1970, Jonathan Jackson entered the Marin County courthouse in San Rafael, California, a gun hidden under his jacket and several others stuffed into a satchel he carried. Convict James McClain was on trial for stabbing a white guard at San Quentin; Assistant District Attorney Gary Thomas was prosecuting the case, with black inmates Ruchell Magee and William Christmas on hand as witnesses.

With the trial in progress, Jackson drew his weapon, tossing guns to McClain, Christmas, and Magee. (Two other black inmates refused to participate in the break.) Judge Harold Haley was kidnapped, a shotgun taped to his neck, with Gary Thomas and three jurors taken along as hostages. Downstairs, the gunmen and their captives piled into a waiting van, but gunfire erupted as lawmen blocked their exit from the parking lot. Judge Haley, Jackson, Christmas and McClain were killed in the shootout; Gary Thomas was paralyzed by a bullet in his spine, and one of the jurors was also slightly wounded. Of the inmates, only Ruchell Magee survived to stand trial on charges of kidnapping and murder.

A routine trace of Jackson's weapons revealed that three had been purchased by Angela Davis at various times, between January 1968 and July 1970. On August 14, a California warrant was issued, charging her with murder and kidnapping; federal charges of unlawful flight were added two days later, and her name was posted to the FBI's "Most Wanted" list on August 18.

On October 13, 1970, FBI surveillance of a male friend from Chicago, David Poindexter, led to Davis's arrest at a motel in New York City. Poindexter, arrested at the same time, was charged with harboring a federal fugitive. (He was acquitted by a federal jury on April 12, 1971.)

While various delays postponed the Davis trial, events were heating up in California's prison system. On August 21, 1971, George Jackson, two other inmates and three prison guards were killed in a bloody shootout at San Quentin. Using a smuggled handgun, Jackson was trying to break out of prison when the scheme blew up in his face, with disastrous results for all concerned.

Abolition of the California death penalty allowed Angela Davis to make bail in February 1972, and her trial opened a month later, on charges of murder, kidnapping, and conspiracy. On June 4, she was acquitted on all counts, the jury accepting her story that Jonathan Jackson—her bodyguard—had taken guns to court without her knowledge or consent. Emerging from the courtroom, Davis hailed the verdict as a "people's victory."

310 ■ DWIGHT ALAN ARMSTRONG
311 ■ KARLETON LEWIS ARMSTRONG
312 ■ DAVID SYLVAN FINE
313 ■ LEO FREDERICK BURT

At 3:40 A.M. on August 24, 1970, police in Madison, Wisconsin, received an anonymous phone call warning that a bomb had been planted at the Army Mathematics Research Center, on the University of Wisconsin campus. Two minutes later, a powerful explosive device was detonated in a stolen truck, parked in an alley beside the research center. Its destructive force demolished the six-story building, killing the solitary occupant, graduate student Robert Fassnacht. Property damage was estimated at $8 million.

Beginning on August 24, leaflets signed and circulated by "The New Year's Gang" attempted to justify the murderous bombing as a "peace" protest, aimed at American military involvement in Vietnam. Federal agents determined that the group's name derived from an abortive bombing raid against the army's ammunition plant at Baraboo, Wisconsin, staged with a stolen airplane on January 1, 1970. From there, it was a relatively simple matter to identify the bombing suspects.

Dwight Armstrong, a high school dropout, had worked at the airport from which the plane was stolen, taking flight lessons in the aircraft itself. Despite his dubious credentials as a "student," Armstrong was identified as a member of SDS. His brother Karleton was also a member, and G-men learned that

Karleton had recently purchased chemicals identical with those used in construction of the August 24 explosive. Informants linked the brothers with two other SDS radicals, Leo Burt and David Fine. On September 2, all four were charged with sabotage, conspiracy to bomb, and destruction of government property. (Karleton Armstrong was separately charged in three other bombings.) Posted to the "Ten Most Wanted" list as special additions on September 4, 1970, they brought the roster to a current all-time high of fourteen names. David Fine, at eighteen years of age, was the youngest person ever added to the list.

On September 5, Fine and Dwight Armstrong were detained by New York state police on charges of operating a vehicle with a faulty muffler. In fact, the car was stolen, but authorities were less than diligent in their examination. Likewise, Fine and Armstrong were not recognized as federal fugitives, and they were soon released, disappearing into the radical underground.

On February 16, 1972, Karleton Armstrong were seized in Toronto by Canadian authorities. He pled guilty, on September 28, 1973, to reduced state charges of arson and second-degree murder, receiving an indeterminate prison term, not to exceed thirty-three years.

David Fine was captured in San Rafael, California, on January 7, 1976, and returned to Wisconsin for trial eight months later. A guilty plea to reduced charges of third-degree murder left him facing a maximum penalty of twenty years in prison, while conviction on federal charges of conspiracy and interstate flight added another seven years to the tab.

The search for Dwight Armstrong and Leo Burt was abandoned in April 1976. Armstrong was struck from the list on April 1, followed by Burt on April 7, but federal charges remained outstanding. Finally arrested in 1977, Dwight Armstrong was sentenced to three years in prison for conspiracy and second-degree murder. Released in 1980, he returned to Madison and enrolled at the university, earning a spot on the dean's list for his grades in electrical engineering.

In March 1987, Dwight Armstrong was indicted again, by Indiana prosecutors, for conspiracy to manufacture and dis-

tribute methamphetamine. He fled to Canada and was captured in Vancouver on July 6, 1987.

314 ■ BERNADINE RAE DOHRN

An active member of SDS, Dohrn declared herself a "revolutionary communist" at the group's annual convention in June
1968, thereafter leading a walkout that resulted in a permanent rift and eventual creation of the violent "Weatherman"
faction. From October 8 to 11, 1969, Weathermen staged riots
in Chicago, dubbed the "Days of Rage," with violence timed
to coincide with the conspiracy trial of protest leaders from
the 1968 Democratic Convention. Dohrn was one of 290 pro-
testers arrested by Chicago police during the riots.

On April 2, 1970, a federal grand jury in Chicago indicted
Bernadine Dohrn and eleven other Weathermen on charges
of conspiracy to cross state lines for the purpose of inciting
riots. She immediately went underground, and was already in
hiding when a second grand jury, in Detroit, indicted her—
with twelve others—on charges of conspiring to transport explosives across state lines. The latter charge grew out of meetings held in December 1968, culminating in the March 1970
explosion of a Weatherman "bomb factory" which killed three
radicals in New York City. Added to the FBI's "Most
Wanted" list on October 14, 1970, Dohrn responded with a
"declaration of war" against the American government.

Three years later, on October 15, 1973, a federal judge in
Detroit granted a United States attorney's request to drop
charges against Dohrn and seven other fugitive radicals. According to the prosecutor, national security would have been
jeopardized by court-ordered exposure of FBI investigative
techniques in the case. Federal process against Dohrn was
dismissed on December 7, 1973, and her name was removed
from the "Ten Most Wanted" list at that time.

In May 1982, having returned from her self-imposed exile,
Dohrn was cited for contempt by a federal judge in New York
City, jailed for her refusal to provide handwriting samples to a
grand jury probing possible terrorist links to the robbery of a

Brinks armored car in October 1981. She was released from
custody in December 1982, still complaining about America's
harsh treatment of "freedom fighters."

315 ■ KATHERINE ANN POWER
316 ■ SUSAN EDITH SAXE

A Denver native, Katherine Power attended Catholic schools
before leaving home to complete her education at Brandeis
University, in Waltham, Massachusetts. There, she met les-
bian Susan Saxe and they soon became lovers, Saxe introduc-
ing Power to feminism, radical politics, and the struggle for
"liberation" in America. Saxe graduated from Brandeis in
June 1970, devoting herself to the movement full-time; Power
was starting her senior year when violence and death inter-
vened to cut short her studies.

Together, Saxe and Power were charged with stealing automatic weapons from the Newbury Port Arsenal, in Massachusetts, during the late summer of 1970. They needed the firepower for "political" bank robberies, and Saxe was
individually charged in connection with a Philadelphia bank
raid which netted $6,240 on September 1, 1970.

Three weeks later, on September 23, the target was a bank
in Boston. Saxe and Power recruited three ex-convicts for
muscle on the job, Katherine waiting with the "switch" car, a
mile away from the scene. Saxe and her three stooges were
leaving the bank when Patrolman Walter Schroeder pulled up
in his squad car, first on the scene in response to a silent
alarm. Cut down in a hail of bullets, Schroeder's death placed
the crime in a whole new perspective.

The three apolitical gunmen were captured in short order.
One was nabbed while disembarking from a cab outside his
home; another was picked up while boarding an airplane in
Grand Junction, Colorado. Number three was caught in
Worcester, Massachusetts, after a wild chase in which he
seized two hostages before surrendering. Feeling no loyalty to
their radical cohorts, the outlaws talked freely. Saxe and
Power were indicted on charges of murder, bank robbery and

theft of government property, topped off with counts of unlawful flight to avoid prosecution. Their addition to the "Ten Most Wanted" roster, on October 17, 1970, brought the list to its all-time maximum of sixteen fugitives.

On March 27, 1975, Susan Saxe was arrested by city police in Philadelphia. On June 9, she struck a bargain with federal prosecutors, pleading guilty to the arsenal theft and the Philadelphia bank job, on condition that she would not be compelled to testify about events since 1969. On June 24, 1975, Saxe pled not guilty to charges of murder and robbery in Boston; a jury disagreed, convicting her of armed robbery and manslaughter. Released from prison in May 1982, Saxe left through a rear exit to avoid members of the press.

Katherine Ann Power remained on the Bureau's "Top Ten" list until June 15, 1984, when her name was quietly deleted. As a former Boston prosecutor told reporters, "Of the five, the weakest case is against her and, well, it's been so long, who'd want to prosecute her?"

317 ■ MACE BROWN

A native of Birmingham, Alabama, born February 21, 1943, Brown was a narcotics user who boasted arrests dating from 1962. His felony convictions included assault and battery on a police officer in New Jersey, along with a contract killing in Washington, D.C., which earned him a sentence of death. The victim in that case was a potential witness in a major narcotics trial, found shot in the back of the head, execution-style. Following his conviction and sentencing, while his death penalty was under appeal, Brown reportedly threatened to murder the trial judge and an Assistant United States Attorney who won the conviction against him.

On October 2, 1972, while sweating out the ultimate result of his appeal, Brown joined seven other inmates—including three accused murderers—in a spectacular escape from the District of Columbia jail. Cutting through steel bars and a metal screen, they smashed a skylight to reach the jail roof, descending from there to the ground by means of a fire hose.

Having come that far, they scrambled over two twelve-foot fences topped with barbed wire, vanishing into the darkness before their flight was discovered.

With his lethal record and recent threats in mind, Brown was named in a federal warrant issued on October 4, charging him with conspiracy and escape from a federal institution. His name was added to the FBI's "Most Wanted" list October 20, but he remained at large until April 18, 1973. Recognized by beat patrolmen in New York, Brown was accosted on the street and chose to shoot it out with the arresting officers. He died in the exchange of gunfire, cancelling all opportunity for him to make good on his list of murder threats.

318 ■ HERMAN BELL

On the night of May 21, 1971, New York City Patrolmen Waverly Jones and Joseph Piagentini were ambushed and shot by two black assailants in uptown Manhattan. Jones was killed instantly, struck by four bullets before he hit the sidewalk; Piagentini took twelve slugs from two different pistols and died en route to a neighborhood hospital. Both officers were stripped of their .38 service revolvers. Communiques released that night claimed "credit" for the murders—and the wounding of two other policemen on May 19—for a militant faction of the Black Liberation Army.

The BLA was organized in early 1972, emerging from a rift in the Black Panther Party. Loyalist Panthers sided with the West Coast leadership of Huey Newton and Bobby Seale, while BLA militants took their cue from Eldridge Cleaver, the party's defecting "Minister of Education," then hiding in Algiers. While Panthers advocated "self-defense" against police and frequently engaged in shootouts on their own, the BLA adopted an aggressive policy of "scoping pigs"—that is, assassination of officers at random—to provoke their hoped-for revolution.

On August 27, 1971, Sgt. George Kowalski was on routine patrol in San Francisco, when a car pulled abreast of his cruiser, a passenger aiming a submachine gun. The weapon misfired and Kowalski gave chase, other officers joining the parade, which climaxed in a crash and shootout. Two suspects —Albert Washington and Anthony Bottom—were captured alive; one of three guns confiscated at the scene was a .38 registered to Patrolman Waverly Jones.

Six days later, with investigation of the East Coast-West Coast connection still underway, nine armed blacks attacked a precinct house in San Francisco's Ingleside district. Sgt. John Young was killed, another officer wounded, but the crude homemade bomb hurled by their assailants failed to detonate. Again, the BLA claimed credit for the raid.

A police lineup soon identified Anthony Bottom as one of the gunmen responsible for killing Jones and Piagentini in New York. Interrogation of Bottom's closest friends identified the second trigger man as Herman Bell, a member of the BLA whose fingerprints matched some recovered from the New York shooting scene in May.

Born in Mississippi during 1958, Bell's football talent earned him a scholarship to Berkeley, but declining grades in high school ultimately kept him out of college. Jailed in Oakland once, in 1969, for holding up a fast-food restaurant with a cap pistol, Bell had begun to see himself as one of the "oppressed." His answer, by the early 1970s, was found in smoking dope and "scoping pigs."

On January 27, 1972, with the search for Herman Bell in progress, New York Patrolmen Gregory Foster and Rocco Laurie were ambushed and murdered by three black gunmen in Manhattan, their service revolvers taken as trophies of the hunt. A few days later, when murder warrants were issued in New York, Herman Bell was one of four men charged with complicity in the deaths of Foster and Laurie. Indicted on murder charges in New York, Bell also faced federal charges of unlawful flight to avoid prosecution. His name was added to the FBI's "Most Wanted" list on May 9, 1973.

On August 25, New Orleans officers arrested twelve black suspects in a local bank robbery, confiscating an arsenal of weapons and sizable quantities of BLA literature. Interrogation of neighbors revealed that a man matching Herman Bell's description was frequently seen at the BLA hideout, and FBI agents established a stakeout. On September 2, Bell was sighted at a nearby intersection and surrounded as he waited for the light to change, surrendering without resistance.

In New York, defendants Bottom, Washington and Bell were each convicted of murdering Patrolmen Jones and Piagentini, receiving two concurrent terms of twenty-five years to life. Herman Bell was also individually convicted in the September 1971 robbery of a San Francisco bank; his prison term in that case was an indeterminate sentence, with twenty-five years maximum.

319 ■ TWYMAN FORD MYERS

On the night of January 27, 1972, New York Patrolmen Gregory Foster and Rocco Laurie were ambushed and murdered on foot patrol, in Manhattan. Witnesses recalled three black men loitering around the murder scene for several hours beforehand, and the owner of a nearby grocery store produced the satchel left inside his store by one of the suspects. It contained dismantled handguns, black extremist literature, and fingerprints belonging to Twyman Myers and Andrew Jackson, known members of the Black Liberation Army. Eyewitness examination of mugshots confirmed Jackson and another BLA member, Ronald Carter, as two of the triggermen in the double murder.

An underground communique, issued on January 28, claimed "credit" in the slayings for the "George Jackson Squad" of the BLA. That night, Patrolman John Bauer was shot four times in Brooklyn, after stopping a black motorist for routine traffic violations, but he managed to survive his wounds. By the end of the week, murder warrants were issued for Jackson, Carter, and fugitive Herman Bell. One of several suspects sought for questioning was Twyman Myers.

On February 14, 1972, four blacks opened fire on St. Louis patrolmen following another routine traffic stop, critically wounding one officer. A high-speed chase and shootout followed, leaving murder suspect Ronald Carter dead and two others in custody. One of ten guns confiscated by police was

Rocco Laurie's missing .38-caliber service revolver. Finger-prints lifted from the suspect vehicle identified Twyman Myers as the one who got away.

On September 12, 1973, Andrew Jackson was captured by New York police officers in the Bronx, dragged out of bed as he slept with a female companion. On September 28, fugitive Twyman Myers was added to the FBI's "Most Wanted" list on charges of unlawful flight to avoid prosecution for attempted murder.

The self-styled guerrilla ran out of time on November 14, 1973. New York detectives, staking out another Bronx apartment used by members of the BLA, saw Myers emerge and fell in step behind him. Spotting his pursuers, Twyman shouted, "Fuck you bastards!" and produced a pistol, wounding both officers before he was killed by return fire. Bullets from his weapon matched the slugs that wounded Patrolman Bauer in January 1972, thus linking the BLA to another attack on law enforcement.

320 ■ RONALD HARVEY
321 ■ SAMUEL RICHARD CHRISTIAN

Harvey and Christian joined the Philadelphia chapter of the Black Muslims in 1959, rising swiftly through the ranks to positions of authority. Within a year, Harvey was second in command of the Philadelphia mosque, while Christian led the paramilitary Fruit of Islam faction. At the same time, they were muscling their way into dominance of the local "Black Mafia," organizing extortion rackets and recruiting a private army of 200 gunmen, murdering competitors, dividing the city into underworld territories. "Dues" were demanded from local drug pushers, and all went well until Tyrone Palmer defied the mob. On April 6, 1972, Palmer and four other persons were killed, with nine wounded, in a wild barroom shootout. Surviving competitors were impressed, and the "Black Mafia" soon expanded its operations to New York, Atlantic City, Washington, D.C.

In Washington, the opposition crystalized along religious

lines, with members of the Hanafi Muslim sect rejecting Harvey and Christian for their corruption of the church. On January 18, 1973, Harvey and six accomplices invaded a communal home occupied by Washington Hanafis. Two men and a ten-year-old boy were shot to death, while four other children—one only nine days old—were deliberately drowned in the bathtub and sink. Two young women were shot in the head but survived their wounds, describing the attackers for police and agents of the FBI.

On June 8, 1973, Harvey, Christian, and two other gunmen entered the home of Major Coxson, a rival Philadelphia mobster residing in Cherry Hill, New Jersey. In the shooting that followed, Coxson and his common-law wife were killed outright; the woman's daughter was mortally wounded, dying two days later, and two other occupants of the house were blinded by bullets.

The body-count kept rising, and that autumn, in Philadelphia, FBI informant Arthur Hadden was shot twelve times, killed instantly, by members of the "Black Mafia" acting on orders from Harvey and Christian. Indictments were finally secured, and both thugs were added to the "Top Ten" list on December 7, 1973.

That very afternoon, in Detroit, FBI agents acting on a tip from undercover agents captured Christian. Three months later, on March 27, a stakeout of Black Muslim properties in Chicago paid off in Harvey's arrest. In custody, the mobster seemed relieved, informing his captors, "Running is a bitch."

New Jersey's murder charge against Christian was ultimately dropped, after a key witness died from an "accidental" overdose of heroin, and the defendant was handed over to authorities in New York. There, convicted of wounding a police officer in 1971, he drew a prison term of fifteen years to life.

In Washington, five of Harvey's triggermen in the Hanafi massacre were convicted on murder charges in July 1974, sentenced to terms averaging 140 years each. Ronald Harvey was tried separately, in October and November, with conviction a virtual foregone conclusion. Sentenced as the mastermind behind the slaughter, he must serve 140 years before he is considered for parole.

322 ■ RUDOLPH ALONZA TURNER

A native of Jacksonville, Florida, born in August 1941, Rudy
Turner had an arrest record dating from age eighteen. His
felony convictions included counts of assault and battery on a
police officer, carrying a concealed weapon, escape, breaking
and entering, plus other assorted crimes. Distinctive in appearance, from the artificial left eye to a little finger he could
never straighten, Turner removed all doubt of his identity for
arresting officers by wearing the name "Rudy" tattooed on his
chest and left forearm.

On August 25, 1973, Turner and three male accomplices
took part in an abortive kidnapping and armed robbery
scheme near Moultrie, Georgia. Wriggling away from his captors, one of the intended victims hailed a passing squad car,
and a Moultrie police lieutenant was shot in the chest, killed
outright, when he sought to apprehend the gunmen.

Local warrants charged Rudolph Turner with the lieutenant's murder, and a federal warrant was issued on August 28,
citing him for unlawful flight to avoid prosecution. Turner was
posted to the FBI's "Most Wanted" list on January 10, 1974,
surviving eight months on the run before he was captured by
federal agents in Jacksonville, Florida, on October 1. Waiving
extradition, he was returned to Georgia for trial and ultimate
conviction on outstanding felony charges.

323 ■ LARRY GENE COLE

Life began to change for Larry Cole when he completed four
years service in the navy, during 1968. He logged his first
arrest that year, in New Orleans, on federal charges of driving
a stolen car across state lines, and conviction brought him
time in jail. Across the next five years, he racked up other
felony convictions, including counts of burglary, receiving
stolen property and parole violation. By late 1973, he was
settled in Roanoke, Virginia, with wife Bonnie Ann, four
years his junior at age twenty-three, but neither of the Coles
had any luck at staying out of trouble.

Bonnie Cole was working as a clerk in a Roanoke department store when $4,630 disappeared from a safe to which she had access. Her disappearance from the building, a quarter-hour before the safe was found open and empty, led police to file charges of grand theft against Bonnie, but they had difficulty tracking her down. Husband Larry, meanwhile, was employed at Frank Van Balen's Virginia Fiberglas Products, also in Roanoke, but like his wife, Cole had his eye on bigger things.

On March 6, 1974, Betty Van Balen—a Roanoke real estate agent and Frank's wife—kept an appointment to show a new client some property listed for sale. Unknown to her, the "client" was Larry Cole, and the business was kidnapping. Producing a gun, Cole took Mrs. Van Balen hostage, communicating ransom demands to her husband by telephone. Frank Van Balen followed instructions, dropping $25,000 in cash at an abandoned railway station, and his wife was released by her captors the following day, in Ansted, West Virginia.

The trip across state lines made it a federal crime, and G-men readily identified the Coles from latent evidence and Larry's prior mug shots. Both were named as federal fugitives, in warrants charging them with kidnapping and extortion. Larry made the Bureau's "Top Ten" list on April 2, and the couple lasted one more day at large.

Alerted that the suspects had been seen in New York state, FBI agents issued an all-points bulletin describing the Coles and their last known vehicle. New York State Police made the collar on April 3, stopping the fugitives on a highway near Buffalo, and the Coles were delivered to federal agents for transportation to Virginia. Formally indicted on April 7, both were convicted a month later, with Larry receiving twenty-five years imprisonment, against Bonnie's sentence of eighteen years. (On May 20, Bonnie Cole was convicted of grand theft in the Roanoke case, a two-year concurrent sentence appended to her outstanding time.) In August 1974, a federal district judge rejected motions to reduce their sentences in length.

324 ■ JAMES ELLSWORTH JONES

In 1972, Jones was convicted on federal kidnapping charges and sentenced to life for the abduction of a Virginia gas station attendant. Kidnapped during a robbery, Jones's victim was found near Martinsburg, Virginia, shot twice in the head and beaten about the face with a claw hammer. In 1973, Jones was transported from a federal prison to the Augusta County jail, in Staunton, Virginia, pending trial on state charges of armed robbery. He escaped on October 16, 1973, and was immediately declared a federal fugitive, on charges of unlawful flight to avoid confinement. Jones was added to the FBI's "Most Wanted" list on April 16, 1974.

Two months later, on June 15, off-duty policeman Steve Fuller was having lunch with friends, in Coral Gables, Florida, when a man and young woman entered the restaurant. Approaching the booth next to Fuller's, they changed their minds and moved to the counter for quicker service, but Fuller had already noticed the man, remarking to companions that the newcomer looked familiar.

Fuller made a point of studying Wanted posters every day, and now a visit to the precinct house confirmed his first suspicion: despite a new mustache, the man in the diner was undoubtedly James Ellsworth Jones. FBI agents were notified, and they reached the cafe before Jones finished his meal. Jones initially identified himself as "James Raynor," a health food salesman, but fingerprint comparisons confirmed his true identity. He was held without bond pending extradition to Virginia, and his innocent companion was released from custody.

325 ■ LENDELL HUNTER

Convicted of numerous felonies in Georgia, Hunter drew three consecutive life terms for rape, ten years each on five separate burglary charges, five years each on five counts of aggravated assault, ten years for kidnapping, and ten years for criminal assault. Rightly viewing himself as a poor parole prospect, Hunter escaped from a prison work camp at Alto, Georgia, on December 20, 1972. Two months later, on February 14, he invaded the Augusta home of Irene DeQuasie, age 78, beating the woman to death in her bed and assaulting her teenage grandson. Federal charges of unlawful flight were added to Hunter's growing rap sheet, and his name was added to the FBI's "Most Wanted" list on June 27, 1974.

A month later, on July 31, Bureau agents caught their man at a YMCA facility in Des Moines, Iowa. Hunter identified himself as "Carey Fontaine Baker," a native of Potts, Oklahoma, who had periodically lived in Des Moines "all my life." Checking into the "Y" on July 8, he had listed his permanent home as Augusta, Georgia, a fact which contradicted his jailhouse claims that "I've never been to Georgia. I've never committed a felony in my life." Fingerprint comparisons proved otherwise, and Hunter's extradition was approved on August 13.

326 ■ JOHN EDWARD COPELAND , JR.

A paunchy sex deviate who preferred rape to courtship, Copeland was born in Newport News, Virginia, on April 3, 1944. By the early 1970s, he had settled in California, working with an accomplice to prey upon the Golden State's plentiful number of female hitchhikers. Displaying a pistol and shotgun, Copeland and his partner would transport their victims to isolated beaches, there inflicting multiple rapes while regaling the terrified women with stories of planned shootouts and airline hijackings. Copeland's beer belly and wheezing, high-pitched voice made him distinctive, but his accomplice was arrested first, leaving Copeland to be named in federal warrants charging unlawful flight to avoid prosecution for rape, robbery, and kidnapping.

Added to the Bureau's "Ten Most Wanted" list on August 15, 1974, Copeland sought safety in distance. Federal officers traced him to Boston on July 23, 1975, taking him into custody with no sign of the promised armed resistance. Copeland was returned to California for trial and ultimate conviction on a long list of outstanding felony charges.

327 ■ MELVIN DALE WALKER

Missouri-born in 1939, Melvin Walker boasted convictions for burglary, robbery, and escape before a bank job earned him fifty-five years in the federal penitentiary at Lewisburg, Pennsylvania. In jail, he was particular about his friends, and one of them was Richard F. McCoy, a former Green Beret and Mormon Sunday school teacher who hijacked a United Airlines flight over Utah in April 1972, bailing out over the desert with a $500,000 ransom. (A conversation with his sister had resulted in McCoy's denunciation and arrest, a few days later.) Other prison pals included Joseph Havel, a sixty-year-old Philadelphian serving ten years, and Larry Bagley, of Iowa, facing twenty years of federal time.

On August 10, 1974, the four inmates scrambled over a prison fence, pulling homemade knives on a guard and convict whom they used as shields against the tower guards. Piling into a prison garbage truck, they crashed through the outer fence and escaped, dumping their conspicuous vehicle ten miles away, in Forest Hill. Invading a private home, the fugitives tied up four residents and hit the road in a stolen sedan.

By August 13, they had surfaced in North Carolina, robbing a Pollocksville bank of some $16,000. Cornered that afternoon, in the Great Dover Swamp near Cove City, Bagley and Havel fought a half-hour duel with police before throwing down their weapons and surrendering, unharmed. Walker and McCoy remained at large, pursued on charges of bank robbery and escape from a federal institution. Walker's name was posted to the "Ten Most Wanted" list October 16, 1974.

Twenty-five days later, G-men acting on a tip converged upon a house outside Virginia Beach, Virginia. They were waiting when the fugitives appeared, McCoy electing to resist with violence. He was hauling out a weapon when the concentrated fire of Special Agents Nick O'Hara, Gerald Houlihan and Kevin McPartland cut him down in his tracks, killing him instantly. Walker took to his heels and was tackled nearby, taken into custody by Special Agents Richard Rafferty and Henry Bolin.

Brought to trial in December 1974, the surviving defendants pled guilty to bank robbery and escape. Walker and Bagley each received twenty-year terms for the Pollocksville robbery and five years for escape, the time to run concurrently with their existing sentences. Havel, in deference to his age, was sentenced to concurrent terms of fifteen years for robbery and five years for escape.

328 ■ THOMAS OTIS KNIGHT

When Miami industrialist Sydney Gans arrived at his office on the morning of July 17, 1974, he found one of his employees waiting to greet him. The circumstance was not unusual, but Thomas Knight was no ordinary employee, the M-1 carbine in his hands no ordinary greeting. Prodded at gunpoint, Gans returned to his car and drove Knight back to the Gans family home, where he parked in the driveway. Under orders from Knight, Gans began tapping the horn on his car, finally attracting his wife's attention and drawing her outside, into range.

With two hostages under the gun, Knight directed Gans to the City National Bank, in downtown Miami, where the executive withdrew $50,000 from his personal account. While the cash was being counted, Gans informed bank president Daniel Gill of his predicament. By the time Gans left the bank, a police helicopter was circling overhead, with squad cars closing on the scene.

Detecting the pursuers, Knight directed Gans to speed away, leading police on a wild chase which ended ten miles from Miami, on a rural expressway. Killing both hostages with single shots to the head, Knight ditched the car and tried to escape on foot. Six hours later, with 200 police and federal agents closing in, he was flushed from the swampy undergrowth by tracking dogs and tear gas, shuttled back to the Dade County jail under guard.

Knight's trial was pending when, on September 19, he escaped from jail in company with eleven other prisoners. Charged in federal warrants with unlawful flight to avoid prosecution for murder and kidnapping, Knight was added to the Bureau's "Top Ten" list December 12. He lasted until New Year's Eve, when FBI agents and local officers traced him to an apartment in Smyrna Beach, Florida, bursting in to catch him by surprise. Though heavily armed at the time of his arrest, Knight had no opportunity to resist in the face of overwhelming firepower. He was returned to Miami for trial and ultimate conviction on murder charges.

329 ■ BILLY DEAN ANDERSON

As a young man, Billy Anderson was interested in art and showed considerable talent. He also tried his hand at preaching in the local churches, meeting with enough success that he considered making the ministry his career. Something changed, however, after Billy left his native Tennessee and spent two years in Indiana. He came home with liquor on his breath, drank heavily, and hung out with a "tough crowd." He talked big in front of his barroom companions, and displayed a new sadistic streak, with tendencies toward sudden violence. His name was linked with robberies in Indiana and Ohio, but authorities in those states would be forced to wait their turn.

On October 26, 1962, Anderson sped past a Tennessee state trooper's car, deliberately weaving across the white line to encourage pursuit. Pulling onto the shoulder a few moments later, Anderson came out shooting, critically wounding Trooper Steve Webb. Webb's partner returned fire, a bullet lodging in Anderson's spine and leaving both legs partially paralyzed. He wore braces to court in January 1963, listening as prosecutors told the jury that he shot Steve Webb "for apparently no other reason than to shoot him." Convicted of attempted murder, Anderson was sentenced to ten years in jail.

Back on the street by 1967, Anderson shot and wounded Fentress County Sheriff Irvin Jones in a second unprovoked attack. In December 1973, he was still running true to form; surprised by Deputy Webb Hatfield as Anderson and his wife were breaking into a bar near Jamestown, Tennessee, Billy bagged his third badge in ten years.

On August 2, 1974, while awaiting trial in the Hatfield shooting, Anderson escaped from jail in Wartburg, Tennessee. Declared a federal fugitive on charges of unlawful flight, his name was added to the FBI's "Most Wanted" list on January 21, 1975.

It took four years and seven months to track the gunman down, but federal agents had a tip that Anderson was planning on a visit to his mother's home, near Pall Mall, Tennessee, on July 7, 1979. Fifteen agents staked out the farm, surprising Anderson as he hobbled across an open field, weighted down by his braces, a loaded rifle, and two pistols tucked in his belt. Instead of halting on command, he raised his weapon, moving toward the nearest agent, and was killed by shotgun blasts discharged in self-defense.

330 ■ ROBERT GERALD DAVIS

Born in November 1947, at Camden, New Jersey, Davis spent his first twenty-six years compiling a record of convictions for illegal possession and sale of narcotics. On July 1, 1974, he changed his M.O., joining three accomplices to rob a Camden grocery store of $10,000. Shooting it out with police as they fled, the bandits killed a thirteen-year-old boy and left five other bystanders seriously wounded.

On July 3, in Pittsburgh, two police officers collared a suspect on charges of failure to appear for trial on a narcotics charge. As they fastened the handcuffs, their man slipped away, sprinting toward a passing car. The officers gave chase, but the vehicle's occupants—Davis and a male companion—opened fire with high-powered weapons, killing one of the policemen instantly. Identified and indicted for murder the same day, Davis was declared a federal fugitive on August 7, 1974. His name was added to the FBI's "Most Wanted" list on April 4, 1975.

Two years and four months later, on August 5, 1977, G-men acting on a tip surprised Davis in Venice, California, taking him into custody without resistance. Returned to Pittsburgh for trial, he was convicted of first-degree murder on July 19, 1978. Twelve days later, he was sentenced to a prison term of life plus forty-five years.

331 ■ RICHARD DEAN HOLTAN

A South Dakota native, born in February 1935, Holtan put his dismal view of life on display for all to see, with identical tattoos on his left wrist and forearm: both read "Born to Lose." When dead-end jobs as an upholsterer and shipping clerk fell short of meeting Holtan's expectations for the future, he decided that violent crime was worth a try.

On November 19, 1973, he held up a bank in Seattle, walking away with $1,000 in cash. Soon arrested and charged with the robbery, Holtan was placed in a "resident release" program for a one-year trial period, in lieu of being sent to prison. Disappearing from the program, he surfaced in Omaha, Nebraska, on November 1, 1974, to rob a local tavern. In the course of the holdup, Holtan fired his pistol repeatedly and without provocation at three unarmed victims, killing the bartender and wounding one of his customers.

Federal warrants charged Holtan with bank robbery, plus unlawful flight to avoid prosecution for robbery and murder. Added to the FBI's "Most Wanted" list on April 18, 1975, he voluntarily surrendered three months later—on July 12—to local police in Kauai, Hawaii. FBI agents took charge of the prisoner, and he was returned to Nebraska for trial and ultimate conviction on charges of murder and robbery.

332 ■ RICHARD BERNARD LINDHORST , JR.

Born in Missouri in March of 1942, Richard Lindhorst wore a dragon tattooed on his chest and earned himself a reputation as a trigger-happy bandit, prone to violence in his robberies. If times were lean, the street talk said, he might not be opposed to taking on a contract murder for variety.

On December 20, 1974, Lindhorst and two male accomplices invaded a bank in Wever, Iowa, firing shots at random as they fled with $20,000 in cash. Attempting to distract pursuers, the escaping bandits burned a local barn. No sooner had the bandits been identified than Lindhorst's name was linked with the brutal, execution-style murders of a man and woman who were gagged and shot to death near Huntsville, Alabama.

Federal warrants charged Lindhorst with bank robbery and unlawful flight to avoid prosecution for murder. Posted to the Bureau's "Top Ten" list on August 1, 1975, he was arrested by FBI agents six days later, in Pensacola, Florida. In custody, he was returned to Alabama for trial on outstanding murder charges, with the bank robbery count held in reserve.

333 ■ WILLIAM LEWIS HERRON , JR.

A native of Paducah, Kentucky, Herron was sentenced to life imprisonment for the fatal shooting of a deputy sheriff who stopped his car on a routine traffic violation outside St. Charles. On April 11, 1975, Herron escaped from a clinic in Madisonville, Kentucky, where he had been transferred for medical treatment. A guard and another inmate were kidnapped during the break-out, later handcuffed to a tree and left unharmed when the inmate refused to follow Herron's orders.

On October 30, 1975, Herron was sighted by federal agents in Peoria, Illinois, and his car was forced to the curb after a brief high-speed chase. Special Agents Elias Williams, Jerome DiFranco, and John Leuck made the arrest, marking their second capture of a "Top Ten" fugitive in Peoria. (The first was Joseph Lloyd Thomas, arrested March 9, 1970.)

In custody, Herron was linked with the murder of Robert Bussen in Springfield, Illinois. A prospective prosecution witness in the narcotics trial of defendant Sidney Rowlett, Bussen was murdered before he had a chance to testify in court.

Rowlett, a close friend of Herron's, was subsequently convicted of hiring Herron to silence Bussen, and additional murder charges were filed against Herron while he awaited extradition to Kentucky.

334 ■ JAMES WINSTON SMALLWOOD

Born December 11, 1949, in Washington, D.C., James Smallwood never journeyed far from home in his pursuit of easy money. By December 1974, he was serving thirty years in Washington, on conviction of robbing two banks, and his trial was pending in Superior Court on further armed robbery charges. On December 19, while being transported from St. Elizabeth's Hospital to a scheduled court appearance, Smallwood produced a .32-caliber revolver and disarmed his escort, a deputy United States marshal, firing a shot at the officer before making his getaway.

Charged in federal warrants as an escaped federal prisoner, Smallwood was added to the FBI's "Most Wanted" list on August 29, 1975. Four months later, on December 15, he surfaced in suburban Seabrook, Maryland, to rob a bank for spending money. Cornered near the crime scene by officers of the Capital Park Police, Smallwood surrendered and was taken into custody, returned to the Washington lockup pending trial on outstanding charges.

335 ■ LEONARD PELTIER

The self-styled "enforcer" of the militant American Indian Movement (AIM), Leonard Peltier was prominent in the organization's activities during the early 1970s. In 1973, with Russell Means, he led AIM's seventy-one-day occupation of the historic battle site at Wounded Knee, South Dakota, during which two FBI agents were wounded by sniper fire from the Indian camp.

Two years later, on June 26, 1975, another shootout occurred between G-men and members of AIM, this time at the Pine Ridge, South Dakota, reservation of the Oglala Sioux. Special Agents Jack Coles and Ronald Williams were killed by automatic rifle fire, and one of Peltier's followers was also fatally wounded in the exchange. Two Indian suspects were acquitted in the case, with charges dropped against a third, but Peltier—named by witnesses as the trigger man—escaped prosecution by going underground. His name was added to the Bureau's "Ten Most Wanted" list on August 1, 1975.

Six months later, on February 6, 1976, the fugitive was captured by Canadian authorities at Hinton, Alberta. Peltier stalled extradition until December, applying for sanctuary on political grounds, but his claims were finally rejected by Alberta's minister of justice. Returned to South Dakota for trial, Peltier was convicted on two counts of murder and sentenced to life imprisonment on each charge.

336 ■ PATRICK JAMES HUSTON

Patrick Huston's record of arrests dated from 1946, with armed robbery dominating the list of felonies. By the early 1970s, he had spent a quarter-century behind prison walls, earning himself a reputation as a ruthless gunman. In 1962, Huston and his gang, based in Sunnyside, Queens, shot it out with New York police after a bank robbery in Manhattan. Twelve years later, he was still running true to form, joining two accomplices to loot a bank in Queens of $50,000. Captured hours later, each of the robbers was armed with a pistol and a .30-caliber carbine.

On March 16, 1975, while awaiting trial on the Queens robbery, Huston and his two accomplices escaped from the federal house of detention in New York City. Hiding in a storage room between floors, they sat out a recreation break and then cut through a mesh enclosure, clearing a skylight and descending to the street on a rope made of knotted bedsheets. Charged with bank robbery and unlawful flight to avoid prosecution, Huston was added to the FBI's "Most Wanted" list on March 3, 1976.

Twenty-one months of intensive investigation finally led agents to Fort Lauderdale, Florida, where Huston had moved. On December 7, 1977, the fugitive left a local tavern, dressed in a blue jogging suit and riding a bicycle. G-men were waiting nearby, and Huston was taken into custody without incident, held in lieu of $250,000 bond pending extradition to New York.

337 ■ THOMAS EDWARD BETHEA

A native of McColl, South Carolina, born November 25, 1937, Thomas Bethea was a violence-prone thief with a history of resisting arrest. Convicted of bank robbery in 1971, he was on parole when he joined the conspiracy to kidnap Miami trucking executive Alan Bortnick for a quarter-million-dollar ransom. The snatch was made on January 24, 1976, with Bortnick's release secured by payment of the designated ransom five days later. Several arrests were made in the case before Bethea was identified as a participant, and he remained at large when his name was added to the list of "Ten Most Wanted" fugitives on March 5, 1976.

Attempting to escape the heat, Tom Bethea had flown to the Bahamas, confident a black man like himself—and one with money—would be welcomed in Nassau. On the contrary, identification of Bethea led to his deportation from the Bahamas as an undesirable alien, and FBI agents were waiting when he stepped off a plane in Miami, on May 5. A search of the fugitive's pockets turned up three $100 bills, identified by serial numbers as part of the Bortnick ransom payment.

338 ■ ANTHONY MICHAEL JULIANO

A prolific thief, Anthony Juliano was linked with a daring holdup gang responsible for twenty-seven bank robberies in Boston and New York City between 1973 and 1975. On November 11, 1975, a federal warrant was issued in Brooklyn,

charging him with conspiracy to rob banks; on November 28, a
second warrant charged him with violating terms of his release from federal prison on a previous conviction. Juliano's
name was added to the "Top Ten" list on March 15, 1976.

A week later, on March 22, FBI agents tipped local officers
in Mecklenburg County, Virginia, that Juliano was headed
their way. At 9:40 that morning, police spotted him at a stop
light in South Hill, trailing him onto the open road outside
town before pulling him over. Juliano surrendered without
resistance and was held in lieu of $1 million bond, pending
extradition to New York.

339 ■ JOSEPH MAURICE McDONALD

An alleged member of a Boston syndicate involved in illegal
gambling and loan-sharking, McDonald was sought by police
in the theft of a stamp collection valued at $50,000. Agents of
the FBI became involved on allegations that the merchandise
had been transported across state lines, and McDonald was
declared a federal fugitive on charges of interstate transportation of stolen property. On April 1, 1976, his name was added
to the "Ten Most Wanted" list.

Six years and five months later, on September 15, 1982, a
tipster fingered McDonald for police and U.S. Customs
agents in New York. Officers were waiting when the fugitive
stepped off a train from Hollywood, Florida, carrying three
Uzi submachine guns in his luggage. McDonald was jailed on
state firearms charges, as well as the federal counts already
pending against him.

340 ■ JAMES RAY RENTON

Renton was born in St. Louis, Missouri, on December 13,
1937. His criminal record spans a quarter-century, including
convictions for assault, burglary, forgery, and narcotics violations. Sought for parole violation and bail-jumping in 1975,

Renton was riding with several male companions when his car was stopped by a rookie patrolman, twenty-three-year-old John Hussey, near Springvale, Arkansas, on the night of December 22.

Producing a gun, Renton disarmed Hussey and used the officer's own handcuffs to secure his wrists, forcing Hussey to kneel before he was killed, execution-style, with four point-blank shots to the head. Branded a federal fugitive on charges of parole violation, bond default, and unlawful flight to avoid prosecution for murder, Renton was added to the FBI's "Most Wanted" list on April 7, 1976.

He survived thirteen months on the run, finally captured by federal agents on May 9, 1977. Conviction on first-degree murder charges brought Renton a sentence of life without parole, in July 1979, but the cop-killer was determined not to serve his time behind bars. On July 12, 1988, he escaped from the Arkansas state penitentiary with three other convicts, leaving a dummy in his bed to deceive guards on the cell block. The inmates climbed out through the ceiling of the prison laundry room, descending a 25-foot wall with the aid of a rope made from bedsheets; outside, they crawled 300 feet to a chain link fence and cut the wire to make their getaway.

One of Renton's cronies was recaptured by authorities July 14, in Memphis, Tennessee. Two others were caught in Iola, Kansas, on July 21. At this writing, James Ray Renton remains at large, although his name has not been posted to the "Ten Most Wanted" list a second time. At age fifty, he is described as a white American male, five feet eight inches tall, with red-brown hair and blue eyes. Distinguishing marks include a large scar on the right side of his face, tattoos depicting a wreath of flowers on his left forearm, the initials "J.R." on his upper right arm, and the name "Smiley" on his right forearm. Renton favors Western-style clothing, and is said to be an avid fisherman.

341 ■ NATHANIEL DOYLE , JR.

A veteran stickup artist, Nathaniel Doyle ran afoul of federal agents in late 1975 and early 1976, earning his place on the "Ten Most Wanted" list through a series of wild daylight robberies. In October 1975, a federal warrant was issued on Doyle in Columbus, Ohio, charging him with unlawful flight to avoid prosecution for armed robbery. Three months later, in January 1976, a second federal warrant charging him with bank robbery was issued in South Bend, Indiana. In March, Doyle robbed a bank at Fresno, California, escaping from California Highway Patrol officers in a high-speed, bullet-punctuated chase. His name was added to the Bureau's "honor roll" on April 29, 1976.

At 10 A.M. on July 15, Doyle and a female accomplice, Barbara Brinkley, held up a bank in Bellevue, Washington, escaping toward Seattle in a gray sedan. An hour later, Brinkley—on probation for credit card forgery—was arrested while returning the getaway car to a Seattle rental agency. (Narcotics were also found in her possession at the time of her arrest.)

Police routinely checked the address on Brinkley's rental contract, confronting her teenage son and fugitive Nathaniel Doyle in the small apartment. Gunfire erupted, wounding Officer Owen McKenna, and Doyle was killed in the exchange, his youthful cohort taken into custody.

342 ■ MORRIS LYNN JOHNSON

Kentucky native Morris Johnson was a stickup artist with a laid-back attitude. Boasting adult convictions for bank robbery, escape and rescue, bank robbery with assault, and assault on a federal officer, Johnson balanced his fondness for easy money and automatic weapons with a passion for freedom. Ever restless in confinement, he was a perennial "rabbit," prone to daring escapes from custody.

Breaking parole on his latest robbery conviction, Johnson was named in federal warrants charging him with bank robbery and bank burglary—both in Atlanta, Georgia—during

August 1975. Briefly recaptured and locked away as a parole violator, he escaped from the federal prison in Atlanta on October 25, 1975.

Named to the Bureau's "Ten Most Wanted" list on May 25, 1976, Johnson lasted a month before federal agents, acting on a tip, captured him in New Orleans on June 26. Held in Selma, Alabama, pending transfer, Johnson confounded his captors by escaping from custody again on November 6. Johnson had promised to send greetings if he ever hit the streets again, and he was true to his word. At Christmas, the fugitive posted cards to the federal judge and prosecutor responsible for his conviction, along with one to the FBI agents instrumental in his arrest. "I do my thing and you do your thing," the cards read. "If we should ever meet again, it's beautiful." At this writing, they still have not.

343 ■ RICHARD JOSEPH PICARIELLO
344 ■ EDWARD PATRICK GULLION , JR.

Picariello and Gullion were active members of a radical "prison reform" group, dubbed the Fred Hampton Unit of the People's Forces. (Hampton was a Chicago Black Panther, killed by police in 1969.) No stranger to prison, Ed Gullion logged his first arrest in 1966, earning probation on charges of breaking and entering, carrying a firearm, and carrying a billy club. A year later, he was sentenced to five years for robbery, in Massachusetts; in 1971, he escaped with a fine of $150 on conviction for hitchhiking and possession of marijuana in Maine. With peculiar logic, members of the self-styled "People's Forces" sought to improve prison conditions through a series of bombings aimed at targets ranging from courthouses to major department stores.

According to the evidence by federal investigators, Picariello and Gullion were linked with bombings in Massachusetts, Maine, and New Hampshire between April and July 1976. Their first target was the Suffolk County courthouse, in Boston, damaged by a blast that injured twenty persons on April 22. Subsequent targets included: the Essex County courthouse, in Newburyport, Massachusetts; a power company building in Maine; the A & P Company's regional headquarters in Boston; and the Polaroid Company's office in Cambridge, Massachusetts. In the first three days of July, "reformist" bombs destroyed two National Guard trucks in Boston, an airliner parked at Boston's Logan Airport, and a post office in Seabrook, New Hampshire.

Accomplices Joseph Aceto and Everett Carlson were arrested by FBI agents on July 4, 1976, naming their cohorts under interrogation. On July 14, the prisoners were indicted, with fugitives Picariello and Gullion, on charges of bombing buildings and transporting explosives across state lines for terrorist purposes. Picariello's name was added to the "Ten Most Wanted" list on July 29, with Gullion following on August 13.

Defendant Aceto pled guilty to three federal counts on September 10, and Carlson was convicted by a jury on October 8, receiving a sentence of ten years in prison. Two weeks later, on October 21, FBI agents captured Richard Picariello outside a Fall River, Massachusetts, motel. They learned that he had been employed for several weeks, with Gullion, at a jewelry store in Providence, Rhode Island.

On October 22, G-men called on Gullion at his place of business, picking him out on sight, despite his insistence on using the name "John Costa." Both fugitives were held without bond for extradition to Massachusetts on bombing charges.

345 ■ GERHARDT JULIUS SCHWARTZ

Born in New York, during May 1929, Schwartz was a compulsive gambler who supported his habit through crime, compiling a record of adult convictions for petty larceny, robbery, and attempted robbery. On April 9, 1976, he joined two companions in raiding a bank in Rochester, New York, threatening clerks and customers with a sawed-off shotgun. On July 5, working with the same accomplices, Schwartz robbed a Rochester supermarket, afterward turning on one of his cronies and stabbing him viciously, leaving the man for dead. In custody, his one-time friends were happy to cooperate with the authorities by naming Gerhardt as their leader.

Indicted by New York authorities for armed robbery and attempted murder, Schwartz was also charged with bank robbery and conspiracy in federal warrants issued July 29, 1976. Posted to the Bureau's "Top Ten" list on November 18, 1976, he lasted four days in the spotlight. On November 22, a telephone call from New Rochelle, New York, led G-men to Gerhardt's hideout in the Bronx. He was taken into custody without resistance and returned to Rochester for trial.

346 ■ FRANCIS JOHN MARTIN

Born December 8, 1946, in Wilmington, Delaware, Frank Martin grew up as a thief and brutal sex offender, compiling a record of convictions for auto theft, burglary, kidnapping, and rape. The latter charges resulted from a string of abductions and sexual assaults, in Delaware, which left one victim dead, but murder charges were deferred in the absence of positive evidence linking Martin with the homicide. On August 21, 1976, Martin joined several other inmates in a breakout from the Delaware Correctional Center at Smyrna. Producing smuggled guns and homemade knives, the convicts overpowered guards and fled the prison grounds, but only Martin succeeded in evading pursuit. Named in federal warrants charging him with unlawful flight to avoid confinement, he was added to the FBI's "Most Wanted" list on December 17, 1976. Precisely two months later, a telephone tip led FBI agents to his hideout in Newport Beach, California, and the fugitive rapist was arrested without incident, returned to Delaware for completion of his outstanding sentence.

347 ■ BENJAMIN GEORGE PAVAN

Born in late December 1939, Ben Pavan logged his first arrest at age seventeen, later chalking up adult convictions for forgery and escape. Unwilling to forsake his roots, the San Francisco native habitually pulled his jobs in northern California, balancing the risks of recognition against the prospects for hiding out on familiar turf. By early 1974, authorities in San Francisco and Burlingame, California, had issued indictments charging Pavan with five armed robberies, three safe burglaries, one auto theft and a count of receiving stolen property. Federal warrants were issued on July 17, charging him with unlawful flight to avoid prosecution for armed robbery, and his name was added to the FBI's "Most Wanted" list on January 12, 1977.

Pavan's downfall, when it came, was a classic example of the "Top Ten" program in action. After nearly three years on the lam, he lasted only thirty-six days in the FBI spotlight. On February 17—the same day agents were surrounding Francis Martin in Newport Beach, California—a telephone tip led other G-men to Pavan's hideaway in Seattle, Washington. Arrested without a fight, the fugitive was returned to California for trial and ultimate conviction on outstanding felony charges.

348 ■ LARRY GENE CAMPBELL

A parolee with fourteen arrests (on multiple charges) since 1962, Campbell's most recent conviction had earned him six years behind bars. By June 1976 he was back on the street, looking for action, and he found it in Buffalo, New York.

On June 9, Campbell invaded a Buffalo apartment, violently assaulting two couples on the premises. Victims Thomas Tunney and Rhona Eiseman were strangled to death, with Eiseman also raped, while Michael Schostick and Teresa Beynart looked on in horror. Turning his attention to the survivors, Campbell stabbed Schostick, piercing a lung. Teresa Beynart, badly beaten, managed to escape from the apartment, her attacker in pursuit, and Schostick seized the opportunity to slip away before his would-be killer could return.

Identified from mug shots, Campbell was indicted on six counts of murder, two counts of robbery, and one count each of burglary, rape, attempted murder, and possession of a weapon. (Only two victims died, but their slayings each fit three legal categories of murder.) On March 18, 1977, his name was added to the FBI's "Most Wanted" list.

Six months later, a resident of the Atlanta ghetto recognized his newest neighbor from a Wanted flyer in the neighborhood post office. FBI agents received several anonymous calls from the tipster, sending him back for more information each time, until they received a detailed description of Campbell's car. The vehicle was found at 3 A.M., September 6, after a search spanning hundreds of blocks in Atlanta. A stakeout was established, and Campbell was apprehended at 12:30 P.M., when he finally returned to the car.

Campbell fought extradition, but his return to New York was ordered on November 15, 1977. Briefly hospitalized in December, following a hunger strike in jail, he was merely postponing the inevitable. Convicted on two counts of murder in 1978, Campbell was sentenced to a term of seventy-five years to life, with his sentence upheld on appeal, four years later.

349 ■ ROY ELLSWORTH SMITH

A native of Painesville Township, Ohio, Smith was deemed "Incorrigible" as a youth. By early adulthood, he had begun to dabble in narcotics and was known as a heavy drinker. Convicted of statutory rape in 1970, he served time in the Ohio state penitentiary and at Lima State Hospital, where psychiatric treatment failed to make a dent in his resentment toward the world at large.

On May 10, 1976, despondent over the collapse of his relationship with girlfriend Sandra Bracken, Smith invaded the woman's home in Kirtland, Ohio, while she was vacationing in Las Vegas. Armed with a ball-peen hammer, Smith murdered Bracken's fourteen-year-old daughter and twelve-year-old son, leaving his fingerprints and bloody weapon at the scene. Last sighted by relatives that evening, when he tried to break into the Fairport Harbor home of his sister-in-law, Smith eluded pursuers and dropped out of sight.

Indicted on murder charges at Kirtland, Smith was declared a federal fugitive on charges of unlawful flight to avoid prosecution. His name was added to the FBI's "Most Wanted" list ten months later, on March 18, 1977.

On June 27, 1977, amateur naturalist Jeff Stenzel was hiking along Red Mill Creek, in Perry Township, when he stumbled on rumpled clothing and human skeletal remains, scattered by predators. Forensic experts identified Smith from dental records, and the local coroner ascribed his death to suicide by hanging.

350 ■ RAYMOND LUC LEVASSEUR

Born in Sanford, Maine, in October 1946, by age twenty-nine Levasseur was a committed radical, bearing a panther's head and "Liberation" tattooed on one arm. On March 12, 1975, he was arrested with "Top Ten" fugitive Cameron David Bishop as they sat outside a bank in Providence, Rhode Island, their vehicle filled with illegal automatic weapons. Bishop was delivered to federal authorities, but Levasseur—still two years away from his own posting to the "Most Wanted" list—was released on bail and promptly went underground.

Within a year, Levasseur had joined the "People's Forces," a violent "prison reform" movement which included "Top Ten" fugitives Richard Picariello and Edward Gullion as members. A leader of the "Sam Melville-Jonathan Jackson Unit," named for two dead radicals. Levasseur joined comrades Thomas Manning, Richard Charles Williams, and West German immigrant Jaan Karl Laaman in a series of bombings aimed at government buildings. Laaman lost the fingertips of his right hand in the bombing of a New Hampshire police station, and Levasseur's fighting unit claimed credit for seven New England explosions between 1976 and 1978. Levasseur, Manning, and Manning's wife were also sought by FBI agents for a series of bank "liberations" committed during the late

1970s. Levasseur's name was added to the "Most Wanted" list on May 5, 1977.

Many American radicals mellowed with age in the latter 1970s and early 1980s, but members of the "People's Forces" were not among them. In 1981, Levasseur and company murdered New Jersey State Trooper Philip Lamonaco following a routine traffic stop. On April 4, 1982, they looted a bank in South Burlington, Vermont, fleeing with a shipment of cash just delivered by armored car. Over the next eighteen months, the pattern was repeated in Utica, Onondaga, Rotterdam and De Witt, New York, netting the bandits a total of $582,000.

On November 4, 1984, Levasseur was surrounded by FBI agents while driving with his common-law wife and their three children in Deerfield, Ohio, near Cleveland. Thirty minutes later, Richard Williams, Jaan Laaman and a female companion were cornered in Cleveland, coaxed out of their rented house without firing a shot. A search of the various homes turned up evidence linking Levasseur and company with the "United Freedom Front," a left-wing group claiming credit for ten bombings around New York City since 1982.

On March 12, 1985, Levasseur and five accomplices were indicted in New York on multiple charges related to ten bombing incidents. The targets included three military facilities and six private corporations, the latter selected for "punishment" on the basis of their military contracts or business dealings with South Africa. A year later, in March 1986, all six defendants were convicted on thirty-three felony counts; a mistrial was declared on thirty-nine other charges.

351 ■ JAMES EARL RAY

Ray, the convicted assassin of Dr. Martin Luther King, Jr., made his second appearance on the FBI's "Most Wanted" list following an escape from the state prison at Brushy Mountain, Tennessee. Serving ninety-nine years on his guilty plea in the King murder, Ray had tried to escape from Brushy Mountain once before, finally making good his attempt on June 10, 1977.

Inmates in the prison yard cooperated in the break by staging a diversion, scuffling and punching one another in the middle of a baseball game, while Ray and six accomplices approached the outer wall, swiftly erecting a make-shift ladder constructed of steel pipe. Guards were slow to notice the escape in progress—and two were later disciplined for negligence—but number seven up the ladder, bank robber Jerry Ward, was shot and wounded as he scrambled for freedom. En route to the prison hospital, Ward confirmed the administration's worst nightmare, shouting, "James Earl Ray got out! Ray got out!"

The state's reaction was immediate and overwhelming. Five of the six fugitives were quickly apprehended in the snake-infested woods surrounding Brushy Mountain, and Ray was added to the FBI's "Most Wanted" list the afternoon of the escape. Acquaintances of Ray—including the authors—were interviewed by federal officers in an attempt to learn if Ray had outside help with his escape. The press was rife with rumors of conspiracy—to liberate King's assassin or, perhaps, to silence him forever with a contract "hit."

The truth was rather less dramatic. On June 13, a team of searchers using bloodhounds found their quarry huddled in the woods, attempting to conceal himself beneath some leaves. Ray offered no resistance as they led him back to prison, but his efforts to escape have continued through the years, without success.

352 ■ WILLIE FOSTER SELLERS

A member of the loose-knit Dawson Gang, renowned for looting banks in northern Georgia through the early 1970s, Sellers was convicted on federal bank robbery charges in 1975 and sentenced to forty-five years in prison. Confined at Marion, Illinois, he was returned to Atlanta in early 1977 to testify in defense of two persons charged with another Georgia robbery. Fulton County deputies intercepted a smuggled shipment of hacksaw blades meant for Sellers on February 25, believing their escape risk had been neutralized.

On March 17, 1977, three armed intruders used bolt cutters to remove the wire screen covering a jail window, passing an acetylene torch through the window to Sellers and convicted bank robber Charles Calvin Garrett. Following his escape, Sellers was linked with robberies netting a half-million dollars from banks in Arkansas, Missouri, North Carolina and Texas. Declared a federal fugitive on charges of bank robbery and unlawful flight to avoid confinement, Sellers was added to the FBI's "Most Wanted" list on June 14, 1977.

Two years later, on June 20, 1979, agents pursuing their investigation of Sellers traced the fugitive to Hartsell Airport, in Atlanta, where he was surrounded in the freight terminal and arrested without resistance. Declining to reveal the source which led them to Sellers, the G-men merely stated that he was visiting the airport on "legitimate business."

353 ■ LARRY SMITH

A quick-trigger gunman and stickup artist, Larry Smith was already serving life in Texas, on conviction of armed robbery and assault with intent to kill, when he was shipped to Michigan for trial on charges of murdering a Detroit man. Complaining of an injured finger, he was moved to the jail ward of a local hospital and escaped from there on May 16, 1977. Federal warrants were issued, charging Smith with unlawful flight to avoid prosecution for murder, and his name was added to the "Ten Most Wanted" list on July 15.

A short month later, on August 20, 1977, police officers in Toronto, Canada, stopped Smith's car after he illegally drove past a street car's open door. A revolver was found in his car, and Smith was identified from fingerprints while being detained on a charge of carrying a restricted weapon in a motor vehicle. A more detailed search of the car also turned up quantities of marijuana, but Smith was delivered to American authorities in lieu of local prosecution. Returned to Detroit for trial on murder charges, he was ultimately convicted and sentenced to prison.

354 ■ RALPH ROBERT COZZOLINO

A notorious Dixie holdup man and escape artist, Cozzolino once served time in Alcatraz but logged most of his years behind bars in Southern prisons, frequently breaking out to commit new crimes. Sentenced to life plus ten years for a robbery at Kingsport, Tennessee, he escaped from the state prison at Nashville in September 1956. In 1958, he was sentenced to thirty years for a robbery in Birmingham, Alabama, breaking out of Kilby prison in a hail of bullets two months later. Back in Georgia, robberies in Fulton and DeKalb counties earned Cozzolino another term of thirty to forty years; he served seven before he was returned to the custody of Alabama authorities. In 1968, he escaped from custody in Georgia twice in three months' time, first fleeing a prison hospital and afterward digging through solid concrete to reach a utility tunnel at Reidsville state prison.

In August 1977, Cozzolino and accomplice Clarence Parker robbed a grocery store in Chattanooga, Tennessee. A policeman, Clarence Hambler, was inside the store at the time, but he had no chance to intervene. Shot once in the face by Cozzolino, Hambler was killed by a second round in the back of his head as he lay helpless on the floor. The store's proprietor, meanwhile, secured a pistol and fatally wounded Parker, putting Cozzolino to flight.

Indicted for murder in September 1977, Cozzolino was declared a federal fugitive on charges of unlawful flight to avoid prosecution. His lengthy record and the brutal violence of his last offense won him a posting to the FBI's "Most Wanted" list on October 19.

Three months later, on January 6, 1978, a flying squad of federal agents captured Cozzolino at a service station in Jonesboro, near Atlanta. Held in lieu of $1 million bail, the fugitive waived extradition and was returned to Chattanooga for trial.

355 ■ MILLARD OSCAR HUBBARD

An habitual criminal whose record spanned thirty years, Hubbard was charged in 1976 with the August 14 robbery of a bank in Tazewell, Tennessee. In short order, his name was also linked with bank jobs in Washington, Pennsylvania, Steubenville and St. Clairsville, Ohio. In December 1976, he held up a supermarket in Lexington, Kentucky. Sought on federal bank robbery charges, Hubbard was added to the FBI's "Most Wanted" list on October 19, 1977.

Two days later, federal agents acting on a tip from residents of Lexington surrounded Hubbard on a visit to the city. Faced with overwhelming numbers, Hubbard grabbed a carbine and was wounded twice, surviving to stand trial in federal court. Conviction on multiple charges—including bank robbery, assault, receipt and possession of a firearm by a convicted felon, and bank robbery with assault—earned him a sentence of thirty-seven years in prison.

In July 1979, Hubbard was transferred from the federal penitentiary at Atlanta, Georgia, to a smaller facility at Marion, Illinois. There, on April 29, 1984, he was beaten by another inmate and died that same afternoon.

356 ■ CARLOS ALBERTO TORRES

A ranking member of the Puerto Rican terrorist group FALN (Armed Forces of National Liberation), Carlos Torres logged his first arrest in Chicago a year before the militant band was organized. Jailed for mob action and disorderly conduct on January 31, 1973, he won dismissal of the former charge, drawing a sentence of one year's supervision on the latter. Arrested again on September 27, 1973, for trespass and interfering with an officer, he saw both charges dismissed nine months later.

By that time, the FALN had collected a hard core of twenty to fifty members, plotting its campaign "to dramatize the strangulation of the Puerto Rican people in the island as well as in the U.S. by the yoke of Yanki imperialism." The group's favorite technique involved bombing, with fifty-one blasts claimed between August 1974 and March 1977. Five Manhattan banks were damaged by the group's explosive packages in October 1974. Two months later, a New York policeman was injured in another blast, but FALN's worst atrocity was committed on January 24, 1975, when a bomb shattered the historic Fraunces Tavern on Wall Street, killing four persons and wounding another fifty-three.

The deadly beat went on, with action shifting to Chicago during 1975. Bombs were detonated in the Windy City during June and October of that year, but the first Illinois casualties were not claimed until June 1976, when five persons were injured in a new series of bombings. More blasts damaged office buildings and a hotel rest room in September, leading FBI agents and local police to redouble their search for the terrorists.

On November 3, 1976, a raiding party swept through Torres's Chicago apartment, uncovering a terrorist bomb factory with evidence linked to recent explosions. Absent from home at the time of the raid, Torres was branded a federal fugitive in warrants charging him with possession of explosives, conspiracy, violation of the National Firearms Act, and unlawful flight to avoid prosecution. His name was added to the bureau's "Ten Most Wanted" list October 19, 1977.

In hiding, Torres continued directing the FALN's violent activities. New York's FBI office was bombed in March 1977; five months later, one person was killed and seven others wounded in a single afternoon of carnage in Manhattan. In July 1978, "explosives expert" William Morales was maimed, losing both hands, when a bomb blew up on his work bench in Queens, leading police to uncover another demolitions factory. More bombs were touched off around Evanston, Illinois, in October 1979, and gangs of FALN adherents raided campaign headquarters of both major political parties during March 1980, vandalizing offices in New York and Chicago.

On April 4, 1980, residents of Evanston, Illinois, complained to local police of "suspicious" activities surrounding a van parked on a residential street. Officers responding to the call arrested Torres and ten other FALN supporters, confiscating a small arsenal of shotguns and pistols from the vehicle and house they had occupied.

But the arrest of Carlos Torres and his cronies did not crush the FALN. In July 1981, imprisoned member Alfredo Mendez exposed a plot to kidnap the son of President Ronald Reagan, trading the information off in a futile effort to shave his own seventy-five-year sentence. Three New York policemen were maimed by FALN bombs in December 1982, and by the following year FALN members were claiming a total of 120 blasts, inflicting $3.5 million in property damage.

357 ■ ENRIQUE ESTRADA

A well-known drug abuser, born in 1941, Estrada launched his criminal career at age eighteen, logging a total of twenty arrests on no less than thirty-two separate felony charges. His seven convictions included counts of burglary, larceny, damage to property, and possession of dangerous drugs. In October and November 1976, Los Angeles authorities sought Estrada in connection with two residential burglaries, resulting in the deaths of elderly female victims. In each case, the women were robbed at knifepoint in their homes, then bound by their assailant and brutally beaten to death.

Indicted for robbery and murder in Los Angeles, Estrada was declared a federal fugitive on charges of unlawful flight to avoid prosecution. His name was added to the FBI's "Most Wanted" list on December 5, 1977, and the resultant publicity paid off at once. In Bakersfield, north of Los Angeles, narcotics officers were following a suspect known as "Hank" Estrada when the federal wanted flyers rang a bell. They trailed him to a local filling station on December 8 and took him into custody, returning him to Los Angeles for trial and ultimate conviction on the more serious charges awaiting him there.

358 ■ WILLIAM DAVID SMITH

Born in Michigan in 1943, Smith was an habitual criminal with multiple convictions on his record by the time he made the FBI's "Most Wanted" list in February 1978. Charged with outstanding counts of bank robbery and parole violation, he finally made the roster through an act of personal violence, shooting his former wife's husband to death at Flint, Michigan, in April 1977 and burning the victim's body before he fled the area. Named to the Bureau's "Top Ten" on February 10, 1978, the same day Gary Warden and serial killer Ted Bundy were added to the list. Smith had eight more months on the road. A telephone tip led FBI agents to his Chicago hideout on October 27, 1978, and the fugitive was taken into custody without resistance, returned to Michigan for trial and ultimate conviction on outstanding murder charges.

359 ■ GARY RONALD WARDEN

Gary Warden, age thirty-two, was serving a forty-year sentence for armed robbery when he escaped from a Florida prison in 1977. Sought on federal charges of unlawful flight to avoid confinement, he was also linked with a series of armed bank robberies in Florida, West Virginia, Missouri, and California following his jailbreak. One of three fugitives posted to the "Ten Most Wanted" list on February 10, 1978, Warden remained at large for exactly three months after his addition to the roster. On May 10, 1978, federal agents and local officers surrounded his hideout, in Cumberland, Maryland, and took Warden into custody without a shot fired in anger. The fugitive was held in federal custody pending disposition of the marathon charges filed against him from coast to coast.

360 ■ THEODORE ROBERT BUNDY

Ted Bundy posed a striking contrast to the general image of a "homicidal maniac": attractive, self-assured, politically ambitious, and successful with a wide variety of women. But his private demons drove him to extremes of violence which make the gory worst of modern "slasher" films seem almost petty by comparison. With his chameleon-like ability to blend, his talent for belonging, Bundy posed an ever-present danger to the pretty dark-haired women he selected as his victims.

Lynda Healy was the first fatality. On January 31, 1974, she vanished from her basement lodgings in Seattle, leaving bloody sheets behind, a blood-stained nightgown hanging in her closet. Several blocks away, young Susan Clarke had been assaulted, bludgeoned in her bed a few weeks earlier, but she survived her crushing injuries and would eventually recover. As for Lynda Healy, she was gone without a trace.

Police had no persuasive evidence of any pattern yet, but it would not be long in coming. On March 12, Donna Gail Manson disappeared en route to a concert in Olympia, Washington. On April 17, Susan Rancourt vanished on her way to see a German language film in Ellensburg. On May 6, Roberta Parks failed to return from a late-night stroll in her Corvallis neighborhood. On June 1, Brenda Ball left Seattle's Flame Tavern with an unknown man and vanished, as if into thin air. Ten days later, Georgann Hawkins joined the list of missing women, lost somewhere between her boyfriend's apartment and her own sorority house in Seattle.

Now detectives had their pattern. All the missing women had been young, attractive, with their dark hair worn at shoulder length or longer, parted in the middle. In their photos, laid out side-by-side, they might have passed for sisters, some for twins. Homicide investigators had no corpses yet, but they refused to cherish false illusions of a happy ending to the case. There were so many victims, and the worst was yet to come.

July 14. A crowd assembled on the shores of Lake Sammamish to enjoy the sun and water sports of summer. When the day was over, two more names would be appended to the growing list of missing women: Janice Ott and Denise Naslund had each disappeared within sight of their separate friends, but this time police had a tenuous lead. Passers-by remembered seeing Janice Ott in conversation with a man who carried one arm in a sling; he had been overheard to introduce himself as "Ted." With that report in hand, detectives turned up other female witnesses who were themselves approached by "Ted" at Lake Sammamish. In each case, he had asked for help securing a sailboat to his car. The lucky women had declined, but one had followed "Ted" to where his small Volkswagen "bug" was parked; there was no sign of any sailboat, and his explanation—that the boat would have to be retrieved from a house "up the hill"—had aroused her suspicions, prompting her to put the stranger off.

Police now had a fair description of their suspect and his car. The published references to "Ted" inspired a rash of calls reporting "suspects," one of them in reference to college student Theodore Bundy. The authorities checked out each lead as time allowed, but Bundy was considered "squeaky clean": a law student and Young Republican active in law-and-order politics, he once had chased a mugger several blocks to make a citizen's arrest. So many calls reporting suspects had been made from spite or simple overzealousness, and Bundy's name was filed away with countless others, momentarily forgotten.

On September 7, hunters found a makeshift graveyard on a wooded hillside several miles from Lake Sammamish. Dental records were required to finally identify remains of Janice Ott and Denise Naslund; the skeleton of a third woman, found with the others, could not be identified. Five weeks later, on October 12, another hunter found the bones of two more women in Clark County. One victim was identified as Carol Valenzuela, missing for two months from Vancouver, Washington, on the Oregon border; again, the second victim would remain unknown, recorded in the files as a "Jane Doe." Police were optimistic, hopeful that discovery of victims would eventually lead them to the killer, but they had no way of knowing that their man had given them the slip already, moving on in search of safer hunting grounds and other prey.

The terror came to Utah on October 2, 1974, when Nancy Wilcox disappeared in Salt Lake City. On October 18, Melissa Smith vanished in Midvale; her body, raped and beaten, would be unearthed in the Wasatch Mountains nine days later. Laura Aime joined the missing list in Orem, on October 31, while walking home in costume from a Halloween party; a month would pass before her battered, violated body was discovered in a wooded area outside of town. A man attempted to abduct attractive Carol Da Ronch from a Salt Lake City shopping mall November 8, but she was able to escape before he could attach a pair of handcuffs to her wrists. That evening, Debbie Kent was kidnapped from the auditorium at Salt Lake City's Viewmont High School.

Authorities in Utah kept communications open with police in other states, including Washington. They might have noticed that a suspect from Seattle, one Ted Bundy, was attending school in Utah when the local disappearances occurred, but they were looking for a madman, rather than a sober, well-groomed student of the law who seemed to have political connections in Seattle. Bundy stayed on file, and was again forgotten.

With the new year, Colorado joined the list of hunting grounds for an elusive killer who apparently selected victims by their hairstyles. Caryn Campbell was the first to vanish, from a ski lodge at Snowmass on January 12; her raped and battered body would be found on February 17. On March 15, Julie Cunningham disappeared en route to a tavern in Vail. One month later to the day, Melanie Cooley went missing while riding her bicycle in Nederland; she was discovered eight days later, dead, her skull crushed, with her jeans pulled down around her ankles. On July 1, Shelly Robertson was added to the missing list in Golden; her remains were found on August 23, discarded in a mine shaft near the Berthoud Pass.

A week before the final, grim discovery, Ted Bundy was arrested in Salt Lake City for suspicion of burglary. Erratic driving had attracted the attention of the police, and an examination of his car—a small VW—revealed peculiar items such as handcuffs and a pair of panty hose with eyeholes cut to form a stocking mask. The glove compartment yielded gasoline receipts and maps which linked the suspect with a list of Colorado ski resorts, including Vail and Snowmass. Carol Da Ronch identified Ted Bundy as the man who had attacked her in November, and her testimony was sufficient to convict him on a charge of attempted kidnapping. Other states were waiting for a shot at Bundy now, and in January 1977 he was extradited to Colorado for trial in the murder of Caryn Campbell, at Snowmass.

Faced with prison time already, Bundy had no time to spare for further trials. He fled from custody in June, and was recaptured after eight days on the road. On December 30 he tried again, with more success, escaping all the way to Tallahassee, Florida, where he found lodgings on the outskirts of Florida State University. Suspected in a score of deaths already, Bundy had secured himself another happy hunting ground.

In the small hours of January 15, 1978, he invaded the Chi Omega sorority house, dressed all in black and armed with a heavy wooden club. Before he left, two women had been raped and killed, a third severely injured by the beating he inflicted with his bludgeon. Within the hour, he had slipped inside another house, just blocks away, to club another victim in her bed. She, too, survived. Detectives at the Chi Omega house discovered bite marks on the corpses there, appalling evidence of Bundy's fervor at the moment of the kill.

On February 6, Bundy stole a van and drove to Jacksonville, where he was spotted in the act of trying to abduct a schoolgirl. Three days later, twelve-year-old Kimberly Leach disappeared from a schoolyard nearby; she was found in the first week of April, her body discarded near Suwanee State Park. On February 10, his name was added to the Bureau's "Ten Most Wanted" list.

Police in Pensacola spotted Bundy's stolen license plates on February 15, and were forced to run him down as he attempted to escape on foot. Once Bundy was identified, impressions of his teeth were taken to compare with bite marks on the Chi Omega victims, and his fate was sealed. Convicted on two counts of murder in July 1979, he was sentenced to die in Florida's electric chair. A third conviction and death sentence were subsequently obtained in the case of Kimberly Leach and it was for this crime that he was eventually electrocuted at 7:16 A.M. on January 24, 1989.

Throughout his long incarceration and extensive legal maneuvering, Bundy maintained his pose of innocence. Despite some verbal sparring with detectives and extensive interviews with authors who recorded his "speculations" on a string of unsolved homicides, he insisted that he was just a victim, that police were using his case to "clear the books" on murders which could never be legitimately solved.

His plea for sympathy, however, was unconvincing; and when he ran out of pleas that would be heard in court, he apparently crumbled, admitting to as many as twenty-eight murders, some of them not previously associated with him.

361 ■ ANDREW EVAN GIPSON

A veteran felon with various jail terms behind him, Gipson was convicted under the Kansas habitual criminal statute for his role in a 1968 bank robbery, during which a state trooper was killed. Upon conviction, Gipson received six concurrent sentences of forty to ninety years in prison, serving nine years before he escaped from the state penitentiary at Lansing, in July 1977. Declared a federal fugitive on charges of unlawful flight to avoid confinement, Gipson was added to the Bureau's "Ten Most Wanted" list on March 27, 1978.

On May 24, 1978—two days before his forty-second birthday—Gipson was traced to Albuquerque, New Mexico, where he had spent the past eight months living and working as "Phillip Daigls." Agents collared him without resistance at his job, where he had lately been promoted as the foreman of a construction crew. Gipson's employers were stunned by the arrest, describing the fugitive as "a damn good worker."

362 ■ ANTHONY DOMINIC LIBERATORE

A lifelong member of the Cleveland underworld, Anthony Liberatore was convicted in 1938—at age sixteen—of participating in the murder of two policemen. His past record of robbery and burglary arrests eliminated any sympathy the court might otherwise have felt for one so young, and he was sentenced to life imprisonment. In 1957, Governor John Brown, filling an eleven-day vacancy in the governor's office, commuted the sentence and Liberatore was paroled.

Returning to Cleveland, Liberatore described himself officially as a laborer. In fact, he was a bomber and "enforcer" on the payroll of local mobsters, rising swiftly to control Local 860 of the laborer's union. Teaming with hoodlum Danny Greene, Liberatore created the Cleveland Trade Solid Waste Guild, blasting his competitors out of the business with dynamite.

In 1972, Governor John Gilligan granted Liberatore a full pardon on his double murder conviction, ignoring evidence that linked Liberatore with the sale of $1 million in bonds stolen during a California bank robbery. Craving respect in his hometown, Liberatore began giving lectures on penal reform, and in 1975 he was appointed by the mayor to serve on the board of a newly-created Regional Sewer District. Meanwhile, Anthony solidified his iron control over local rackets and corrupt labor unions, frequently resorting to violence in the face of opposition.

On October 6, 1977, one-time ally Danny Greene was vaporized by a remote-control car bomb in Cleveland. FBI informants fingered Liberatore as the man behind the contract, and federal warrants were issued. Liberatore vanished at once, and was declared a fugitive on charges of unlawful flight to avoid prosecution for murder and conspiracy. His name was added to the "Ten Most Wanted" list on May 26, 1978.

On April Fool's Day, 1979, FBI agents traced Liberatore to the home of an associate in Eastlake, Ohio. (His host, accused of arson and assorted other felonies, was a member in good standing of the Cleveland underworld.) A search of the home turned up blank birth certificates and driver's licenses, suggesting that Liberatore did not plan to surrender voluntarily. He was held in lieu of $1 million bail, pending trial on state and federal charges.

363 ■ MICHAEL GEORGE THEVIS

An Atlanta-based pornography tycoon, Mike Thevis boasted more than 100 arrests for distributing obscene material. In 1974, he was convicted of transporting pornography across state lines, drawing a sentence of eight and a half years in federal prison. Confined at Terre Haute, Indiana, he was moved to the more comfortable prison hospital at Lexington, Kentucky, in 1977, with assistance from Georgia politicians who received an estimated $400,000 in campaign contributions from Thevis the previous year.

In April 1977, Thevis lost a civil suit in Louisville, Kentucky, stemming from an arson fire that leveled the establishment of a competing porno merchant. A jury ordered Thevis to pay $667,000 to the victim and several insurance companies —the first time on record that punitive damages were ever awarded to an insurer. On April 28, Thevis escaped from a local jail in New Albany, Indiana, after deputies left him alone to make a private phone call. Charged with unlawful flight to avoid confinement, Thevis made the "Top Ten" list on July 10, 1978.

By that time, a federal grand jury in Atlanta had issued indictments charging the fugitive with fourteen counts of racketeering and mail fraud. According to the charges, Thevis had used murder, arson and extortion to control the Georgia porno industry and spread his tentacles across the nation, consolidating a chain of 200 outlets that grossed between $5 and $10 million annually. Among other crimes, he was charged with the 1970 murder of business partner Kenneth Hannah, found shot in the trunk of his own car, and the subsequent slaying of rival James Mayer, Jr. On October 25, 1978, with Thevis still at large, chief prosecution witness Roger Underhill was assassinated by hit men near Atlanta. (The gunners also murdered an innocent bystander, Isaac Galanti, in the shotgun attack.)

On November 9, 1978, bank tellers in Bloomfield, Connecticut, became suspicious and summoned police after a new depositor, "Arbi Jonathan Evans," tried to withdraw $31,500. Swiftly identified as Thevis, the fugitive explained that he had borrowed his alias from the brother of his latest female travel-

ing companion. Both were taken into custody; their car, outside the bank, contained a .38 revolver, $600,000 in cash, and
close to $1 million worth of jewelry.

364 ■ CHARLES EVERETT HUGHES

A major drug smuggler, Hughes was sought in the murders of
two adult men and two teenaged sisters in Bay County, Florida. On January 23, 1977, the four victims accidentally witnessed Hughes and associates in the act of unloading thirty-
two tons of marijuana—valued at $1.2 million—along a re-
mote stretch of Florida coast. Shot execution-style, the bodies
were weighted and dropped in a sink hole nearby, from which
they were recovered during August 1977. A federal warrant
was issued for Hughes on January 24, 1978, charging him with
unlawful flight to avoid prosecution for murder, and his name
was added to the "Top Ten" list on November 19, 1978.

On April 30, 1981, FBI agents traced Hughes to an auto
body shop in Myrtle, Mississippi, where he was employed under the alias of "George Hacker." The arrest startled many of
"Hacker's" new friends in the community, and residents of
Myrtle raised $3,000 for his legal defense, sparking a local
controversy between Hughes sympathizers and strict advocates of law and order. Meanwhile, Hughes was returned to
Florida for trial on murder charges.

365 ■ RONALD LEE LYONS

The arrest record on Ron Lyons dates from 1967; by 1973, he
was serving a fifty-year prison term on conviction of robbing
Moose lodges in Jackson and Dickson, Tennessee, at gunpoint. Prison authorities, monitoring phone calls to and from
their institution, were aware that Lyons planned a break in
1978, but they apparently dismissed the possibility that he
would be successful in his efforts to recruit outside assistance.

On September 13, 1978, Lyons accompanied other inmates

on a recreational outing to a bowling alley in Dickson, Tennessee. Entering the rest room with convicts Larry Chism, George Bonds, and Floyd Brewer, he recovered sawed-off shotguns which accomplices had hidden in the ceiling. As a guard approached, the inmates came out shooting, wounding an officer and an innocent bystander. Prison guards returned the fire, until their targets seized Carolyn Barnette, a snack bar employee, to use as a human shield, fleeing the scene in a stolen car.

Lyons and company drove their hostage to the Dickson airport, where they released her and promptly kidnapped airport manager Mel Romine, forcing him to fly them to Lee County, Arkansas, leaving eight kidnapped hostages and six commandeered vehicles in their wake. Three of the inmates were soon recaptured: Chism escaped again, from an Arkansas jail, in December 1978, while Bonds and Brewer pled guilty on all counts, receiving added terms of thirty years in prison. Ronald Lyons was added to the FBI's "Most Wanted" list on December 17, 1978, charged with air piracy, kidnapping and conspiracy. (Eight residents of Nashville, Memphis and Lenior City were also charged with conspiracy for supplying the money and weapons used in the breakout.)

On September 10, 1979, Lyons was arrested by Washoe County sheriff's deputies at Hungry Valley, Nevada, not far from Reno. Hiding in a rural desert home, he offered no resistance and was handed over to the FBI. Pleading guilty to aircraft piracy in November, Lyons received an additional term of 30 years.

366 ■ LEO JOSEPH KOURY

A prominent Virginia businessman of Lebanese extraction, Koury held a virtual monopoly on Richmond's gay bars and nightclubs in the early 1970s. When various competitors began to threaten that monopoly by opening their own establishments, Koury launched a campaign of retaliation aimed at driving all his rivals out of business. According to the federal charges filed against him, his unorthodox "business techniques" included murder, arson and extortion.

Koury reportedly launched his campaign in March 1975, when he ordered the execution of a rival gay bar's bouncer. The victim, shot to death and wired to heavy weights, was subsequently fished out of a nearby river. Another shooting incident, arranged by Koury, claimed the life of one patron and wounded two others in a rival establishment, on January 15, 1977.

When he was not engaged in crude guerilla warfare with his competition, Koury followed other criminal pursuits. A favorite was insurance fraud, with Koury wrecking several cars, torching a pleasure boat, and arranging the theft of his own jewelry in order to reap insurance benefits from unwitting companies. On the side, between August 1 and October 1, 1975, he also plotted the kidnapping of Richmond businessman E. Claiborne Robbins, intending to demand $500,000 ransom. The snatch was aborted when one of Koury's co-conspirators was picked up by the FBI on unrelated charges.

On October 30, 1978, a federal grand jury indicted Leo Koury on fifteen counts of racketeering, murder, attempted murder, extortion, arson, conspiracy to commit kidnapping, armed robbery, mail fraud, loan sharking, threatening a grand jury witness, and obstructing justice. Koury disappeared before he could be taken into custody, and he was added to the FBI's "Most Wanted" list on April 20, 1979. At this writing, he is still at large.

Leo Joseph Koury was born in Pittsburgh, Pennsylvania, on July 14, 1934. He is described as a white male, five feet eleven inches tall, weighing 240 pounds, with black hair, brown eyes, and a dark complexion. A diabetic, he requires daily injections of insulin. Koury frequents Lebanese restaurants whenever possible, and has worked part-time as a baseball umpire in the past. He sometimes uses the alias "Mike Decker," in conjunction with Social Security number 224-38-4566. Known to carry a revolver in an ankle holster, Koury is considered armed and extremely dangerous.

367 ■ JOHN WILLIAM SHERMAN

A member of the radical "George Jackson Brigade," linked with numerous West Coast bombings and bank robberies during the 1970s, Sherman shot it out with police on at least two occasions. Once, during a 1976 Seattle bank robbery, he was wounded by police and subsequently arrested. Sherman escaped on that occasion when an accomplice, dressed as a medical assistant, wounded the guard assigned to escort Sherman from a local hospital. Back on the street, Sherman resumed his career of terrorism, ultimately robbing fourteen banks and touching off eleven high-explosive charges in the name of "liberation." Captured at a Tacoma drive-in restaurant, in March 1978, Sherman was dressed as a priest when FBI agents surrounded his car and took him into custody. Upon conviction of bank robbery and escape charges, he was sentenced to ten years in prison.

On April 24, 1979, Sherman escaped from prison at Lompoc, California, and was declared a federal fugitive on charges of unlawful flight to avoid confinement. His name was added to the Bureau's "Most Wanted" list on August 3, 1979.

Thirty-two months later, after completing extensive investigations in Seattle and Portland, Oregon, federal agents traced Sherman to his hideout in Golden, Colorado. He was taken into custody without incident, surrendering meekly to his captors. Also arrested were Sherman's wife, Marianne, and another female traveling companion, Paula Botwinick. Both women were held on charges of aiding a federal fugitive.

368 ■ MELVIN BAY GUYON

At age nineteen, Guyon was charged with aggravated robbery, aggravated kidnapping and rape, following his brutal assault on a Chicago-area woman. Evidence of interstate travel resulted in issuance of a federal warrant, charging Guyon with unlawful flight to avoid prosecution, and FBI agents had traced their man to Cleveland, Ohio, by the second week of August 1979.

On August 9, Special Agents Johnnie L. Oliver and William Tenwick entered a run-down housing project in East Cleveland. They cornered Guyon in an apartment crowded with children, unable to fire as Guyon panicked and drew a pistol. His first shot misfired, but the second struck Agent Oliver in the chest, inflicting a mortal wound. Agent Tenwick got off a shot as Guyon crawled through a window, causing Guyon to drop his gun outside before he fled.

The killer of a federal agent, Melvin Bay Guyon was added to the "Most Wanted" list on August 10, a massive search already under way across Ohio. On August 16, G-men received a tip that Guyon was hiding in Youngstown, and teams began scouring the city at 6:30 P.M. Two hours later, staking out a suspect house, the agents saw Guyon emerge and step into a sidewalk phone booth. The fugitive's identity was confirmed by an agent who "casually" strolled past the booth for a close-up inspection.

While Guyon was on the phone, agents hatched a plan to trap him in the booth. A van would pull up on the sidewalk, tip the booth, and pin Guyon inside while agents hastily surrounded him and made the collar. In the actual event, the booth refused to tip, and Melvin squeezed off several shots while he was scooting down the sidewalk on a one-way ride. Escaping from the booth at last, he raced across a nearby vacant lot and disappeared amid the unkempt shrubbery.

While federal agents and police were scouring the lot and nearby buildings, Guyon barged into a private residence some blocks away. Unarmed, he huddled in a chair and grudgingly agreed to let the resident transport him to a local hospital. Once there, Guyon surrendered to a hospital security guard, and federal agents were summoned to take him away. A charge of first degree murder was added to the felony counts already pending against Guyon in Chicago.

369 ■ GEORGE ALVIN BRUTON

Of all the fugitives to grace the FBI's "Most Wanted" list, George Bruton is the only one thus far to set a precedent for handling of prosecutions in a federal case. Appealing a 1968 conviction to the Supreme Court in *Bruton vs the United States,* Bruton won a ruling that confessions taken by police from an accomplice to a crime were not admissible, per se, in the pursuit of a conviction. Simply put, the so-called "Bruton doctrine" holds that a defendant may not be convicted on the testimony of a co-defendant if said co-defendant is not cross-examined on the witness stand, in open court.

The legal victory did not prevent Bruton's conviction and imprisonment on subsequent felony charges, but a decade later, on November 22, 1978, he was paroled from the federal penitentiary at Leavenworth. Wasting no time on the streets, he joined forces with former cellmate Steven Parnell on December 21, launching a crime spree which included burglary, theft of cars and weapons, kidnapping of hostages, and the wounding of two law enforcement officers in Utah. Parnell was caged December 24, but Bruton managed to escape on foot, a federal warrant charging him with unlawful flight to avoid prosecution.

Shortly after his escape in Utah, Bruton surfaced in Kansas City, moving in with another fellow inmate, Michael Walker, and Walker's girlfriend. Togetherness proved taxing on the fugitive, and Bruton's benefactors were found days later, Walker shot in the head, his lover strangled. In the absence of concrete evidence, local authorities issued new warrants, seeking Bruton as a material witness in the double murder.

Added to the FBI's "Most Wanted" list on September 20, 1979, Bruton evaded pursuers until December 14, when G-men and local officers flushed him out of his hideout in Fort Smith, Arkansas. Arrested without resistance, the fugitive was returned to Utah for trial on outstanding felony charges.

370 ■ EARL EDWIN AUSTIN

A native of Tacoma Park, Maryland, Austin spent much of his adult life in prison, racking up convictions for grand larceny, forgery, aggravated assault, bank robbery, escape, and threatening the President of the United States. The latter charge resulted from a letter Austin sent to Lyndon Johnson from a penitentiary in Idaho; it cost him five more years in custody. A jail-break artist with a history of firing on police when he was cornered, Austin won parole in February 1979, from Kansas City, and immediately headed south to launch another crime spree.

On February 25, Earl Austin robbed a bank in Houston, Texas, of $86,000, making a clean getaway. By mid-July, he was linked with at least five other bank jobs in Southern states, ranging from Kentucky to Florida. Already sought by federal agents on charges of bank robbery and unlawful flight to avoid prosecution, Austin's name was added to the "Top Ten" list on October 12, 1979.

Five months of investigation paid off for FBI agents on March 1, 1980, when they traced Austin to his rented apartment in Tucson, Arizona. Surrendering without a struggle, Austin carried a loaded pistol and more than $10,000 in cash at the time of his arrest; a portion of the loot was marked, and thus directly traceable to the Houston bank job in February. Charged in three of his known holdups, Austin was held in lieu of $350,000 bond.

371 ■ VINCENT JAMES RUSSO

An ex-policeman and deserter from the United States Marine Corps, born in St. Albans, New York, in July 1954, Russo was sought by federal agents on charges of unlawful flight to avoid prosecution for robbery, kidnapping, and attempted murder. The charges resulted from Russo's raid on a Ramona, California, liquor store, December 22, 1978. After cleaning out the till, Russo abducted the lone clerk and drove him to an isolated area where he was forced to lie down on the ground. With the sole witness prostrate before him, Russo fired multiple rounds from a .45-caliber pistol, leaving his victim for dead as he drove from the scene. Incredibly, the clerk survived his wounds and furnished a description of the gunman which ultimately led to Russo's identification.

Added to the FBI's "Most Wanted" list on December 21, 1979, Russo remained at large for five years. Federal agents visited his home in Beaver Falls, Pennsylvania, on January 4, 1985, and found the triggerman unarmed. Arrested without incident, Russo was returned to California for his trial on outstanding felony charges.

372 ■ ALBERT LOPEZ VICTORY

A Coney Island native with ties to organized crime in New York, Albert Victory earned a reputation as "one of the most vicious criminals ever to be jailed in New York state." In 1968, New York Patrolman John Varecha stopped Victory and a male companion for a routine traffic infraction and was shot in the face at point-blank range by Victory's crony, reportedly at Victory's instigation. Both men were convicted of murder, with Victory drawing a sentence of twenty-five years to life.

On May 5, 1978, two correctional officers escorted Victory from Green Haven prison, at Stormville, New York, to see a private dentist. Hours later, they returned without him, claiming three armed men had freed their prisoner, but first one guard and then the other swiftly changed his tune. In fact, they had accepted a $500 bribe to let Victory stop at a nearby motel, for sex with a female attorney, and their man had slipped away while they were sipping drinks in an adjacent bar. Both officers were jailed for perjury, while Albert Victory —a federal fugitive on charges of unlawful flight to avoid confinement—was added to the FBI's "Most Wanted" list on March 14, 1980.

Eleven months later, on February 23, 1981, a federal drug enforcement agent, Dan Addario, received a phone call from New York state police at his office in San Francisco. According to the callers, Albert Victory was in the neighborhood, his presence double-checked and solidly confirmed by wire-taps. Agents of the DEA met New York officers next morning, at the airport, with news that Victory's phone number had been traced to an address in nearby Lafayette.

An exclusive hillside neighborhood, luxurious Lafayette is a

hideaway for the rich and not-so-famous. Victory had rented
lodgings there, complete with swimming pool and sporty gold
Mercedes-Benz, using the alias of "Ali" to satisfy his landlord.
Surprised by a raiding party before breakfast, on February 24,
Victory surrendered without incident and was taken into cus-
tody for extradition to New York.

373 ■ RONALD TURNEY WILLIAMS

The son of a West Virginia coal miner, Ronald Williams had a
tested IQ of 145, but raw intelligence never kept him out of
trouble with the law. By 1975, he had spent half of his life
behind bars, on convictions for armed robbery, kidnapping
and arson. Numerous jailbreaks only added to his prison time,
but Williams never seemed to learn. In 1975, he shot and
killed Sergeant David Lilly, of the Berkley, West Virginia, police, and was sentenced to life.

On November 7, 1979, Williams and fourteen other inmates
staged a daring mass escape from the state prison at Moundsville. Inmate barber Jack Hart set the ball rolling, entering the
cell block control center to store his tools, producing a pistol
and covering the duty officer while a second inmate slipped in,
armed with a knife. Using the officer's keys, they entered a
corridor leading to the prison waiting room, there surprising a
second guard and taking him hostage. With two prisoners in
hand, the convicts seized more weapons, demanding that the
outer gates be opened. As administrators bowed to their demand, another thirteen inmates suddenly emerged from hiding, rushing through the open gates.

Outside, the convicts stopped a passing car, driven by off-
duty police officer Philip Kasner. Kasner and one of his attackers were killed in a brisk exchange of gunfire, before several inmates piled into the officer's car and escaped, leaving
their comrades behind. More than half the escapees were recaptured within the hour; only Ronald Williams remained at
large by the end of the month, and his name was added to the
"Ten Most Wanted" list on April 28, 1980.

Over the next eighteen months, Williams traveled the country, taunting authorities with sarcastic correspondence. He was linked with a murder in Arizona, during March 1980, and with other crimes in Colorado and Pennsylvania. Throughout this period, the fugitive was also getting messages from one of his pursuers, Rev. Tom Cook, an ordained minister and the sole member of the West Virginia Department of Corrections Fugitive Department. Using contacts on the fringes of the underworld, Cook had enjoyed past success in convincing escapees to surrender, but Williams was less amenable to the idea. He was still considering Cook's offer when federal agents found him in June 1981.

On June 8, acting on a tip, FBI agents staked out a small hotel in New York City. One G-man was posing as the desk clerk when Williams arrived, and he struck up a conversation with the fugitive. Growing suspicious of the "clerk's" pointed questions, Williams suddenly drew a revolver. The agent produced his own weapon, with a shout of, "FBI! Drop your gun!"

"Drop dead!" the fugitive responded. "You drop yours!"

Williams squeezed the trigger on his .38, producing a loud click as the weapon misfired. His opponent fired three shots, striking Williams in the head, chest and arm, but none of the wounds proved fatal, and doctors reported him in satisfactory condition at a neighborhood hospital the next day. Upon recovery, the fugitive was returned to West Virginia to complete his sentence of life imprisonment.

374 ■ DANIEL JAY BARNEY

Born in 1953, Dan Barney was a violent and unstable felon with a record of violence against women. Jailed in Wisconsin on charges of armed burglary and sexual assault, he escaped from jail on February 24, 1980, and was named in federal warrants charging unlawful flight to avoid prosecution before being added to the FBI's "Most Wanted" list on March 10, 1981.

On April 19, 1981, Barney invaded the Denver condominium occupied by Paul Debroeck, twenty-eight, and a female companion. Brandishing a pistol, he bound Debroeck and led the woman into an adjoining room, intending rape, but Debroeck freed himself with a small knife attached to his key ring, escaping from the flat to call police. Besieged by officers, Barney panicked and shot himself in the head. His identity was confirmed from fingerprints on April 20, and his file was permanently closed.

375 ■ DONALD EUGENE WEBB

Number two (after Leo Joseph Koury) on the January 1989 issue of the "Ten Most Wanted" list, Donald Webb was born July 14, 1928, in Oklahoma City. A longtime jewelry thief with several prison terms behind him, the fugitive is sought on charges of unlawful flight to avoid prosecution for attempted burglary and first-degree murder. The latter charge refers to the slaying of Gregory Adams, chief of police in Saxonburg, Pennsylvania. On December 4, 1980, Chief Adams was shot twice at close range, then brutally beaten about the head and face with a blunt instrument, left to die by an assailant subsequently identified as Donald Webb.

Webb is described by the FBI as a white American male, five feet nine inches tall, approximately 165 pounds, with brown eyes, a medium complexion, and grayish-brown hair. He has a small facial scar on his right cheek, and another scar on his right forearm. Tattoos include the names "Don," on the back of his right hand, and "Ann," on his chest. Webb is known for his flashy attire, love of dogs, and his reputation as a big tipper. Described by police as a "master of assumed identities," his aliases include A. D. Baker, Donald Eugene Perkins, Donald Eugene Pierce, Stanley J. Pierce, John S. Portas, Stanley John Portas, Wilfred Y. Reams, Eugene Donald Webb, and Stanley Webb, among others. He normally uses Social Security number 462-48-0452. He may be accompanied by another federal fugitive, Frank Joseph Lach, and both men are considered dangerous.

376 ■ GILBERT JAMES EVERETT

Born June 26, 1939, Everett worked variously as a car salesman, a map maker and topographer when not involved in
crime, but his first love was bank robbery. Arrested for a robbery at Knoxville, Tennessee, in September 1980, Everett escaped from federal custody later that month and fled to Alabama in a stolen car, racking up new charges for violation of
the Dyer Act. Further warrants were issued in November, after he took down another bank in Orlando, Florida, and Everett's name was added to the FBI's "Most Wanted" list on May
13, 1981.

Undaunted by his notoriety, Everett robbed yet another
bank—this one in Sacramento, California—during January
1983. The money was his traveling stake, and Everett was
northbound, shaking pursuit as he lost himself in the wilds of
Alaska. It took the better part of three more years, but federal
agents traced him to his hideaway and took Everett into custody on August 12, 1985.

377 ■ LESLIE EDWARD NICHOLS

Holding a criminal record dating from 1963, Nichols was involved in organized narcotics traffic from his teens. By 1980,
he was moving major shipments through the capital of Arkansas and running lethal errands for the leaders of the mob in
other states. His posting to the FBI's "Most Wanted" list resulted from a string of homicides in Little Rock, which em-
phasized the dealer's taste for violence.

The first of five known victims was John Phelan, a used car
dealer, abducted from his job on June 13, 1980. A Volkswagen
minibus was stolen from the lot when Phelan disappeared,
and officers found it two days later, abandoned in an area of
played-out mining pits, west of town. That afternoon, they
stumbled over Phelan's body, hands and feet bound with boot
laces, gagged and severely beaten, garroted with a piece of
wire. According to detectives, robbery appeared to be the motive.

Drugs were uppermost on Nichols' mind in other homicides that month. Victim Sheila Bishop was a "protected" federal witness, relocated in Arkansas after she testified in a Maryland drug trial, but enemies traced her to Little Rock and Nichols accepted the contract. When police discovered Bishop's body in the woods, her hands were bound with twisted coathangers, a bullet fired into her head at close range, execution-style.

On June 16, two dead men were recovered from an auto trunk in Little Rock, each bound and shot in identical fashion with Sheila Bishop's murder. These were no innocent witnesses, however. Carl Jackson and Leonard Jones both possessed extensive criminal records in Arkansas; Jones had been sentenced to death on a rape conviction in 1960, but his life was spared when the Supreme Court overturned his sentence.

Two days after discovery of the double murder, a final victim was discovered in a roadside ditch. Rosemary Jones—wife of victim Leonard Jones—had been killed by a close-range shotgun blast, around the same time that her husband and Carl Jackson died.

Three Nichols accomplices were identified in the four drug-related murders, and all were convicted while Nichols remained at large. Billy Gene Stephenson received six consecutive life sentences for his role in the crimes, while Charles V. Moorman drew only five. Luther Hall broke out of jail before his murder trial, but he was soon recaptured and received a term of life without parole. The "mastermind" behind the murders, Leslie Nichols, earned a posting to the FBI's "Most Wanted" list on July 2, 1981, charged with unlawful flight to avoid prosecution for murder.

Five months later, on December 18, FBI agents and Los Angeles police crashed into the fugitive's apartment following an all-night party. Bleary-eyed and wasted, Nichols raised his hands, surrendering without a struggle. He was held in lieu of $500,000 bail, and subsequently extradited to Arkansas for trial. December 18, which also featured the arrest of John Sherman in Colorado, marked the only time that two unrelated "Top Ten" fugitives have been arrested on the same date.

378 ■ THOMAS WILLIAM MANNING

Born at Beverly, Massachusetts, in June 1946, Manning was a cohort of fugitive Raymond Luc Levasseur (# 350) in the "Sam Melville-Jonathan Jackson Unit" of the self-styled "United Freedom Front." A committed leftist radical, he was initially sought by federal agents for the September 1976 robbery of a bank in Portland, Maine. Money "liberated" in that holdup (and others) was used to sustain the radicals in hiding, financing a campaign of terrorist bombings aimed at multinational corporations and United States government targets along the East Coast.

On December 21, 1981, Manning and fellow "liberation warrior" Richard Williams were driving through Warren County, New Jersey, when their vehicle was stopped by a lone state trooper, Philip Lamonaco. In the burst of gunfire that followed, Lamonaco was wounded eight times, dying at the scene while his assailants sped away. Named in federal warrants charging him with bank robbery and unlawful flight to avoid prosecution for murder, Manning was added to the FBI's "Most Wanted" list on January 29, 1982.

A federal grand jury raised the ante in March 1985, indicting Tom Manning and seven other radicals on seventy-two counts related to terrorist bombings in New York state. Arrested in Virginia on April 24 of that year, Manning was held in New York pending a series of marathon trials resulting from various charges filed against him.

In March 1986, Manning was one of six terrorists convicted of terrorism by a federal jury in Manhattan. After reviewing the government's case, jurors found Manning guilty of five bombings and one attempted bombing, planned and executed between May 1983 and September 1984. Removed to New Jersey for his murder trial, nine months later, Manning testified that he shot Trooper Lamonaco "in self-defense," but a jury failed to buy the argument. Convicted of murder, Manning was sentenced to life imprisonment on February 18, 1967.

379 ■ DAVID FOUNTAIN KIMBERLY , JR.

A native of Nashville, Tennessee, born in 1946, David Kimberly was a fugitive from robbery charges in Alabama when he made the FBI's "Most Wanted" list in January 1982. Sought for holding up a Mobile antique store, Kimberly was recognized by a U.S. Park officer in Prince Georges County, Maryland, on October 25, 1981, responding with gunfire when the officer detained him for questioning. Kimberly's victim would survive, but the incident made him a federal fugitive, named in warrants charging him with unlawful flight to avoid prosecution for robbery and attempted murder.

Posted to the "Top Ten" list on January 29, 1982, Kimberly remained at large for five months. On July 8, federal agents caught him in Miami, Florida, as Kimberly pulled his rented car into the parking lot of a local realtor's office. Kimberly refused to identify himself before a federal magistrate, but fingerprint comparisons removed any doubt of his identity, and he was held for trial on outstanding state and federal charges.

380 ■ MUTULU SHAKUR

On October 20, 1981, a flying squad of "revolutionaries," joined by several mercenary pros, ambushed a Brinks armored truck outside of Nanuet, New York, in Rockland County. Peter Paige, a Brinks guard, was killed in the initial blast of automatic gunfire. Racing to the scene in response to a distress call, Sgt. Edward O'Grady and Patrolman Waverly Brown were killed before the bandits escaped with $1.6 million in cash.

Fleeing from the scene, four members of the holdup gang were captured by an off-duty corrections officer and held for police. Among those apprehended were ex-Weathermen Judith Clark, David J. A. Gilbert, and Kathy Boudin (sought by federal officers since 1970, when she escaped the accidental blast which demolished an SDS bomb factory in New York City). The fourth suspect, Samuel Brown, had no radical connections, but his record of felony convictions spanned a quarter-century, including prison terms for larceny and weapons violations. Federal officers knew they were dealing with no ordinary robbery.

Three days later, in the borough of Queens, police officers surrounded a dwelling where members of the holdup gang were said to be hiding out. Barricaded inside, Samuel Smith and a companion, Sekou Odinga, opened fire on police, sparking another firefight. Smith was killed in the exchange of fire, Odinga surrendering after he was wounded, and the suspect in custody provided a major break for officers working the case.

Under his given name, Nathaniel Burns, Odinga had once joined the Black Panther Party, later gravitating into the more militant Black Liberation Army. Over the next few weeks, evidence was collected revealing a new coalition of black and white radicals, drawing members from the BLA and the defunct Weather Underground. BLA participants in the Brinks robbery included Smith, Odinga, and Donald Weems, backed up by mercenaries including Sam Brown, William Johnson, Ricky Marcos Blanchard and his common-law "wife," Wendy Heaton. (Blanchard was a fugitive from San Bruno, California, where he escaped from jail after an arrest for raping his ten-year-old niece. Heaton, meanwhile, was wanted on charges of first-degree murder in Eureka, New York.)

The "brains" behind the operation, based on evidence collected by the FBI, had been an ex-Panther and BLA stalwart named Mutula Shakur. Born Jeral Wayne Williams in 1951, Shakur had abandoned his "slave name" on enlisting with the militant cause. Charged with bank robbery and conspiracy in federal warrants issued on April 21, 1982, ringleader Shakur was added to the FBI's "Most Wanted" list on July 23.

Meanwhile, the web of conspiracy continued to unravel. Wendy Heaton was arrested in New Orleans on June 4, 1982, carrying a list of local armored car companies and their schedules for pick-ups and deliveries at area banks. FBI agents arrested Ricky Blanchard four days later, also in New Orleans, and November saw William Johnson in custody, shipped back from his point of arrest in Central America.

By autumn 1983, the several cases were prepared for trial.

David Gilbert, Judith Clark and Donald Weems were convicted on various charges in September, drawing terms of seventy-five years to life, and Gilbert married Kathy Boudin on the day of his conviction, thus "legitimizing" their three-year-old son. Sekou Odinga was acquitted of participation in the Brinks conspiracy, but a conviction for attempted murder in Queens earned him a sentence of twenty-five years to life in prison. Kathy Boudin-Gilbert filed a guilty plea on May 3, 1984, receiving concurrent prison terms of twenty years to life (for second-degree murder) and twelve to fifteen years (for robbery). Convicted on all counts a month later, Sam Brown was ordered to serve seventy-five years before he was eligible for parole.

Mutulu Shakur remained at large while the others were drawing prison terms for the robbery he engineered. Arrested by federal agents in California, on February 11, 1986, he was returned to New York state for trial and ultimate conviction on outstanding felony counts, resulting in imposition of the maximum sentence.

381 ■ CHARLES EDWARD WATSON

A native of Johnson City, Tennessee, born in October 1946, Watson was convicted as an accessory after the fact in the August 9, 1975 shotgun slaying of a Maryland state trooper, drawing life plus ninety-five years on counts which included murder, rape, kidnapping, and handgun violations. He had served six years of his sentence when he escaped from the Patuxent Correctional Institution on June 22, 1982. A federal warrant was issued two days later, charging Watson with unlawful flight to avoid confinement, and his name was added to the Bureau's "Top Ten" list on October 22, 1982.

Watson lasted another year on the run, before he was apprehended in Slatington, Pennsylvania, twenty miles north of Allentown. He worked periodically in the construction field, until October 25, 1983, when a team of federal agents descended on his home, making the arrest without incident. Watson was returned to Maryland for completion of his outstanding sentence, with extra time added to cover his recent escape.

382 ■ LANEY GIBSON , JR.

Born August 28, 1950, in Clay County, Kentucky, Laney Gibson logged two murder convictions by the time he turned thirty. On February 26, 1981, he was charged with assault after shooting a male resident of Manchester, Kentucky, in the head with a 9mm pistol. The victim remained paralyzed until his death, several months later, at which time Gibson's charge was altered to another count of murder.

On August 7, 1983, while awaiting trial on his latest homicide, Gibson escaped from the Clay County jail with three other inmates, overpowering a jailer and locking him up in a cell. Gibson's companions in the break included: his brother Stanley, held on drunk driving charges; Jerry Hinkle, charged with armed robbery; and Larry Knuckles, awaiting transfer to state prison after his guilty plea on charges of murder and robbery. The other three were soon captured, but Laney Gibson was still at large four days later, when a federal warrant was issued charging him with unlawful flight to avoid prosecution.

On September 13, 1983, while still a fugitive, Gibson abducted a woman in Elgin, Ohio, later dumping her body alongside the road. Local authorities filed indictments charging Gibson with kidnapping and aggravated murder; his name was added to the Bureau's "Ten Most Wanted" list on November 16, 1983.

A month later, on December 18, FBI agents found Gibson at a small motel in a suburb of Montgomery, Alabama. Surrounded and outnumbered, Gibson surrendered without a struggle and was returned to Kentucky for trial and conviction in the Manchester case.

383 ■ GEORGE CLARENCE BRIDGETTE

A native of Long Beach, California, born in July 1946, Bridgette's record listed adult convictions for armed robbery, forgery, auto theft and parole violation. In September 1977, with accomplices James E. Cade and Willie Thomas, Bridgette invaded a Long Beach home, blasting five persons with shotguns at close range. Four of the victims, including a three-year-old child, were dead at the scene; a survivor managed to identify the gunmen in what authorities described as a drug-related massacre.

Cade and Thomas were arrested swiftly, tried and sentenced for their role in the murders, but Bridgette remained elusive. Federal warrants charged him with unlawful flight to avoid prosecution on multiple counts of murder and assault with a deadly weapon, while Long Beach authorities sought to arrest him as a parole violator. On January 14, 1984, his name was added to the FBI's "Most Wanted" list.

By that time, George Bridgette had already settled in Miami, living there for two years as "James Freeman," working various jobs which included a stint with the juvenile court system. On January 30, 1984, a local resident recognized his mug shot in the post office, rushing to phone the FBI. Taken into custody that afternoon, Bridgette stubbornly denied his true identity until a fingerprint comparison removed all doubt.

384 ■ SAMUEL MARKS HUMPHREY

A Detroit native, born in August 1949, Samuel Humphrey compiled an impressive record of convictions on charges including postal law violations, aiding and abetting, uttering and publishing a forged U.S. Treasury check, and jumping bond. When not in jail, he was a heavy user of cocaine and heroin, a habit shared with his favorite female traveling companion, Luvenia Marie Carter.

On March 17, 1977, a Detroit resident was shot and killed during the robbery of his home, and the available clues pointed to Sam Humphrey as the killer. He was still at large

five years later, running with Luvenia Carter, when he robbed
a jewelry store in San Diego on November 16, 1982. Humphrey surfaced in Rochester, New York, on January 3, 1983,
looting a bank of $5,799. Two months later, on March 8, he
robbed another bank in Atlanta, Georgia, taking a teller hostage to make good his escape.

Federal warrants charged Humphrey and Carter in both
bank jobs, the San Diego robbery adding a further charge of
interstate transportation of stolen property. Murder warrants
in Detroit provided the basis for charges of unlawful flight to
avoid prosecution, and Humphrey was added to the FBI's
"Most Wanted" list on February 29, 1984.

Three weeks later, on March 22, Humphrey was arrested in
Portland, Oregon, while visiting an inmate in the city jail.
Luvenia Carter was waiting in a car, a block from the jail,
when officers spotted her and took her into custody without
resistance. Tried first in Atlanta, both defendants were convicted of bank robbery and sentenced to twenty-four years in
prison. A second conviction at Rochester, in December 1984,
added concurrent terms of fifteen years to their existing sentences.

385 ■ CHRISTOPHER BERNARD WILDER

Born March 13, 1945, Christopher Wilder was the product of
an international marriage, between an American naval officer
and his Australian wife. A sickly child from the beginning,
Wilder was given last rites as an infant. Two years later, he
nearly drowned in a swimming pool; at age three, he suffered
convulsions while riding with his parents in the family car, and
had to be resuscitated.

By his teens, the boy had problems of a different sort. At
seventeen, in Sydney, Wilder and a group of friends were
charged with gang-raping a girl on the beach. He pled guilty
to carnal knowledge and received one year's probation, with a
provision for mandatory counseling. The program included
group therapy and electroshock treatments, but it seemed to
have little effect.

Wilder married at age twenty-three, but the union lasted only a few days. His bride complained of sexual abuse, and finally left him after finding panties (not her own) and photographs of naked women in a briefcase Wilder carried in his car. In November 1969, he used nude photographs to extort sex from an Australian student nurse; she complained to the police, but charges were ultimately dropped when she refused to testify in court.

Australia was growing too hot for Wilder, so he moved to the United States. Settling in southern Florida, he prospered in the fields of construction and electrical contracting, earning (or borrowing) enough money to finance fast cars and a luxurious bachelor pad, complete with hot tub and a private photo studio. The good life visibly agreed with Wilder, but it did not fill his other hidden needs.

In March 1971, at Pompano Beach, Wilder was picked up on a charge of soliciting women to pose for nude photos; he entered a plea of guilty to disturbing the peace and escaped with a small fine. Six years later, in October 1977, he coerced a female high school student into oral sex, threatening to beat her if she refused, and he was jailed a second time. Wilder admitted the crime to his therapist, but confidential interviews are inadmissible in court, and he was later acquitted. On June 21, 1980, he lured a teenaged girl into his car with promises of a modeling job, then drove her to a rural area where she was raped. A guilty plea to charges of attempted sexual battery earned him five years probation, with further therapy ordered by the court. Following his last arrest in Florida, the self-made man complained of suffering from blackouts.

Visiting his parents in Australia, Wilder was accused of kidnapping two fifteen-year-old girls from a beach in New South Wales on December 28, 1982, forcing them to pose for pornographic snapshots. Traced through the license number of his rented car, Wilder was arrested on December 29, charged with kidnapping and indecent assault. His family posted $350,000 bail, and Wilder was permitted to return to the United States, his trial scheduled for May 7, 1983. Legal delays postponed the case, but Wilder was scheduled to appear in court for a hearing on April 3, 1984.

He never made it.

On February 6, Rosario Gonzalez, 20, disappeared from her job at the Miami Grand Prix. Chris Wilder was driving as a contestant that day, and witnesses recall Gonzalez leaving with a man who fit Wilder's description. Her body has never been found.

On March 4, twenty-three-year-old Elizabeth Kenyon vanished after work from the school where she taught in Coral Gables. She was seen that afternoon, with Wilder, at a local gas station, and his name was found in her address book. Kenyon's parents remembered her speaking of Wilder as "a real gentleman," unlike the various photographers who asked if she would model in the nude. As in the February case, no trace of Kenyon has been found.

Wilder celebrated his thirty-ninth birthday on March 13, treating himself to the peculiar gift of a 1973 Chrysler. Three days later, the *Miami Herald* reported that a Boynton Beach race driver was wanted for questioning in the disappearance of two local women. Wilder was not named in the story, but he got the point. Missing his scheduled therapy on March 17, he met with his business partner the following night. "I am not going to jail," he vowed, tearfully. "I'm not going to do it." Packing his car, Wilder dropped off his dogs at a kennel and drove out of town, headed north.

Indian Harbour lies two hours north of Boynton Beach. On March 19, Terry Ferguson, twenty-one, disappeared from a local shopping mall where witnesses remembered seeing Wilder. Her body was recovered four days later, from a Polk County canal.

On March 20, Wilder abducted a university co-ed from a shopping mall in Tallahassee, driving her across the state line to Bainbridge, Georgia. There, in a cheap motel, she was raped repeatedly and tortured with electric shocks, her eyelids smeared with super glue. Wilder fled after his captive managed to lock herself in the bathroom, screaming and pounding on the walls to draw attention from the other guests.

The killer touched down next in Beaumont, Texas. Terry Walden, twenty-four, informed her husband on March 21 that a bearded man had approached her between classes at the local university, soliciting her for a modeling job. She thanked him and declined the offer, but the conversation struck a chord of memory when Terry disappeared March 23. Her body, torn by multiple stab wounds, was recovered from a canal three days later.

On March 25, twenty-one-year-old Suzanne Logan disappeared from a shopping mall in Oklahoma City. Her body was found the next day, floating in Milford Reservoir, near Manhattan, Kansas. Raped and stabbed, the victim had apparently been tortured prior to death.

Sheryl Bonaventura was the next to die, abducted from a shopping mall in Grand Junction, Colorado, on March 29. Another shopper placed Wilder in the mall, soliciting women for modeling jobs, and he was seen with Sheryl at a nearby restaurant that afternoon. She joined the missing list as Wilder worked his way across the country, killing when he paused to rest.

On April 1, seventeen-year-old Michelle Korfman vanished from a fashion show at the Meadows Mall, in Las Vegas, Nevada. Snapshots taken at the time show Wilder smiling from the sidelines, watching as the teenaged girls parade before him in their miniskirts.

At last, it was enough. Linked with three murders, one kidnapping, and four disappearances, Wilder was described by FBI spokesmen as "a significant danger." His name was added to the Bureau's "Ten Most Wanted" list on April 3, 1984.

The following day, he abducted sixteen-year-old Tina Marie Risico in Torrance, California, raping her that night and through successive evenings as they stayed in various motels, working their way eastward. Subjected to threats and abuse, living continually in the shadow of death, Risico agreed to help Wilder find other victims as he continued his long flight to nowhere.

On April 10, Dawnette Wilt was lured away from a shopping mall in Merrillville, Indiana, raped and tortured through the course of that day and the next. Wilder tried to murder her on April 12, stabbing Dawnette and leaving her for dead outside Rochester, New York, but she managed to survive and staggered to the nearest highway, where a passing motorist discovered her and drove her to a hospital.

Wilder's final victim was Beth Dodge, abducted near Victor,

New York, on April 12 and shot to death in a nearby gravel pit. Following the murder, Wilder drove his teenage captive to Boston's Logan Airport, purchasing a one-way ticket to Los Angeles and seeing her off at the gate.

Wilder's sudden attack of compassion remains unexplained, but he wasted no time in searching out another victim. On April 13, he brandished his gun at a woman near Beverly, Massachusetts, but she fled on foot, unharmed. Continuing his aimless hunt, the killer stopped for gas that afternoon in Colebrook, New Hampshire, unaware that he had reached the end of his run.

Passing by the service station, state troopers Wayne Fortier and Leo Jellison recognized Wilder's car from FBI descriptions. Approaching the vehicle, they called out to Wilder and saw him break for the car, diving inside as he went for his pistol. Jellison leaped on the fugitive's back, struggling for the .357 magnum, and two shots rang out. The first passed through Wilder and pierced Jellison's chest, lodging in his liver; the second snuffed out Wilder's life, resulting in what a coroner termed "cardiac obliteration."

Wilder's violent death, ironically, did not resolve the tangled case. Sheryl Bonaventura's body was uncovered in Utah, on May 3, the victim of a point-blank gunshot wound. Michelle Korfman was found in the Angeles National Forest on May 11, but another month would pass before she was identified, her family's fears confirmed. No trace has yet been found of Wilder's early victims in Miami and environs.

With his death, Chris Wilder was inevitably linked with other unsolved crimes. A pair of girls, aged ten and twelve, identified his mug shot as the likeness of a man who snatched them from a park in Boynton Beach, in June of 1983, and forced them to fellate him in the nearby woods. His name was likewise linked with other deaths and disappearances across two decades, in Australia and America.

In 1965, Marianne Schmidt and Christine Sharrock accompanied a young man matching Wilder's description into the beachfront dunes near Sydney; strangled, raped and stabbed, their bodies were discovered in a shallow grave, but no one has been charged to date. In 1981, teenagers Mary Hare and Mary Optiz were abducted from a mall in Lee County, Florida; Hare was later found, stabbed to death, while Optiz remains among the missing. During 1982, the skeletal remains of unidentified women were unearthed on two separate occasions near property owned by Wilder, in Loxahatchee; one victim had been dead for several years, the other for a period of months.

And the list goes on. Tammi Leppert, teenaged model, kidnapped from her job at a convenience store on Merritt Island, July 6, 1983. Melody Gay, nineteen, abducted on the graveyard shift of an all-night store in Collier County, Florida, on March 7, 1984, her body pulled from a rural canal three days later. Colleen Osborne, fifteen, missing from the bedroom of her home in Daytona Beach, March 15, 1984. Chris Wilder was seen in Daytona that day, propositioning "models."

There was a final, ghoulish twist to Wilder's story. Following an autopsy on April 13, 1984, Dr. Robert Christie, the New Hampshire pathologist in charge of Wilder's case, received a phone call from a man claiming to represent Harvard University. Wilder's brain was wanted for study, the caller explained, in order to determine whether defect or disease had sparked his killing spree. Dr. Christie agreed to deliver the brain on receipt of a written request from Harvard. Two weeks later he was still waiting, and spokesmen for the university's medical school denied making any such request.

386 ■ VICTOR MANUEL GERENA

Born in New York City during June 1958, Gerena had a spotless record prior to 1983, but there is evidence that he enjoyed a secret life, maintaining contact with a group of Puerto Rican terrorists who call themselves Los Macheteros—"the machete-wielders." Spokesmen for the group claimed "credit" for assassinating two American naval officers in 1979, along with the 1981 bombing of nine military jets at an American base near San Juan.

On September 12, 1983, while employed as a security guard for the Wells Fargo company, Gerena pulled a gun on two fellow employees at the company's depot in West Hartford,

Connecticut. Handcuffing and binding his captives, Gerena also injected them with a drug to render them senseless, afterward lending a hand while his terrorist cronies looted the Wells Fargo vault of more than $7 million.

A federal warrant was issued for Gerena on September 13, charging him with bank robbery, theft from an interstate shipment, and unlawful flight to avoid prosecution for armed robbery. Los Macheteros took credit for the heist in 1984, publicly naming Gerena as one of their own, and his name was added to the FBI's "Most Wanted" list on May 14, 1984.

On August 23, 1985, a federal grand jury in Hartford formally indicted Gerena and two other men for the Wells Fargo job. Gerena's accomplices were named as Juan Enrique Palmer and Filiberto Ojeda Rios, the latter a known terrorist associated with Puerto Rico's Armed Forces of National Liberation (FALN) and its violent offshoot, the Armed Independence Revolutionary Movement (MIRA). Arrested in 1970 after several bombings in San Juan, Rios had jumped bail and disappeared. He was suspected of involvement with a New York tavern bombing, claimed by the FALN, which killed five persons and wounded fifty-three in 1975.

On August 30, federal officers arrested fourteen suspects in connection with the Wells Fargo holdup. Eleven—including Rios—were seized in Puerto Rico, following a shootout that left one officer wounded by automatic fire. Others were picked up in Massachusetts, Mexico, and Texas, where Palmer was captured at the Dallas-Fort Worth International Airport.

Still at large and listed as a "Top Ten" fugitive, Gerena is believed to be in Cuba, where communist agents are suspected of sharing his stolen cash and supporting the FALN in its violent anti-American campaigns. He is described as a white male, five foot six or seven and 169 pounds, with a stocky build, brown hair, and green eyes. Wells Fargo has offered a $250,000 reward for recovery of the stolen money, and $100,000 for information leading to Gerena's arrest.

387 ■ WAI-CHIU NG

The first Asian criminal to rate a "Top Ten" listing, Wai-Chiu (Tony) Ng was a British citizen, born in Hong Kong on November 26, 1956. He came to the United States with his family, as a child, settling in Seattle where his father opened a successful Chinese restaurant.

On February 19, 1983, Tony Ng and two accomplices invaded the Wah Mee Club, a private gambling establishment in Seattle's Chinatown. Fourteen customers were hog-tied, robbed, and shot repeatedly in their heads at close range with a .22-caliber revolver before the trio fled. Unknown to the assassins, one of their intended victims would survive to testify.

Within twenty-four hours, police had arrested Willie Mak and Benjamin Ng (no relation to Tony) in connection with the massacre. Both were ultimately convicted, Mak earning a sentence of death, while Ben Ng's jury failed to agree on a penalty, thus granting him an automatic term of life without parole. Tony Ng was still at large when federal warrants were issued on March 31, 1983, charging him with unlawful flight to avoid prosecution for murder, and his name was added to the "Ten Most Wanted" list on June 14, 1984.

On October 4, officers of the Royal Canadian Mounted Police traced Ng to his rented lodgings in Calgary, Alberta, taking him into custody without incident. Held on charges of illegal immigration, he was subsequently deported to the United States, convicted on multiple murder charges, and sentenced to die.

388 ■ ALTON COLEMAN

Born Elton Coleman in November 1955, the middle of five children from a prostitute in the Waukegan ghetto, the future terror of the Midwest was raised by his maternal grandmother. Dubbed "Pissy" by his playmates, for a childhood tendency to wet his pants, Coleman grew up running with street gangs, cultivating an unsavory reputation. A black who preferred blacks as victims, his numerous arrests were concentrated in the area of sex crimes, a propensity which led him on a lethal crime spree and, eventually, to the death house.

In January 1974, Coleman was arrested for the abduction, rape, and robbery of an elderly woman in Waukegan. A bargained guilty plea to simple robbery earned him a sentence of two to six years in Joliet prison, where he was later accused of molesting male inmates. A prison psychiatric profile dubbed Coleman a "pansexual, willing to have intercourse with any object, women, men, children, whatever." Free on parole, he was charged with rape again in 1976 and 1980, winning acquittal each time when a jury believed that his victims consented to sex. His record reveals a total of four rape charges, two counts of deviate sexual assault, five of unlawful restraint, and one count for indecent liberties with a child. The latter victim was a niece of Coleman's; an angry mother filed the charge, but later changed her mind in court. The judge, dismayed, branded her new story "completely implausible." "I think," he declared, "the woman as she stands here today is terrified by this man."

Briefly married, Coleman was abandoned by his teenaged wife, who sought police protection when she went to claim her various belongings from their home. She "just couldn't take it no more," and years later, in court, she would offer descriptions of Coleman's obsession with bondage, young girls, and perverse, violent sex.

In February 1980, Coleman was accused of raping a Waukegan girl at knifepoint, and while never indicted, he was also suspect in the rape and strangling of Gina Frazier, age fifteen, in 1982. Reduction of his bail in the Waukegan case put Coleman on the street in time to launch a rampage which would place him on the FBI's "Most Wanted" list.

Coleman's young accomplice in the weeks to come was Debra Denise Brown, age twenty-one. The fifth of eleven children from a respectable home, she had been engaged to marry another man when she met Coleman and fell into a semblance of love. Breaking off her engagement, she became Coleman's live-in lover—and, later, his confederate in crime.

On May 29, 1984, Vernita Wheat, age nine, convinced her mother to let her accompany "Robert Knight" and his girlfriend to Waukegan, fifteen miles from their home in Kenosha, Wisconsin. The purpose of the trip was to retrieve a stereo, described by Vernita and "Knight" as a belated Mother's Day present. When the three had not returned next morning, officers were notified. A photo lineup readily identified "Robert Knight" as Alton Coleman; his companion had been Debra Brown.

With Coleman's sinister record in mind, a federal grand jury indicted both suspects on kidnapping charges, and the FBI went to work. On June 18, Tamika Turks, age seven, and her nine-year-old aunt were walking near their home in Gary, Indiana, when Coleman and Brown pulled in to the curb, asking directions. Money was offered in exchange for help, and both girls climbed into the car. Confronted with a knife, they were driven to a wooded area twelve miles away, where Coleman raped and choked Tamika Turks, while Debra held her down. Tamika's aunt was also raped and beaten, but she managed to escape. Selection of familiar photographs by the survivor added further charges to the growing list, and still the fugitives remained elusive.

The strangled body of Vernita Wheat was found on June 19, in an abandoned building in downtown Waukegan. That same afternoon, police in Gary received a missing-person report on Donna Williams, twenty-five, a local beauty operator. She had last been seen en route to pick up a "nice young couple from Boston," who had agreed to visit her church. None of them showed for the service, but witnesses identified photos of Coleman and Brown as recent visitors to the salon where Williams worked. On June 27, the missing woman's car was located in Detroit, but Coleman and Brown had already surfaced in Motor City, with a vengeance.

On June 24, the couple accosted a Detroit woman outside her home, brandishing knives and demanding that she drive them to Ohio. The intended victim saved herself by deliberately crashing into a parked truck, fleeing on foot while the killers took off in her damaged vehicle.

On June 28, Coleman and Brown invaded the home of Palmer and Maggie Jones, in Dearborn Heights, surprising the middle-aged couple at breakfast. The latest victims were beaten with a club, robbed of $86, and left bleeding on the floor while the fugitives fled in their car. Two days later, a pair of Detroit men offered the couple a ride. When Coleman drew a gun, the driver grappled with him briefly and escaped. His passenger, an invalid, was tossed out on the street, amazingly unharmed.

Verified sightings of Coleman and Brown were recorded every day between July 2 and 7. On July 2, a middle-aged Detroit couple were attacked in their home, beaten with a pipe and subjected to Coleman's incoherent harangue on how blacks were forcing him to murder other members of his race. The victims' stolen car was dropped off in Toledo, where another couple was assaulted, handcuffed in their home, relieved of transportation. A Toledo bartender reportedly exchanged shots with Coleman, after the fugitives tried to abduct one of the bartender's patrons.

On July 7, Coleman and Brown spent the night with Virginia Temple, thirty, and her ten-year-old daughter, Rochelle, in Toledo. Before they left next morning, both were strangled, the girl raped, their bodies stuffed into a crawlspace beneath the looted home.

Four days later, on July 11, the remains of Donna Williams were discovered in Detroit. She had been strangled with a pair of pantyhose. That afternoon, the FBI announced that Coleman had been elevated to a most unusual eleventh place on its "Most Wanted" list, an option used when vicious crimes in progress mark a suspect as particularly dangerous.

And the body-count kept rising. In Cincinnati, Tonnie Storey, age fifteen, had last been seen with individuals resembling Brown and Coleman; four days later, when her corpse was found, she had been stabbed repeatedly, with two shots in the head. On July 13, Marlene Walters, forty-four, became the first white victim of the crime spree, bludgeoned in her home at Norwood, Ohio, a Cincinnati suburb. Harry Walters, gravely injured, managed to describe the killers of his wife as two young blacks who had arrived on ten-speed bikes and talked their way inside the house, expressing interest in the purchase of a camper. When they fled, they had been driving Harry's car.

On July 16, Coleman and his sidekick abducted Oline Carmichal, a Lexington college professor, driving him back to

Dayton, Ohio, where they left him unharmed, locked in the trunk of his car. Rescued on July 17, Carmichal described his kidnappers as *two* black men and a woman. The mystery was cleared up shortly, with the arrest of Lexington native Thomas Harris, who explained that he was "kind of forced" to help the fugitives. Harris claimed he had talked Coleman and Brown out of killing their latest prisoner.

A half hour after Carmichal was freed, an elderly minister and his wife were found, battered but breathing, in their Dayton home. Investigation showed that Coleman and Brown, using pseudonyms, had met the couple a week earlier, spending two nights in their home and parting on amiable terms when the minister drove to Cincinnati "for a prayer meeting." On July 17, the couple had returned, beating their former hosts severely and making off with the minister's station wagon.

The latest stolen vehicle was dumped next day in Indianapolis, beside a car wash, where owner Eugene Scott, seventy-seven, and *his* car were reported missing. Scott was found by searchers hours later, in a ditch near Zionsville; he had been stabbed repeatedly, shot four times in the head.

The long trail reached its end in Evanston, Illinois, on July 20, 1984. An anonymous tip from a "friend" of the fugitives alerted police to their presence in the neighborhood, and they were soon spotted at a local park. Five officers surrounded the couple, relieving Coleman of two bloody knives and lifting an unloaded .38 from Brown's purse. That afternoon, Eugene Scott's missing car was found in Evanston, five blocks from where the suspects were arrested. Debra Brown had left her fingerprints inside.

In Chicago, a federal magistrate set bond in the Wheat case at $25 million in cash. "This nation has been under a siege," he declared. "This nation has been under a reign of terror not knowing when the next victim was going to be taken. I am going to make sure no other victim will be subject to this man." Another bond of $20 million cash was set for Debra Brown.

The magistrate need not have worried. Tried separately for the murders of Marlene Walters and Tonnie Storey, in Cincinnati, both were convicted and sentenced to death in each case.

In Indiana, Coleman picked up another death sentence for the murder of Tamika Turks; 100 years was added for the rape and the attempted murder of her aunt. Debra Brown was also convicted in that case, hoping for a lighter sentence when she slipped the judge a note that read: "I am a more kind and understandable and lovable person than people think I am." Unmoved, the judge pronounced matching sentences of death, on the murder charge, and consecutive forty-year terms on charges of kidnapping and child-molesting. Illinois supplied the *coup de grace,* sentencing Coleman to die for the kidnap and murder of Vernita Wheat.

"I'm dead already," Coleman told the court before pronouncement of his sentence in Waukegan. "You are talking to a dead man." Satisfied that he was right, authorities declined to prosecute the couple in their four outstanding homicides.

389 ■ CLEVELAND McKINLEY DAVIS

A native of Enfield, North Carolina, Davis was born in April 1942. While undergoing treatment for periodic bouts of severe depression, he also chalked up convictions for armed robbery, possession of a sawed-off shotgun, malicious assault, coercion and unlawful imprisonment, burglary, breaking and entering, escape, and parole violation. In 1968, with two accomplices, he robbed a grocery store in Virginia Beach, Virginia, trading shots with the police before he was subdued. Davis escaped from the city jail with two other inmates, and was not seen again until 1970, when New York police picked him up for armed robbery. Sentenced to ten years on that charge, he was returned to Virginia Beach for trial and drew another twenty-five, later reduced to fifteen years maximum.

While serving his time in New York, Davis emerged as a ringleader of the 1971 riots at Attica prison, where he was charged with killing another inmate. Plea bargains and reduced charges left him with an additional four years of prison time, and he was returned to the custody of Virginia authorities in 1973. Paroled three years later, Davis was subsequently pardoned by New York's governor for his role in the Attica revolt. In celebration, Davis married the female attorney who had defended him during his latest series of trials.

On March 11, 1984, Davis invaded the Virginia Beach home of Raymond Stith, joined by accomplices Robert Green and Curtis Norfleet. The trio hoped to walk away with drugs and money, but they quickly had a battle on their hands as Stith resisted the intrusion. Davis suffered stab wounds in his leg and shoulder, but his life was spared when Norfleet shot Stith in the head, killing him instantly. Davis's wounds were stitched up by Green, and he struck off for New York, leaving his comrades behind.

Both Green and Norfleet were in custody by early April, tried and finally convicted for their parts in killing Raymond Stith. Green drew a prison term of twenty-five years, while Norfleet—as the trigger man—went up for forty-five. Cleveland Davis, still at large, was named in federal warrants as a fugitive from justice, and his name was added to the "Ten Most Wanted" list on October 24, 1984.

Three months later, on January 25, 1985, FBI agents and New York police surrounded Davis in his rented apartment. Despite promises that he would never be taken alive, Davis surrendered without a fight and was packed off to Virginia Beach for trial. On August 6 he was convicted of involvement in the murder and consigned to prison for another quarter-century.

390 ■ CARMINE JOHN PERSICO ; JR.

Dubbed "The Snake" by his associates in New York's underworld, Carmine Persico began his criminal career as a member of Joseph Profaci's Mafia "family." In 1961, unhappy with Profaci's stern demands for tribute from subordinates, he joined a revolt led by Nicholas Forlano and the deadly Gallo brothers. Persico participated in the abduction of five Profaci loyalists, including brother Frank Profaci and mob counselor Joseph Magliocco, but the hostages were later released, despite Carmine's urgings that they be executed.

Waging war against Profaci was a risky proposition, and the

tide soon turned against the insurrectionists, prompting a change of heart from The Snake. On August 21, 1961, he was arrested on suspicion of attempting to strangle Larry Gallo in a New York tavern, thereby demonstrating loyalty to Profaci. A dozen men were killed and scores wounded before the fighting petered out in 1963, and one of them was Persico, hit by snipers on May 19 of that year. As evidenced by the indictments later filed against him, Carmine's brush with death did nothing to deter him from pursuing a career in crime.

By 1970, Joseph Colombo was in charge of the old Profaci mob, beating the drum against FBI "persecution" of Mafia members and stumping New York on behalf of the mob-owned Italian-American Civil Rights League. Persico stood second in line for the throne, but he was facing problems with the federal government, in the form of a hijacking conviction which earned him fourteen years in prison. In January 1971, Persico also helped to shelter hoodlum Joseph "Fatty" Russo, charged with gunning down two black domestics in the middle of a dinner party. "The guy's all right," Persico told his associates. "He just blew his top and killed two blacks."

In June 1971, Joe Colombo was shot and critically wounded during an "Italian unity" demonstration in New York. Persico was next in line to rule the family, but his luck and his appeals ran out in January 1972. Continuing to offer sage advice from the federal pen in Atlanta, he was soon charged with conspiracy in the case of Fatty Russo, returned to New York for yet another trial.

Local jailers proved to be so accommodating—providing Persico with such luxuries as steaks and liquor in return for payment—that the felon was eventually ordered back to prison in Atlanta, while his lawyer's pretrial motions were eliminated. Special U.S. Attorney Michael Pollock charged Persico with exercising a corrupting influence over his keepers in New York, and the court agreed. As Judge George Rosling remarked, "I suppose he could corrupt the whole jail." "It's not that he could," Pollock replied. "He is presently doing so."

Free on parole in 1984, Persico was generally regarded as the ruler of the Profaci-Colombo family. In that capacity, he was indicted by a federal grand jury on October 23, charged with racketeering, conspiracy, and bribing a public official, while using threats, force and violence to further his criminal enterprises. Persico went underground in lieu of submitting to arrest, and he was added to the FBI's "Most Wanted" list on January 17, 1985.

One month later, on February 15, federal officers traced Persico to an estate on Long Island, where he was quietly taken into custody. New indictments, issued on February 26, named Persico and eight other men as the leaders of New York's "five families." Eventually convicted on all counts, the ruling mafiosi drew prison terms which averaged better than 100 years for each defendant.

391 ■ LOHMAN RAY MAYS , JR.

Born February 19, 1943, in Dallas, Texas, Mays was a soft-spoken felon with a long record of violent crimes behind him. Variously convicted of murder, armed robbery, aggravated assault, and concealing stolen property, by early 1969 he was confined for life as an habitual criminal, linked with the February 22 murder of a man in Kannapolis, North Carolina. Mays escaped from prison on July 1, 1984, afterward robbing banks in Spartanburg, South Carolina, on July 16, and in Orleans, Vermont, on September 14. Named in federal warrants charging him with bank robbery and unlawful flight to avoid confinement, Mays was added to the FBI's "Most Wanted" list on February 15, 1985.

Agents stalked their man with caution, conscious of the fact that he had shot and wounded a policeman in the past. Mays was alleged to travel with an attack dog and a small arsenal of weapons, but he offered no resistance when a flying squad of G-men traced him to Wyoming on September 23, 1985, and arrested him. Returned to North Carolina for completion of his life sentence, the fugitive faced additional prison time for the robberies committed after his escape.

392 ■ CHARLES EARL HAMMOND
393 ■ MICHAEL FREDERIC ALLEN HAMMOND

The fourth and latest set of brothers added to the FBI's "Most Wanted" list since its inception, Charles and Michael Hammond were a pair of hard-case felons sought in connection with a drug related massacre in Kansas City, Missouri. Five persons had died, with a sixth gravely wounded, when the guns went off on May 29, 1980, evidence recovered at the scene naming Charles and Michael as the executioners. Five years after the fact, local authorities had made no progress in their case, and the Hammonds made the "Top Ten" list together, on March 14, 1985.

Charles was the older of the two, born December 16, 1942, in Seattle; two years younger, Michael had been born on January 3, 1945, in Redding, California. In flight, the brothers traveled with Carolyn Mae Hammond, Charles's wife, two years his senior, who was sought by U.S. marshals for parole violation in her own right.

Charles and Michael Hammond remained on the "Ten Most Wanted" list for seventeen months before their federal warrants were dismissed, at the request of Kansas City prosecutors, on August 4, 1986. Such a move normally indicates that subjects are believed to be deceased, or else that crucial witnesses and evidence pertaining to their case have been eliminated over time, rendering prosecution impossible.

394 ■ ROBERT HENRY NICOLAUS

Born in 1933, Robert Nicolaus was an avid jogger, weight lifter and physical fitness enthusiast who graduated from college with a major in child psychology. He had little opportunity to use that expertise on his job with the California Department of Highways, which employed him as an economic analyst, but it is probably just as well. In his private life, application of the Nicolaus psychology had resulted in unmitigated disaster.

The father of two children by his first marriage, Nicolaus was divorced and remarried by 1960, that union producing a third child. That year, without apparent motive, he attempted suicide by slashing his wrists and spent seventy-two hours in a county hospital's psychiatric ward. Things went from bad to worse over the next four years, and wife Charlyce left Nicolaus on May 23, 1964. The following day, Robert took his three children—ages two, five, and seven—to a Sacramento toy store; buying them gifts before he drove them to a vacant field north of town. Urging them into the car's trunk, allegedly seeking a "lost key," he snuffed out their lives with a barrage of ten bullets, pausing once to reload his five-shot revolver.

In custody, Nicolaus told arresting officers that his children were "better off in heaven" than with either of his wives. Convicted on three counts of first-degree murder, he was sentenced to death on September 25, 1964. Three years later, the state supreme court reduced his conviction to murder in the second degree, ruling that, while Nicolaus was obviously sane, he could not grasp the full enormity of his crime. The standing death sentence was commuted to three concurrent terms of five years to life. Despite a recommendation from his trial judge that Nicolaus never be released from prison, the killer was paroled on August 15, 1977.

On February 22, 1985, Nicolaus cornered ex-wife Charlyce Robinson in a Sacramento alley, blocking her car with his own and shooting her twice with a .38-caliber revolver while the woman's three-year-old daughter looked on, horrified. The wounds were fatal, but Robinson named her killer for police before she died. A search of the fugitive's home produced a hit list of future targets, including his first wife (now living in Texas) and a Sacramento couple Nicolaus suspected of reporting him for welfare fraud in 1984.

Federal warrants charged Nicolaus with unlawful flight to avoid prosecution for murder, and his name was added to the Bureau's "Top Ten" list on June 11, 1985. On July 19, Nicolaus checked into the YMCA at York, Pennsylvania, planning to attend the scheduled funeral of York Barbell Company's founding father. G-men were waiting when he left the "Y" next morning, and Nicolaus surrendered without resistance.

Convicted of another murder charge in California, he was sentenced to death a second time on June 23, 1985.

395 ■ DAVID JAY STERLING

A native of Vancouver, Washington, born in January 1945, David Sterling was an ex-marine and violent sex offender, with convictions for rape, sodomy, sexual abuse and assault. A string of brutal sex attacks in Clark County, Washington, led to his arrest and conviction, in 1982, on charges of rape and assault. Confined to Western Washington State Hospital, in Stellacoom, as a sexual psychopath, Sterling had made little or no progress toward rehabilitation at the time of his escape, on February 28, 1985. Six days later, federal warrants charged him with unlawful flight to avoid confinement, and Sterling's name was added to the "Top Ten" list on August 13, 1985.

Psychiatrists in Washington expressed concern that Sterling's taste for rape would lead to further sexual assaults, but in his flight the fugitive seemed more concerned with money. Teaming with accomplice Ronald Johnson, twenty-three, Sterling was suspected of participation in four bank robberies by the time state police officers collared the pair near Covington, Louisiana, on February 13, 1986. Sterling was returned to maximum security in Washington, with further trials outstanding on the crimes committed after his escape.

396 ■ RICHARD JOSEPH SCUTARI

A product of the post-war "baby boom," Scutari grew up as a virulent racist and anti-semite. He joined a paramilitary neo-nazi group, The Order, shortly after it was formed in 1983, with fellow members drawn from the Ku Klux Klan, the Aryan Nations, and other white supremacist cliques. Committed to eradication of Jews and "mud people"—i.e., blacks—The Order declared open war on the "ZOG," the so-called Zionist Occupational Government based in Washington, D.C. When an inner, hard-core unit of The Order was created, dubbed the "Bruder Schweigen" (Silent Brotherhood), Scutari was among the charter members. Code-named "Mr. Black," after his black belt in karate, he allegedly participated in the Bruder Schweigen's raids on banks and armored cars between December 1983 and July 1984, netting more than $4 million for the racist warriors.

Major crimes attributed to the Silent Brotherhood include the June 1984 assassination of Alan Berg, a controversial Jewish talk-show host in Denver, Colorado, and the robbery of a Brinks truck at Ukiah, California, a month later. In the latter crime, one Brinks employee was, in fact, a member of The Order, feeding crucial information to his cronies as they planned their raid, escaping with $3.6 million in a bullet-punctuated heist.

On April 12, 1985, Scutari was named in federal warrants charging him with racketeering, conspiracy, and transportation of stolen money across state lines. Some of the charges were founded on testimony from Charles Ostrout, the Brinks employee and one-time Order stalwart, who pled guilty to conspiracy charges on April 29. A few days later, Scutari and others were also indicted for interfering with interstate commerce by means of threats and violence. Scutari's name was added to the "Ten Most Wanted" list on July 11, 1985.

Eight months later, on March 19, 1986, federal agents traced their man to a brake shop in San Antonio, Texas, where he had found employment as "Larry Cupp." Known by fellow employees as a "nice guy," Scutari had no opportunity to reach the .45 automatic hidden under the driver's seat of his car.

In September 1986, Scutari and others were convicted on federal racketeering charges, the one-time fugitive drawing a sentence of forty to 100 years imprisonment. Subsequent trials, in the Berg assassination and on federal sedition charges, resulted in acquittal for Scutari, but it scarcely mattered now. With forty years to serve before he was considered for parole, the would-be fuhrer was not going anywhere.

397 ■ JOSEPH WILLIAM DOUGHERTY

A veteran bank robber since the 1960s, Dougherty joined accomplice Terry Lee Conner (#402) in perfecting the technique of holding bank officers and their families hostage, thereby gaining access to cash hidden in vaults. In December 1982, the duo held an Oklahoma City bank manager and his wife prisoner in their home for eight hours before looting the victim's bank of $706,000. Conner earned 25 years in prison for that score, but Dougherty remained at large, raiding banks in Phoenix (January 25, 1984), Salt Lake City (May 3, 1984), and Reno (February 19, 1985) before his ultimate arrest on federal bank robbery and conspiracy charges.

On June 19, 1985, the partners were en route from the federal prison at El Reno, Oklahoma, to a court in Oklahoma City, where Dougherty faced trial on the 1982 robbery. Concealing a handcuff key and a razor blade in his mouth, Conner managed to free himself, holding the blade to a deputy U.S. marshal's throat and demanding a detour. Stripping their captives of guns and official ID, the fugitives dumped the stolen car and left their hostages cuffed to a tree, commandeering fresh wheels at a nearby truck stop. Using federal badges to invade a private home, Dougherty and Conner stole fresh clothing before moving on.

New charges filed against the fugitives included escape, theft of government property, and assaulting federal officers, but the runners were not finished, yet. On August 12, 1985, they raided a St. Louis bank for $27,000, reverting to form for another strike on September 2. That evening, Dougherty and Conner invaded the home of Richard Woodcock, a bank manager in the Milwaukee suburb of West Allis, Wisconsin. Holding Woodcock's family hostage through the night, they struck his bank next morning, walking out with $574,119 in cash. Some $34,000 was later found in the abandoned getaway car, but the loss did not spoil Dougherty's mood; he had promised that stolen deposit slips would be returned to the bank, and they arrived by mail September 7, safe and sound.

Joe Dougherty was posted to the FBI's "Most Wanted" list on November 6, 1985—Conner would wait for another vacancy, nine months later—but with cash in his pocket, the new publicity did not slow him down. On June 30, 1986, the robbers barged in on bank manager Raymond Deering, in the Vancouver suburb of Hazel Dell, Washington, covering his family through the night with a pistol and a submachine gun. Next morning, Conner and Dougherty looted Deering's bank of $225,000 before making good their escape.

Friendship would be Dougherty's undoing, in the end. Federal agents had established surveillance on one Robert Butcher, a crony of Joe's from old prison days, and the trap was sprung on December 18, 1986, when Dougherty met Butcher at a Laundromat in Antioch, California. United States marshals were backing the FBI's play, since Conner and Dougherty held the distinction of placing on both the Bureau's "Top Ten" and the U.S. Marshal's "Top Fifteen" lists. Taken into custody without resistance, Dougherty and Butcher, with a third accomplice, faced additional charges of plotting to rob a bank in Antioch.

398 ■ BRIAN PATRICK MALVERTY

Born in 1959, Brian Malverty logged his first arrest at age sixteen, moving on from there to collect adult convictions for assault, aggravated assault on a police officer, narcotics violations and weapons offenses. His involvement in the drug trade centered on Atlanta, Georgia, where the endless quest for "easy" money led him into homicide by early 1985.

On April 23 of that year, acting with accomplices Anthony Scott Willingham and Tony Ray Albertson, Malverty abducted two male victims with robbery in mind, subsequently shooting each victim in the head, chest and back with a .25-caliber handgun. In an effort to forestall identification, the bodies were then doused with gasoline and set on fire, but evidence recovered at the scene would point a finger at the killers over weeks to come.

In the wake of the double murder, Malverty, Willingham and Albertson traveled to Queens, New York, but Willingham got homesick in May and returned to Atlanta. (Officers were waiting to arrest him there, and he was subsequently sent to prison for the murders.) In New York, Tony Albertson had developed loose lips, talking carelessly about the killings in Atlanta, and Malverty decided that his "friend" would have to go.

On June 14, 1985, a pair of joggers in Queens discovered two men in a park, apparently digging a grave for a body wrapped in a sleeping bag. Discovered, the joggers were assaulted and beaten with shovels before they managed to escape, reporting the incident to police. The latest victim was identified as Tony Albertson, shot twice in the head with a .25-caliber pistol, and Brian Malverty leaped to the top of the suspect list.

Already charged in federal warrants with unlawful flight to avoid prosecution for murder (in Georgia), Brian Malverty was elevated to the "Ten Most Wanted" list on October 10, 1985. Six months later, on April 8, 1986, federal agents traced him to a small apartment in San Diego, California, and took him into custody without resistance. For Malverty, it remained a toss-up whether Georgia or New York would try him first on counts of murder in the first degree.

399 ■ BILLY RAY WALDON

Billy Waldon scarcely knew his mother. During 1957, at the tender age of five, he was delivered to his grandmother's care, and the older woman raised him as her own around Tahlequah, Oklahoma, teaching him the values which she hoped would guide his steps through life. Enlisting in the navy out of high school, Waldon had fourteen years of service behind him when he was discharged, as a first petty officer, in January 1985. One-quarter Cherokee, he was described by friends and neighbors as "a brilliant man" who "spent more time listening to others than talking about himself." If Waldon had a quirk, it was his fascination with the subject of AIDS, a compulsive quest for knowledge which encouraged some associates to think he might be homosexual.

The death of Waldon's grandmother, in 1985, appeared to be the trigger incident for an astounding, lethal shift in Billy's personality. A quiet, unassuming man by all accounts before her death, he changed dramatically in later weeks, like Mr. Hyde emerging from the passive Dr. Jekyll. With the change of seasons into autumn, Billy launched a one-man reign of terror that would claim four lives and leave at least eight other persons injured.

The rampage began in Tulsa, close to home. Police suspect that Waldon was the gunman who wounded an elderly man outside a neighborhood grocery store on October 10, 1985. The following day, they believe, he robbed three persons at a shopping mall, rebounding for an unsuccessful robbery attempt on October 15. Witnesses were hazy on descriptions of their assailant, but the crimes fit an emerging pattern, and there would be no doubt of Waldon's involvement in the next outbreak.

Laying off a month from his activities, the phantom gunman surfaced on November 15, firing a single shot that grazed twenty-eight-year-old Cynthia Bellinger's skull outside her parents' Tulsa home. Two days later, Annabelle Richmond, age fifty-four, was cut down by four .25-caliber bullets outside her apartment. The shooting continued in Broken Arrow, on November 23, when Waldon confronted Frank Hensley and Tammie Tvedt in a parking lot, demanding cash, wounding them both when they refused to pay up.

The heat was on in Tulsa, and Waldon fled west, presumably to visit his ex-wife and their two small children in Gardenia, California. Drifting into San Diego, refreshing old memories of his navy days, Billy picked up his crime spree where he had left off in Tulsa. By mid-December, he would be suspected of three rapes, five robberies, two burglaries, and one count of receiving stolen property.

On December 7, a gunman invaded the home of forty-two-year-old Dawn Ellerman, shooting her in the neck with a .25-caliber pistol, beating her dogs and locking them inside a bathroom, then setting the house on fire before he fled with a personal computer and other valuables. Erin Ellerman, thirteen, came home from babysitting to find the house in flames, and she died in a futile attempt to save her mother's life.

Two weeks later, on December 20, a masked man tried to rob a San Diego woman in a parking lot. Foiled in the attempt, he fled on foot, veering through a yard where two men were working on a car. Frustrated again in his attempt to steal the vehicle, the gunman killed Charles Wells, fifty-nine, and critically wounded John Copeland, thirty-six, with a spray of .25-caliber bullets. Eluding 150 officers in a seven-hour manhunt, the killer still left traces of himself behind. Police recovered the Ellerman computer and an abandoned car registered to Billy Waldon, along with Waldon's military passport and other pieces of ID.

Communication with police in Tulsa matched the murder slugs from San Diego with the Oklahoma shootings. On January 3, 1986, a federal warrant charged Waldon with unlawful flight to avoid prosecution for murder, attempted murder, robbery, burglary, rape, and arson. His name was added to the FBI's "Most Wanted" list on April 23.

By that time, Billy had performed an eerie disappearing act. His latest stolen car, picked off a street December 20, had been discovered outside Tijuana on January 27. There was no other trace of the fugitive before June 16, when San Diego officers routinely stopped a car with a defective brake light. They had planned to let the driver off with a warning, but his face was familiar, and Waldon's use of the alias "Steven Midas" fooled no one at police headquarters.

Waldon was ordered to trial on multiple charges in San Diego. Jailers discovered his effort to tunnel through a wall of his cell, and fellow inmates proved dangerous. On July 24, 1986, Waldon was severely beaten by cellmates, hospitalized for two days, after he refused their orders to kill another prisoner. The motive for the bungled contract? Jailers noted that the target was unpopular with other cons because of his attitude, which was "basically anti-social."

400 ■ CLAUDE LAFAYETTE DALLAS , JR.

A rugged individualist and self-styled "mountain man," Claude Dallas was born March 11, 1950, and grew up in love with the wilderness, learning to live off the land in his native Idaho and neighboring states. In Claude's view, laws were artificial things, imposed on men when they decide to congregate in cities; he had little patience with restrictions of his own behavior, designated hunting seasons and the like. When Idaho game wardens Bill Pogue and Conley Elms sought to arrest Dallas for poaching deer and bobcat, on January 1, 1981, he greeted them with gunfire, dropping both men in their tracks.

Clinging to his beloved wilderness, Dallas evaded pursuit on the double murder charge for sixteen months, becoming a legend of sorts in the West. Two books were written about his exploits, one shamelessly romanticizing the killer and turning him into a kind of twisted "folk hero." Cornered and wounded on April 18, 1982, Dallas was held for trial in Idaho, insisting that he shot the game wardens down in "self-defense," after one of them went for his weapon without provocation.

Jurors appeared to buy the argument, convicting Dallas on a reduced charge of voluntary manslaughter. Sentenced to 30 years in the state penitentiary, Dallas was a "model" prisoner until Easter Sunday 1986. Taking advantage of the confusion produced by holiday visits, he slipped away from guards and cut through two chain-link fences to make his escape. Hours passed before he was missed, and by that time the mountain man had a long head-start on pursuers.

Federal warrants were issued on March 31, 1986, charging Dallas with unlawful flight to avoid confinement, and his name was added to the FBI's "Most Wanted" list on May 16. In hiding, Claude retained his outlaw mystique, acquaintances spreading the story that he had been "a marked man" in prison, with officers threatening his life, watching every move he made and yearning for a chance to use their guns.

On March 9, 1987, federal agents trailed Dallas to a small convenience store in Riverside, California. Emerging with two bags of groceries in his arms, he was wrestled to the ground before he had another opportunity to break away. Dallas faced an additional five years in prison if convicted on escape charges, but he found himself another sympathetic jury, pouring out his tale of official abuse and intimidation. Acquitted of breaking jail, he was returned to the state prison for completion of his original sentence.

401 ■ DONALD KEITH WILLIAMS

A native of Lincoln, Nebraska, Williams faced his first arrest, on larceny charges, in 1952. Convicted of burglary in Missouri, during 1961, he rolled on from there to collect a prison sentence for armed robbery in Oklahoma. Paroled in 1968 on that conviction, he was subsequently hauled back to prison as a parole violator. Between 1983 and '86, Williams was named as the bandit in thirty-four bank robberies, netting more than $100,000 from raids in California, Colorado, Illinois, Minnesota, Oregon and Washington. Fifteen of those robberies occurred in Los Angeles, where Williams was dubbed the "Veil Bandit," after the cloth veil he wore as a disguise, suspended from a baseball cap. (The veil concealed a distinctive muscular affliction, which caused Donald's right eye to squint.) He also sported body armor on occasion, to deflect police bullets, and he sometimes wore radio earphones, as if tuning in to local law enforcement bulletins.

Named a federal fugitive on bank robbery charges in May 1984, Williams was elevated to the FBI's "Most Wanted" list on August 8, 1985. In Los Angeles twelve days later, an alert citizen recognized published photographs and directed G-men to the fugitive's Mar Vista apartment, in West L.A. Three pistols were seized in the raid, but Williams made no effort to resist arrest. At age fifty-seven, facing a potential 950 years in prison on various charges, his long run was finally over.

402 ■ TERRY LEE CONNER

A veteran stickup artist from the 1960s, Terry Conner was suspected of ten bank robberies in Arizona during 1972 alone, including two jobs where bank officials and their families were held hostage overnight. Ten years later, in August 1982, Conner was one of three bandits who held a bank officer and his family prisoner in Bountiful, Utah, before looting the vault next morning. Perfecting the hostage technique with accomplice Joseph Dougherty, Conner joined Joe for an identical job in Oklahoma City four months later, waltzing out of the bank with $706,000 in cash.

Convicted of both robberies, Conner was sentenced to 25 years in the federal penitentiary at El Reno, Oklahoma. Dougherty joined him there in 1985, and they were en route to Joe's trial when Conner pulled his Houdini routine on June 19, escaping from handcuffs and threatening their escorts with a razor blade while Dougherty went for their guns. More robberies followed, in Missouri, Wisconsin, and Washington, with Dougherty making the FBI's "Top Ten" list on November 6, 1985. Conner was forced to wait until August 8, 1986, for a vacancy on the dishonor roll, supplied by dismissal of federal warrants against the Hammond brothers on August 4.

By early December 1986, federal agents had focused their search on Chicago, where Conner had roots. On the morning of December 9, an anonymous phone call led G-men to a motel in suburban Arlington Heights, where Conner was taken without resistance, emerging from his room to seek a cup of coffee. Unarmed at the time of his arrest, he had left his .45 in the motel room. Formally indicted six days later, on charges of escape, kidnapping, theft of government property and assaulting federal officers, he faced a maximum sentence of life imprisonment and a $1.5 million fine.

403 ■ FILLMORE RAYMOND CROSS , JR.

A ranking member of the Hell's Angels motorcycle gang and one-time president of the group's San Jose chapter, Cross was nicknamed "Crazy" by his fellow bikers. In September 1964, he was briefly charged with the rape of two teenaged girls at Bass Lake, California, but charges were dismissed when the witnesses proved "unreliable." Ten years later, Cross launched a highly-publicized effort to rid the San Jose Angels of drug abusers, but his posturing did not prevent liaisons with members of the California Mafia. Adult convictions in Cross's file include counts of battery and assault with a deadly weapon, plus conspiracy to distribute and sell cocaine and amphetamines.

On October 1, 1984, two thugs employed by Cross abducted a Santa Cruz, California, businessman, beating him almost to death in an effort to extort $100,000 from their victim. Cross was named in federal warrants on March 6, 1986, charging him with unlawful flight to avoid prosecution for extortion and assault with a deadly weapon. Five months later, on August 8, his name was added to the "Ten Most Wanted" list. The fugitive surrendered voluntarily to authorities in California, on December 23, 1986, and was held for trial on pending felony charges.

404 ■ JAMES WESLEY DYESS

Born June 10, 1956, in Laurel, Mississippi, Dyess became a heavy drinker and had adult convictions for theft, larceny and grand larceny. By early 1986, he was confined in Clarke County, Mississippi, sentenced to seven years as a burglar and habitual criminal.

On April 25, 1986, Dyess escaped from custody in Clarke County, invading a private residence the next night and shooting both occupants to death with a .22-caliber revolver. A federal warrant was issued in Jackson, Mississippi, on May 8, charging Dyess with unlawful flight to avoid prosecution for murder, and his name was added to the FBI's "Most Wanted" list on September 29, 1986.

Running for the West Coast, Dyess managed to elude pursuit for nearly two years. Federal agents ran him down in California, on March 16, 1988, and he was taken into custody without resistance, facing extradition to Mississippi and trial on pending charges of first-degree murder.

405 ■ DANNY MICHAEL WEEKS

A native of Roswell, New Mexico, born January 19, 1954, Danny Weeks grew up in association with drug addicts and "outlaw" bikers, hanging around the fringes of motorcycle gangs like the Hell's Angels and the Bandidos. Boasting adult convictions for burglary, escape, and possession of marijuana, by 1986 he was confined in Louisiana, convicted of armed robbery and murder for hire. On August 23 of that year, he joined two other inmates in breaking out of Louisiana's state prison; two days later, federal warrants charged him with unlawful flight to avoid confinement.

In flight across Texas, Weeks kidnapped female hostages in two separate instances, releasing his hostages unharmed in each case. He was identified as the gunman who held up a savings and loan office in San Antonio, moving on from there to rob a bank in Tucson, Arizona. His name was added to the FBI's "Most Wanted" list on September 29, 1986.

Sixteen months later, Weeks was still at large when the new Fox television network introduced a weekly program called "America's Most Wanted," profiling desperate fugitives from justice. His case was featured on the program's broadcast of February 28, 1988, and federal agents found him three weeks later, on March 20, pursuing leads provided by a viewer of the program. Apprehended in Washington state, Weeks was held for transportation to Louisiana, facing prosecution on more recent felony counts in Texas and Arizona.

406 ■ MICHAEL WAYNE JACKSON

Born in Mississippi in 1945, Mike Jackson had reached the Midwest by the time he entered his teens. In 1962, with two other youths, he was arrested for robbing an Indianapolis cab driver. Over the next two decades, he logged at least thirty-five arrests in Indiana, Tennessee, and Missouri, serving time on convictions for rape, sodomy, kidnapping, auto theft, assault and battery, shoplifting, and firearms violations. A violence-prone paranoid schizophrenic, Jackson was several times institutionalized without apparently benefitting from therapy. Twice married and divorced from the same woman, Jackson had two small daughters whom he saw only three times in his life.

Arrested for shoplifting in Indianapolis, on March 1, 1985,

Jackson faced more serious problems a week later, when federal officers retrieved a home-made shotgun and four Molotov cocktails from his pickup truck. A guilty plea on weapons charges sent him to the Medical Center for Federal Prisoners, at Springfield, Missouri, and he was paroled in April 1986, against the best advice of staff psychiatrists.

Federal probation officer Thomas Gahl had trouble rousing Jackson when he dropped by Michael's Indianapolis home unannounced, on the morning of September 22, 1986. Spot-checks are not uncommon, but the outcome of this visit was a tragedy. Emerging wild-eyed, with a shotgun in his hands, Jackson leveled Gahl with his first blast, afterward firing another to finish the job as the officer lay pleading for his life.

A half-hour later, grocer J. B. Hall was murdered in his market, the till looted before Jackson escaped in a bread delivery truck, holding the terrified driver at gunpoint. Dropping his hostage at the Indianapolis airport, Jackson dragged another motorist from his car and roared off into a residential area, there abducting a woman and taking her car on a wild drive to Frankfort, Indiana. There, Jackson's hostage leaped from the moving vehicle, escaping with her life at the cost of a broken leg.

In Frankfort, Jackson stole another car, briefly abducting the female driver and her son, releasing both after he took the woman's money and her wedding ring. Rolling on through St. Peter, Missouri, he shot and killed forty-seven-year-old Earl Finn after mistaking the victim's car for an unmarked police cruiser.

Nightfall brought Jackson to O'Fallon, Missouri, forty miles north of St. Louis, where he assaulted two women and stole three cars in the space of an hour, driving on toward Wright City in a hot Cadillac, its owner locked in the trunk. Police in Wright City gave chase, one of them wounded in the fierce running battle, but Jackson was forced to abandon his wheels north of town. The Caddy's owner was released, unharmed, but bullet holes and bloodstains indicated that the gunman had been wounded.

A massive ground search was begun around Wright City, federal agents joining the hunt after Jackson was declared a fugitive on charges of unlawful flight to avoid prosecution.

Still at large nine days after the shootings, Jackson was added to the FBI's "Most Wanted" list on October 1, 1986.

Next day, the searchers were scouring an abandoned farm site, a mile and a half from where Jackson had dumped his last car, when gunfire erupted from the barn. SWAT teams laid siege to the decrepit building, alternately calling for Jackson's surrender and pouring tear gas through every available opening. That night, when officers rushed the barn, they found Jackson dead inside, his skull shattered by a self-inflicted shotgun blast.

407 ■ THOMAS GEORGE HARRELSON

A firearms and explosives expert linked with the Aryan Nations movement, Harrelson was another of those home-grown nazis who seek to "defend the white race" by robbing banks. Between October 1985 and February 1987, he robbed at least nine banks, in six states, assisted by his fiancee and fellow hardcore facists. By autumn of 1986, Harrelson's raiders had bagged close to $90,000 for "the cause," and his efforts won him a posting to the FBI's "Top Ten" list on November 26.

Addition to the Bureau's honor roll made Harrelson nervous, prompting him to cancel his scheduled wedding. Pregnant and disappointed, fiancee Cynthia Ehrlich understood her man's commitment to the struggle. Her own father, Robert Miles, had served time in prison for bombing school buses in Michigan, as a protest against integration, and he would soon be indicted with other "aryan" leaders across the country for conspiracy to overthrow the American government.

On January 13, 1987, Harrelson's raiders robbed a bank in Little Rock, Arkansas, making their getaway with $11,018 in cash. Four weeks later, on February 9, Harrelson robbed a small bank in Warren, Minnesota. Backed up by Cynthia Ehrlich and "aryan" Stuart Skarda, he was pursued from the scene by bank employees in private cars, losing his own vehicle when it bogged down in mud on a rural track. Commandeering a grain truck with four hostages, the bandits rolled on toward Argyle, where a police roadblock stopped them cold.

Veering into a ditch after a brisk exchange of gunfire, the fugitives surrendered when they found themselves surrounded.

In custody, Harrelson struck a bargain with federal prosecutors, seeking reduced time in return for a marathon guilty plea. Aside from the holdups in Warren and Little Rock, he confessed to bank robberies in Fowlersville, Michigan ($7,825); Leslie, Michigan ($13,000); Springport, Michigan ($2,733); Delta, Ohio ($9,800); Rossville, Illinois ($43,911); Drayton, North Dakota ($2,807); and a previous stick-up in Warren ($9,800). His "reward" for the guilty plea was a sentence of thirty-four years in the federal penitentiary at Leavenworth.

408 ■ ROBERT ALAN LITCHFIELD

Born in 1948, Robert Litchfield was a truck driver who turned to armed robbery in 1983. Over the next two years, he raided at least fifteen banks in Florida, drawing a sixty-year sentence upon his conviction in 1985. Confined to the federal prison at Talladega, Alabama, Litchfield escaped on February 4, 1986, returning to the "trade" which he knew best. Over the next six months, he robbed three more banks in Florida and Michigan, resulting in issuance of new federal warrants on August 29, charging Litchfield with bank robbery and escape from a federal institution. His name was added to the FBI's "Top Ten" on January 20, 1987.

Four months later, on May 14, Litchfield entered the First Security Bank in Boise, Idaho, drawing a pistol and threatening employees with a shoe box which allegedly contained a bomb. In fleeing with a briefcase full of cash, he dropped a business card belonging to his one-time federal parole officer, based in West Palm Beach, Florida. Descriptions of the bandit rang a bell, and the parole officer tentatively identified Litchfield, recalling that "hoax" bombs were employed in several of the fugitive's Florida robberies.

Narrowing their search patterns, G-men were ready to move when they received a telephone tip on May 20, placing

Litchfield and his wife near Lake Tahoe. FBI agents and federal marshals descended on the residence in force, capturing Litchfield without a struggle. His wife, Donna, was also taken into custody on a charge of jumping bail, the fugitives returned to Alabama pending disposition of their latest felony indictments.

409 ■ DAVID JAMES ROBERTS

A native of Perth Amboy, New Jersey, born in January 1944, Roberts logged his first adult arrest at age twenty-two. Preying on women in Gary and Crown Point, Indiana, he had raped and robbed at least two victims, leaving them locked in the trunks of their cars before police picked him up. Conviction on reduced charges of armed robbery earned him a twelve-year sentence in the state reformatory, where Roberts took part in a bloody 1969 riot. Listed as one of the forty-six wounded, he carried scars from knife and bullet wounds sustained in the melee. After serving half his sentence, Roberts was paroled on December 12, 1972.

Eight months later, he purchased a set of new tires from a White River, Indiana, shop and drove off without paying. Manager Bill Patrick signed a complaint against his elusive customer, but Roberts was still at large on the night of January 20, 1974, when he dropped by Patrick's home with cans of gasoline in hand. Smoke inhalation was listed as the cause of death for Patrick, his wife Ann, and their year-old daughter Heidi.

Indicted on triple murder charges in March 1974, Roberts was held without bond until September 17, when a sympathetic judge set bail at $10,000. Undaunted by the prospect of a death sentence, Roberts reverted to type in early November, abducting a nineteen-year-old Indianapolis woman, raping her twice before leaving her locked in the trunk of her car. The victim's six-month-old son was abandoned in some nearby woods, where he died of exposure during the night.

Roberts was armed with a pistol when police picked him up on new felony charges, and this time there would be no bail.

Convicted on four counts of murder, with additional charges of kidnapping, arson, and rape, the defendant was sentenced to die. Subsequent commutation of his sentence left Roberts facing six terms of life imprisonment, but the killer had no intention of serving his time.

In October 1986, Roberts complained of breathing difficulties, requesting a medical examination. Returning from a local hospital on October 24, he drew a gun on his escorts, handcuffed both officers, and drove them to Hammond, Indiana, where they escaped after Roberts stopped to make a phone call. (Both officers were subsequently disciplined for negligence in handling their prisoner; one of the guards confessed to trafficking in contraband for prisoners and was summarily dismissed.)

Federal warrants charged Roberts with unlawful flight to avoid confinement, his name reaching the "Ten Most Wanted" list on April 27, 1987, but the fugitive was nowhere to be found. On February 7, 1988, his case was profiled on the first edition of a new television program, "America's Most Wanted." By February 11, at least seventy-five callers had identified Roberts as one "Robert Lord," director of a shelter for homeless men on Staten Island, New York. Federal agents arrested Roberts on the job, from which he had been earning $18,000 yearly, and he was returned to Indiana for completion of his sentences.

410 ■ RONALD GLYN TRIPLETT

Born in Alabama in July 1949, Triplett spent most of his life in the vicinity of Detroit, Michigan, holding down jobs in automobile plants and various area health clubs. The latter jobs were good for meeting women, but Triplett's style left something to be desired, his approach consisting primarily of violent sexual assault. On October 11, 1978, he held up a restaurant in Trenton, Michigan, wounding a female employee with gunfire before he fled the scene. Convicted of armed robbery, attempted murder, and interstate flight, Triplett was confined to Southern Michigan Prison, escaping from custody on June 14, 1984.

Surfacing in the Southwest, Triplett continued his practice of preying on women. New Mexico authorities accused him of kidnapping, aggravated assault, sexual assault and possession of stolen property, following a May 13, 1986, incident in which a woman was raped, her male companion locked inside the trunk of an automobile. Arrested on May 21, following another rape attempt and a high-speed chase, Triplett—using an alias—was allowed to post $100,000 cash bond before police learned his true identity. Failing to appear for his arraignment, he was added to the FBI's "Most Wanted" list on April 27, 1987.

Less than three weeks later, on May 16, federal agents found Triplett in Tempe, Arizona, where he had been working as a construction laborer, using the alias "James R. Triplett." Five G-men surrounded the fugitive's car at a local intersection, slapping the cuffs on Triplett before he could reach a 9mm pistol concealed in the vehicle.

411 ■ CLAUDE DANIEL MARKS
412 ■ DONNA JEAN WILMOTT

May 22, 1987, marked the first time in FBI history that a man and woman were added to the list of "Ten Most Wanted" fugitives on the same date. Recipients of the dubious honor, Claude Marks and Donna Wilmott, are described as members of the terrorist FALN organization (see Carlos Torres, #356), allegedly involved in a conspiracy to liberate one of their radical compatriots from the federal prison at Leavenworth, Kansas. Warrants issued in Chicago, on December 12, 1986, charge both fugitives with conspiracy to violate laws prohibiting prison escape, damage and destruction of government property, receipt and transportation of explosives, interstate travel to promote criminal activity, and possession of unregistered firearms. At this writing, both are still at large, ranking numbers four and five on the January 1989 "Top Ten" list.

Born Claudio Daniel Makowski on December 31, 1949,

"Marks" is a native of Buenos Aires, Argentina, described as a white male, six feet tall and 190 pounds, with brown hair, brown eyes, and a heavy build. He has a distinctive mole on his neck, speaks fluent Spanish, and alternates between wearing glasses and contact lenses. A martial arts enthusiast, Marks is knowledgeable in electronics and automobile maintenance, weapons, explosives, and the reloading of ammunition. He has held employment as a fast food cook, radio announcer, auto mechanic and printer, using Social Security numbers 551-80-8393, 129-62-4064, and 287-03-2916. Aliases on file for this subject include John Chester Clark, Edward Cole, Charles Everett, Michael Hamlin, C. Henly, Dale Allen Martin, Tony McCormick, Michael Prentiss, and Brian Wilcox.

Donna Wilmott was born June 30, 1950, in Akron, Ohio. She is described as a white female, five feet tall and 105 pounds, with brown hair, brown eyes, and a petite build. She wears corrective lenses, and is known to wear wigs or dye her hair in an effort to change her appearance. A student of martial arts, she has worked as a hospital technician, nurse, lab technician, acupuncturist and housekeeper, using Social Security numbers 270-50-0840, 360-62-8763, and 360-42-8736. Aliases used by this fugitive include J. Billings, Marcie Garber, Marcia Gardner, Jean Gill, Dona J. Krupnick, Donna Wilmiet, and Terry Young.

413 ■ DARREN DEE O'NEALL

Born in Albuquerque, New Mexico, on February 26, 1960, O'Neall grew up a drifter and pathological liar with a taste for violent sex. He traveled widely, favoring the West and avidly devouring the novels of best-selling Western writer Louis L'Amour. On the road, assuming various identities, O'Neall frequently lifted his latest alias from favorite L'Amour characters.

On March 28, 1987, twenty-two-year-old Robin Smith left a Puyallup, Washington, tavern to attend a party with new acquaintance "Herb Johnson." She never came home, and police were alarmed when they found Johnson's car abandoned near Marysville, north of Seattle, on May 31. A search of the trunk turned up Robin's bloodstained jacket, plus several human teeth; a check on the vehicle's registration revealed it had been stolen two months earlier, in Nampa, Idaho.

The owner was a trucker, who recalled the thief in detail. Young and blond, with the word "JUNE" tattooed across the knuckles of his left hand, the drifter had been thumbing rides when the truckdriver picked him up and offered him a place to spend the night. Next morning, he was gone, along with his benefactor's car and a Ruger .357 magnum revolver, stolen from the trucker's home.

The "JUNE" tattoo rang bells with law enforcement, leading to identification of the drifter as Darren O'Neall, a fugitive from child support payments after abandoning his wife and child six years earlier. His whereabouts were presently unknown, but officers suspected he was hunting other female victims.

On April 29, 1987, Wendy Aughe, twenty-nine, disappeared after leaving her beauty school night class to keep a date with the bartender from a neighborhood restaurant in Bellingham, Washington. It was the bartender's first day of work, and he never returned to pick up his paycheck, but fingerprints lifted from his job application identified the man as Darren O'Neall. Wendy's car turned up days later, outside a tavern in Eugene, Oregon, and federal warrants were issued charging O'Neall with unlawful flight to avoid prosecution for murder.

By that time, there were other warrants pending, including a federal charge of unlawful flight to avoid prosecution for sexual assault, in Colorado Springs, Colorado. A female victim there identified O'Neall as her assailant, and the list of charges grew longer when skeletal remains of Robin Smith were discovered on May 25, near Greenwater, Washington, north of Mt. Rainier.

On June 9, 1987, Lisa Szubert disappeared from a truck stop at Mountain Home, Idaho. Last seen with a young man bearing the familiar knuckle tattoo, she was found dead on June 13, southeast of La Grande, Oregon. A week later, O'Neall was linked with the bungled abduction of a woman in

Burly, Idaho. His name was added to the FBI's "Most Wanted" June 25.

In flight, O'Neall was drawing attention from law enforcement agencies across the nation. Three women had been shot to death in Salt Lake City over the past year, each killed with the same small-caliber gun, and witnesses recalled seeing them last with a man bearing the "JUNE" tattoo on his knuckles. Speculative body-counts were climbing into double digits by the time FBI agents captured O'Neall in Florida, on February 3, 1988. He was returned to Washington for trial on murder charges, and the disposition of his case is pending.

414 ■ LOUIS RAY BEAM

A native of Lufkin, Texas, born August 20, 1946, Beam had no use for blacks or Jews. By age thirty, he had attained the rank of Grand Titan—commander of a congressional district—in the Texas Ku Klux Klan, instituting paramilitary training courses for his Klansmen and exhorting them to "reclaim Texas for the white man." "It will take fresh blood," he declared in 1977, "but, by God, a lot of it will be the blood of our enemies. Get ready!" A leader of violent protests against Vietnamese refugees who settled along the Texas Gulf Coast, "invading" the shrimp industry, by the early 1980s Beam had set his sights on bigger things, consorting with various "aryan" groups nation-wide. A pioneer in the use of computers to link racist cliques, he established more than a dozen computerized bulletin boards for the faithful, stocking the menus with diatribes assailing the "Zionist Occupational Government" in Washington, D.C.

On April 21, 1987, federal indictments were returned against Beam and thirteen other militant white supremacists, charging them with a seditious conspiracy to overthrow the government of the United States with specific acts of murder, armed robbery and sabotage. Eleven of the suspects were swept up in FBI dragnets on April 23, but Beam slipped through the net with his wife and daughter, absconding to

Guadalajara, Mexico. His name was added to the "Ten Most Wanted" list on July 14, 1987.

The list of those indicted for sedition reads like a *Who's Who* of the neo-Nazi "survivalist" movement in America. Fully half of the defendants were already in jail, charged or convicted with various armed robberies and murders, including the assassination of Denver radio personality Alan Berg. "Bruder Schweigen" stalwarts David Lane, Andrew Barnhill and Richard Scutari (#396) were included on the list. So was David Snell, a fanatic member of the Covenant, Sword, and Arm of the Lord, sentenced to death for killing an Arkansas pawnbroker, his sentence backed up with another of life without parole, in the murder of a black state trooper. Richard Butler, founding father of the Aryan Nations, was included on the roster, along with ex-Klansman and convicted arsonist Robert Miles, lately self-styled "pastor" of the right-wing Mountain Church, in Cohoctah, Michigan.

Federal agents traced Louis Beam to Guadalajara on November 6, 1987, surrounding his home in a joint operation with Mexican Federal Judicial Police. Beam surrendered quietly, but his wife opened fire on the arresting officers, wounding one Mexican policeman before she was disarmed.

Returned to Arkansas for trial, Beam stood beside twelve fellow defendants when a jury returned its verdict on April 7, 1988. Unimpressed with the evidence of conspiracy and collusion, jurors acquitted the thirteen racists on all counts, setting them at liberty. Scooping up his wife as she began to faint, Beam emerged from the courtroom all smiles, vowing to continue his fight against "ZOG" and the "mud people."

415 ■ TED JEFFREY OTSUKI

Listed at number six on the FBI's January 1989 "Most Wanted" list, Otsuki was the second Oriental fugitive to make the roster since its inception in 1950. In 1979, at Los Fresno, Texas, Otsuki invaded the small town's police station, overpowering the officers inside and destroying their communications equipment before crossing the street to loot a bank.

Convicted on charges of armed robbery, bank robbery, and as a felon in possession of a firearm, he was sentenced to a lengthy term in Leavenworth. A federal parolee, he has continued his career in crime since winning conditional release from the penitentiary.

Confronted by Boston police officers in 1986, Otsuki killed one and wounded another before fleeing the city. Federal agents traced him to Dayton, Ohio, and from there to Chicago, filing charges of unlawful flight to avoid prosecution. By the time his name was added to the "Top Ten" list, on January 22, 1987, Otsuki had left tracks in Harlingen, Texas, and in San Francisco, where a rented self-storage locker yielded two suitcases filled with explosives. Outstanding federal warrants included charges of unlawful flight, felon in possession of a firearm, and possession of an unregistered firearm.

Otsuki was captured October 10, 1988 in Harlingen, Texas, and was returned to Boston for trial. In May 1988, he was convicted of murder and sentenced to life.

416 ■ PEDRO LUIS ESTRADA

A one-time professional boxer, Pedro Estrada is listed as number seven on the FBI's January 1990 "Most Wanted" roster. Born November 17, 1963, in Brooklyn, he boasts adult convictions for disorderly conduct and criminal possession of a weapon. His nomination to the "Top Ten" list results from Estrada's alleged involvement in the New York narcotics trade —dealing both heroin and "crack"—including homicides related to the daily conduct of his illicit business.

On June 15, 1986, Estrada and two male accomplices reportedly visited the Bronx apartment of a former gang member, now a competitor attempting to establish his own "crack" dealership in New York. Suspecting his target of a drug rip-off, Estrada allegedly shot and killed the man, next turning his gun on two female witnesses. One of the women survived her wounds, while the other was killed at the scene. Later that same afternoon, Estrada and his backup gunners allegedly visited a second acquaintance, also suspected of involvement in the rip-off scheme, adding another homicide to their list of accomplishments for the day. Federal warrants issued on November 21, 1986, accuse Estrada of unlawful flight to avoid prosecution for murder, and his name was added to the "Top Ten" list on April 15, 1988.

Estrada is described as muscular, between five-feet-ten and six feet tall, 160 pounds, with brown hair and brown eyes. Distinctive marks include a scar above his right eye, with a one-inch tattoo of the initials "PE" on his upper left arm. In addition to boxing, Estrada has been employed as a cab driver and construction worker. Known aliases include Pablo Estrada, Pedro Epstrade, Junior Rivera, Pablo Rivera, Pete Rivera, "Moe," and "Pistola." Last seen in New York City, Estrada is believed to be traveling with his girlfriend, Desiree Morales, and their two-year-old son, Christian Luis Estrada.

417 ■ JOHN EDWARD STEVENS

Listed as number eight on the FBI's January 1989 roster of "Most Wanted" fugitives, Stevens is described as a loud-talking, abusive bank robber who typically threatens employees with a pistol before vaulting over the counter to loot the cash drawers himself. Linked with twenty-two bank robberies in eight states, netting an estimated half-million dollars, Stevens was one of three fugitives added to the "Top Ten" list on May 29, 1988, when FBI Director William Sessions appeared on the weekly broadcast of "America's Most Wanted." At this writing, Stevens is still at large.

418 ■ JACK DARRELL FARMER

A convicted drug dealer and reputed boss of a Chicago-based gang known as the "Little Mafia," Farmer was indicted for racketeering activities which included two murders, drug trafficking, several robberies, armed home invasions, false credit transactions, and intimidation of prosecution witnesses. Held without bail pending trial, Farmer was released to his lawyer's custody on a series of day visits in April 1987, to help prepare his case. During one of those visits, Farmer and his wife assaulted the lawyer, leaving him bound and gagged as the fugitive made his escape.

Posted to the "Ten Most Wanted" list on May 29, 1988, Farmer was one of those profiled on the weekly airing of the Fox network's program, "America's Most Wanted." Three days later, on June 1, a viewer's telephone call led federal agents to Farmer's Florida hideout, where he was taken into custody without resistance. Returned to Chicago for trial, Farmer mugged for the cameras, adopting a philosophical tone as he explained that he was being "framed by the FBI."

419 ■ ROBERT LEE JONES

Ranking ninth on the FBI's January 1989 list of "Ten Most Wanted" fugitives, Robert Jones has been arrested and charged with sexually molesting three children, videotaping his crimes for personal amusement and potential sale to other pedophiles. After posting bond on the charges, he failed to appear for his scheduled trial in November 1986, thereby rating a new federal charge of unlawful flight to avoid prosecution. Described as a sexual deviant who endears himself to neighborhood children, thereafter luring them into escalating levels of sexual contact, Jones was added to the "Top Ten" list on May 29, 1988, his case profiled on an episode of "America's Most Wanted." At this writing, he is still at large.

420 ■ TERRY LEE JOHNSON

An ex-marine and reputed drug addict, Johnson allegedly supports his habit by dealing in mid-level narcotics distribution. In 1976, he was convicted of murdering an Alabama farmer, shooting his victim with a high-powered rifle after the farmer denied Johnson permission to hunt on private property. Confined to the Limestone Correctional Facility at Elmore, Alabama, he escaped in 1986 and continues to elude capture. Federal warrants have been issued, charging Johnson with unlawful flight to avoid confinement, and his name was added to the "Ten Most Wanted" list on June 12, 1988. Reportedly adept in wilderness survival, living off the land, he is, at this writing, still at large.

PROFILES OF THE FBI'S "MOST WANTED" FUGITIVES 1950–1988

This listing of "Top Ten" profiles is complete within the limitations of material obtainable from FBI and media sources. Ages at listing were unavailable for 34 of the 420 fugitives. In recent years, the FBI has released only perfunctory descriptions of "Top Ten" fugitives, with the last three combined on a single sheet, typed double-spaced; missing information is therefore more prevalent in recent listings.

Geographical notations are specific where possible. In some cases, only a state is named as the location of a particular offense or arrest. Where nomadic fugitives are sought in numerous localities for the same crime, we've listed their venue as "Nationwide," "Midwest," etc.

The following FBI abbreviations are used to denote individual crimes:

AWDW = assault with a deadly weapon
CRV = conditional release violation (similar to parole violation)

EFP = escaped federal prisoner
FFA = Federal Firearms Act violations
ITOM = interstate transportation of obscene materials
ITSMV = interstate transportation of stolen motor vehicles (Dyer Act)
ITSP = interstate transportation of stolen property
PV = parole violation
RICO = racketeering influence in corrupt organizations
UFAC = unlawful flight to avoid confinement (with specific charge)
UFAP = unlawful flight to avoid prosecution (with specific charge)

NOTE: Fugitives are listed in chronological order confirmed from two lists supplied by the FBI. One individual surrendered before his listing was published, but publication went ahead regardless, for reasons unknown. At least two others—#11 (Sutton) and #291 (Gentile)—show listing dates earlier than that of their immediate predecessor, but our inquiries have failed to resolve the apparent discrepancy, and we've stuck with the order and dates recorded in FBI files.

NAME	AGE	LISTED	OFFENSE	LOCATION	ARRESTED	LOCATION
Holden, Thomas	55	3/14/50	UFAP-Murder	Chicago	6/23/51	Beaverton, OR
King, Morley	48	3/15/50	UFAP-Murder	San Luis Obispo, CA	10/31/51	Philadelphia, PA
Nesbit, William	50	3/16/50	UFAC-Murder	So. Dakota state pen	3/18/50	St. Paul, MN
Mitchell, Henry	55	3/17/50	Bank robbery	Williston, FL		Dropped from list 7/18/58
Pinson, Omar	31	3/18/50	UFAC-Murder	Hood River, OR	8/28/50	Pierre, SD
Downs, Lee	43	3/20/50	UFAP-Burglary	San Jose, CA	4/7/50	Daytona Beach, FL
Jackson, Orba	43	3/21/50	EFP	Leavenworth, KS	3/22/50	Aloha, OR
Wright, Glen	50	3/22/50	UFAP-Robbery	McAlester, OK	12/13/50	Salina, KS

NAME	AGE	LISTED	OFFENSE	LOCATION	ARRESTED	LOCATION
Shelton, Henry	40	3/23/50	Kidnap.; ITSMV	Paducah, KY	6/23/50	Indianapolis, IN
Guralnick, Morris	35	3/24/50	UFAP-Assault	NY City	12/15/50	Madison, WI
Sutton, William	51	3/20/50	UFAC-Armed robbery	NY City	2/18/52	NY City
Davenport, Stephen	43	4/4/50	EFP; ITSMV	Leavenworth, KS	5/5/50	Las Vegas, NV
Tollett, Henry	—	4/11/50	EFP	McNeil Island, WA	6/3/51	Redding, CA
Tenuto, Frederick	35	5/24/50	UFAC-Murder	Philadelphia, PA	Dropped from list 3/9/64	
Kling, Thomas	44	7/17/50	UFAP-Attempted Armed robbery	NY City	2/20/52	NY City
Dembin, Meyer	—	9/5/50	Bank robbery; ITSMV	Sparkill, NY	11/26/51	NY City

Name	Age	Date Listed	Crime	Captured	Date Captured	Hometown
Taylor, Courtney	42	1/8/51	CRV; ITSP	Nationwide	2/16/51	Mobile, AL
Brent, Joseph	24	1/9/51	UFAP-Robbery	San Diego	8/29/52	Texas City, TX
Burton, Harry	49	3/9/51	UFAP-Murder	L.A.	2/7/52	Cody, WY
Cato, Joseph (Surrendered before his listing was published)	48	6/27/51	UFAP-Murder	San Francisco, CA	6/21/51	Cleveland, OH
Brancato, Anthony	36	6/27/51	UFAP-Robbery	Las Vegas, NV	6/29/51	San Francisco, CA
Peters, Fred	65	7/2/51	ITSP; PV	Tampa, FL	1/15/52	Wash., DC
Tait, Ernest	40	7/11/51	UFAP-Burglary	New Castle, IN	7/12/51	Miami, FL
Embry, Ollie	22	7/25/51	Bank robbery; ITSMV; ITSP	Columbia, IL	8/5/51	Kansas City, MO
Baccolia, Giachino	—	8/20/51	Obstructing justice	Detroit	12/10/51	NY City
Young, Ray	39	11/12/51	UFAP-Burglary	L.A.	11/16/51	Denver, CO

NAME	AGE	LISTED	OFFENSE	LOCATION	ARRESTED	LOCATION
Hill, John	49	12/10/51	UFAP-Murder	Willoughby, MD	8/16/52	Hamtramck, MI
Heroux, George	22	12/19/51	Bank robbery	Kansas City	7/25/52	El Portal, FL
Martin, Sydney	30	1/7/52	UFAP-Murder	Belchertown, MA	11/27/53	Corpus Christi, TX
Puff, Gerhard	37	1/28/52	Bank robbery	Kansas City	7/26/52	NY City
Young, Thomas	34	2/21/52	Bank robbery	Santana, KS	9/23/52	Lowman, ID
Maurer, Ken	20	2/27/52	UFAP-Murder	Detroit	1/8/53	Miami, FL
Beausoleil, Isaie	46	3/3/52	UFAP-Murder	Monroe Co., MI	6/25/53	Chicago
Zalutsky, Leonard	37	8/5/52	UFAC-Murder	Miami, FL	9/8/52	Beaver Falls, PA
Martin, William	42	8/11/52	ITSMV	Olathe, KS	8/30/52	St. Louis, MO

Name	Age					Dropped from list 12/14/61
Diggs, James	39	8/27/52	UFAP-Murder	Norfolk, VA		
Montos, Nick	37	9/8/52	UFAP-Armed robbery	Alma, GA	8/23/54	Chicago
Byrd, Theodore	27	9/10/52	ITSP	Nationwide	8/21/54	El Reno, OK
Kemper, Harden	50	9/17/52	ITSMV	Santa Fe, NM	1/1/53	Glendale, AZ
Brennan, John	33	10/6/52	Bank robbery	Lyons, IL	1/23/53	Chicago
Shue, Charles	—	1/15/53	Bank robbery	Lyons, IL	2/13/53	Chicago
Butler, Lawson	42	1/22/53	UFAC-Armed robbery	Salem, OR	4/21/53	Los Angeles
Brletic, Joe	25	2/9/53	UFAP-Robbery	St. Louis	2/10/53	Lancaster, CA
Taylor, David	—	3/3/53	UFAC-Murder	Jasper, AL	5/26/53	Chicago
Miller, Perlie	31	3/4/53	UFAC-Armed robbery	N. Carolina	3/5/53	Somersworth, NH

NAME	AGE	LISTED	OFFENSE	LOCATION	ARRESTED	LOCATION
Bowerman, Fred	60	3/5/53	Bank robbery	Chicago	4/24/53	St. Louis, MO
Mathus, Robert	37	3/16/53	UFAP-Armed robbery	Alma, GA	3/19/53	Duson, LA
Hill, Floyd	40	3/30/53	UFAP-Robbery	Ft. Worth	4/18/53	Dallas, TX
Levy, Joseph	56	5/1/53	PV; CRV; ITSP	Baltimore	4/30/53	Louisville, KY
Hinson, Arnold	40	5/4/53	UFAP-Murder	Millegan, MT	11/7/53	Memphis, TN
Cooper, Gordon	32	5/11/53	UFAP-Armed robbery	Poplar Bluff, MO	6/11/53	St. Louis, MO
Current, Fleet	29	5/18/53	UFAP-Robbery	Minneapolis	7/12/53	Omaha, NE
Fitterer, Don	28	6/8/53	UFAP-Murder	Denmark, IA	6/21/53	Oakland, CA
Cooke, John	29	6/22/53	Kidnapping	Lowell, MA	10/20/53	Detroit, MI
White, Jack	—	7/6/53	UFAP	Florida	8/27/53	Seattle, WA

Name	Age	Date	Charge	Location	Date	Location
Bryant, Alex	48	7/14/53	ITSMV	Jackson, MI	1/26/54	Los Angeles
Krendich, George	29	7/27/53	UFAP-Murder	Akron, OH	Found dead 10/11/53	
Russell, Lloyd	31	9/8/53	UFAC-Murder	Marquette, MI	8/3/54 (killed)	Spokane, WA
Garrison, Ed	53	10/26/53	UFAC-Burglary	Atmore, AL	11/3/53	Detroit, MI
Wilson, Frank	—	11/2/53	UFAP-Armed robbery	Chicago	1/18/54	Chicago
Johnson, Charles	46	11/12/53	Bank robbery	Lakesville, NC	12/28/53	Long Island, NY
Massingale, Thomas	20	11/18/53	UFAP-Kidnapping	Wichita, KS	11/26/53	Las Vegas, NM
Kenzik, Peter	47	12/7/53	UFAP-Murder	Chicago	1/26/55	San Diego, CA
Dickerson, Tom	30	12/10/53	UFAP-Robbery	Bethesda, MD	12/21/53	Verdunville, WV

NAME	AGE	LISTED	OFFENSE	LOCATION	ARRESTED	LOCATION
Davenport, Chester	31	1/6/54	UFAC-Robbery	Locust Grove, OK	1/7/54	Dixon, CA
Whitmore, Alex	45	1/11/54	UFAP-Robbery	Norfolk, VA	5/10/54	Seattle, WA
Kreuger, Everett	31	1/25/54	ITSMV	Jackson, WY	2/15/54	Las Cruces, NM
Chapman, Apee	35	2/3/54	UFAP-Murder	Cleveland	2/10/54	Silver Spring, MD
Duncan, Nelson	32	2/8/54	ITSMV; FFA	Atlanta	2/21/54	Atlanta, GA
Falzone, Charles	42	2/24/54	UFAP-Robbery	No. Tonawanda, NY	8/17/55	New Bedford, PA
Beck, Basil	21	3/1/54	UFAP-Burglary	Kansas City	3/3/54	San Pablo, CA
Lofton, James	43	3/16/54	UFAC-Armed robbery	Atmore, AL	3/17/54	Morgan City, LA

Name	Age	Date	Crime	Location	Date	Location
Dye, Clarence	43	3/8/54	UFAP-Armed robbery	Akron, OH	8/3/55	Milwaukee, WI
Groom, Sterling	50	4/2/54	UFAP-Murder	Winston, VA	4/21/54	Baltimore, MD
Menard, Ray	27	5/3/54	UFAP-Burglary	St. Louis	5/5/54	New Orleans, LA
Hopkins, John	43	5/18/54	UFAP-Murder	Wickenburg, AZ	6/7/54	Beowawe, NV
Loel, Otto	44	5/21/54	UFAP-Murder	Oklahoma City	1/17/55	Sanford, FL
Keegan, David	35	6/21/54	ITSP	Mondamin, IA		Dropped from list 12/13/63
Wilkinson, Walter	30	8/17/54	UFAP-Kidnapping	Corinth, NY	1/12/55	Los Angeles
Allen, John	45	9/7/54	UFAP-Robbery	Birmingham, AL	12/21/54	Ft. Smith, AR
Belew, George	41	1/4/55	ITSP	Hays, KS	1/24/55	Springfield, IL

NAME	AGE	LISTED	OFFENSE	LOCATION	ARRESTED	LOCATION
Carpenter, Ken	43	1/31/55	Bank robbery	Independence, MO	2/4/55	E. Arlington, TN
Payne, Flenoy	46	2/2/55	UFAP-Murder	Toledo, OH	3/11/58	Crittenden Co., AR
Morset, Palmer	49	2/7/55	UFAP-Robbery	Chicago	3/2/56	Indianapolis, IN
McDermott, Pat	57	2/9/55	UFAC-Murder	Canton, OH	7/19/55	NY City
Daniels, Garland	50	2/18/55	EFP; ITSP	Lexington, KY	3/29/55	Los Angeles
O'Connor, Dan	27	4/11/55	ITSMV	Great Falls, MT	12/26/55	El Cajon, CA
Raymond, Jack	34	8/8/55	ITSP	Walla Walla, WA	10/14/55	Denver, CO
Everhart, Dan	30	8/17/55	UFAP-Robbery	Akron, OH	10/9/55	Denver, CO

Name	Age		Crime			
Ranels, Charles	32	9/2/55	Bank robbery	Louisville, KY	12/16/56	Pine Bluff, AR
Green, Thurman	35	10/24/55	ITSMV	Walla Walla, WA	2/16/56	Nashville, TN
Kendrick, John	55	11/2/55	UFAP-Assault	Washington, DC	12/5/55	Chicago
Bagnola, Joe	39	12/19/55	UFAP-Murder	New Orleans	12/30/55	Chicago
Montos, Nick	39	3/2/56	EFP	Parchman, MS	3/28/56	Memphis, TN
Faherty, James	44	3/19/56	UFAP-Armed robbery	Boston	5/16/56	Boston
Richardson, Thomas	48	4/12/56	UFAP-Armed robbery	Boston	5/16/56	Boston
Newman, Eugene	30	5/28/56	UFAP-Robbery	Buffalo, NY		Dropped from list 6/11/65
Di Biase, Carmine	35	5/28/56	UFAP-Murder	NY City	8/28/58	NY City

NAME	AGE	LISTED	OFFENSE	LOCATION	ARRESTED	LOCATION
McCollum, Ben	49	1/4/57	UFAC-Murder	McAlester, OK	3/7/58	Indianapolis, IN
White, Alfred	53	1/14/57	UFAP-Assault	Hamlin, WV	1/24/57	Memphis, TN
Green, Robert	27	2/11/57	UFAP-Burglary	Draper, UT	2/13/57	St. Paul, MN
Cole, George	32	2/25/57	UFAP-Murder	San Francisco	7/6/59	Des Moines, IA
McCracken, Eugene	43	3/26/58	UFAC-Murder	Nashville, TN	3/27/58	Baltimore, MD
Leftwich, Frank	36	4/4/58	UFAC-AWDW	Lumberton, NC	4/18/58	Chicago
Kilburn, Quay	34	4/16/58	CRV	Leavenworth, KS	6/2/58	Los Angeles
Scialo, Dominick	32	5/9/58	UFAP-Murder	NY City	7/27/59	NY City
Pero, Angelo	53	6/16/58	UFAP-Murder	NY City	Warrant dismissed 12/2/60	

Name	Age	Date	Charge	Location	Date	Location
Dunn, Fred	54	7/29/58	UFAP-Burglary	Westphalia, IA		Found dead 9/7/59 Ellsworth, KS
Sprenz, Frank	29	9/10/58	UFAP-Robbery	Akron, OH	4/15/59	Laredo, TX
Thurston, Dave	30	1/8/59	UFAC-Robbery	New York	2/6/59	NY City
Freeman, John	—	2/17/59	ITSMV	Nationwide	2/18/59	Hillside, MD
Garrison, Ed	60	3/4/59	UFAC-Robbery	Atmore, AL	9/9/60	St. Louis, MO
Kervan, Emmett	51	3/29/59	Bank robbery	E. Norwalk, CT	5/13/59	El Paso, TX
Hunt, Richard	27	5/27/59	ITSMV	Brownsville, OR	6/2/59	Thermopolis, WY
O'Donnell, Walter	57	6/17/59	UFAP-Robbery	Norfolk, VA	6/19/59	Norfolk, VA
Williams, Bill	32	7/10/59	UFAP-Kidnapping	New York	3/4/60	NY City

NAME	AGE	LISTED	OFFENSE	LOCATION	ARRESTED	LOCATION
Jenkins, James	37	7/21/59	Bank robbery	Philadelphia, PA	8/12/59	Buffalo, NY
Pope, Harry	39	8/26/59	UFAP-Burglary	Phoenix, AZ	9/2/59	Lubbock, TX
Duffy, James	51	8/11/59	UFAP-Armed robbery	Philadelphia, PA	8/25/59	Philadelphia, PA
Brown, Robert	41	9/9/59	ITSP	Chicago	1/11/60	Cincinnati, OH
Seno, Fred	52	9/24/59	UFAP-Armed robbery	Chicago	9/24/59	Miami, FL
Hudson, Smith	32	10/7/59	UFAC-Murder	Harrisburg, PA	7/31/60	Cozad, NE
Thomas, Joe	48	10/21/59	Bank robbery	Pelzer, SC	12/10/59	Pelzer, SC
Lawson, Ken	27	1/4/60	UFAC-Armed robbery	Fresno, CA	3/20/60	Laredo, TX
Rinehart, Ted	33	1/25/60	UFAC-Armed robbery	California	3/6/60	Granada Hills, CA

Name	Age	Date	Charge	Location	Date	Location
Rogers, Charles	31	3/18/60	UFAC-Murder	Chattahoochee, FL	5/11/60	Minneapolis, MN
Corbett, Joe	31	3/30/60	UFAP-Murder	Morrison, CO	10/29/60	Vancouver, B.C.
Mason, William	34	4/6/60	UFAP-Murder	Detroit	4/27/60	Milwaukee, WI
Reily, Edward	38	5/10/60	Bank robbery	Logansport, IN	5/24/60	Rockford, IL
Fields, Harold	44	5/25/60	UFAC-Burglary	Champaign, IL	9/5/60	Schererville, IN
Wagner, Peter	42	6/23/60	EFP	Sandstone, MN	6/25/60	Ray, MN
Warjac, John	34	7/19/60	UFAC-Burglary	California	7/22/60	Los Angeles
Tait, Ernest	49	8/16/60	UFAP-Burglary	Crawfordsville, IN	9/10/60	Denver, CO
Raby, Clarence	27	8/19/60	UFAP-Murder	Andersonville, TN	8/28/60	Heiskell, TN

NAME	AGE	LISTED	OFFENSE	LOCATION	ARRESTED	LOCATION
Beans, Nathaniel	39	9/12/60	UFAP-Murder	Oakland Pk., FL	9/30/60	Buffalo, NY
Fitzgerald, Stanley	39	9/20/60	UFAP-Murder	Truckee, CA	9/22/60	Portland, OR
Payne, Donald	42	10/6/60	UFAP-Rape	Houston, TX	Dropped from list 11/26/65	
Higgins, Charles	54	10/10/60	UFAC-Robbery	Canon City, CO	10/17/60	Kirkwood, MO
Schultz, Robert	38	10/12/60	EFP	Sandstone, MN	11/4/60	Orlando, FL
Gall, Merle	37	10/17/60	UFAP-Burglary	Great Falls, MT	1/18/61	Scottsdale, AZ
Economou, James	40	10/31/60	UFAC-Robbery	San Quentin, CA	3/22/61	Los Angeles
Tate, Ray	27	11/18/60	Bank robbery	Newark, NJ	11/25/60	Vancouver, B.C.

Name	Age	Date	Charge	City	Date	City/State
Everhart, John	41	11/22/60	UFAC-Murder	Lexington, GA	11/6/63	San Francisco, CA
Huffman, Herbert	32	12/19/60	UFAP-Murder	Chicago	12/29/60	Euclid, OH
Cindle, Ken	48	12/23/60	UFAP-Armed robbery	Wichita, KS	4/1/61	Cochran Co., TX
Viola, Tom	48	1/17/61	UFAC-Murder	Columbus, OH	3/27/61	Detroit, MI
Cole, William	22	2/2/61	UFAP-Armed robbery	New Orleans	2/6/61	Gulf Breeze, FL
Hughes, William	46	3/15/61	UFAP-Murder	Detroit	8/8/61	Pocatello, ID
Nichols, William	30	4/6/61	UFAC-Robbery	Bainbridge, GA	4/30/62	Homestead, FL
Bradley, Geo.	40	4/10/61	Bank robbery	Stuart, FL	5/1/61	Davenport, IA
Lanormandin, Philip	54	4/17/61	UFAP-ADW	Reading, MA	4/17/61	Hackensack, NJ

NAME	AGE	LISTED	OFFENSE	LOCATION	ARRESTED	LOCATION
Sharp, Kenneth	29	5/1/61	UFAP-Murder	Chicago	7/3/61	Philadelphia, PA
Fede, Anthony	47	5/22/61	UFAP-Kidnapping	Cleveland, OH	10/28/61	Los Angeles
Marquette, Richard	26	6/29/61	UFAP-Murder	Portland, OR	6/30/61	Santa Maria, CA
Schuette, Robert	39	7/19/61	UFAC-Robbery	Baltimore	8/2/61	Chicago
McGonigal, Chester	46	8/14/61	UFAP-Attempted murder	Aspen, CO	8/17/61	Denver, CO
Morse, Hugh	31	8/29/61	UFAP-Attempted murder	Reseda, CA	10/13/61	St. Paul, MN
Dillon, John	—	9/1/61	UFAP-Narcotics	Coweta, OK	3/2/64	Chelsea, OK
Sawyer, John	30	10/30/61	Bank robbery	Omaha, NE	11/3/61	Arizona

Name	Age		Crime			
Edwards, Ed	28	11/10/61	Bank robbery	Akron, OH	1/20/62	Atlanta, GA
Alltop, Frank	28	11/22/61	UFAP-Armed robbery	Huntington, WV	2/2/62	Kansas City, KS
Brannan, Francis	36	12/27/61	UFAP-Murder	Rushville, IL	1/17/62	Miami, FL
Linaweaver, Delbert	30	1/30/62	UFAC-Burglary	Salina, KS	2/5/62	Floydada, TX
Young, Watson	30	2/5/62	UFAP-Murder	Indianapolis	2/12/62	Salina, KS
Smith, Lyndal	38	2/14/62	Escape	San Quentin	3/22/62	Baltimore, MD
Grove, Harry	35	2/19/62	UFAC-Robbery	Toledo, OH	1/26/63	Uhrichsville, OH
Wilcoxson, Bobby	33	2/23/62	Bank robbery	Washington, DC	11/10/62	Baltimore, MD
Nussbaum, Al	28	4/2/62	Bank robbery	Washington, DC	11/4/62	Buffalo, NY
Holland, Tom	31	5/11/62	UFAC-Robbery	Baltimore	6/2/62	La Harpe, KS

NAME	AGE	LISTED	OFFENSE	LOCATION	ARRESTED	LOCATION
Maps, Edward	39	6/15/62	UFAP-Murder	Stroudsburg, PA	Dropped from list 12/1/62	
Jacubanis, David	52	11/21/62	Bank robbery	Dedham, MA	11/29/62	Arlington, VT
DeJarnette, John	41	11/30/62	UFAP-Obtaining drugs by fraud	Louisville, KY	12/3/62	Hollywood, CA
O'Connor, Mike	—	12/13/62	UFAP-Murder	Jersey City	12/28/62	NY City
Taylor, John	29	12/14/62	UFAP-Robbery	Champaign, IL	12/20/62	Chicago
O'Brien, Harold	58	1/4/63	UFAP-Murder	Fox Lake, IL	Dropped from list 1/14/65	
Rush, Jerry	—	1/14/63	Bank robbery	Perth Amboy, NJ	3/25/63	Bay Harbor Is., FL
Chrisman, Marshall	38	2/7/63	Bank robbery	Toledo, OH	5/21/63	Los Angeles

Barnard, Howard	38	4/12/63	UFAP-Robbery	Orland, CA	4/6/64	Sacramento, CA
Frazier, Leroy	44	6/4/63	EFP	Washington, DC	9/12/63	Cleveland, OH
Close, Carl	48	9/25/63	Bank robbery	Baltimore	9/26/63	Anderson, SC
Haddar, Tom	22	10/9/63	UFAP-Murder	Jessup, MD	1/13/64	Oklahoma City, OK
Oponowicz, Al	37	11/27/63	Bank robbery	Cleveland	12/23/64	Painesville, OH
Couts, Arthur	32	12/27/62	UFAP-Robbery	Philadelphia, PA	1/30/64	Philadelphia, PA
Gilbert, Jesse	38	1/27/64	Bank robbery	Alhambra, CA	2/26/64	Philadelphia, PA
Ammons, Sam	29	2/10/64	UFAP-Forgery	Tennessee	5/15/64	Cherokee, AL
Dumont, Frank	42	3/10/64	UFAP-Assault	Pocatello, ID	4/27/64	Tucson, AZ
Hughes, William	34	3/18/64	Escape	Montgomery, AL	4/11/64	Bylas, AZ

NAME	AGE	LISTED	OFFENSE	LOCATION	ARRESTED	LOCATION
Kilburn, Quay	40	3/23/64	UFAC-Robbery	Salt Lake City, UT	6/25/64	Ogden, UT
Bryan, Joseph	25	4/14/64	Kidnapping	Hallandale, FL	4/28/64	New Orleans, LA
Bailey, John	44	4/22/64	UFAC-Robbery	Hot Springs, AR	5/4/64	Hayward, CA
Zavada, George	58	5/6/64	Bank robbery	Los Angeles	6/12/64	San Jose, CA
McLaughlin, George	37	5/8/64	UFAP-Murder	Boston	2/24/65	Dorchester, MA
Collins, Chester	51	5/14/64	UFAP-Assault	Winter Haven, FL	Dropped from list 3/30/67	
Nivens, Ed	42	5/28/64	UFAP-Robbery	Toledo, OH	6/2/64	Tampa, FL
Vasselli, Lewis	34	6/15/64	UFAP-Narcotics	Chicago	9/1/64	Calumet City, IL
Galloway, Tom	43	6/24/64	UFAP-Murder	St. Louis	7/17/64	Danville, VA

Name	Age		Crime			
Wahrlich, Alson	28	7/9/64	Kidnapping	Tucson	10/28/67	Treasure Is., FL
Christiansen, Kenneth	33	7/27/64	UFAC-Robbery	Chino, CA	9/8/64	Silver Spring, MD
Cable, William	40	9/11/64	Escape	Nashville, TN	3/1/65	Charlotte, NC
Greeson, Lloyd	40	9/18/64	UFAP-Murder	Wilkes-Barre, PA	9/23/64	Elsinore, CA
Wyngaard, Ray	27	10/5/64	UFAP-Armed robbery	Detroit	11/28/64	Madison, WI
Gorham, Norman	45	12/10/64	Bank robbery	Boston	5/27/65	Los Angeles
Clouser, John	32	1/7/65	ITSMV	Montgomery, AL		Dropped from list 8/1/72
Parman, Walter	32	1/15/65	UFAP-Murder	Washington, DC	1/31/65	Los Angeles
Webb, Gene	38	2/11/65	UFAP-Attempted murder	Chicago	2/12/65	Chicago

NAME	AGE	LISTED	OFFENSE	LOCATION	ARRESTED	LOCATION
Veney, Samuel	26	2/25/65	UFAP-Murder	Baltimore	3/11/65	Garden City, NY
Veney, Earl	32	3/5/65	UFAP-Murder	Baltimore	3/11/65	Garden City, NY
Heien, Donald	28	3/11/65	UFAC-Murder	San Quentin	2/3/66	Newton Center, MA
Pierce, Arthur	28	3/24/65	UFAP-Murder	Indianapolis	3/25/65	Spring Valley, NY
Rainey, Donald	40	3/26/65	Bank robbery	Del Rey, CA	6/22/65	Nogales, AZ
Ashley, Leslie	28	4/6/65	UFAC-Murder	San Antonio	4/23/65	Atlanta, GA
Harris, Charles	69	5/6/65	UFAP-Murder	Fairfield, IL	6/17/65	Fairfield, IL
Tahl, William	27	6/10/65	UFAP-Murder	San Diego	11/5/65	St. Louis, MO
Pope, Duane	22	6/11/65	Bank robbery; Murder	Big Springs, KS	6/11/65	Kansas City, MO

Name	Age	Date	Charge	Location	Date	Location
Haugsted, Allan	34	6/24/65	UFAP-Murder	Willmar, MN	12/13/65	Houston
Brechtel, Theodore	27	6/30/65	EFP	New Orleans	8/16/65	Chicago
Woodford, Robert	26	7/2/65	UFAC-Robbery	San Francisco	8/5/65	Seattle, WA
Osborne, Warren	45	8/12/65	UFAP-Murder	Nashville, TN	9/9/65	Mt. Washington, KY
Black, Holice	21	8/25/65	UFAP-Armed robbery	Chicago	12/15/65	Miami, FL
Watkins, Ed	47	9/21/65	Bank robbery	Cleveland	12/2/65	Florence, MT
Singer, Joel	22	11/19/65	UFAP-Robbery	Syracuse, NY	12/1/65	Montreal
Kennedy, James	28	12/8/65	Bank robbery	Ohio	12/23/65	Worcester, MA
Higgins, Lawrence	52	12/14/65	Bank robbery	Covina, CA	1/3/66	Emigrant Gap, CA

NAME	AGE	LISTED	OFFENSE	LOCATION	ARRESTED	LOCATION
Cobb, Hoyt	34	1/6/66	UFAP-Murder	Tampa, FL	6/6/66	Hialeah, FL
Bishop, James	47	1/10/66	UFAP-Armed robbery	Phoenix, AZ	1/21/66	Aspen, CO
Van Lewing, Robert	45	1/12/66	Bank robbery	St. Louis	2/6/67	Kansas City, MO
Wright, Earl	51	1/14/66	Bank robbery	Kenova, WV	6/20/66	Cleveland, OH
Roberts, Jesse	46	2/3/66	Bank robbery	Quapaw, OK	2/8/66	Laredo, TX
Gove, Charles	—	2/16/66	Escape; Bank robbery	Vacaville, CA	2/16/66	New Orleans, LA
Owen, Ralph	—	2/16/66	Escape	Vacaville, CA	3/11/66	Kansas City, MO
Parker, Jimmy	30	2/25/66	UFAC-Murder	Asheboro, NC	3/4/66	Detroit, MI
Sayadoff, Jack	30	3/17/66	Kidnapping; ITSMV	Chicago	3/24/66	Indianapolis, IN
Buick, Robert	—	3/24/66	Bank robbery	California	3/29/66	Pecos, TX

Name	Age	Date	Crime	Location	Date	Location
Taylor, James	44	4/4/66	UFAP	Baltimore	4/4/66	Baltimore, MD
Meares, Lynwood	53	4/11/66	Escape	Carey, NC	5/2/67	Winston-Salem, NC
Ringrose, James Robert	24	4/15/66	Interstate check fraud	Minneapolis	3/29/67	Osaka, Japan
Lesczynski, Walter	35	6/16/66	UFAP-Robbery	Chicago	9/9/66	Chicago
Smelley, Don	36	6/30/66	UFAP-Armed robbery	Albuquerque	11/7/66	Hollywood, CA
Edmondson, George	29	9/21/66	UFAC-Armed robbery	Jefferson City, MO	6/28/67	Campbells Bay, Quebec
Biggs, Everett	30	9/21/66	UFAP-Armed robbery	Tulsa, OK	12/1/66	Brownfield, CO
Jennings, Gene	31	12/15/66	UFAC-Armed robbery	Eddysville, MD	2/14/67	Atlantic City, NJ
McFarland, Clarence	—	12/22/66	Bank robbery	Washington, DC	4/4/67	Baltimore, MD

NAME	AGE	LISTED	OFFENSE	LOCATION	ARRESTED	LOCATION
Hickson, Monroe	58	2/17/67	UFAC-Murder	Aiken, SC	1/30/68	Chapel Hill, NC
Laws, Clyde	40	2/28/67	Kidnapping	Wheaton, MT	5/18/67	Raytown, MO
Ervin, Chas.	—	4/13/67	UFAC-Armed robbery	Jackson, MI	7/25/67	Hawksbury, Ontario
Ervin, Gordon	41	4/13/67	UFAC-Armed robbery	Jackson, MI	6/7/69	Winnipeg, Canada
Dorman, Tom	35	4/20/67	Kidnapping	Wheaton, MD	5/20/67	Grantsburg, IN
Young, Jerry	24	5/12/67	Bank robbery	Asheville, NC	6/15/67	Akron, OH
Newman, Joseph	31	6/2/67	EFP; ITSMV	Washington, DC	6/29/67	Jersey City, NJ
Gagliardi, Carmen	26	6/9/67	UFAP-Murder	Boston	12/23/67	Medford, MA
Bussmeyer, Donald	—	6/28/67	Bank robbery	Los Angeles	8/24/67	Upland, CA

Name	Age	Date	Crime	Location	Date	City
Mationg, Florencio	33	7/1/67	UFAP-Murder	California	7/16/67	Los Angeles
Bono, Victor	28	7/1/67	UFAP-Murder	California	7/16/67	Los Angeles
Cooper, Al	—	7/27/67	UFAP-Robbery	Cinnaminson Twnsp., NJ	9/8/67	Boston
Slayton, John	41	8/2/67	UFAP-Assault	Oroville, WA	12/1/67	Harquahala Valley, AZ
James, Jerry	28	8/16/67	UFAP-Armed robbery	Amarillo, TX	1/24/68	Tucson, AZ
Anderson, Richard	27	9/7/67	UFAP-Murder	St. Louis	1/19/68	Toronto, Ontario
Young, Henry	56	9/21/67	UFAC-Armed robbery	Walla Walla, WA	1/9/68	Kansas City, MO
Sparks, Don	—	11/13/67	UFAP-Armed robbery	Mobeetie, TX	1/24/68	Tucson, AZ
King, Zelma	25	12/14/67	UFAP-Murder	Chicago	1/30/68	Phoenix, AZ

NAME	AGE	LISTED	OFFENSE	LOCATION	ARRESTED	LOCATION
Peacock, Jerry	30	12/14/67	UFAC-Robbery	Soledad, CA	3/5/68	Mesquite, NV
Storck, Ron	28	1/19/68	UFAP-Murder	Silverdale, PA	2/29/68	Honolulu, HI
McCain, Robert	26	1/31/68	Bank robbery	Dallas, TX	2/23/68	Gulfport, FL
Allen, William, II	—	2/9/68	UFAC-Murder	Nashville, TN	3/23/68	NY City
Herron, Chas.	31	2/9/68	UFAP-Murder	Nashville, TN	6/18/86	Jacksonville, FL
Spears, Leonard	31	2/13/68	UFAP-Murder	Springfield, IL	3/2/68	Tampa, FL
Bornman, Wm.	40	2/13/68	UFAP-Armed robbery	Cleveland	2/13/68	Covington, KY
Patterson, John	23	2/26/68	UFAP-Murder	E. St. Louis, IL	3/17/68	Milwaukee, WI
Martin, Troy	41	3/8/68	Kidnapping	Toledo, OH	3/19/68	Seattle, WA

Name	Age	Date	Crime	Location	Date	City
Williams, George	56	3/18/68	Bank robbery	Newcastle, CA	6/19/68 (fd. dead)	Lovelock, NV
Sanders, Mike	28	3/21/68	UFAP-Armed robbery	Salinas, CA	4/8/68	NY City
Johnson, Howard	52	3/21/68	UFAP-Murder	Summerfield, AL	4/24/68	Louisville, KY
Wells, Geo.	53	3/28/68	UFAP-Murder	Independence, MO	5/27/69	South Point, OH
Evans, David	24	4/3/68	Bank robbery	Bethlehem, PA	4/26/68	Philadelphia, PA
Paris, Frank	34	4/9/68	UFAP-Burglary	Bakersfield, CA	5/21/68	Lakehead, CA
Neff, David	32	4/18/68	Bank robbery	Beverly, MA	4/25/68	NY City
Ray, James	40	4/20/68	Conspiracy	Memphis, TN	6/8/68	London, England
Shannon, John	32	5/7/68	Bank robbery	Northfield, NJ	6/5/68	Camden, NJ

NAME	AGE	LISTED	OFFENSE	LOCATION	ARRESTED	LOCATION
Teaford, Taylor	33	5/10/68	UFAP-Murder	North Fork, CA	Dropped from list 5/24/72	
Jones, Phil	27	6/5/68	Bank robbery	Bakersfield, CA	6/26/68	San Mateo, CA
Smith, John	—	6/20/68	ITSMV	Pensacola, FL	6/24/68	Ocean Springs, MS
Rice, Byron	32	7/5/68	UFAP-Murder	Mtn. View, CA	10/2/72	Chicago
Lindblad, Robert	34	7/11/68	UFAP-Murder	Dayton, NV	10/7/68	Yerrington, NV
Scully, James	48	7/15/68	Bank robbery	Covina, CA	7/23/68	Arcadia, CA
White, Billy	25	8/13/68	UFAP-Murder	Budsville, NM	8/17/68	Wood River, IL
Yokom, Fred	22	8/29/68	UFAP-Armed robbery	Miami	9/6/68	Los Angeles
Evans, Harold	23	9/19/68	UFAC-Armed robbery	Norristown, PA	1/2/69	Chicago

Carr, Robert	22	10/18/68	UFAP-Robbery	Sunbury, PA	11/4/68	South Gate, CA
Washington, Levi	36	11/15/68	Bank robbery	New Orleans	12/9/68	Jackson, MI
Tingler, Richard	28	12/20/68	UFAP-Murder	Cleveland	5/19/69	Dill City, OK
Gentile, Geo.	66	6/18/68	Extortion	Denton, TX	12/17/68	NY City
Krist, Gary	23	12/20/68	Kidnapping	Atlanta	12/22/68	Punta Gorda, FL
Eisemann-Schier, Ruth	26	12/28/68	Kidnapping	Atlanta	3/5/69	Norman, OK
Estolas, Baltazar	31	1/3/69	UFAP-Murder	Stockton, CA	9/3/69	Langtry, TX
Bryant, Billy	30	1/8/69	Escape	Lorton, VA	1/8/69	Washington, DC
Schales, Billy	29	1/27/69	UFAP-Murder	Houston	1/30/69	Bossier City, LA

NAME	AGE	LISTED	OFFENSE	LOCATION	ARRESTED	LOCATION
Lucas, Tom	24	2/13/69	Bank robbery	Baltimore	2/26/69	Washington, DC
Reddock, Warren	43	3/11/69	UFAP-Murder	Chicago	4/14/71	Pacifica, CA
Blue, George	—	3/20/69	Bank robbery	Evansville, IN	3/28/69	Chicago
Bishop, Cameron	24	4/15/69	Sabotage	Colorado	3/12/75	East Greenwich, RI
Arrington, Marie	36	5/29/69	UFAP-Murder	Leesburg, FL	12/22/71	New Orleans, LA
Paddock, Ben	43	6/10/69	EFP	La Tuna, TX	Dropped from list 5/5/77	
Hohimer, Francis	41	6/20/69	UFAP-Burglary	Denver	12/20/69	Greenwich, CT
Thomas, Joe	—	9/12/69	Bank robbery	Terre Haute, IN	3/8/70	Peoria, IL

Name	Age	Date	Crime	Location	Date	Location
Byrnes, James	42	1/6/70	Kidnapping	Stafford, KS	4/17/70	Huntington Beach, CA
Devlin, Ed	—	3/20/70	Bank robbery	Norwalk, CT	8/15/70	Manchester, NH
Plamondon, Lawrence	22	5/5/70	Destruction of government property	Ann Arbor, MI	7/23/70	Mackinac Co., MI
Brown, Hubert	23	5/6/70	UFAP-Arson	Cambridge, MD	10/16/71	NY City
Davis, Angela	26	8/18/70	UFAP-Murder	San Rafael, CA	10/13/70	NY City
Armstrong, Dwight	19	9/4/70	Destruction of government property	Madison, WI	Removed from list 4/7/76	
Armstrong, Karleton	22	9/4/70	Destruction of government property	Madison, WI	2/16/72	Toronto, Ontario

NAME	AGE	LISTED	OFFENSE	LOCATION	ARRESTED	LOCATION
Fine, David	18	9/4/70	Destruction of government property	Madison, WI	1/8/76	San Rafael, CA
Burt, Leo	22	9/4/70	Destruction of government property	Madison, WI	Dropped from list 4/7/76	
Dohrn, Bernadine	28	10/14/70	UFAP-Conspiracy	Chicago	Dropped from list 12/7/73	
Power, Katherine	21	10/17/70	Bank robbery; Murder	Boston	Dropped from list 8/15/85	
Saxe, Susan	26	10/17/70	Bank robbery; Murder	Boston	3/27/75	Philadelphia, PA
Brown, Mace	29	10/20/72	UFAP-Murder	NY City	Killed 4/18/73	NY City
Bell, Herman	—	5/9/73	UFAP-Murder	NY City	9/2/73	New Orleans, LA

Name	Age	Date	Crime	Location	Date	Location
Myers, Twyman	22	9/28/73	UFAP-Murder	NY City	11/14/73	NY City
Harvey, Ron	—	12/7/73	UFAP-Murder	Washington, DC	3/27/74	Chicago
Christian, Samuel	—	12/7/73	UFAP-Murder	Washington, DC	12/11/73	Detroit, MI
Turner, Rudolf	—		UFAP-Murder	Moultrie, GA	10/1/74	Jacksonville, FL
Cole, Larry	27	4/2/74	Kidnapping	Roanoke, VA	4/3/74	Buffalo, NY
Jones, James	40	4/16/74	UFAP-Armed robbery	Augusta, GA	6/15/74	Coral Gables, FL
Hunter, Len	21	6/27/74	UFAC-Rape	Augusta, GA	7/31/74	Des Moines, IA
Copeland, John	30	8/15/74	UFAC-Rape	California	7/23/75	Boston
Walker, Melvin	35	10/16/74	EFP	Lewisburg, PA	11/9/74	Virginia Beach, VA

NAME	AGE	LISTED	OFFENSE	LOCATION	ARRESTED	LOCATION
Knight, Tom	23	12/12/74	Kidnapping; Murder	Miami, FL	12/31/74	New Smyrna Beach, FL
Anderson, Billy	40	1/21/75	Escape	Morgan Co., TN		Killed 7/7/79 Pall Mall, TN
Davis, Robert	28	4/4/75	UFAP-Murder	Pittsburgh, PA		Killed 8/5/77 Venice, CA
Holtan, Richard	40	4/18/75	Bank robbery; Murder	California	7/12/75	Kauai, HI
Lindhorst, Richard	33	8/4/75	Bank robbery	Wever, IA	8/7/75	Pensacola, FL
Herron, William	29	8/15/75	UFAP-Murder	Nashville, TN	10/30/75	Peoria, IL
Smallwood, James	25	8/29/75	EFP	Washington, DC	12/5/75	Seabrook, MD
Peltier, Leonard	31	12/22/75	UFAP-Murder	Pine Ridge, SD	2/6/76	Hinton, Alberta

Name	Age	Date	Charge	City	Date	Location
Huston, Pat	47	3/3/76	Bank robbery	NY City	12/7/77	Ft. Lauderdale, FL
Bethea, Tom	39	5/5/76	Kidnapping	Washington, DC	5/4/76	Miami, FL
Juliano, Anthony	53	3/15/76	Bank robbery	NY City	3/22/76	Mecklenburg Co., VA
McDonald, Joe	59	4/1/76	ITSP	Boston	9/15/82	NY City
Renton, James	38	4/7/76	PV; UFAP-Murder	Springvale, AR	5/9/77	Aurora, CO
Doyle, Nathaniel	30	4/29/76	UFAC-Bank robbery	Columbus, OH		Killed 7/15/76 Seattle, WA
Johnson, Morris	38	5/25/76	Escape	Selma, AL	6/26/76	New Orleans, LA
Picariello, Richard	28	7/29/76	Conspiracy; Explosives	New England	10/21/76	Providence, RI
Gullion, Edward	—	8/13/76.	Conspiracy; Explosives	New England	10/22/76	Providence, RI

NAME	AGE	LISTED	OFFENSE	LOCATION	ARRESTED	LOCATION
Schwartz, Gerhardt	47	11/18/76	Bank robbery	Rochester, NY	11/22/76	NY City
Martin, Francis	31	12/17/76	Escape	Smyrna, DE	2/17/77	Newport Beach, CA
Pavan, Ben	38	1/12/77	UFAP-Armed robbery	San Francisco, CA	2/17/77	Seattle, WA
Campbell, Larry	35	3/18/77	UFAP-Murder	Buffalo, NY	9/6/77	Atlanta, GA
Smith, Roy	26	3/18/77	UFAP-Murder	Kirtland, OH	6/2/77	Perry Twnsp., OH
Levasseur, Raymond	31	5/5/77	Bank robbery	Providence, RI	11/4/84	Cleveland, OH
Ray, James	50	6/10/77	Escape	Petros, TN	6/13/77	Petros, TN
Sellers, William	43	6/14/77	Escape	Atlanta, GA	6/20/79	Atlanta, GA

Name	Age	Date	Crime	Location	Date	Location
Smith, Larry	23	7/15/77	UFAP-Murder	Detroit, MI	8/20/77	Ontario, Canada
Cozzolino, Ralph	54	10/19/77	UFAP-Murder	Chattanooga, TN	1/6/78	Atlanta, GA
Hubbard, Millard	49	10/19/77	Bank robbery	Tazewell, TN	10/21/77	Lexington, KY
Torres, Carlos	24	10/19/77	Explosives	Chicago	4/4/80	Evanston, IL
Estrada, Enrique	36	12/5/77	UFAP-Robbery	Los Angeles	12/8/77	Bakersfield, CA
Smith, William	35	2/10/78	UFAP-Murder	Detroit, MI	10/27/78	Chicago
Warren, Gary	32	2/10/78	UFAP-Armed robbery	Nationwide	5/12/78	Cumberland, MD
Bundy, Ted	32	2/10/78	UFAP-Murder	Snowmass, CO	2/15/78	Pensacola, FL
Gipson, Andy	41	3/27/78	Escape	Lansing, KS	5/24/78	Albuquerque, NM
Liberatore, Anthony	57	5/26/78	UFAP-Murder	Cleveland, OH	4/1/79	E. Lake, OH

NAME	AGE	LISTED	OFFENSE	LOCATION	ARRESTED	LOCATION
Thevis, Mike	46	7/10/78	ITOM; UFAP-Conspiracy	Atlanta, GA	11/9/78	Bloomfield, CT
Hughes, Charles	46	11/19/78	UFAP-Murder	Atlanta, GA	4/29/81	Myrtle, MS
Lyons, Ron	34	12/17/78	Air piracy; Kidnapping	Dixon, TN	9/10/79	Washoe Co., NV
Koury, Leo	45	4/20/79	RICO	Richmond, VA	Still at large	
Sherman, John	39	8/3/79	EFP	Lompoc, CA	12/17/81	Golden, CO
Guyon, Melvin	19	8/9/79	Kidnapping	Chicago	8/16/79	Youngstown, OH
Bruton, George	37	9/28/79	UFAP-Burglary	Utah	12/14/79	Ft. Smith, AR
Austin, Earl	38	10/12/79	Bank robbery	Tampa, FL	3/1/80	Tucson, AZ
Russo, Vincent	24	12/24/79	UFAP-Robbery	San Diego, CA	1/4/81	Pennsylvania
Victory, Albert	40	3/14/80	Escape	New York	2/24/81	Lafayette, CA

Name	Age	Date	Crime	Location	Date	Status
Williams, Ronald	—	4/16/80	Escape	Moundsville, WV	6/8/81	Washington, DC
Barney, Daniel	28	3/10/81	UFAP-Sexual assault	Wisconsin		Suicide 4/19/81 Denver, CO
Webb, Don	50	5/4/81	UFAP-Murder	Saxonburg, PA		Still at large
Everett, Gil	42	5/13/81	Bank robbery	Knoxville, TN	8/12/85	Alaska
Nichols, Les	38	7/2/81	UFAP-Murder	Little Rock, AR	12/17/81	Little Rock, AR
Manning, Tom	36	1/29/82	Bank robbery	S. Burlington, VT	7/8/82	Virginia
Shakur, Mutulu	32	1/29/82	Bank robbery	NY City	7/8/82	California
Kimberly, David	32	7/23/82	UFAP-Murder	Prince Georges Co., MD	2/11/86	Miami, FL
Watson, Chas.	37	10/22/82	Kidnapping	Baltimore	10/25/83	Sterling, PA
Gibson, Laney	33	11/16/83	UFAP-Murder	Manchester, KY	12/18/83	Montgomery, AL

NAME	AGE	LISTED	OFFENSE	LOCATION	ARRESTED	LOCATION
Bridgette, George	37	1/13/84	UFAP-Murder	Long Beach, CA	1/30/84	Miami, FL
Humphrey, Samuel	35	2/29/84	Bank robbery	Atlanta, GA	3/22/84	Portland, OR
Wilder, Chris	39	4/5/84	Kidnapping; Murder	Nationwide	8/13/84	Colebrook, NH
Gerena, Victor	26	5/14/84	Bank robbery	Hartford, CT	Still at large	
Ng, Wai-Chiu	27	6/15/84	UFAP-Murder	Seattle, WA	10/24/84	Calgary, Alberta
Coleman, Alton	29	10/24/84	Kidnapping; Murder	Midwest	1/25/85	Evanston, IL
Davis, Cleveland	42	6/15/84	UFAP-Murder	Virginia Beach, VA	10/24/84	NY City
Persico, Carmine	57	1/31/85	RICO	NY City	2/15/85	Long Island, NY
Mays, Lohman	41	2/15/85	Escape	Nashville, TN	9/23/85	Wyoming

Name	Age	Date	Charge	Location	Date	Location
Hammond, Charles	43	3/14/85	UFAP-Murder	Kansas City, MO	8/4/86	Florida
Hammond, Mike	40	3/14/85	UFAP-Murder	Kansas City, MO	8/4/86	Florida
Nicolaus, Robert	52	6/28/85	UFAP-Murder	Sacramento, CA	7/20/85	York, PA
Sterling, David	30	9/30/85	UFAC-Rape	Vancouver, WA	2/13/86	Covington, LA
Scutari, Richard	38	9/30/85	UFAP-Armed robbery	Ukiah, CA	3/19/86	San Antonio, TX
Dougherty, Joseph	46	11/6/85	Bank robbery	Oklahoma City, OK	12/19/86	Antioch, CA
Malverty, Brian	35	3/28/86	UFAP-Murder	Atlanta, GA	4/7/86	California
Waldon, Bill	33	5/16/86	UFAP-Murder	Tulsa, OK	6/16/86	San Diego, CA
Dallas, Claude	36	5/16/86	Escape	Idaho state prison	3/8/87	Riverside, CA

NAME	AGE	LISTED	OFFENSE	LOCATION	ARRESTED	LOCATION
Williams, Don	—	7/18/86	Bank robbery	Chicago	8/20/86	California
Conner, Terry	43	8/8/86	Bank robbery	Oklahoma City, OK	12/9/86	Arlington Hts., IL
Cross, Fillmore	44	8/8/86	Extortion	Santa Cruz, CA	12/23/86	California
Dyess, James	30	9/29/86	UFAP-Murder	Jackson, MS	5/16/88	California
Weeks, Danny	32	9/29/86	UFAC-Kidnapping	Houston, TX	3/20/88	Washington
Jackson, Mike	41	10/1/86	UFAP-Murder	Indianapolis, IN	Suicide 10/2/86 Wright City, MO	
Harrelson, Thomas	29	11/28/86	Bank robbery	Danville, IL	2/9/87	Marshall Co., MN
Litchfield, Robert	38	1/20/87	EFP	Talladega, AL	5/20/87	Zephyr Cove, NV

Name	Age	Date	Crime	Location	Date	Status/Location
Roberts, Dave	43	4/27/87	UFAC-Murder	Indianapolis, IN	2/11/88	NY City
Triplett, Ron	38	4/27/87	UFAC-Armed robbery	Jackson, MI	5/16/87	Tempe, AZ
Marks, Claude	38	5/22/87	Conspiracy	Leavenworth, KS		Still at large
Wilmott, Donna	37	5/22/87	Conspiracy	Leavenworth, KS		Still at large
O'Neall, Darren	27	6/25/87	UFAP-Murder	Pierce Co., WA	2/3/87	Florida
Beam, Louis	41	7/14/87	Sedition	Houston, TX	11/6/87	Guadalajara, Mex
Otsuki, Ted Jeffrey	35	1/22/87	UFAP-Murder	Boston	10/10/88	Harlingen, TX
Estrada, Pedro	25	4/15/88	UFAP-Murder	NY City		Still at large
Stevens, John	—	5/29/88	Bank robbery	Nationwide		Still at large

NAME	AGE	LISTED	OFFENSE	LOCATION	ARRESTED	LOCATION
Farmer, Jack	—	5/29/88	RICO	Chicago	6/1/88	Florida
Jones, Robert	—	5/29/88	UFAP-Child molesting	Interstate		Still at large
Johnson, Terry	—	6/12/88	Escape	Elmore, AL		Still at large

INDEX